296.7
St 8   Strassfeld, Michael.
        A book of life.

## Temple Israel Library
### Minneapolis, Minn.

_____

Please sign your full name on the above card.

Return books promptly to the Library or Temple Office.

Fines will be charged for overdue books or for damage or loss of same.

# A BOOK OF LIFE

ALSO BY MICHAEL STRASSFELD

*The First Jewish Catalog:*
*A Do-It-Yourself Kit*

*The Second Jewish Catalog:*
*Sources and Resources*

*The Third Jewish Catalog:*
*Creating Community*

*The Jewish Holidays:*
*A Guide & Commentary*

*A Night of Questions:*
*A Passover Haggadah*

# A
# BOOK
# OF LIFE

### EMBRACING JUDAISM
### AS A SPIRITUAL PRACTICE

## Michael Strassfeld

SCHOCKEN BOOKS, NEW YORK

Copyright © 2002 by Michael Strassfeld

All rights reserved under International and Pan-American Copyright
Conventions. Published in the United States by Schocken Books,
a division of Random House, Inc., New York, and simultaneously
in Canada by Random House of Canada Limited, Toronto.
Distributed by Pantheon Books, a division of Random House, Inc.,
New York.

Schocken and colophon are registered
trademarks of Random House, Inc.

Owing to limitations of space, permissions to reprint previously
published material can be found following the note on sources.

A Cataloging-in-Publication record has been established
for *A Book of Life* by the Library of Congress.

ISBN: 0-8052-4124-8

www.schocken.com

Book design by M. Kristen Bearse

Printed in the United States of America
First Edition
2   4   6   8   9   7   5   3   1

FOR JOY


Love is alone sufficient by itself.
It pleases by itself, and for its own sake.
It is itself a merit, and itself its own recompense.
It seeks neither cause, nor consequence, beyond itself.
It is its own fruit, its own object and usefulness.
I love, because I love.
I love that I may love.

— BERNARD OF CLAIRVAUX

# CONTENTS

# ACKNOWLEDGMENTS

A few years ago, I took up paper-cutting. (My copies of old paper-cuts serve as the art for this book.) As you cut out the myriad pieces of an intricate paper-cut, the design slowly emerges. The process is a slow revelation of a work of art that is composed in equal parts of what is taken away and what remains. Only in the end is the total work complete.

The writing of this book feels like a similar process. It took many years to write and feels like the culmination of all that I have learned and experienced until this moment. I feel indebted to all of my teachers and all the communities that have helped shape who I am.

It begins with my parents, Meyer and Ruth Strassfeld. It continues with my day-school teachers, Rabbis Wohlgemuth, Simon, and Blau, and Mr. Gerry. The Saturday night *shiurim* of Rabbi Joseph Soloveitchik. The music of Shlomo Carlebach. Professors Nahum Glatzer, Alexander Altmann, and Nahum Sarna at Brandeis. Professors Tikva Frymer-Kensky, Nili Gold, Shulamit Magnes, Nancy Fuchs-Kreimer, Linda Holtzman, and Neil Danzig at the Reconstructionist Rabbinical College. A special thanks to my *hevruta* study partners David Rosenn, Arnie Eisen, Edward Feld, Burt Visotzky, Barry Holtz, Ed Greenstein, Paula Hyman, Alan Mintz, Nessa Rapaport, Marcia Lind, Michael Paley, and the rabbis' study group. Others whom I have studied with or learned from include: Rob Agus, Harlene Appelman, Saul Berman, Tzvi Blanchard, Yitzhak Buxbaum, Michael Cohen, Diane Cohler-Esses, David Cooper, Shoshana Cooper, Ilan Ezrahi, Sue Fendrick, Nancy Flam, David Gedzelman, Everett Gendler, Mary Gendler, Elliot Ginsberg, Shefa Gold, Robert Goldenberg, Shai Held, Richard Hirsch,

Lawrence Hoffman, Dick Israel, Sherry Israel, Jan Kaufman, Bill Kavesh, Naami Kelman, Levi Kelman, Wolfe Kelman, Sharon Kleinbaum, Adina Kling, Shira Kober Zeller, Irwin Kula, Larry Kushner, Allan Lehmann, Michael Lerner, Shaul Magid, Danny Matt, Deborah Mowshowitz, Solomon Mowshowitz, Joseph Newirth, Jonathan Omerman, Saul Pavlin, Peter Pitzele, Judith Plaskow, Joel Rosenberg, Joe Rosenstein, Jeff Roth, Zalman Schachter-Shalomi, Drorah Setel, Steve Shaw, Carl Sheingold, Chuck Simon, Jacob Staub, Betsy Teutsch, David Teutsch, Esther Ticktin, Max Ticktin, Judith Turner, Nina Wacholder, Brian Walt, Arthur Waskow, Sheila Weinberg, Trude Weiss-Rosmarin, Elliot Wolfson, and Joel Ziff.

I have been especially influenced by the communities I have been part of, including: The *kavanah minyan,* Weiss's Farm, the National Havurah Institutes, Derekh Re'ut, the spirituality *hevra,* the West Side Minyan, and Minyan M'at. A special mention should be made of Debbie Friedman and our monthly healing services. My years in Havurat Shalom still remain essential to my religious life. Discussions with participants in the Metivta Spirituality Institute and the experience of its retreats were very helpful in the final formation of this book.

A special thanks to Rabbi Rachel Cowan, who started me on the latest version of my path. Also to Rabbi Art Green, lifelong friend and teacher, for helping me find my way from the Sons of Lithuania to my present moment. Most especial thanks to Sylvia Boorstein, who taught me how to meditate and how meditation was not the answer, only the opening question.

Thank you to Seymour Rossel, my editor, and to Bonny Fetterman, Arthur Samuelson, Susan Ralston, and Altie Karper, my editors at Schocken. Thanks to the Schocken staff, including Dassi Zeidel, Archie Ferguson, Kristen Bearse, Stefanie Breitling, and Kathleen Fridella.

Last but most important, thank you to my children, Kayla, Noam, Ben, Sara, and Ruthie, who remain my greatest and most challenging teachers.

# INTRODUCTION

## *Avodah she-be-gashmiyut,* Spirituality through the everyday

When the great Rabbi Israel Baal Shem-Tov saw misfortune threatening the Jews it was his custom to go into a certain part of the forest to meditate. There he would light a fire, say a special prayer, and the miracle would be accomplished and the misfortune averted.

Later, when his disciple, the celebrated Magid of Mezritch, had occasion, for the same reason, to intercede with heaven, he would go to the same place in the forest and say: "Master of the Universe, listen! I do not know how to light the fire, but I am still able to say the prayer." And again the miracle was accomplished.

Still later, Rabbi Moshe-Leib of Sasov, in order to save his people once more, would go into the forest and say: "I do not know how to light the fire, I do not know the prayer, but I know the place and this must be sufficient." It was sufficient and the miracle was accomplished.

Then it fell to Rabbi Israel of Rizhyn to overcome misfortune. Sitting in his armchair, his head in his hands, he spoke to God: "I am unable to light the fire and I do not know the prayer; I cannot even find the place in the forest. All I can do is tell the story, and this must be sufficient." And it was sufficient. [Elie Wiesel, *The Gates of the Forest*]

In a way, this tale seems to describe today's Judaism—a truncated version of a once-vibrant and rich tradition. For many of us, Judaism is about old stories often told in a language that even the tellers hardly comprehend. Knowing the prayer, building the fire, relating to God, meditating in the face of a crisis—all these seem beyond the repertoire of most contemporary Jews. Instead, Judaism sometimes appears to be an annual summer stock revival of an old chestnut, enjoyed by its audience just because it is so familiar. There are few surprises in the production or staging; in fact, careful attention is paid to mounting it exactly as has been done according to the memory of the oldest member of the cast. (Occasionally, some people feel like they have to go in when the child of a friend is cast in a one-time bit part known as a bar/bat mitzvah.)

Those without a nostalgia for this past, or those seeking a transformational experience, or those searching for contemporary answers to the questions of their life, often choose to bypass the theater after a glimpse at the marquee. This despite the increasingly desperate pleas of the ushers urging them to enter.

As one who has spent a lifetime either acting in or attending this theater, however, I rebel against the notion, so lyrically portrayed in the opening story, that Judaism is diminished by each passing generation. Telling the story is *not* sufficient. If we no longer know the place in the forest, it is up to us to discover new places. If we no longer know the prayer, we need to write new prayers. Clearly our hearts have not lost the ability to speak. If we no longer remember how to build the fire, it is up to us to establish new rituals. We can begin, as did the Baal Shem Tov, by meditating on who we are and who we want to be. Within the forests of the world, we can rediscover, both in the richness of the Jewish past and the richness of the contemporary moment, how to overcome misfortune *and* take advantage of the opportunities that life presents us.

I believe that we all struggle to answer one simple question: What makes my life meaningful? If we go beyond merely repeating the story of our ancestors, merely preserving Jewish traditions, merely attempting to ensure "continuity," we may find, in the accumulated wisdom of over three thousand years, answers to that question.

One enduring anwer is the realization that each of us is created in the image of God. The Jewish assertion that all human beings are fundamentally equal teaches us how to treat one another. Being created in the Divine image also suggests, that through our relationship to God, we must strive for holiness in the world. Jewish tradition refers to this as *tikkun olam*, "repairing" or "healing the world."

*Tikkun olam* is often associated with the word *spirituality*, a word with an extraordinarily imprecise meaning. Spirituality is sometimes defined in contrast to religion. If religion is seen as a set of beliefs, laws, and institutions (including clergy), spirituality is viewed as being beyond all these trappings. It is defined as our sense of connection to something larger than our own selves. Compared to religion, which is objective, distant, and formal, spirituality is understood to be subjective, personal, and informal. Within the religious world, however, the word *spirituality* describes the life of the spirit. In this context, spirituality is not contrasted to religion, but rather to the material world. The more spiritual you are the more you are connected to God and religion, and the less you are connected to worldly things. For much of the history of religion, the material world has been conceived of as the enemy of the spirit. It is the flesh that tempts or corrupts the soul.

In this book, I attempt to delineate a different path—one that sees the point of religion as fostering the spiritual, that understands Judaism as a spiritual practice meant to awaken us to life's potential. Viewed this way, the practice of Judaism encourages engagement with the world rather than withdrawal from it. It is in the ordinary rather than in the extraordinary that we should seek holiness and meaning.

A precedent for this approach can be found in the religious movement known as Hasidism. Hasidism emerged in the eighteenth century as a form of Jewish mysticism that fired the imagination and captured the allegiance of most of Eastern European Jewry. While contemporary Hasidism is a historical descendant of eighteenth-century Hasidism, spiritually it has retreated from most of the radical teachings of its past. One of these doctrines was *avodah she-be-gashmiyut*, "worship" or "service through the everyday." Hasidism diverged from earlier Jewish mystical movements that had often been ascetic in their approach to the world. Hasidism taught that God was everywhere, in everything: "there is no place where God is absent." The potential to encounter the divine was present at every moment. Everything ordinary contained a spark of holiness. Eating, conversation, work—in fact all mundane activities—had the potential to be made holy. In the Hasidic worldview, the life task of the Jew was to make that potential actual. This was done not by saying special prayers or doing things in a special Jewish way, but by being acutely aware of the potential in every moment. Thus the term *avodah she-be-gashmiyut* meant serving God through the material world. *Avodah,* "service," is the same word used for prayer. All acts become a form of prayer. That was what the philosopher Abraham Joshua Heschel had in mind when he explained why he joined civil rights demonstrations: while marching, he said, he was praying with his feet.

This book sees life as a spiritual path from waking in the morning to retiring at night, from traversing one whole year to traversing a life span from birth to death. For each "life moment," I try to present traditional teachings that can guide us on our path. For some life moments the tradition is replete with rituals; for others, traditional rituals are sparse or nonexistent. In these cases, I offer new teachings and suggest new rituals gleaned from my own study and my own experience. The teachings and the rituals, traditional and nontraditional, have a common aim: to bring us to awareness as we journey through the real world.

The point of Judaism is not to pray three times a day or to observe the Sabbath or the holidays. Rituals should not be observed because we are "supposed to" observe them, but rather because they help us achieve the real goal: awareness. To be a good Jew is not to do all the particular Jewish things perfectly. It is to live a life of goodness and holiness inspired by the teachings and structured by the traditions of Judaism.

A spiritual practice of Judaism strives for awareness of the moment, every moment, helping us to live life to its fullest. With that awareness, we can discover moments of self-awareness. With that awareness, we can truly hear those who are speaking to us and strive to respond to them in an openhearted way. With that awareness, we can feel the presence of God as our Beloved Companion. Out of that awareness, we can perform deeds of *tikkun olam,* "restoring the world" to wholeness and healing.

*Bekhol derakhekha da'ehu,* "in all your ways, in everything you do, know God" (Prov. 3:6), and in that knowing you will live a life of meaning and purpose.

## A Little About My Own Journey

I grew up in an Orthodox family. My father is a rabbi. I attended Maimonides School, an Orthodox day school in Boston. Ideologically, my family belonged to the left wing of Orthodoxy. My father marched for civil rights in Selma and the whole family campaigned for an independent peace candidate for the U.S. Senate. When I was entering my junior year of high school, we moved to Marblehead, a suburb north of Boston, where my father became the rabbi of a Conservative congregation. My adolescent rebellion was to refuse to pray in his Conservative synagogue with its mixed seating.

I spent my freshman college year at Yeshiva University, where it became clear to me that I was no longer an Orthodox Jew. I transferred to Brandeis University to study Jewish texts from a critical perspective. In 1971, my wife and I joined Havurat Shalom, a religious community in Somerville, Massachusetts. One of the first *havurot* (*havurah* means "fellowship," *havurot* is the plural form), Havurat Shalom explored new approaches to Judaism while seeing the Jewish past as an essential resource. It was in the *havurah* that my Jewish life for the next twenty-five years was shaped.

Havurah Judaism was egalitarian (i.e., it provided equal roles for men and women), participatory, contemporary, and yet traditional. It was not defined by being part of an organized branch of Judaism, though it was certainly liberal rather than Orthodox. Out of that *havurah* experience the *Jewish Catalogs* were born. The Judaism as presented in the *Catalogs* struck a chord with thousands of Jews who were not part of any *havurah.*

My wife and I moved to New York City and had three children. At the age of thirty-nine I decided to enter rabbinical school. I attended the Reconstructionist Rabbinical College and, upon graduation, became the rabbi of Congregation Ansche Chesed in Manhattan. My two older children went off to college. My wife and I were divorced. My youngest child became bar mitzvah. I remarried. After ten years of being rabbi at Ansche Chesed, I decided it was time to move on. I wanted to find a setting that was open to the exploration of a new approach to Judaism, the approach reflected in this book. I became the rabbi of the Society for the Advancement of Judaism, a synagogue deeply rooted in both tradition and innovation.

Some years ago, I was approached by an editor with the idea of writing a new *Jewish Catalog*. After all, it had been more than two decades since the *Catalog* had first appeared and the book needed updating in terms of both content and tone. Clearly, the first *Catalogs* had emerged out of the *havurah* movement. What, then, should be the central focus of this new book?

In the summer and fall of 1995 I decided to travel the highways and byways of American Jewish life and seek my new focus. I attended gatherings as diverse as the Aleph Kallah of Jewish Renewal and the General Assembly of Jewish Federations. I discovered that there was a single subterranean thread running through American Jewry—a search for spirituality. It was mentioned wherever I spoke with Jews. It made striking appearances, such as when six hundred "regular" Jews at the General Assembly performed hand movements as they sang as part of the opening of an institute on Jewish identity. In some places, *spirituality* was a word that evoked snide comments suggesting it was a cliché. For some folk, the word itself seemed embarrassing, similar to talking about God in a casual conversation. We who are so university trained, so modern, so intellectual, seemed embarrassed to speak of the spirit— just as Jews once joked about the body, as in jokes about Jews in sports. Yet I found that I didn't know what spirituality meant either.

After all my travels I came home and tried to write the book, but I still felt directionless. Then I was invited to a three-day retreat for rabbis. I hesitated about going, especially after I heard it was going to be a silent retreat. "Can't we chat at night?" "No. No talking beginning Sunday night until Wednesday morning. No writing or reading either."

I had done a little bit of meditating, but it never seemed to work for me. My mind was always racing around. I decided to go because I thought I might learn something that I could use in my congregation, and if nothing else it would be a precious opportunity, a couple of days to reflect on my life and its issues.

Fourteen rabbis attended the retreat. I knew most of them. The retreat was led by Sylvia Boorstein, an author and teacher of meditation. The style of meditation was Vipassana, a form of Buddhist meditation, though we were taught it without the larger context of Buddhist teachings. It consisted basically of forty-five minutes of sitting meditation alternating with forty-five minutes of walking meditation. I spent most of the first day discovering that I was actually able to meditate—not that I could levitate myself or feel filled with light but that I didn't sit there waiting desperately for the forty-five minutes to be over.

Most of the time the bell that signaled the end of the forty-five-minute periods came as a surprise. I found that by concentrating on my breathing I could stay focused. When my mind wandered, I would take a deep breath to refocus. Finally, I had the time just to be more aware of things—my breath, silence. I loved the walking meditations because the center was surrounded by fields, stone walls, and forests. The woods of New England have always been for me the landscape of my soul.

I came away from the retreat with some important insights (another name for this style of meditation is "insight meditation"). I realized that this meditation could be a wonderful spiritual discipline. As a Jew, I wondered how this discipline could be incorporated in my Jewish life even without daily meditation. Then the obvious occurred to me. *Judaism is meant to be a spiritual discipline,* even though we don't talk about it that way. The word *halakhah* (usually translated as Jewish "tradition" or "law") is from the root meaning "to walk" or "to go." *Halakhah* is meant to be a path to follow through life. Somewhere that way of looking at Judaism got disconnected from Jewish practice. The modern Jew's fear of spirituality, the intangible, and God made *halakhah* into a practice, but not a spiritual practice.

I realized that there was a whole variety of Jewish practices that I observed because they added meaning to my life and/or because I grew up doing them, yet they did not feel like a spiritual discipline.

If Judaism is supposed to make us aware of the holy at all times and help us to act accordingly, this rarely happened to me. For example: I observed Shabbat every week in a fairly traditional manner. I enjoyed it. It set the rhythm of the week for my family and me. It was pleasant and did not feel like a burden most of the time. Yet it did not feel very spiritual—not that I think every Sabbath can be a spiritual paradise. Still, too much of Judaism has become first a ritual and then a rote ritual. It had lost the purpose of being a spiritual discipline, of making me more aware, more mindful, as my meditation teacher would say.

Even among those who follow Orthodox practice daily, we can see the danger of ritual that is empty of spiritual content. *Halakhah* is a discipline of Orthodox Jews, but one that too often seems far from a sense of the Presence of God. For too many ritually observant Jews what goes into your mouth is more important than what comes out of it, often in the form of gossip.

Sitting and walking at the retreat, I had begun to wonder whether there was a way to reconstruct Judaism as a spiritual discipline or a spiritual devotion or practice. I imagined a practice, a *halakhah,* not because God commanded it at Sinai, but because God wants us to be holy and because we actively strive to be holy. I imagined a Judaism that would encourage an awareness, a mindfulness, as we go through our daily lives—a practice not for spiritual masters or adepts, but for all of us. It would not require mystical visions, or sainthood, or withdrawing from the world either to a monastery or to a separatist community like Boro Park. I imagined a practice that would take up only little bits of our time and yet have two simple goals: to make us better human beings and to engage us with the presence of God. These goals would be reached by using much of the Jewish tradition but by trying to recapture its original *kavanah,* its "intention."

This was what I had been seeking in my quest through the world of American Jewry—a spiritual devotion based on Judaism as practiced by the Jewish people through the centuries.

I added this new element to the chapters I had already written. I worried that it might seem too "flaky" to some people. I worried that all this talk about God and spirituality would frighten people away. I questioned my own life, my Jewish life. I still have plenty of questions about it. Yet the approach through spirituality seemed right.

One question often arises: Isn't this awareness stuff really Buddhist? Is it authentically Jewish?

In response, allow me to cite a seemingly unlikely source, one of the most legalistic traditional Jewish texts. The *Shulhan Arukh,* the classic code of Jewish law, opens by stating:

> One should strengthen oneself like a lion to get up in the morning for the service of the Creator. . . . *Shiviti YHVH le-negdi tamid,* "I have placed God before me always" (Psalm 16:8). This verse states an important principle in Torah and among the righteous who walk before God. For the way in which such a person sits and behaves, and does his business when he is alone in his home is not the same as if he conceives of himself before a great king. . . . All the more so if a person understands in her heart it is the Great King, the Holy One whose glory fills the whole earth, that stands before her and sees what she does. . . . Even when lying in bed, know before Whom you lie, and when you get up, get up with diligence to worship your Creator.

The goal of life as expressed in this code is not just to observe the minutiae of Jewish ritual and law. It is to fulfill the precept of *Shiviti YHVH le-negdi tamid,* "to place God before us at all times" (Ps. 16:8). We are called to walk through life with a consciousness of the presence of the Holy One always. We are to do so as we walk, do business, and interact with people—in other words, when we are engaged in all of the "mundane" activities of daily life. For the *Shulhan Arukh,* awareness is the goal of life. The whole rest of this book is commentary on how to achieve that awareness.

The prophet Micah says (ch. 6:8): "What does God ask of you? To do justice, to love kindness, and to walk humbly before God." It is that simple.

May the writings of my heart and the teachings of Torah help you on your journey.

Part One

# AWAKENING TO THE DAY

# DAWNING

*Only that day dawns to which we are awake.*
— THOREAU

We begin with the act of waking up. The *Shulhan Arukh*, the classic code of Jewish law, urges us to arise at dawn, at the moment of transition from night to day. Sunrise is a clear reminder that this is a moment of transition, a moment repeated every day and yet never exactly the same. Though we have substituted the face of the clock for the face of the sun, we can still rise to greet the dawn of our new day whenever we actually get up. It is a moment of transition from sleep to awareness; a moment to orient ourselves for a new day. For humans, the new day means life and consciousness. By opening our eyes each morning, we become awake to the world and to our being.

## Getting Up on the Right Spiritual Side of the Bed

Even as we struggle to awaken and shake off the vestiges of sleep, we begin to engage the new day. Our mind goes to our "to do" list for the day while we engage in the mundane tasks of getting ready. As we shower, dress, make coffee, and prepare lunch, our mind is trying to focus on the many things we need to do at work, the errands we need to accomplish, and the problems and challenges ahead. Nevertheless, we can orient our day and thus have an impact on its quality by taking a

3

brief moment for reflection. We can create a spiritual "to do" list. To whom do we want to be sure to express love, caring, warmth, friendship, or just appreciation on this day? How can we be slightly more conscious in our behavior toward others? To what spiritual place can we be a little closer at the end of this day? This spiritual reckoning requires just a moment—as we wash our hands or take a shower, as we put all the things we need for the day in our briefcase. Find a moment that seems right for you and create a daily ritual. What follows are a number of suggested rituals for awakening to the day, some traditional and some contemporary. They are suggestions for practice. You may use these to create your own ritual or liturgy, or you may simply set aside time for silent reflection and meditation. Make your own choices but understand that how you start the day can make a difference.

To renew your faith in the morning, do not involve yourself in any worldly activity or speech when you get out of bed; just go to the bathroom, wash, then meditate, thinking of the Creator of the world with full concentration—that God is One, Single, and Unique.

Look through your window at the sky and the earth and recall the verse "Lift up your eyes on high and see—who created all this?" (Isa. 40:26), and think that God created it all out of absolute nothingness. And think, "How many are Your works, O Lord, with wisdom have You made them all; the earth is full of Your creations" (Psalm 104:24). Think of how great God's works are, in the creation of the heaven and the earth and all that is in them—inanimate and animate—plants, animals, humans, creatures great and wonderful. "God created the ocean and all that is in it, the awesome whales, God formed the mountains and created winds and fire" (*Kitzur Shnei Luhot ha-Brit*).

**Modeh ani**—*an awakening ritual*    Upon waking up, say: *Modeh ani lefanekha melekh hai ve-kayam she-hehezarta bi nishmati be-hemlah, rabbah emunatekha.* "I give thanks to You, Source of life and existence, that you have once again placed my soul within me, great is your faith (in me)."

Alternatively: "As the sun rises to reawaken the world, let wonder and possibility be the blessing of my life this day renewed."

The *modeh ani* prayer reflects a belief that God renews creation daily. We too are seen as a *beriah hadashah,* "a new creation." There is a traditional belief that the soul leaves the body during sleep and "checks in with the home office" up in heaven. This prayer is, then, an expression of gratitude to God for literally returning our soul to us each morning. Traditionally, too, sleep was seen as analogous to death and therefore we are thankful to awaken alive for a new day.

> The Hasidic master, the Apter Rebbe, when asked why he had not begun the morning service even though it was already noon, replied: "I woke up this morning and began to praise God, saying, 'I offer my thanks before You [the *modeh ani*]; but immediately I began to wonder: Who am I? And who is the You before Whom I am I? I'm still pondering this, and haven't been able to go onward.' " [*Jewish Spiritual Practices,* p. 78]

*Washing the hands*   Water is a symbol of life, because it nourishes all living things. It is also a symbol of birth, as it reminds us of the fluids that accompany birth. It is used as a means of symbolic cleansing in a variety of settings. It is a traditional Jewish practice to wash our hands upon awakening by first taking a cup of water in one hand and pouring it over the other hand, then switching hands and repeating the process. (Some people do this three times for each hand.) Ritually anointing our hands is a symbol of the renewal of creation as well as a spiritual cleansing in preparation for the work of the new day.

In addition to the traditional prayer, we may add a *kavanah,* a word or concept, a poem or meditation, or even a chant, to "direct" our attention to the extraordinary holiness of an ordinary moment. The word *kavanah* has the inner meaning of "direction" or "intention," but a better translation for English speakers is "a focus."

*KAVANAH*

Water flows over these hands
  May I use them skillfully
  as I construct and shape this day *[based on a prayer by Thich Nhat Hanh]*
  Or:
  *Ve-yehi noam Adonai eloheinu aleinu, u-ma'aseh yadainu konenah aleinu, u-ma'aseh yadainu konenaihu.*
  "May the favor of Adonai our God be upon us, let the work of our hands prosper, O prosper the work of our hands!" [Psalm 90:17]
  While slowly drying your hands, recite the *berakhah*/blessing:
  *Barukh attah Adonai eloheinu melekh ha-olam asher kidshanu be-mitzvotav ve-tzivanu al netilat yadayim.*
  "Praised are You, Eternal One, our God, source of the universe, who has made us holy through the commandments and commanded us concerning the washing of hands."

### Washing the face and mouth

A person should wash her face, her hands, and her feet every day for the sake of her Maker, as is said, "Adonai has made everything for God's own purpose" (Prov. 16:4). [Talmud, *Berakhot* 50b]

In addition to the hands, some wash the face upon arising, and the *Mishneh Berurah*, a commentary on the *Shulhan Arukh*, says that just as we anoint our hands we should also rinse our mouths. For most of us, the mouth is the most significant vehicle in our interaction with others in the world. Rinsing the mouth, in this case, is not intended to cleanse it, but to purify it symbolically in preparation for the words we will vocalize during the day. (Some Jews, therefore, observe the custom of being silent before they wash in the morning.)

*KAVANAH*

May I see the image of the Holy One reflected in this face and in
the faces of all those whose eyes will reflect mine this day.
    May the words of my mouth be pleasing to all who have listen-
ing ears.
    May I take care of this body, Your creation, and a vessel for
the holy.

Although this anointing of the hands, face, and mouth is only symbolic, you might choose to use the above *kavanot* or "focusings" during your morning shower.

### Attitudes toward the body

The body is the soul's house. Shouldn't we therefore take care of
our house so that it doesn't fall into ruin? [Philo, *The Worse Attacks the Better,* section 10]

While traditional Judaism believes in a soul that survives beyond
death, the body is not seen as the enemy of spirituality or even as something that weighs down the spirit. The body is the vessel that contains
the soul; it is also the vehicle that creates opportunities to serve God and
to effect *tikkun olam,* the repair of the world. For Judaism, all of life is
part of God's world—a corollary of monotheism—since there is only
one God who created everything in the universe. This is true of even the
most mundane and seemingly base activities. Thus there is a blessing to
be recited after going to the bathroom in the morning. (Traditionally,
the blessing is said after each visit to the bathroom.) The blessing expresses an appreciation for the workings of the human body and the
delicate balance that maintains it, something we often take for granted.

Praised are You, Eternal One, our God, source of the universe,
who has formed a human with wisdom, and created in her openings

and vessels. It is well known before Your glorious throne, that if one of these is opened or if one is closed that it would be impossible to exist. Praised are You, who heals all creatures in a wondrous fashion.

Judaism's concern with care of our bodies is also reflected in issues of physical appearance and well-being. Societal standards determine what constitutes modest attire, and many of the specific statements in our tradition no longer seem applicable. In broad terms, however, the tradition attempts to maintain an appreciation for the beauty of the body and its sensuality while consistently reminding us that we are more than just bodies. Each of us is created in the Divine image. It is natural for us to want to be attractive to others and to be noticed by those around us.

Unlike secular society, Judaism does not have an idealized model of beauty. We are all created in God's image. In all our diversity, fat and thin, tall and short, we are all equally God's creations. As the vessel that holds our soul, Judaism seeks most of all to have our outside selves be a reflection of our inner beings. Our inner beauty is what counts and it is always reflected on the outside. The important thing is to focus on who we are and how we live rather than how we look. Indirectly, Judaism addresses those who may be dissatisfied with their outward body by pointing out that all individuals differ:

> Therefore people were created unique, in order to proclaim the greatness of the Holy One. For if a person strikes many coins from one mold, they are all exactly alike. But though the King of kings, the Holy One, has fashioned every person in the stamp of the first human, not a single one of them is exactly like another. [Talmud, *Sanhedrin* 37a]

This is not to deny that our body image is important or that it may often be a conflicted part of our self-image. Nor does it mean that clothes don't make a difference in how we feel about ourselves or how others feel about us.

> When you dress or otherwise do something to improve your appearance, putting on nice clothes or ornaments, your intention

should be holy and for the sake of heaven—to beautify and adorn the Divine Image. . . . *[Noam Elimelekh]*

Nor does Judaism's focus on inner beauty release us from our obligation to care for our bodies. This is especially true with regard to matters of health, such as eating the right foods, losing excess weight, and regular exercise. In fact the tradition regards the body as a precious gift to us from God.

"He who does good to his own person is a person of piety" (Prov. 11:17). Such a one was Hillel the Elder. After taking leave of his disciples, he proceeded to walk along with them. His disciples asked him, "Master, where are you going?" He answered, "To perform a precept." "What precept?" "To bathe in the bathhouse." "But is this a precept?" "It is indeed. King's statues set up in theaters and circuses are scoured and washed down by the official specially appointed to look after them who receives a salary for the work. More, he is esteemed as one of the notables of the empire. How much more am I required to scour and wash myself, who have been created in God's image and likeness, as it is written: "In the image of God, God made people" (Gen. 9:6)! [Midrash, *Leviticus Rabbah* 34:3]

So doing good to one's self is not regarded as being "self-indulgent," but rather as being pious, for we are created in the Divine image. Almost paradoxically, Judaism asks us to accept and appreciate ourselves as creatures of the Creator and yet calls on us to strive to improve ourselves.

Finding the correct balance is not always easy. This is especially true when it comes to feelings about our bodies and our appearance. Nevertheless, the tradition is clear about the need to refrain from self-destructive activities. Judaism calls on us to alter habits, such as overeating or excess drinking, which may endanger our lives. For this reason, in recent halakhic literature a prohibition on cigarette smoking has been promulgated.

By keeping the body in health and vigor one walks in the ways of God. Since it is impossible during sickness to have any understanding or knowledge of the Creator, it is therefore a person's duty to avoid whatever is injurious to the body and cultivate habits conducive to health and vigor. [Maimonides, *Mishneh Torah, Hilkhot Da'ot* 4:1]

All of our morning preparations can lead to a more conscious sense of self and of our bodies. Washing, putting on makeup, shaving, combing our hair, putting on deodorant, and brushing our teeth are all ways to connect with our body, and with our desire to make our exterior reflect the beauty of our soul. All of these activities are expressions of caring for ourselves. They are also expressions of concern about how others will view us. In that sense, they are preparations for leaving home and journeying out into the world.

## On the Soul

As the Holy One fills the entire world, so the soul fills the entire body. As the Holy One sees but is not seen, so the soul sees but is not seen. As the Holy One sustains the entire world, all of it, so the soul sustains the body. As the Holy One is pure, so the soul is pure. As the Holy One dwells in chambers that are innermost, so the soul dwells in chambers that are innermost. [Talmud, *Berakhot* 10a]

Judaism has no single doctrine regarding the soul. Beginning in rabbinic times, there was a notion of the soul as distinct from the body. One view is that God breathed the soul into Adam at creation and subsequently each human being is born with a soul. Jewish tradition states that unlike the body, the soul continues to exist after death. Among the sages, some believed that the soul exists before the body, waiting for the birth of its human form. In a frequent metaphor, the body is that which houses the soul during life.

The body is not, however, merely a housing. As much as the soul's importance is stressed, the body is seen as having its own intrinsic value. In fact, the rabbis believed that both the body and the soul together will be resurrected in the end of days.

*KAVANAH*

Every day a person is formed by God, every day a person is born;
every day a person lives, every day a person dies; every day a person's soul is taken from them (during sleep) and deposited with
the soul's true Owner; every day a person is fed out of the fruit of
their deeds, just as the infant is fed out of their mother's breast.
[*Tanna deve Eliyahu Zuta* 1 5]

*A prayer for the soul*    *Elohai neshamah*, "O God, the soul . . . ," is a
*berakhah,* a "blessing," that sets forth the themes of *modeh ani* at
greater length.

O God, the soul that You have given me is pure. You created it;
You formed it; You breathed it into me; You sustain it within me.
You will take it from me in the future (and restore it to me in the time
to come) [an allusion to the doctrine of the resurrection of the dead].
So long as my soul is within me I give thanks to You, Adonai, my
God and God of my ancestors, master of all creation, lord of all
souls. Praised are You Adonai, in whose hands are the souls of all living things and the spirit of all human beings [or the traditional *berakhah*: "who restores the souls to the dead"].

## *Birkhot ha-shahar,* Morning Blessings

Awareness of the body is reflected in *birkhot ha-shahar,* a series of
"morning blessings." Originally, these blessings were voiced in con-
junction with the physical acts that follow awakening—opening eyes,
putting feet on the floor, getting dressed, and so on. Later, they were
incorporated into the daily synagogue liturgy. The medieval commentator Maimonides was critical of this change, correctly noting that blessings are intended to be recited at the moment of action rather than at
some later time.

The *berakhot* are as follows:

When she hears the cock crowing she should say: *Praised is the One who has given the cock understanding to distinguish between day and night.* When he opens his eyes, he should say: *Praised is the One who opens the eyes of the blind.* When she stretches herself and sits up, she should say: *Praised is the One who frees the bound/ imprisoned.* When he dresses, he should say: *Praised is the One who clothes the naked.* When she stands erect, she should say: *Praised is the One who straightens those that are bowed down.* When he puts his feet to the ground, he should say: *Praised is the One who spreads forth the ground over the waters.* [There was a belief that the earth rested upon water, see Genesis 1.] When she walks, she should say: *Praised is the One who guides the steps of people.*

When he puts on his shoes, he should say: *Praised is the One who provides for all my needs.* When she puts on a belt, she should say: *Praised is the One who girds Israel with strength.* When he puts on a hat, he should say: *Praised is the One who crowns Israel with glory.* [Talmud, *Berakhot* 60b]

A number of additional blessings are often found in traditional prayer books. Three of these are normally changed by liberal communities to reflect positive statements about our identity: "who has made me in God's image" (rather than, for men, "who has not made me a woman"); "who has made me a Jew" (rather than "who has not made me a Gentile"); and "who has made me a free person" (rather than "who has not made me a slave").

It is striking that, despite their being connected to specific physical acts, the blessings themselves are metaphorical. We don't thank God for our eyes. Instead we speak about God opening the eyes of the blind. The *birkhot ha-shahar* thus link the physical and the spiritual on many levels. For example, saying the *berakhah* on opening our eyes sensitizes us to the blessing of having sight, reminds us of those who are literally blind, and impresses us with the notion that blindness is more than a physical state. Thus each blessing reflects issues that connect us with the psychological and spiritual journey of our lives.

*KAVANOT* TO ACCOMPANY THE *BIRKHOT HA-SHAHAR*

- *distinguishing between night and day*—perceiving clearly our choices
- *opening eyes*—preparing us to see in places we have been blind
- *clothing the naked*—feeling clothed rather than naked or shamed
- *freeing the bound*—releasing us from places we feel constricted
- *straightening the bowed down*—enabling us to rejoice in our selves, enabling us to stand straight in a metaphorical sense
- *setting the earth*—feeling solid ground beneath our feet (both a sense of self-worth and a sense of the support provided by strong relationships
- *providing our needs*—helping us to achieve a realistic sense of our needs
- *guiding our steps*—reassuring us that there is a path and that God is our constant companion
- *girding us*—reminding us that faith provides courage
- *crowning us*—reaffirming our exalted nature as creations of God and reminding us that we can crown ourselves with respect
- *giving us strength*—making us aware that faith brings strength to the weary—an acknowledgment of how hard the journey is

We need to engage in that journey with determination and yet we need to be forgiving of ourselves for all the missteps and for feeling too weary to go on. If we are able to give ourselves both a sense of forgiveness and the strength to continue, we have the potential to discover who we are and understand who we are meant to be. Therefore, we say three additional blessings that affirm basic notions about our selves: (1) that we are created in God's image; (2) that we are Jews; and (3) that we are free—free to make choices about who we are.

One additional *berakhah* is added at the end of this series, praising God as the One who removes sleep from our eyes and drowsiness from our eyelids. It seems strange that this is not the first blessing. Yet, following the metaphorical meanings, its place here at the end is a call to awareness. It is all too possible to go through life asleep or at least drowsy. Only by actively engaging with the issues raised by these *berakhot* can we walk through the world with eyes open to understanding and awareness.

## Creating a Daily Spiritual Practice

Regularly setting aside time in the morning for spiritual practice is an ancient custom. It is a spiritual awakening to the day, but more, it helps to create a spiritual orientation for everyday life. As we have seen, the most common traditional practice is prayer, but others, such as meditation and Torah study, also have ancient precedents.

*Daily prayer*   Traditionally, Jews prayed three times a day. While prayer with a *minyan* (a congregation of ten or more individuals), a community of worshipers, was ideal, praying as an individual was certainly an acceptable way to fulfill one's obligation. The morning service, *shaharit,* is the longest of the daily services. Prayer in its fixed liturgical form is an important component of spiritual practice. If you can attend a morning *minyan* or set aside time for prayer on your own in the morning, you will provide a means for carrying awareness and holiness into the day. (For more about prayer in general and about the daily services, see "*Avodah:* The Path of Prayer," pp. 176–205.) What follows is a variety of suggestions beyond the full traditional *shaharit* service.

While encouraging people to pray the complete service, the rabbis of the Talmud were aware that work schedules or other circumstances could make this difficult (see *Berakhot* 28b). They therefore created a number of abbreviated forms of worship for use in special circumstances. Two examples are:

Hear the supplication of Your people Israel and speedily fulfill their request. Praised are You, God, who listens to prayer.

May it be Your will, Adonai our God, to give to each one their sustenance and to each body what it lacks. Praised are You, God, who hearkens unto prayer.

A number of commentators have pointed out that the *birkhot ha-shahar* are eighteen in number (when the three blessings for washing hands, going to the bathroom, and *elohai neshamah* are included). The preliminary service, in which the morning blessings are found, also includes blessings over Torah study (see below) and the recitation of the first line of the Shema: "Hear O Israel, Adonai our God, Adonai is one." Thus, in abbreviated form, the *birkhot ha-shahar* provide the semblance of the structure of the entire morning service—beginning with thankfulness to God, blessings that encourage us to reflect upon ourselves, the recitation of the Shema—our fundamental statement of belief—and the study of Torah. The latter is also the equivalent of the Torah reading performed every Monday and Thursday morning as part of the daily service. (For further suggestions about a morning prayer practice see "*Avodah:* The Path of Prayer," pp. 185–86.)

Whether you use one of these traditional liturgies, create your own, or resort to spontaneous prayer, setting aside a regular time for prayer/meditation can center you spiritually as you are about to engage the world on a new day.

*Other disciplines*    In some pietistic and mystical circles, meditation has been a traditional Jewish practice. As meditation has become more popular in the contemporary world, the practice of Jewish meditation or general meditation as a Jewish ritual has become more common. A good resource on traditional meditation is *Jewish Meditation: A Practical Guide,* by Aryeh Kaplan (Schocken, 1985). *Discovering Jewish Meditation: Instruction and Guidance for Learning an Ancient Spiritual Practice,* by Nan Fink Gefen (Jewish Lights, 1999), is a good how-to guide for getting started.

There are various techniques and schools of meditation, but one technique that easily recommends itself is concentrating on the breath and the simple activity of breathing to help the mind become focused. You need not breathe in a particular fashion or sit in a special way. Simply paying attention to the most repeated activity in our day, breathing, reminds us to pay attention to even the simplest things that happen every day. This approach to meditation is not necessarily intended to provide the practitioner with extraordinary experiences. The goal is not to fill us with light or enable us to hear a divine voice; rather it is to allow us to become aware of the present moment. Simply sit in meditation for fifteen to thirty minutes each day, constantly returning your attention to your breathing whenever your attention wanders.

Two other recent practices (also with roots in the tradition) are chanting and the singing of *niggunim*, Hasidic melodies. Both use repetitive singing as a spiritual preparation for the day. Chanting the same phrase or verse over and over again focuses us on its particular theme. Some people create their own simple chant; others use chants composed by contemporary musicians and teachers of chant such as Shefa Gold. *Niggunim* are chanting melodies employed by Hasidic communities. They are often wordless repetitions of simple melodic lines. They were (and still are) composed as sacred music. They can be upbeat or contemplative. *Niggunim* are intended as a means to move beyond words and to express that which cannot be expressed in language. The melody is repeated in a seemingly endless way, until the power of the *nigun* opens a door that reaches deep inside us and seems to stretch all the way to heaven. Our souls are singing the *nigun*, the song of the universe, and for a moment we have joined the universal chorus of oneness. (I have just produced a CD entitled *Songs to the Soul*, available from S.A.J., 15 West 86th St., New York, NY 10024, for $18.)

Different forms of meditation and prayer reinforce each other. Often people incorporate a mixture of practices. For example, some people begin by singing a *nigun* or chanting for ten minutes. Then they pray the highlights of the morning service for ten minutes, followed by silence for ten minutes. Others employ meditation as a preparation for reciting parts of the liturgy. With some experimentation, you may find a combination of practices that particularly resonates with your soul.

*Torah study*    For many, Torah study is the best means of spiritual preparation for the day ahead. As Jews we are commanded to be constantly engaged with Torah. (See "Torah: The Path of Study," pp. 139–75.) Therefore, we begin our day with a series of *berakhot* or blessings for the *mitzvah* of studying and engaging in Torah.

The first two blessings seem particularly appropriate *kavanot* (intentions) for our engagement in Torah:

Praised are You, Eternal One, our God, source of the universe, who has sanctified us through the commandments and commanded us to occupy ourselves in the words of Torah.

May the words of Torah, Eternal One, our God, be sweet in our mouths and in the mouths of all Your people Israel. Then we and our descendants and the descendants of Your people, the house of Israel, will all know You through the study of Torah for its own sake. Praised are You, Eternal One, who teaches Torah to the people of Israel.

Praised are You, Eternal One, our God, source of the universe, who has chosen us from among all nations by giving us the Torah, Praised are You, Eternal One, who gives the Torah.

In the last two *berakhot,* God is described in the present tense as teaching or giving us Torah. Thus, the giving of Torah is not relegated to the Revelation at Sinai but conceived as an ongoing experience.

After these blessings the *Siddur* gives examples of Torah study from the Bible and Talmud. You may make your own choice of passages for daily Torah study.

It is an old tradition to prepare for the Torah reading on Shabbat by reading the portion of the week over the course of the week. This is easily accomplished by using the traditional division of the Torah portion into seven sections (this division is clearly marked in Hebrew editions of the Torah). Each day, one *aliyah* or section is read. (See "*Avodah:* The Path of Prayer," pp. 176–205, for details regarding the Torah cycle.) If you have difficulty finding the time to read a whole section, reading even one verse can suffice. Whether we accompany our study with the *berakhot* or not, whether we study in Hebrew or in English, the study of Torah engages us with the primary text of the Jewish people. When we start our day with Torah study, we are reminded that in our getting up and lying down and all through the day we are to be engaged in the study of Torah as well as living in the light of Torah.

Will there be some message from God to you answering a problem facing you that day? Probably not, unless your long-distance carrier is a lot better than mine. But over time, you will begin to learn the

Torah text and reading that verse will connect you to the cycle of the Torah reading and Shabbat. And occasionally, you will be struck by a verse resonating with your own experience.

*The discipline of* musar *practice*   Another tradition of Jewish spiritual practice is called *musar*. *Musar* literally means "instruction" or "teaching," but it has come to mean a focusing on character development. *Musar* literature, followed in the nineteenth century by the *musar* movement, called upon Jews to develop *middot*, "qualities" such as patience, humility, and forbearance, in order to improve our character. One method employed by *musar* is *heshbon ha-nefesh*, "examining the soul." This involves a systematic daily review, usually focusing on one personal quality at a time. For example, you might read or recite a summary statement about this particular quality each morning to bring the quality to consciousness for the day. If you wanted to focus on the quality of *menuhat ha-nefesh*, "calmness" or "equanimity," you might recite the following: "When faced with a setback that you have no control over, do not make things worse by useless worrying." At the end of the day, you could review how well you did on that quality during the day. (I set out a complete model for this practice in the chapter "The End of the Day.")

## Breaking Fast

Our special relationship with food is covered in "Eating and Food" (pp. 66–93).

## Coming and Going

After all of our preparations to greet the new day, we are ready (or, in any case, need) to venture out into the world of work or school. Judaism encourages us to be aware of the transition from home to work through the *mitzvah*/practice of the mezuzah.

> You shall inscribe them on the doorposts of your house and on your gates. [Deut. 11:20; see also 6:9]

This verse is understood literally—we are to inscribe words of Torah on our door frames—*mezuzot* in Hebrew. Traditionally, we attach a container known as a mezuzah (plural: mezuzot) to the doorpost of our house. Inside is a parchment with Deut. 6:4–9 and 11:13–21 handwritten by a Hebrew scribe.

These are the first two paragraphs of the Shema, the central prayer of Jewish liturgy. The selection also contains the verses that require us to put mezuzot on our doors.

It is traditional to place a mezuzah on every door in the home (excluding bathrooms). It is also traditional to ritually kiss the mezuzah as we pass it by touching it with our fingers and then bringing our fingers to our lips. This reflects an awareness of the transition involved in leaving home and entering the outside world, and in leaving the outside world to return home. Home provides us with a sense of familiarity, safety, and family, of "ourness." On the other hand, the outside world is a place of opportunity, challenge, unclear boundaries, even of risk and danger, populated with people known and unknown. Kissing the mezuzah marks that transition at the boundary line of our door.

Our *kavanah* then is to be aware of the movement from home to world, a journey fraught with dangers real and imagined. It is a journey that promises opportunities for growth and success, along with opportunities for bringing holiness to all our interactions.

The traditional prayer normally voiced when embarking on a long journey seems equally appropriate for our daily journey. My composite of a number of versions follows. Say one of the following *kavanot* and then kiss the mezuzah.

*KAVANAH*

May it be Your will, Eternal One, our God and God of our ancestors, to guide us in peace and to lead our steps in peace. Bring us to our desired destination in life, happiness, and peace, and return us to our home in peace. Save us from every danger lurking on the road. Send blessing on the work of our hands. May we find favor, kindness, and love in Your eyes and in the eyes of all whom we meet. Hear our prayer, for You listen to prayers. Praised are You, Eternal One, who hears prayer.

Or:

God will guard your goings and your comings, now and always. [Psalm 121:5. Some recite this verse before starting their car]

*Some traditions concerning mezuzot*    The key component of the mezuzah is not the container but the parchment. The parchment should be written by a scribe. Printed copies of the text, while widely available, are not traditionally acceptable. The container can be made of any material—metal, wood, and ceramic are often used.

One side of the parchment contains the text from Deuteronomy; the other side is inscribed with the word *Shaddai,* a traditional name of God. The name is interpreted as an abbreviation for the phrase *Shomer Daltot Israel,* "Guardian of the doors of Israel." The parchment is rolled so that the Shema is at the beginning and the word *Shaddai* is visible. Some mezuzot have a hole so that the word can be seen. Others have the Hebrew letter *shin* on the mezuzah representing the name *Shaddai.*

Some mezuzot also have the words *kuzu be-mukhsaz kuzu* on the same side of the parchment as *Shaddai.* This is actually a magical/ mystical name of God. It is known as the fourteen-letter name of God. It is created by a code that substitutes each letter in the Hebrew alphabet with the following letter (*bet* replaces *aleph,* and so on). Decoded, the phrase forms the traditional names of God, *yhvh elohainu yhvh.*

The mezuzah is affixed on the right-hand side of the door as one enters. It is placed in the upper third of the doorway (with allowances sometimes being made for children's rooms) with the container on a slant, its top part closer to the interior of the house.

A mezuzah should be put in place within thirty days of moving into a new home. There is a tradition not to remove the mezuzah when you move if the new tenant or the person buying the house is Jewish.

The blessing said before affixing the mezuzah is:

Praised are You, Eternal one, our God, source of the universe, who has sanctified us with the commandments, commanding us to affix the mezuzah.

The *sheheheyanu* blessing is also recited.

Technically, mezuzot are required only in homes, not in workplaces or even synagogues. But it has become customary to place mezuzot on the front doors of Jewish institutions.

The mezuzah has become one of the most popular symbols of Judaism. And many Jews wear a mezuzah as a pendant around their neck.

As we leave home, we are challenged to bring with us the awareness of the opportunities for holiness in all our activities of the everyday.

# SPEECH

In the beginning, God spoke and the world came into being. We might think that this power to create a world out of nothing through speech distinguishes God from human beings. In actuality, however, we create our world every day through speech. What we convey in our communications with others has a powerful effect on our world. Speech can either be helpful, clarifying, and positive, or it can be muddling and destructive. Speech can heal and speech can damage.

### Lashon ha-ra, Gossip

The tradition's term for gossip and slander is *lashon ha-ra,* literally, "an evil tongue." The rabbis prohibited gossip based on their interpretation of Lev. 19:16, "You shall not be a tale-bearer among your people." Their prohibition against *lashon ha-ra* included not only slanderous falsehoods but also gossip even when it is true. They understood the deleterious effect that gossip can have on a community.

> R. Samuel bar Nahman said: Why is the evil tongue called a thrice-slaying tongue? Because it slays three persons: the person speaking, the person spoken to, and the person spoken of. [Talmud, *Arakhin* 15b]

In this triangle all the parts are connected in a destructive way. Of course, the gossiper is guilty, but also the one who listens to gossip is a willing and a necessary accomplice. The victim may never become aware of the gossip. Yet his or her place in the community can be affected. Profound changes may take place, but gossip is a secret crime and it is very hard to repair its damaging effects. The victim is often unable to defend him- or herself. Gossip spreads, so even confronting the originator of the gossip may not undo the damage. Once pronounced, gossip has a momentum that is difficult to stop.

A story is told that once a person went to a rabbi wanting to make amends for some gossip he had told. The rabbi said, "Take a pillow and walk through town. As you walk, drop the pillow's feathers one by one on the ground, and then return to me." When the gossiper returned, the rabbi said, "Now go and collect the feathers you dropped." This time, when the person returned, he was carrying only a few feathers. "These were all I could find," he said. "The wind scattered the rest." The rabbi said, "So it is with gossip—once loosed on the world there is no way to take it all back."

> The tongue is like an arrow. Why? Because if a person takes his sword in hand to slay his neighbor, who then pleads with him and begs for mercy, the would-be slayer can change his mind and return the sword to its sheath. But once the would-be slayer has shot and let fly an arrow, it cannot be brought back even if he wants to do so. [*Midrash Tehillim*, 120:4]

The rabbis also observed that gossip can be subtle. How things are said, in what context, and with what intonation can make the difference between an innocent comment and gossip. Such indirect gossiping is known by the rabbis as "the dust of *lashon ha-ra.*" Maimonides gives two examples: "Don't say: 'Who would have thought of so and so that he would be as he is now.' Or 'I will be silent about so and so. I do not wish to tell what happened, etc.' " (*Hilkhot De'ot,* 7:4). The rabbis warn against praising a person in front of her enemy, for they understood that it could be done to provoke the enemy to speak ill of her.

Reflect for a moment how often you speak badly of other people. *Lashon ha-ra* is so much a part of our daily conversation that it seems harmless. Sometimes we speak ill of whole groups of people—a race, a social class, or a profession. Other times it is more personal—we may speak ill of people in our workplace or among our circle of acquaintances. It sometimes seems that society itself revels in gossip. Certainly magazines and talk shows specialize in it. I was struck by the negative effect of talk shows a number of years ago when I was on an all-night radio call-in program. The host spent the night confirming, feeding, and expanding upon his callers' worst opinions by telling them that not only was their specific story "true," but their experience reflected a larger "truth." Thus, *all* politicians were corrupt; *all* lawyers were only after our money, etc.

On a more personal level, we often gossip even about people we like: "You know how John is, he's always late." "Typical of Sarah, she can never get her act together in a relationship." Gossip seems to be intrinsic to the very fabric of our conversations. Why? Why do we do it?

There are a number of reasons. Certainly, some gossip is malicious. It is a way to hurt another person or, at least, to express anger toward someone. Since it is done secretly, this is a passive-aggressive form of angry expression. Or gossip can be deliberate, intended to damage another person's reputation, as when we gossip to someone's friends to undermine the subject's relationships.

Gossip is also a way of creating and defining social groups. This is often done out of a sense of insecurity. Afraid of being an outsider, we gather others around us by portraying someone else as the outsider. By gossiping or criticizing others, we enter into a secret alliance with those who will listen. Sometimes these are fairly fixed alliances; at other times the gossip is fluidly promiscuous, flowing in this direction and that direction from one person to the next. Gossip, then, can be used as a tool to define who is a member of an inner circle. This is most obvious when it is used to characterize whole groups of people in stereotypical ways by race, ethnicity, religion, or gender. Gossip is turned against shifting groups of outsiders—"all people on welfare are lazy," "men don't know how to have relationships," and so on. This kind of stereotyping is still prevalent in every part of our society.

Gossip is also related to power. To have knowledge that others do not have and then to choose with whom to share it is a way to wield power. Employed in this fashion, information and gossip are not only ways of forming groups, but also sources of power within a group.

Gossip also seems to be inimical to the fabric of our discourse. It comprises a significant portion of daily conversation. We talk about the weather and we talk about each other. It seems part of the natural order. Is it really possible not to gossip? I shouldn't tell you this, but even the rabbis of the Talmud gossiped a lot. Oops, I just gossiped about them.

R. Amram said in the name of Rav: "No person escapes— not even for one day—committing three transgressions: unchaste thought, insistence on God's immediate response to prayer, and slander. Slander, you say? Yes, at the very least, the fine dust (the overtones) of slander."

R. Judah said in the name of Rav: "Most people are guilty of some cheating, a few of unchastity, but all of slander. Slander, you say? Well, at least the fine dust (the overtones) of slander." [Talmud, *Bava Batra* 164b]

R. Yohanan said in the name of R. Yose ben Zimra: "The one who speaks slander is as though he denied the existence of God." [Talmud, *Arakhin* 15b]

The company of those who speak slander cannot greet the *Shekhinah* [God's Presence]. [Talmud, *Sotah* 42a]

Behold, how vicious is slander! It is more vicious than murder, unchastity, and idolatry put together. . . . [Talmud, *Sotah* 5a]

Gossip is prevalent and destructive, yet it seems only realistic to accept it as common practice, like taking sweeteners from restaurants, overeating, or driving just above the speed limit. But imagine for a moment how different the world would be if gossip were to disappear! A gossip-free workplace, for instance, would be spiritually healthy just as a smoke-free workplace is physically healthy. As human beings, created in the image of the Divine, we are ultimately more alike than unalike.

Gossip only serves to sidetrack us from confronting both our own goodness and our own flaws.

The challenge is great, but it is easy to get started. Just ask yourself the question, "Is this information I am about to pass on really necessary?" That will usually remove you from the role of gossiper. As for being an accomplice, if people begin to get a sense that you don't enjoy hearing gossip, they will share it with you less frequently. If you seem uninterested in gossip, people soon take the point.

Is there ever a time when gossip is permissible? Some Jewish authorities, in their attempt to discourage *lashon ha-ra*, hold the position that gossip is permissible only when it may save someone from physical or financial harm. Yet it seems to me that there are other times when it is important to share information about another person. A number of criteria would apply. The information, though negative, should be truthful. The sharing needs to be helpful to the listener. Clearly, motivation is a critical factor. To be malicious or just to idly share information is to gossip. To respond honestly to a request for a job reference, an employee evaluation, and so on, can have an entirely different and important purpose. Similarly, to describe your feelings about another person in the context of therapy is a sharing both in confidence and for the purposes of healing. More complex, but still appropriate, is the human need to share with a friend when someone has hurt you emotionally. Here, too, the overall purpose is healing.

Like God, we have the ability to re-create the world every day with words. The challenge for us is what will follow the words that initiate creation: "Let there be . . ." Will we, at the end of each day, be able to echo the Creator's words: There was evening and there was morning, one day, *ki tov,* "and it was good"?

## Reproof, Hatred, and Love

Two questions are raised by the situations discussed above. What should you do if you see someone hurting another person? And what should you do if a person is hurtful to you?

The biblical verses that follow "you shall not be a tale-bearer among your people" set out ways to deal with these complexities.

You shall not be tale-bearer among your people. You shall not stand idly by the blood of your neighbor: I am the Lord. You shall not hate your kinsfolk in your heart. Reprove your kinsman. Incur no guilt because of him. You shall not take vengeance or bear a grudge against your countrymen. Love your neighbor as yourself. I am the Lord. [Lev. 19:16–18]

Let us examine each of these verses through the eyes of the traditional commentaries. We begin with a call to cease from gossip, since this pervasive practice is so destructive to the social fabric. We are then told not to stand idly by the blood of our neighbor. We move from a negative commandment, do not gossip, to a positive commandment calling for our involvement in the life of the community. In the face of injustice or wrongdoing, we are told not to stand idly by. We must actively attempt to better the situation.

Whence is it derived that if you are in a position to testify on behalf of your friend, you are not permitted to remain silent? From: "You shall not stand idly by the blood of your neighbor." *[Torat Cohanim]*

How are we to feel about the person who is hurting another person? And to return to one of our initial questions, What if the person is hurting you? What if you catch someone in the act of gossiping about you? Then you cannot stand idly by. If it is about you, you are involved.

The next verse sets out the ideal response. "You shall not hate your kinsfolk in your heart. Reprove your kinsman. Incur no guilt because of him." The Torah asks something very difficult of us. It is not just an act such as eating *matzah* or keeping kosher, but rather an emotion (or lack of one) that is required. Do not hate!

The rabbis taught: "Do not hate"—I might think the meaning is not to strike him, not to smite her, not to curse him; it is, therefore, written: "You shall not hate your kinsfolk *in your heart*—scripture is speaking of hatred in the heart." [Talmud, *Arakhin* 16b]

In other words, it matters what you feel in your heart even if you do not express it. Instead of hatred, the Torah tells us to express reproof. *Hokha'ah tokhiah.* "Reprove, surely reprove," as the doubling of the verb in the Hebrew is usually translated. Do not stand idly by, but confront the wrongdoer.

The traditional commentaries discuss whom we are obligated to reprove. One understanding is that we are to reprove those who hurt us. Instead of bearing hate in our heart toward people, we are to confront them and explain to them how they have hurt us. At the least, this process may enable us to avoid hating another person. At its best, a greater understanding and reconciliation are possible, leading us to *tikkun,* to a "repair" in the breach of the human relationships involved. In this understanding, the last part of the verse, "incur no guilt because of him," instructs us to engage in reproof to avoid hating another person. For if you hate someone, you incur guilt or sin through your hatred.

A second understanding incorporates the first but adds another layer. We are to reprove not only someone who has wronged us but also those who wrong anybody. This verse, then, is seen as directly tied to the previous verse about "not standing idly by." Whether done to us or to anyone in society, we are called not to hate the wrongdoer but rather to reprove him or her. The last part of the verse indicates that avoiding reproof "incurs guilt" because by silence we become accomplices to the wrongdoing.

The Talmud provides some guidelines for reproof:

1) Reprove and reprove again even up until a hundred times, that is, until the person hears the reproof (Talmud, *Bava Metzia* 31a).
2) Up to which point should you reprove? Until the other person hits you to make you stop (Talmud, *Arakhin* 16b).
3) Just as it is a *mitzvah,* a commandment, to reprove someone who will heed the reproof, so too is it a *mitzvah* not to say what will not be heeded (Talmud, *Yevamot* 65b).

These guidelines demonstrate that the rabbis understood both the importance of reproving a person and the difficulties involved. To be fully successful, the reproof must be heard. Only in this way is change possible. Even for the reprover, a sense of full satisfaction is only present when the reproof is fully heard and an apology is offered. Thus these guidelines set out contradictory notions: We should reprove if there is a chance of success and also continue to reprove until the one reproved "punches us." Perhaps that is why one interpretation is that we are obligated to reprove only someone who has hurt us directly. If someone has hurt us, in most cases, a previous relationship existed. Friendship or acquaintance provides a context for the reproof. It is more likely that a reproof will be heard if it comes from someone we know. It is less likely that the reproof of a total stranger will be effective. *Sefer Hasidim* (the medieval *Book of the Pious*) states that we should reprove only a person we love. On the one hand, with someone we love there is a great deal of past history and the reproof will often evoke a counter-reproof. Most often, for couples this is in fact round number 3,426 of the same fight that they have had for years. But on the other hand, those moments when we speak to the other out of love rather than hurt or anger are moments when those we love can hear the criticism because it is wrapped in our love. Love makes it possible for reproof to be absorbed.

There are two other benefits to reproof that are worth mentioning. First, reproof forces you to focus your anger on the person who hurt you rather than displacing it on others. Second (as the medieval commentator Ibn Ezra points out), the act of reproof allows for the possibility that you can discover that the other person is in fact totally innocent. It may be that you misunderstood what was spoken and that there is no real reason to be angry with the other person. If you hesitated to reprove the one you think wronged you, those mistaken feelings of hurt would only fester.

All told, the ideal reproof is expressed more out of concern for the other than out of our own hurt. This kind of reproof can begin the process of transformation for both parties, the reprover and the reproved. After all, the tradition could have just said, "Do not hate." Without a notion of reproof, the tradition could have called us to forgive the one who wronged us, to let go of the hurt and the anger. If we could do that then we could move on in our lives without being eaten up by hurt and hatred. However, this is not enough in Judaism. In community, it is not enough for one of us to move on. We are to reprove the other so that both of us can move on, both of us can work at repairing the breach.

Simple, then? Not at all.

> Rabbi Tarfon said: I wonder if there is anyone in this generation capable of giving reproof. For if anyone says to another: "Take the chip from between your teeth," the other retorts, "Take the beam from between your eyes." Rabbi Eleazar ben Azariah said: I wonder whether there is anyone in this generation capable of accepting reproof. Rabbi Akiva said: I wonder whether there is anyone in this generation that knows how to give reproof without humiliating the one reproved. [Talmud, *Arakhin* 16b]

To complicate things further, Rabbi Akiva's comment is related to the rabbinic concern that just as you should be relentless in your reproof, you also must not humiliate the one reproved. Thus there is in fact a third understanding of the last part of our verse "Incur no guilt because of him." It means that we should not embarrass the one being reproved, because to embarrass another person is to commit a sin. This concept is expanded to include anyone, not just one who is reproved. To shame someone is considered a very serious wrongdoing.

> She who shames her neighbor human being in public is as though she shed blood. [Talmud, *Bava Metzia* 58b]

To embarrass someone publicly is to reveal that you have an inappropriate motive for reproof. Instead of reconciliation and healing, your purpose is to hurt the other person. Embarrassing someone publicly is also the opposite of gossip, which is done behind a person's back. Yet even though this is done openly and to a person's face, it is at least as destructive as gossip.

The tradition sets out a manner of relationship that encourages us to process feelings and hurts through a positive confrontation with the one that hurt us, while at the same time discouraging gossip, hatred, indifference, and humiliation. The question still remains, however: How are we to relate to someone who has hurt us deeply? How are we to relate to the person who cannot hear our reproof? How are we to relate to a person who has done evil deeds?

> The rabbis taught: "You shall not hate": But if he sees in him something indecent it is permitted to hate him. Rabbi Nahman bar Yitzhak said: It is a *mitzvah* to hate him, as it is written (Prov. 8:13): "The fear of the Lord is to hate evil." [Talmud, *Pesahim* 113b]

Once again, the tradition reflects the complexity of human existence. We should not hate. We should reprove both those who hurt us and those who bring hurt into the world. We should reprove in such a way that it can be taken in by the one reproved. We certainly should not reprove in a way that is publicly embarrassing. *Except* if the person cannot hear the reproof. *Except* if there is a legitimate reason to hate the person. *Except* if the person should be publicly shamed for his or her deeds.

In regard to the latter, it does seem to make a difference whether the person is a public figure or not. To report on allegations of wrongdoing by a public figure in a newspaper is not perforce either gossip or public embarrassment. It obviously needs to be done with care and with some reason to believe that there is substance to the accusations. Even here there are limits. Recently it has been widely debated whether a discussion of the personal lives of public figures, particularly politicians, is a legitimate area of the public's "right to know." While a politician's taking a bribe is newsworthy, are a politician's sexual indiscretions relevant to his or her qualifications for the job?

The last verse in our selection from Leviticus carries these notions of proper relationship one further step. "You shall not take vengeance or bear a grudge against your countrymen. Love your neighbor as yourself. I am the Lord."

> It was taught: Which is vengeance and which is bearing a grudge? If one said: Lend me your scythe, and she was refused; and the next day the other said to her: Lend me your spade—If she replied: I

will not lend it to you, just as you did not lend it to me—this is vengeance; and if she replied: Here it is—I am not like you, who do not lend—this is bearing a grudge. [Talmud, *Yoma* 23a]

In the concepts of vengeance and bearing a grudge, we can see the playing out of broken relationships. There is neither gossip nor hatred. There is no great hurt and the vengeance being described is not of the Hatfield and McCoy kind. What is described is the everyday interactions of people. It involves keeping score and generosity. The difference between vengeance and bearing a grudge as understood by the rabbis is clear. Vengeance is acting in a tit-for-tat fashion—I won't lend something to you because you wouldn't lend to me. Bearing a grudge is a verbal withholding and attack. It also seems to put us on the high moral ground, though really our act of generosity isn't generous at all. Either way, by withholding or by giving grudgingly, we are responding to the other person's need improperly. We have become locked by them, and thereby with them, in a cycle of revenge—an endless loop until someone breaks it.

There is another reason that this verse about vengeance and bearing a grudge follows the previous verse about reproof. What if you attempt to reprove someone and they just don't hear you? What if the next day they come over to borrow something from you?

Our verse teaches that even if past hurts are unresolved, there is still a proper way to act. You should lend your scythe or your bowl of sugar. You are not to do so ungraciously. The first part of the verse does not tell you what you should be feeling as you lend this person your scythe. It just tells you to do it and what not to say. However, the verse does end with an ideal goal—that is, to love others.

The cycle of revenge is in stark contrast to the cycle of love set out at the end of the verse in the words "Love your neighbor as yourself." The cyclical nature of the latter is emphasized by the addition of the word *kamokha*, "as yourself." The verse would have been clear if it had said "Love your neighbor," period. Adding "as yourself" creates a cycle between you, the other, and yourself.

This is one of the most famous verses in the Torah. It is Rabbi Akiva's choice as *the* verse in the Torah. Similarly, when a convert asked Hillel to teach him the whole Torah while standing on one foot, Hillel quoted him a restatement of this verse.

The highest ideal, as well as a summary of all that comes before, lies in these words: "Love your neighbor as yourself." How are we to understand this *mitzvah*?

The simplest understanding, the most literal, is that the verse asks us to do unto others what we would have them do unto us. What does it mean to "love" your neighbor? It means to act toward her in a loving way by being helpful and generous toward her just as we would want her to be helpful and generous toward us. Perhaps, after all, it is not so much a *feeling* of love as a *behaving* in a loving way. We then know how to fulfill this *mitzvah* in an almost utilitarian fashion: think how we want to be treated and act to the other accordingly.

RaMBaN (Nahmanides, a medieval Bible commentator) sees a potential problem with this approach and adds another layer to it. He defines this verse as asking us to want for our neighbor whatever we would want for ourselves. He then highlights a problem of this linkage of *kamokha*, "as yourself." We may want good things for those we care for, but the "as yourself" could become a limit. I want good things for you but I want the best for me either out of a sense that there is not enough "best" to go around equally to everyone or simply out of a competitive feeling. Instead, *kamokha*, "as yourself," teaches us that we should love the other as much as ourselves. We should move beyond the constricting coils of jealousy to a place of wanting the best for all those around us.

There is still another interpretation that moves the understanding of *kamokha*, "as yourself," even further away from being "you"-centered. This understanding suggests that we should love our neighbor as ourself because our neighbor is just like us. We are all created *be-tzelem elohim*, "in the image of God." We are commanded to love everyone because we are all fundamentally alike, all images of God. The mystics would say love the other because you and they are a part of the great Oneness of the world.

Love is relational and so is this commandment. We are called not just to cultivate an attitude of loving the other as some abstract principle. The love is in relation to the other. If we are to visit the sick because of this verse (as Maimonides states), we are only to visit the sick who want to be visited. This is not some absolute commandment to be fulfilled whether the other person wants it or not. The other person matters. It is a commandment that can only be fulfilled in relationship to the other. This love of the other is an affirmation of the self and the other.

When I teach this text, someone always asks me about the person who doesn't love herself. Ought she to hate the other as she hates herself? The answer is she probably does. True love is an affirmation both of the self and the other. The tradition contrasts this to another kind of love that is dependent on something: *Ahavah teluyah ba-davar,* "love that is conditional." This is love that treats the other as an object. True love is *unconditional* because the other is just "like you," *kamokha.* *Kedushah* or "holiness" is found when any two people are profoundly connected.

True love is not so common, yet the Torah calls us to try to remember who we are and who the other really is. The more we remember that we are all equal, all created in the image of God, the harder it will be to stereotype others, to want to gossip about them, to want to take revenge upon them. Instead, we recognize in their failings and foibles echoes of our own—that mixture of the divine and the flawed mortal.

In the end, the challenges of these verses from Leviticus can still seem overwhelming. Stop gossiping and love everyone! Yet each step in that direction is important. Each word of gossip left unsaid, each act of generosity, each word of loving reproof that brings change—each of these is of incalculable importance even amid all the times we do the opposite.

The Jewish tradition was aware both of how much was being asked of us and also of how little steps in the right direction can make a difference. The rabbinic comments on "love your neighbor" are not glowing paeans to love. Instead there are a series of comments along the following lines:

R. Yehudah said in the name of Rav: One is forbidden to marry someone before you see them, for perhaps you will find something in them that is unattractive which will make them displeasing to you;

and the Torah has written: "And you shall love your neighbor as yourself." [Talmud, *Kiddushin* 41a]

Even in the act of executing a criminal, the principle of "love your neighbor" applies—not to forgive him but to grant him a humane death:

The stoning platform [the condemned were thrown from the platform] was two floors in height. Was so much height needed to kill him? R. Nahman said: " 'And you shall love your neighbor as yourself'—choose a humane death for him." [That is, the greater height made for a quicker death.] [Talmud, *Sanhedrin* 45a]

Thus, in every moment the potential to act from the context of these principles is present for us. We need to act in the everyday world in the confidence that every small positive act always makes a difference.

There is a tradition to recite as a *kavanah* (intention) every morning the words *ve-ahavta le-re'akha kamokha*, "love your neighbor as yourself." This *kavanah* was introduced by the mystics of Safed as a prelude to the daily *minyan*. "Only by accepting upon ourselves the obligation to love others as ourselves are we allowed to enter the human community of prayer" (Arthur Green). Accepting this commandment can also be a *kavanah* for relating to every person we meet in the course of every day of our lives.

## ONE AT A TIME

A friend of ours was walking down a deserted Mexican beach at sunset. As he walked along, he began to observe a native in the distance. As he drew nearer, he noticed that the native kept leaning down, picking something up and throwing it out into the water. Time and again he kept hurling things out into the ocean.

As our friend approached even closer, he noticed that the man was picking up starfish that had been washed up on the beach and, one at a time, he was throwing them back into the water.

Our friend was puzzled. He approached the man and said, "Good evening, friend. I was wondering what you are doing."

"I'm throwing these starfish back into the ocean. You see, it's low tide right now and all of these starfish have been washed up on shore. If I don't throw them back into the sea, they'll die up here from lack of oxygen."

"I understand," my friend replied, "but there must be thousands of starfish on this beach. You can't possibly get to all of them. There are simply too many. And don't you realize this is probably happening on hundreds of beaches all up and down this coast? Can't you see that you can't possibly make a difference?"

The local native smiled, bent down and picked up yet another starfish, and as he threw it back into the sea, he replied, "Made a difference to that one!" [Jack Canfield and Mark V. Hansen, *Chicken Soup for the Soul*]

# WORK

Rabbi Israel of Salant was once sitting with his close followers and discussing with them the ways of life, and speaking words of ethical teaching. They began to consider the question of who is higher—someone who sits in the *Bet Midrash,* the house of study, turning his nights into days and occupying himself full time with Torah study and prayer and other Divine service, or someone who sits in his store and conducts his business dealings in faithfulness to the Torah's teachings? "It is known," said Rabbi Israel, "that there is nothing higher than doing business in faithfulness. But that being so, how sad when someone in business spends his time thinking he should have his attention on the kerosene or the salt or the salted fish [rather than the spiritual tasks involved]!" [*Midor Dor,* vol. 2 #1366]

For many people, "work" and "spirituality" negate and contradict each other; they are polar opposites that come from two entirely different universes. . . .

To them, "work" is wholly practical, rooted in the necessities of this world and geared toward providing for self and family. "Spirituality," on the other hand, is otherworldly, ethereal, and has little bearing on what seems to be one of the most mundane, demanding, and unavoidable aspects of our lives: our jobs and our professions.

For them, the concept of spirituality has to be reconstructed, almost from the ground up. [Rabbi Jeffrey Salkin, *Being God's Partner*]

Do we work because we have to or because we want to? The answer is yes. Most of us work first and foremost because we need to earn a living in order to survive. We no longer live in a Garden of Eden where all is provided. Instead, as Genesis predicts, "by the sweat of your brow shall you get bread to eat" (Gen. 3:19). Our lives are destined to be filled with toil until we "return to the ground" (Gen. 3:19) from whence we came.

Long before the modern world, with its emphasis on work as a basic human right (socialism) or as a means of personal fulfillment (American "careerism"), work was a way of being in the world. We spend much of our lives at work. It is the arena in which we interact with the wider world. Little wonder, then, that we want to feel pride in our accomplishments. Our accomplishments and our children may be our only means to leave a legacy that will survive our death. So we all share the Psalmist's hope, *ma'aseh yadaynu konnenahu,* "let the work of our hands establish us" (Psalm 90:17).

Jewish tradition places a high value on work. If you lack it, then you are missing a basic element of life. "Sages of the school of R. Ishmael taught: 'Choose life' (Deut. 30:19) means: choose a craft" (Jerusalem Talmud, *Peah* 1:1, 15c). "R. Judah said: 'When people do not teach their children a craft, it is as though they were teaching them to be brigands'" (Talmud, *Kiddushin* 29a). But the tradition also understands that it is difficult to earn a living.

> R. Shezbi said in the name of R. Eleazar ben Azariah: "The maintenance of people in their daily bread is as awesome as the splitting of the Red Sea." [Midrash, *Genesis Rabbah* 20:9]

> Our masters taught: There are three whose life is no life: one who must look to the table of others, one whose spouse rules over her or him, and one whose body is racked by suffering. [Talmud, *Bava Metzia* 32b]

> R. Ahai ben Josiah said: One who eats of their own is [as much at ease] as an infant raised at a mother's breast. He also used to say:

When people eat of their own, their minds are at ease. But people's minds are not at ease when they eat even at their father's table, their mother's table, or their children's table, let alone at a stranger's table. [*Avot de Rabbi Nathan* 30]

Our sense of self is inextricably bound up in work and feeling good about work. More than a livelihood is at stake here. "Sell yourself to work that is alien to you rather than depend on the [handouts of] others" (Jerusalem Talmud, *Berakhot* 9:3, 13d). Or "Flay a carcass in the marketplace to earn a wage and do not say, 'I am a priest, I am an important person, and such work is degrading to me' " (Talmud, *Bava Batra* 110a). Who we are and how we perceive ourselves is deeply dependent on our work. "When you eat the labor of your hands, happy you shall be and it shall be well with you" (Psalm 128:2).

Work then has this dual nature: it is the human curse to have to struggle to survive and the human blessing to be born with hands that can shape, mold, and create. The more successful we become at earning enough for our basic needs, the more complex are the issues surrounding the meaning of our work. Is the time we spend seeking fulfillment in our work detrimental to our families, our relationships, and our inner selves? Is fulfillment through work a possible or ever-elusive goal? How should we relate to employers? To employees? To customers and clients? And what impact does our work have on the world at large?

In the beginning, the First Contractor said: "Let there be!" And a world was created down to the smallest detail. For six days God labored at creating the world, resting only on the seventh day, Shabbat. These six days of creating are re-created weekly. This is another way in which we are created in the image of God.

Unlike the Creator, however, most of our work does not establish an eternal legacy. Yet it may have an impact, as we learn from the following:

"And when you come into the Land, you shall plant" (Lev. 19:23). The Holy One said to Israel: Even though you find it full of all kinds of good, you are not to say, "We will stay put and not plant." But be sure to plant saplings. Even as, when you entered, you found saplings that others planted, so you are to plant for your children. [*Midrash Tanhuma, Kedoshim* 8]

In the main, however, the purpose of our work lies not in the future, but in the present moment. Our job is to continue creation through the work of our hands. What we create may not equal Michelangelo's *Moses,* but in truth the world is created and sustained in its details.

Just as important as knowing that our task is to continue the work of God's creation, we need to recognize the ultimate fact that we cannot finish creation. At the end of the "week" of our lives, when we come to our final rest, the job is not complete. As the Mishnah points out, "You are not obligated to finish the task, neither are you free to neglect it" (*Ethics of Our Ancestors,* 2:21). The best we can hope for in the end is to be able to echo the Creator by saying *ki tov,* "and it was good."

To say our work was good is not to say our task was completed. It is to say that we performed the task we were given with care, diligence, and responsibility. Our work benefited those whose lives it intersected. It inched forward the work of God's creation. In this sense, work is intrinsic to, and not separate from, our spiritual lives.

## TEACHINGS ON THE NECESSITY OF WORK

Shemaiah says: Love work. . . . What does this mean? This teaches that a person should love work and no one should hate work. For even as the Torah was given as a covenant, so was work given as a covenant; as it is said, "Six days you shall labor and do all your work, but the seventh day is a Sabbath of the Lord your God" (Exod. 20:9–10).

R. Simeon ben Eleazar said: Even Adam tasted nothing before he worked, for Scripture says, "And God put him into the Garden of Eden to till it and tend it" (Gen. 2:15), and only after that, God told him, "Of every tree of the Garden of Eden you may eat freely" (Gen. 2:16). [*Avot de-Rabbi Nathan*]

> R. Tarfon said: The Holy One did not cause God's presence to dwell among Israel until they did some work, for Scripture says, "And let them make Me the Sanctuary, then shall I dwell among them" (Exod. 25:8).
>
> R. Yose said: A human dies only out of idleness. [*Avot de-Rabbi Nathan* 11]

## Work as a Spiritual Path

Work as a spiritual path involves two large components: our relationship to our work and our impact on the people and the world around us.

Not so long ago, most people had a direct relationship with the product of their work. The farmer knew his land and its product in a very intimate way. The craftsperson in a shop could take personal pride in the work of his hands. Industrialization tended to lead to an "alienation of labor" as the connection between worker and product became distanced in factories and agribusinesses. Workers less often produced a complete product. Workers less often owned the finished product. The result was a kind of alienation.

A friend visiting the Soviet Union in the late 1960s bought a tape recorder in a store in Moscow to give to a Soviet Jew as a present. When the gift was presented, they discovered that it didn't work. My friend returned to the store and explained to the salesperson that the recorder didn't work. "No problem," responded the salesperson, reaching into the display case and taking out another recorder. My friend immediately tested the new tape recorder to ensure that it worked. "Have a nice day," the salesperson said as he placed the broken tape recorder back on the shelf in the display case along with all the other new tape recorders!

In the modern Western world, the alienation illustrated in this story is prevalent, even if in less extreme forms.

If work is to have spiritual meaning, or at least not be deadening to the spirit, it cannot be drudgery. The challenge is to find work that feeds our souls. We need to enjoy our jobs at least some of the time. We need to feel both that we are doing a good and competent job and that our work is purposeful.

The Midrash says that the Egyptians would have the Israelite slaves do meaningless work. They would tell them to dig a big hole and then fill it back in. Even a slave, one with no choice, could take pride in building a city, but no one's spirit could survive a life of absolutely meaningless work.

When we feel related to our work, it becomes a meaningful enterprise. When we feel related, we can also tell when we are doing a good job. Without such relatedness, an enormous hole develops in our sense of self, since competency in work gives us a sense of general competency and self-worth. For the unemployed, all of this seems a luxury. They may need to take any job, no matter how unsatisfying, because economically they have no choice. Judaism is hardly ignorant of this harsh reality.

> The torments of poverty deprive people of their good sense and of the capacity to acknowledge their Creator. [Talmud, *Eruvin* 41b]

> No portion in life is harder to bear than poverty, for a person who is crushed by poverty, is as one beset by all the afflictions of the world, indeed as one stricken by all the curses listed in Deuteronomy [see ch. 28]. Our masters added: Were all the afflictions in the world gathered on one side and poverty on the other, poverty would outweigh them all. . . . [Midrash, *Exodus Rabbah* 31:12]

All the same, for anyone with a job, no matter what the job is, it is essential to feel competent in that job. Yet doing a job well is not just about performance. It also has to do with that job's impact on others and on the world. If I am doing my job well, then my co-workers are happy to work with me. The people who work for me feel that I am a fair boss and even a person who cares about their lives outside of work. The clients and customers feel that I am not just out for their money but that I am honest, will try to respond to a complaint, and will treat them like human beings instead of numbered invoices. A healthy workplace is a pleasant environment that greets the public with genuine concern.

Such a workplace, whatever its product, is helping to create the world. It is a place that respects the fact that everyone is created in the Divine image and should be treated as such. A healthy workplace affirms life.

A true story: I hate going to my local post office. There is always a long line. Recently I waited until after the Christmas rush to go to buy stamps. Sure enough, a line of eight people stood ahead of me. There were only two tellers working, one of whom spent twenty minutes with a person speaking a foreign language. As usual, you could see three other tellers doing something but not opening their windows. The people on line became increasingly restless. Finally the person behind me switched from muttering to yelling out loud, "Let's get moving." Of course, nothing happened. Looking at the tellers' faces, it seemed to me that they were as unhappy as the customers. An atmosphere of negativity prevailed in this office. The postal employees were regularly berated by irate customers. Presumably understaffed, the employees responded to a bad situation by approaching their job with a great deal of passivity. I could try to avoid the post office by getting my stamps by mail, but they could only show up for their daily round of giving and receiving abuse. This is a prime example of an unhealthy workplace. It is a shame that the postal workers were unfamiliar with Rabbi Judah: "On his way to the house of study, R. Judah used to carry a pitcher on his shoulder, saying 'Great is labor, for it honors the laborer' " (Talmud, *Nedarim* 49b).

In other words, our attitude to work, combined, of course, with the reality of our work situation (fair boss, fair pay, good colleagues, etc.), can make the time spent in work one that nurtures the soul and our sense of self.

But there is yet another attitude that needs to be cultivated to put work in its proper perspective. While some people may find their work tedious and meaningless and cannot wait to get home, at the opposite extreme there are others who never seem to leave work. A workaholic is simply someone who lives to work. Even in our society, there are people who work more hours than their grandparents did. Why? For some, it is an economic necessity required by the demands of a particular profession, as in the case of a corporate lawyer. For others, it is a "legitimate" way not to be home when home is an empty apartment or an empty relationship. For still others, it is the only way to have enough money to acquire all the things they desire. Yet for all of these workaholics, success, whether professional or financial, always seems to be just over the next hill. In the end, it is always necessary to achieve a correct balance between economic need, professional success, and self-worth. As Rabbi Jeffrey Salkin has observed, "If we judge ourselves and judge others only by the goods or services that we produce, if we believe that to *be* more is to *do* more, then we are truly slaves to what we do. Work becomes an end in itself."

### A TEXT STUDY ON WEALTH

Who is wealthy? A person who is satisfied with his lot. [Talmud, *Shabbat* 32a]

Our masters taught: Who is wealthy? One who is content with her wealth—so said R. Meir. But R. Tarfon said: One who has one hundred vineyards, one hundred fields, and one hundred slaves working in them. R. Akiva said: One who has a spouse comely in deeds. R. Yose said: One who has a privy not far from his table [at that time, only the wealthy could afford a private privy]. [Talmud, *Shabbat* 25b]

Abbaye said: We have a tradition that only one who lacks knowledge is poor. [Talmud, *Nedarim* 41a]

R. Joshua ben Levi said: "All the days of a poor person are evil" (Prov. 15:15) if he is irascible; "but contentment is a feast without end" (ibid.), [even for a poor person] when he is content. [Talmud, *Bava Batra* 145b]

When you hear that your neighbor is dead, believe it; [when you hear] that your neighbor got rich, do not believe it. [Talmud, *Gittin* 30b]

All parts of the body depend on the heart. But the heart depends on what's in the purse. [Jerusalem Talmud, *Terumot* 8:10, 46b]

A person's possessions should not be more precious to her than her person. [Talmud, *Bava Kamma* 117b]

A lover of money never has his fill of money, nor a lover of wealth his fill of income. That too is futile. As his substance increases, so do those who consume it; what, then, does the success of its owner amount to but feasting his eyes? A worker's sleep is sweet, whether he has much or little to eat; but the rich person's abundance doesn't let him sleep. . . . She must depart just as she came. As she came out of her mother's womb, so must she depart at last, naked as she came. She can take nothing of her wealth to carry with her. So what is the good of her toiling for the wind? [Eccles. 5:9–11, 14–15]

How easy it is to fall into the trap of a never-ending desire for more money and more possessions. This is a need that can never be satisfied. These texts point out that a sense of satisfaction comes from a certain attitude. If you are grateful for what you have, your sense of appreciation can provide enjoyment of, and satisfaction with, your life. It is not that desire itself can be, or even should be, eliminated. It is rather that wealth comes more from a "sense" that you have enough rather than a "sense" that you are a have-not or that you have but others have more.

The second text quotes four different opinions about who is wealthy. While R. Meir upholds the notion that wealth comes from satisfaction, R. Tarfon suggests that there is an empirical definition of wealth that is related to possessions. R. Akiva's opinion is that wealth is not material possessions but rather a good relationship with your spouse (his wife left her family to marry him when he was poor, and she even supported him while he studied). The last opinion, that of R. Yose, agrees that there is an empirical notion to wealth but suggests that it is also subjective. Having the comfort of a bathroom close by may be a form of wealth even if you do not own a hundred vineyards. For some of the sages, wealth comes from satisfaction and happiness. For others, material possessions are the source of wealth. R. Yose's opinion suggests that possessions have a purpose: wealth is not about owning many things but rather about owning those things that make life comfortable. His opinion postulates a relationship between meeting basic needs and being satisfied with your lot.

Whether wealth is based on owning many things, on a general sense of happiness in life, or on having enough to live comfortably, all of the opinions recognize that without a sense of satisfaction, whatever its source, possessions can come to possess you.

The text about believing news of a neighbor's death but not news of his becoming wealthy is a reflection of the danger of trying to keep up with the Joneses. One way to understand this statement is that while death is objective, becoming wealthy is not. Jealousy of another's good fortune is an attitude all of us too easily acquire. Our want for more should be based on what we need, what would give us pleasure, rather than on what another person has.

Ultimately, the tradition provides a fine balance. Satisfaction comes from attitude, but attitude is related to what we own. The next text states that all the parts of the body are dependent on the heart, suggesting that how we feel about things is more important than objective "reality." Yet the one thing that is not dependent on the heart is money. While some individuals can be poor and be satisfied with their lot, for most of us there is a correlation between financial well-being and emotional well-being. The tradition's bottom line is to remember that our possessions are ultimately less important than our selves. Kohelet (Ecclesiastes) reminds us of this ultimate truth: we leave the world as we came into it, naked and possessionless. There are no pockets in *takhrihin*, the traditional Jewish shroud. Unlike Kohelet's cynical view, we can strive for a satisfaction with our lot, even as we take pleasure in all the beautiful things that this world has to offer. Perhaps we can own some of those beautiful things, but most of life's beauty, whether it is a sunset or a Rembrandt, can be enjoyed without being possessed.

## Whose World Is It Anyway?

Kohelet reminds us that we are temporary sojourners on this planet. Whatever we own is really on temporary loan. Yet at least as far back as the Egyptian pyramids, people have tried to use wealth to "defeat" death, irrationally believing that immortality can be purchased. Instead, Judaism reminds us that "the earth is the Lord's." Even land, which in the ancient world was the most important and basic possession, is not ours. The Promised Land for which we wandered in the desert for forty years is only leased to us by God. When the Israelites finally reached the land, each family was given a plot to till. Every seven years (the Sabbatical) we are to let it lie fallow and every fifty years (*yovel*, "the Jubilee year") all land returns to its original owners. Because of the Jubilee you could never buy or sell land in a permanent way. Every fifty years the economic game started all over again with everybody equal. The metaphor is eloquent. Our job here as tenant farmers is to take care of the world and each other, not to build empires.

The laws of the Jubilee are no longer applicable even in Israel. However, Arthur Waskow has recently suggested applying these ancient concepts to other areas of economic life. See his book *Down-to-Earth Judaism* (William Morrow, 1995, pp. 147–239).

## Work Ethics

The second component of our relationship to work is the way we behave in our work. Do we work in an honest and ethical way? In the last chapter, we spoke of speech and gossip. Clearly, the workplace is one area where destructive talk can thrive. But beyond speech and all the ways that we are to behave in a caring manner to all human beings, there are a number of specific demands related to honesty in business.

If you will heed the Lord your God diligently, doing what is upright in God's sight, giving ear to God's commandments and keeping all God's laws . . . (Exod. 15:26). What does "doing what is upright" refer to? It refers to being engaged in the give-and-take of business. The verse implies that when people act in business with integrity (and the spirit of their fellow creatures delights in them), it is accounted to them as if they had fulfilled the entire Torah, all of it ["keeping *all* God's laws"]. [Mekilta de-Rabbi Ishmael, *Be-Shallah, Va-yassa,* 1]

Let the property of your fellow be as precious to you as your own. [*Ethics of Our Ancestors* 2:12]

Naturally, Judaism has prohibitions against dishonest business relations. It is in the details of these and other commandments that a spiritual approach to business ethics is revealed.

## Theft

R. Yohanan said: When a person robs his fellow even the value of a *perutah* [penny], it is as though he had taken his life away from him, as it is said, "So are the ways of everyone that is greedy of gain, which takes away the life of the owners thereof" (Prov. 1:19). [Talmud, *Bava Kamma* 119a]

The Torah instructs us not to steal or deal dishonestly (Lev. 19:11) and not to use false weights or measures (Lev. 19: 35–36). Most people would affirm that not stealing and not cheating are important moral principles and, if asked, would deny engaging in such practices. Yet the tradition realizes that it is not grand theft but the category of petty theft that involves the average person. As R. Yohanan says above, in the eyes of the tradition there is no such thing as petty theft. The consequences of theft are twofold: one on the victim, the other on the thief. The victim is deprived of something that was hers. The thief is burdened with the knowledge that he has done something wrong. The thief then enters a world (even if only temporarily) of fear of discovery and of corrupting self-justification. One justification is to say that it is "only" a penny, that is, to posit that what was stolen is not valuable or important to its owner. In truth, we seldom have an accurate idea of a thing's value or importance to its owner. Related to this justification are the claims that the owner is rich and therefore the item won't be missed and perhaps that the thief deserves it more. How often have you heard someone say that it is okay to do x because "they" are a large corporation. Whom does it hurt to use a cable descrambler in order to get pay TV channels for free? This justification misses the point. Whether the one being cheated is an individual or a corporation, as the tradition points out, any theft is wrong.

Jewish tradition is also concerned with the impact of theft on society. Taken together, small petty thefts create a social norm accepting or even approving of such activities. This is the "everybody does it" syndrome. As members of such a society, we participate in stealing by indirectly supporting it. I remember unloading our truck of household goods when we moved to Manhattan and being approached by someone who wanted to sell me a color television of unknown provenance. The tradition understands the consequences of buying stolen goods: the end result is a general corruption of the social fabric.

The tradition is also concerned with the welfare of the thief. Theft is a corrupting process supported by two factors: escaping punishment and justifying thievery. Certainly, one deterrent to stealing is the fear of being caught. First you steal a penny, then, if you get away with it, you think it is "safe" to steal more. The second factor is the thief's need to create a justification to explain why it is permissible to steal. One justification, already mentioned, is that the one being robbed is so wealthy that the thing being stolen will not be missed. There are many other justifications, of course, but they all rely on a process of "othering" the intended victim. For the rabbis in premodern times, the "other" was non-Jews, hence they taught:

Torah was given only to hallow God's great name, as it is said, "God said unto me: 'You are My servant, Israel, through whom I shall be glorified'" (Isa. 49:3). [By your deeds, you will glorify Me among all people.] Hence, the sages said, a person should keep away from dishonesty in dealing, whether with Jew or Gentile; indeed with anyone in the marketplace. Besides, a person who steals from a Gentile will in the end steal from a Jew; a person who cheats a Gentile

will in the end cheat a Jew; a person who swears [falsely] to a Gentile will in the end swear [falsely] to a Jew; a person who acts deceitfully toward a Gentile will in the end act deceitfully toward a Jew. . . .
[*Tanna de-Bei Eliyyahu*, p. 140]

One understanding of this text would suggest that it is worse to steal
from a Jew than from a Gentile, but it can also be demonstrating how
we allow ourselves to cross moral boundaries by creating distinctions.
By treating the victim as "other," theft is easier to justify. If "they" are
not the same as "you," then they are lesser and you are more deserving.
Obviously, once you begin to steal you are on a slippery slope. The tradition therefore teaches that there is no justification for stealing, not
even to right a wrong. Thus:

Once, four hundred jars of wine belonging to R. Huna turned
sour. The sages came to visit him and said, "Let the master examine
his [past] actions." He asked them, "Am I suspect in your eyes?"
They replied, "Is the Holy One suspect of imposing judgment without justice?" He said to them, "If anyone has heard something
against me, let him speak up." They replied, "We have heard that the
master does not give his tenant his [lawful share of] vine shoots."
R. Huna replied, "Does he leave any of them for me? He steals them
all!" They said to him, "That is exactly what the proverb says: 'Even
if you steal [what is your own] from a thief, you are also a bit of a
thief!' " He said to them, "From now on, I pledge myself to give
them to him." Some say that then and there the vinegar turned back
into wine. [Talmud, *Berakhot* 5b]

## Dishonesty

"You shall not insult the deaf, or place a stumbling block before
the blind. You shall fear your God: I am the Lord" (Lev. 19:14). This
verse is understood as a statement about treating those with disabilities
with special care, but most rabbinic commentary on it focuses on the
expanded understanding that all of us are "blind" and liable to be
deceived.

"You shall not place a stumbling block before the blind," [not just the physically blind, but] one who is "blind" in a particular matter. . . . If people seek your counsel, do not give them counsel that is not right for them. Do not say to them, "Leave early in the morning," so that brigands will rob them. Do not say to them, "Leave at noon," so that the sun will strike them. Do not say to them, "Sell your field and buy a donkey," so that you may circumvent them and take the field away from them [for your own gain]. If you protest, "But it is sensible counsel I am giving them," remember that the matter is known to the One who knows your heart, for the verse ends by saying, "You shall fear your God." [*Sifra,* ed. Weiss, p.88d]

One is forbidden to beautify the article being sold in order to create a false impression. . . . One is not allowed to paint old baskets to make them look new nor is one allowed to soak meat in water to make it white and look fat. [*Shulhan Arukh, Hoshen Mishpat,* Laws of Theft, ch. 358]

When we deceive another, we are taking advantage of a kind of blindness. Our motives are often mixed, and partly selfish. Yet it is easy to convince ourselves that what we are doing is also for the other person's benefit. The verse reminds us that God knows what is really in our hearts. We are meant to strive for clarity about our motives, but if there is deception involved, then we are putting a stumbling block before the blind. The deception does not need to be dramatic. We are prohibited from taking advantage of a person in any way.

The stumbling block can also be a temptation. "It was taught: R. Nathan says: Whence is it derived that one should not stretch forth a cup of wine to a Nazirite (who has taken an oath not to drink wine) . . . from 'You shall not place a stumbling block before the blind' " (Talmud, *Pesahim* 22b). The same goes for placing a luscious dessert before a dieter or wine before a recovering alcoholic.

Similarly, "R. Yehudah said in the name of Rav: All who lend money without witnesses are in transgression of the precept 'You shall not place a stumbling block before the blind' " (Talmud, *Hullin* 7b). To lend money without witnesses (or a contract signed by both parties) is to tempt the borrower to deny that any loan was transacted. The intent is to avoid tempting others, since, at one level or another, all of us are susceptible to temptation.

It is not just that we must not steal or cheat in business. We must not prey on people because of their blindness. This places a challenging demand on honesty in business transactions. While recognizing that each side has its self-interest and that it is certainly legitimate to earn a profit, the transaction still must be fair to both parties. The ideal in the tradition is described as *zeh neheneh ve-zeh lo haseir,* "one party benefited but the other party also did not lose." In modern idiom, it is a "win-win" situation.

In addition to the principle of not placing a stumbling block, there are several broad ethical categories regarding business. The first relates to stealing, including the principle of *ona'ah,* "economic exploitation" (Lev. 25:14–17). *Ona'ah* refers to "overreaching," making excessive profit. It is also interpreted as taking advantage of a weaker party (the Torah conventionally defines this as the stranger, the poor, the widow, and the orphan; e.g., see Lev. 19:33). Weaker parties are those without legal redress or, in our society, without the money to hire a decent lawyer. They are therefore vulnerable to economic oppression. The concept of *ona'ah* is applied even to speech *(ona'at devarim),* that is, using speech to "oppress" or take advantage of another. A contemporary example would be "reminding" someone that she or he served time in jail. In the same way, sexual harassment is also a form of *ona'ah. Ona'ah* is creating or taking advantage of any inequality. It is a form of stealing, of taking something away from another person.

> Just as there is wronging in business, so there is wronging in speech. People should not ask, "How much is this article?" if they do not intend to buy it. If a person is a penitent, one is not to say [to him], "Remember the way you used to act." If a person is the child of converts, one should not taunt, "Remember the way your parents acted. . . ." [Talmud, *Bava Metzia* 58b]

> R. Yohanan said . . . : Wronging through speech is more heinous than wronging in money matters. . . . R. Samuel bar Nahmani said:

For the second, restitution is possible; but not for the first. [Talmud, *Bava Metzia* 58b]

When R. Dimi came [from the land of Israel], he said: How do we know that when someone is his neighbor's creditor for a *maneh,* and he knows that the neighbor does not have the money to repay it, he may not even pass in front of the neighbor? From the verse "Do not act toward him as a creditor" (Exod. 22:34). [Talmud, *Bava Metzia* 75b]

Related to this is *genevat da'at,* literally, "stealing thoughts," which means misleading a person to think that you are doing a favor when you are not. This form of theft most often involves only words. An example is inviting guests when you know that they cannot come. This kind of pretense is also a form of theft, as the rabbis observed:

There are seven kinds of thieves—the foremost among them is the person who steals the good opinion of people. [Mekilta de-Rabbi Ishmael, *Mishpatim, Nezikin* 13]

We have been taught that R. Meir used to say: People should not urge a friend to dine if they know the friend will not do so. Nor should they offer gifts if they know the friend will not accept them. People should not make believe that it is for the guest's sake that they are broaching a cask of wine that in fact they intend to turn over to a shopkeeper to be sold. . . . they should not say to a guest, "Anoint yourself with oil," when they know that the oil jar is empty. [Talmud, *Hullin* 94a]

Another broad category of business ethics involves *oshek,* "fraud." *Oshek* is withholding from people that which is legitimately theirs. "You shall not defraud your fellow. You shall not commit robbery. The wages of a laborer shall not remain with you until morning" (Lev. 19:13). The Bible prohibits the withholding of a day laborer's wages; it appreciated the need for money of such workers, who were often poor. The principle is understood more broadly by the rabbis to include the withholding of any item that is legitimately owed to another person. "Whoever withholds an employee's wages, it is as though they have taken the person's life from them" (Talmud, *Bava Metzia* 112a).

> If a person hires workers and asks them to work in the early morning or late evening, at a place where it is not the local custom to work early or late at night, one cannot force the workers to do so. Where it is customary to provide food for the workers, one must do so. If it is customary to give them dessert, one must do so. It all depends on local custom. [Talmud, *Bava Metzia* 83a]

A third area of business ethics covered in rabbinic literature concerns responsibility and liability. There are a number of verses regarding the responsibility a person has for property left in their safekeeping. These laws revolve around the concept of *shomer,* "a watchman." Once again, this concept was understood broadly by the rabbis. You don't have to be hired to watch over something to have responsibility for guarding what is given to you. With responsibility comes a potential liability if the object is lost or damaged. The concept is part of a larger regard for the property of your neighbor (not letting your animals graze in his fields) and returning found objects. In business, it affects your responsibility for money given to you to invest or goods that you are buying and selling.

One famous biblical law forbids usury or lending money at interest. The rabbis defined this prohibition as applying only to Jews lending money to other Jews. In the Middle Ages, because the Catholic Church frowned upon Christians lending at interest to other Christians, Jews filled an increasingly important economic role as moneylenders to Christians. Both religions saw usury as an unfair and immoral method of making money. People should lend money out of a desire to help their neighbor. Nevertheless, as capitalism grew, moneylending became an integral part of commerce. The rabbis responded by developing a legal device called a *heter iska* (literally, a "permission to operate"), which allows one Jew to lend to another Jew at interest. This formality is still observed among traditional Jews.

### Employee and Employer

A level of mutual responsibility exists between employer and employee. The employer is to treat employees with respect and pay them a fair wage. The employee must treat the employer with respect and not take unfair advantage. The employer is entitled to an honest day's work. An employee who takes office supplies home, speaks at length to friends on the phone, or plays solitaire on the computer violates the employee/employer relationship.

> Just as the employer is enjoined not to deprive poor workers of their hire or withhold it from them when it is due, so are workers enjoined not to deprive the employer of the benefit of their work by idling away their time, a little here and a little there, thus wasting the whole day deceitfully. Indeed, the worker must be very punctual in the matter of time, seeing that the Sages were so solicitous in this matter that they exempted the worker from saying the fourth benediction of grace. [Maimonides, *Mishneh Torah*, Laws Concerning Hiring 13:7]

Maimonides here underscores the importance of a worker's time even over statutory prayer. While the daily liturgical obligation is still incumbent on workers, the rabbis stated that workers should recite an abbreviated version of the Grace after Meals and of the daily prayers to ensure a minimal loss of work time.

The tradition also reminds us of the need to be compassionate in employer/employee relations. There are even times when we should not stand on our rights.

> Some porters [accidentally] broke a cask of wine belonging to Rabbah bar Bar Hanah. So he seized their clothes. When they went and complained to Rav, he said to Rabbah, "Return their clothes." Rabbah: "Is that the law?" Rav: "Yes—'that thou mayest walk in the way of good people'" (Prov. 2:20). So Rabbah returned the clothes to the porters, who then said, "We are poor people. We worked hard all day. We are hungry and have no money [for food]." Rav then said

to Rabbah, "Go and pay them their wage." Rabbah: "Is that the law?" Rav: "Yes—'keep the path of the saintly' " (ibid.). [Talmud, *Bava Metzia* 83a]

While "the law" is clearly on the side of Rabbah, nevertheless Rav uses a "higher" law to adjudicate this dispute. His proof texts are from Proverbs, which is neither a legal text nor a text that carries the sanctity of the Torah. He tells Rabbah that he must go beyond the letter of the law to ensure that poor workers have money for food. Thus, the tradition shows that compassion is part of the business relationship.

Rabbi Simeon ben Shetah once purchased a donkey from an Ishmaelite. His disciples discovered a pearl entangled in its neck. They said to R. Simeon: "Master, 'The blessing of God makes a person rich' " (Prov. 10:22). R. Simeon replied: " I have purchased a donkey, but I have not purchased a pearl." He went and returned the pearl to the Ishmaelite. [Midrash, *Deuteronomy Rabbah* 3:3]

## Work as a Spiritual Practice

For criticizing the Roman government, the sage R. Simeon bar Yohai was sentenced to death. He fled with his son to a cave. The following was told:

A miracle occurred—a carob tree and a well were created for them. They would remove their garments and sit up to their necks in sand, and study the entire day. When it was time for prayer, they put on their garments, wrapped themselves in their prayer shawls, and prayed. Afterward, they again removed their garments, so that [the garments] would not wear out.

They dwelled twelve years in the cave. Then the prophet Elijah came and, standing at the entrance to the cave, announced, "Who will inform the son of Yohai that Caesar is dead and his decree is annulled?" So they went out, and, seeing people plowing and sowing, R. Simeon exclaimed, "These people forsake life eternal and engage in life temporal!" Whatever they cast their eyes upon was immediately incinerated. At that, a divine voice went forth and said, "Have you come out to destroy My world? Return to your cave!" [Talmud, *Shabbat* 3b–34a]

The story teaches that the ordinary work of the world is of higher value even when compared with devotion to Torah. While a few exceptional individuals may live in a "cave" or pursue lives of holiness, most people need to work in the real world. It is in that real world that Torah is challenged as we try to live up to its precepts of honesty and fair dealings.

A contrasting story:

Rabbi Yitzhak of Vorki told of how once he was together with his master, Rabbi David of Levov, at sunrise. The Rebbe was enrobed in a *tallit* and crowned in *tefillin*, ready to pray the Morning Prayer, when a gentile came in, pounded on the table and asked that he sell him a quantity of liquor. [His house was also an inn.] There was no one else in the house then to sell it to him, so the Rebbe himself went with alacrity, measured it out himself, and put it before the man. [When asked about why he left his prayer preparation to do business,] the Rebbe explained to him softly, "Listen to me, my sweet friend. My path in the service of God is 'Know God in all your ways.' . . . So when I went to measure out the liquor, my whole intention was to fulfill the Torah's *mitzvah* about honest measures and to give pleasure to God by this; and that is why I happily ran to do it with such haste." [*Kodesh Hillulim*, pp. 150–151]

"I shall walk before the Lord in the land of the living" (Psalm 116:9). Rav Judah said: That means the marketplaces. [Talmud, *Yoma* 71a]

Rav Judah said: A person who wishes to be pious must fulfill the laws of the tractates of *Nezikin* [those dealing with business]. [Talmud, *Bava Kamma* 30a]

True piety is determined by one's attitude toward money, for only one who is reliable in money matters may be considered pious. [Zevi Hirsch Koidonover, *Kav ha-Yashar*]

Likewise, the tradition is not at all ambivalent about business, nor even about the accumulation of wealth.

Rabbi Yehudah said: "The merchant may not distribute roasted wheat or nuts to children or to the servants, since he accustoms them to buy from him." However, the sages permit this practice, since the merchant can say to his competitors, "I distribute nuts, you can distribute other gifts." Rabbi Judah added: Similarly, he may lower his prices. [Mishnah, *Bava Metzia* 4:12]

Nevertheless, the acquisition of wealth must be accomplished by honest means that neither cheat, deceive, nor take advantage of others.

Most people are not outright thieves, that is, do not actually seize their neighbor's property and transfer it to their own premises, yet in their dealings with one another they have a taste of the sin of theft, insofar as they permit themselves to unfairly profit at their neighbor's expense, claiming that this profit has nothing to do with theft. . . . So many a person without actually intending to steal finds it hard to be absolutely cleanhanded. This is the case because, instead of the heart controlling the eyes so that they should not desire what belongs to others, the eyes seduce the heart to condone wrong committed for the sake of owning beautiful and desirable things. . . . "But," you will say, "how, in the course of bargaining, can we avoid trying to convince our neighbor that the article we want to sell is worth the price we are asking?" There is an unmistakable distinction between fraudulent and honest persuasion. It is perfectly proper to point out to the buyer any good quality that the thing for sale really possesses. Fraud consists in hiding the defects in one's wares. . . . [*Mesilat Yesharim*, ch. 11]

While acknowledging that the two parties in business dealings have differing self-interests, the tradition believes that transactions can be accomplished fairly without recourse to deception. The tradition is opposed to outright deception, but it does acknowledge the buyer's responsibility to ask questions and examine the transaction carefully.

The bottom line is the spirit in which the negotiation and the deal takes place. A transaction between two people is not a war or a contest to see who can outsmart the other. Judaism is concerned with more than outright illegal behavior. A person can oppress another person with words, by creating an inequality, by taking an unfair advantage. Thus the process surrounding the transaction is as important as the transaction itself. A person can be the victim of theft not only by gun or pen but by deceptive words that create a false atmosphere of camaraderie through *genevat da'at*. It is a challenge to live up to these principles, but by following them we acknowledge that the other party in any transaction is created in God's image just as we are.

### *Avodah* as Work

The word for work in Hebrew, *avodah*, is the same word used for prayer. *Avodah* connotes service. (It is also the word for slavery, which is involuntary service.) Work is not only a necessary part of life, it is a form of service to the world, to the rest of humanity, and to God. We are meant to be of service, to be partners with God in the ongoing creation of the world. Yet even as we serve God, we also serve our fellow human beings, as set forth in this second story about the Hasidic master Rabbi David of Levov:

> Rabbi Yitzhak of Vorki was once traveling with the holy rabbi, David of Levov, and they came to the town of Elkish at night, at one a.m. Rabbi David did not want to wake anyone to ask for a place to sleep, for (as is famous) his love for all Jews was so great [he did not want to wake anyone for his own benefit]. "So," the Vorker said, "we went to Reb Berish's bakery [for he would be awake and at work]. When we arrived there we found him at work, by the oven,

and Reb Berish was embarrassed at being found this way [in the midst of such lowly manual labor]. But the holy Levover said to him, 'Oh, if only God would let me earn my living by the work of my hands! For the truth is that every one of Israel in their innermost hearts, which even they themselves don't know, wants to do good to their fellow human being. So everyone who works—as a shoemaker or tailor or baker, or whatever, who serves others' needs for money— on the inside they don't do this work in order to make money, but in order to do good to others—even though they do receive money for their trouble; but this is secondary and unimportant, because it is obvious that they have to accept money in order to live. But the inner meaning of their work is that they want to do good and show kindness to their fellow human beings.' " [GMvGhTz, *Helek* 2, p. 14]

Though work is our vocation, it has the potential to accomplish *tikkun olam*, "repair of the world." Every job, every work interaction has value. There are those who believe that each of us is chosen for a particular task to perform in the world.

Rav Zutra said: What is the meaning of this verse: "God made everything beautiful in its time" (Eccles. 3:11)? This teaches that the Holy One made everyone's craft appear beautiful in their eyes. [Talmud, *Berakhot* 58a]

This is reflected in a story told by Rabbi Jeffrey Salkin:

The boss of the moving crew was a delightful, crusty gentleman, a dead ringer for Willie Nelson. I had never met anyone so enthusiastic about his or her work, and I asked him the source of that enthusiasm.

"Well, you see, I'm a religious man," he answered, "and my work is part of my religious mission."

"What do you mean?" I asked.

"Well, it's like this. Moving is hard for most people. It's a very vulnerable time for them. People are nervous about going to a new community, and about having strangers pack their most precious possessions. So, I think God wants me to treat my customers with love and to make them feel that I care about their things and their life. God wants me to help make their changes go smoothly. If I can be happy about it, maybe they can be, too." [Salkin, *Being God's Partner*]

Seeing the value in work only heightens the question of how to balance the demands and challenges of work with the rest of our lives—our family, friends, etc. For the rabbis the question was different: how to balance Torah/Judaism and work. If, after all, the highest Jewish value is Torah study, which is a lifelong occupation, then shouldn't we minimize our time at work? For the rabbis, the question was how much work to fit into a life of Torah, while for us the question is how much life to fit into a world of work! Yet despite their love of Torah, work occupied a central place in the rabbis' lives.

Rabbi Zadok taught: "Do not make the Torah a spade wherewith to 'dig' [i.e., make a living]" (*Ethics of Our Ancestors* 4:7). Each of the talmudic rabbis had real jobs, none of them made their living as rabbis. They understood that the success of the Torah depended upon putting its ideals to work in "real" life. *The tradition is only worthwhile if it works during the week, not just on Shabbat.*

> Rava said: When they escort people to their Heavenly tribunal after their death, the tribunal asks: "Did you conduct your business transactions faithfully? [only then are you asked] Did you set aside fixed times for Torah study? [Talmud, *Shabbat* 31a]

Today we often think of religion as that which takes place in the synagogue or within the realm of ritual. Religion in America can be consigned to the leisure-time activities, allocated to the Sabbath. Instead, we are taught the following:

> Joshua said: If people recite two *Halakhot* in the morning and two *Halakhot* in the evening, and the rest of the day is occupied with their work, it is imputed to them as though they [meditated upon it day and night, and thus] fulfilled the entire Torah, all of it.

"Thou shall meditate therein day and night" (Josh. 1:8) [a precept that is impossible to fulfill]. Hence R. Simeon ben Yohai said: Only to people who ate manna [whom God provided sustenance] was the Torah given to study intensely, since such people had no need to engage in craft or business. Otherwise, could a person sit and study Torah, not knowing where their food and drink would come from or where they would get their clothes or coverings? . . . [Mekilta de-Rabbi Ishmael, *Be-shallah, Va-yassa* 3]

These texts reflect the tradition's essential attitude toward work. Work is not just necessary to earn a living, it is a way, perhaps *the* way, to engage in Torah. Thus the very verse that is often understood to mean that we should engage in Torah study continuously—day and night—is reinterpreted to refer not to Torah study but to living a life of Torah. Why? Because it is impossible in the "real" world to spend all of one's time in Torah study. The Torah is meant to be lived, not studied. We are to meditate on it day and night, night and day, not by withdrawing from the world into the *beit midrash*, "the house of study," but rather by engaging fully in the world while meditating on the Torah and its teachings regarding honesty and living with awareness.

Man's livelihood requires his active participation. Apart from the period of the wandering in the wilderness, or other instances of miraculous intervention for limited periods, there is no manna from heaven. This active participation of man in the creation of his own wealth is a sign of man's spiritual greatness. In this respect, he is an imitator of God. [Bahya ibn Pakuda, in Salkin, *Being God's Partner,* p. 83]

That other challenge still remains. How shall we balance work with family? Here, the tradition's model of balancing can serve our needs. Work is essential to our lives. Work also provides an essential arena in which to live a life of Torah, of ethics and caring. Yet work is only a part of life, not the whole thing. To be a workaholic means to be an *oveid avodah zarah,* "an idol worshiper." It is to place the acquisition of money, possessions, fame, or power above all else. But there is only one thing which is above all else, the Holy One who asks us to be partners in creation. We are to spend our week working at creating like God. Work has a sacred weekly limit, Shabbat, which was created to remind us not to lose perspective.

With a clearer view of what work is and is not, we can strive for a life that balances work, relationships, and leisure. The answer to the question of what my life is all about is never as simple as the career we choose. Living a full life with meaning places a striving for an awareness of the holy at the core. It recognizes that many pathways lead to that awareness, including work, relationships, leisure, etc. As complex beings created in the image of God, we need to travel all of these paths to live a life of *avodah*, "service."

## Practice

Before you go to work, have a time of preparation to make yourself ready to be careful about all forbidden things and ready to fulfill God's warning, and not transgress, God forbid, such things as theft and robbery, fraud, lying, cheating, false weights and measures.

After eating the midday meal, and before you go back to work, prepare yourself again as you did in the morning, going over in your mind the various things to avoid. And happy are you if you fulfill all this. [R. Hayyim Yosef David Azulai, *Avodat ha-kodesh, Moreh b'Etzba* 3–97 and 3–122]

I heard that a merchant who had gone to be with a certain *tzaddik* explained to him apologetically that he was so involved in his business that he did not have any time to compose himself [and think of religious things]. He was told that whenever he went to the basement to get some wine [to sell] he should stand there for a few minutes in meditation [on why he had come into this world, and how he was spending his time] [*Likkutim Hadashim*, p. 4a]

We need to take moments to prepare ourselves to enter into the world of work. It does not require a review of all the laws regarding business dealings nor a lengthy ritual. As suggested above, it involves just a moment to remember who you are—a partner in God's creation—and what you are here to do—interact with honesty and decency with all the other images of God you will encounter this day.

A suggested *kavanah* follows, but feel free to create your own.

---

*KAVANAH*

O God let me be careful with my speech and with my deeds conveying caring rather than hurt to all the lives I touch this day. Let me not get angry unnecessarily, nor judge others harshly. Let me not imagine slights. Let me not be anxious in dealing with those for whom I work. And if necessary to respond critically, let me do so in a clear and calm manner. Let me always try to remember that all of us are flawed and wounded creatures even as we are also all created equally in Your image. I hope for success in my striving to earn a living even as I hope that success is not unnecessarily at the expense of others. May the words of my mouth and my inner thoughts this day be acceptable unto You as reflecting that which is holy and best within me, your servant and partner in creation.

Another focus might center on thankfulness for having employment and appreciation for the work of others from whom your life benefits.

Ben Zoma: How many exertions did Adam, the first human, make until Adam found a garment to wear! Adam sheared the wool, cleaned it, disentangled it, spun it into threads, wove the threads, and afterwards found a garment to wear. But I rise early in the morning and find all these labors already prepared before me. Indeed, members of all the trades diligently come to the entrance of my house and I rise early in the morning and find all of them before me. [Talmud, *Berakhot* 58a]

---

Try to find moments during the day, not just in the morning, to come back to an awareness of living Torah through work. We don't all go down to a wine cellar during the workday, but we all have such moments. They may come before a meeting begins or before an important phone call. They may come as part of coffee or bathroom breaks. Certainly lunch (even if it is a business lunch) can provide a moment of transition.

While some may say the *minhah* (afternoon) service, others may want to take five minutes just to step back from the business and routine of the day. For a while I was part of a group whose members would recite Psalm 30 every day at 3:00 p.m., each in her or his own workplace. It was helpful to know that other people around the city were doing what I was doing. You might also use your break for a study/reading of the week's Torah portion. Silence, prayer, or study, all can serve as a call to attention.

### In Summary

Rabban Gamliel son of R. Judah the Patriarch said: "Study of Torah combined with an occupation is good, for labor at both keeps sin out of one's mind. But study of Torah alone, without an occupation, will in the end come to naught, and even occasion sin." [*Ethics of Our Ancestors* 2:2]

Elazar ben Azariah said: No sustenance, no Torah. No Torah, no sustenance. [*Ethics of Our Ancestors* 3:21]

Torah sets a limit on our striving for sustenance and offers guidance on earning a living in an ethical manner. Yet without sustenance not only would we starve, we would not engage the world armed with the teachings of Torah.

### For Further Reading

*Being God's Partner: How to Find the Hidden Link Between Spirituality and Your Work,* by Rabbi Jeffrey Salkin (Jewish Lights, 1994), helped inform this chapter.

The laws related to business are complex. A good guide to them is *With All Your Possessions: Jewish Ethics and Economic Life,* by Meir Tamari (Free Press, 1987).

# EATING AND FOOD

The main service of God is through eating—so have I heard from my masters; and it is similar to prayer. [*Darkei Tzedek,* p. 18]

Contrary to what one might think, it is possible some times to come closer to God when you are involved in material activities like eating and drinking than when you are involved with "religious" activities like Torah study and prayer. Because when the heart opens up due to the sense of pleasure, and there is a feeling of satisfaction and happiness, then is the fit time to come close to holiness. [Abraham of Slonim, *Torat Avot,* p. 195]

As we go through our day, we eat. Our relationship to food is a basic aspect of our lives. For you who are reading this book, the ability to obtain enough food has no doubt become a given. For much of the world today, this is not true. Nor was it always true for our ancestors. Having enough to eat was a constant concern, either because of poverty or because of the whims of nature. A successful harvest, therefore, has generally been a time for rejoicing. In societies lacking our resources and our sophisticated system of food distribution, people are closely connected to the agricultural cycle whether or not they are farmers, since food is obtained locally. The success or failure of the local farmers, then, is of immediate concern to everyone living in such a community.

Our concern may be the opposite, namely, having too much food. For one thing, our society places a high value on appearance, idealizing thin women and men, and bombarding us with images of "beautiful" people. What, when, and how we eat have become subjects of a focus on our bodies that would hardly be understood by our ancestors.

Judaism values eating, first and foremost, as an act necessary for survival. It also validates the pleasure we get from food and encourages us to enjoy food at special occasions. The tradition marks eating as a spiritual enterprise through *berakhot* or blessings. Judaism also limits what we can eat and when we can eat certain foods (through the laws of keeping kosher). Naturally, Judaism urges us to be concerned with our health and to take care of our bodies. On the other hand, while acknowledging that there are handsome and beautiful people in the world, Judaism sets no definition of beauty, nor are we encouraged to strive to be beautiful. Instead, we are encouraged to make eating, like all the mundane activities of our lives, into an act of holiness—an act that nourishes the soul as well as the body.

Let us begin our examination of eating and food at the beginning—with creation. On the sixth day, God instructed the newly created humans: "See, I give you every seed-bearing plant that is upon all the earth, and every tree that has seed-bearing fruit; they shall be yours for food" (Gen. 1:29). The first thing God said to humans after "be fruitful and multiply" was that all growing things are available for human consumption. From this we learn that food is an essential part of human existence.

By saying nothing about eating animals, the Torah implies that animals were not created for human consumption. Indeed, God equates humans and animals: "And to all the animals on land, to all the birds of the sky, and to everything that creeps on earth, in which there is the breath of life, I give all the green plants for food" (Gen. 1:30). According to this initial version of the creation story, human beings and animals were apparently meant to be vegetarians.

The second chapter of Genesis, however, points to a difference between animals and human beings. It begins: "When the Lord God made earth and heavens—when no shrub of the field was yet on the earth and no grasses of the field had yet sprouted, because the Lord God had not sent rain upon the earth and there was no human to till the soil." By implication, though no human yet existed, the verse maintains that human beings are intrinsic to creation. Humans would till the soil and transform the earth. Animals would eat off the land, while humans were destined, through the art of agriculture, to attempt to shape nature to their own needs.

Before the age of agriculture commenced, God planted an idyllic garden and placed Adam and Eve in it. Everything was provided. There was only one catch—the creation of the first diet plan. God commanded: "Of every tree of the garden you are free to eat; but as for the tree of knowledge of good and bad, you must not eat of it, for as soon as you eat of it, you shall die" (Gen. 2:17). The rest, as we know, is history. Adam and Eve ate of the tree whose fruit (unspecified in the text, its identification as an apple is from the Middle Ages) was more likely to be chocolate cream pie or French fries than a fig or an apple. They then had the knowledge of good and evil; despite that, they wanted to eat more of what God had called evil.

Perhaps Adam and Even knew they were naked because they noticed they were gaining a little weight. Almost at once, they became concerned about whether they would still be attractive to each other. At first God wanted to let nature take its promised course: "as soon as you eat of it, you shall die." But God had a second thought: if, whenever humans ate food that wasn't good for them, their bodies would shut down and die, there would be no real choice, no free will, no struggle; no tree standing in the midst of the garden that contained both good and evil. So God changed the rules. From now on, there would be good *and* bad things to eat. There would also be many good things of which it would be bad to eat too much. Choices would abound. Food, eating, and bodies would never be simple again.

> Cursed be the ground because of you;
> By toil shall you eat of it
> All the days of your life:
> Thorns and thistles shall it sprout for you.
> But your food shall be the grasses of the field;
> By the sweat of your brow
> Shall you get bread to eat,
> Until you return to the ground—

For from it you were taken.
For dust you are,
And to dust you shall return. [Gen. 3:17–19]

The obtaining of food would become a struggle. Mere survival could no longer be taken for granted. However, the dynamic of the tree continues writ large. We will desire that which we cannot have or at least that which is hard to obtain. We will want food not just to survive but because we lust for what we cannot have and for what we imagine that food gives us. We will struggle to feed ourselves emotionally as well as nutritionally.

The human story continues as the Torah tells us: "The earth became corrupt before God; the earth was filled with lawlessness." Therefore, God regretted all the creatures God had made and decided to destroy them with a flood. What was the corruption? The text is not explicit. Perhaps we can infer the answer from the laws that God promulgates after the flood. One of these states that anyone who commits murder should be executed in punishment. Therefore, some commentators conclude that the corruption that led to the flood involved murder. God also tells us: "Every creature that lives shall be yours to eat; as with the green grasses, I give you all these" (Gen. 9:3). No longer will animals and humans be equal. Human beings are given explicit permission to be predators: "The fear and dread of you shall be upon all the beasts of the earth and upon all the birds of the sky—everything with which the earth is astir—and upon all the fish of the sea; they are given into your hand" (Gen. 9:2). So, despite suffering a common fate in the flood, human beings emerge as antagonists to animals rather than as co-equals!

From the context it would seem that this concession allowing humans to eat flesh is somehow related to the lawlessness that preceded the flood. The eating of animal flesh may be a concession to the blood-lust rampant in humans. In this regard, the laws after the flood also take a number of steps to discourage murder. First, murder is established as a capital crime. Second, though humans are allowed to eat any animal, "You must not, however, eat flesh with its life-blood in it" (Gen. 9:4). As the Torah states later on: "For the life of all flesh—its blood is its life" (Lev. 17:14). Therefore, while we are given permission to eat meat, we cannot eat its blood (or eat the limb of a living animal, which is also how this verse is understood). We are to focus on what constitutes life and death, particularly because God gives the life of other creatures into our hands. We are instructed to honor life by not consuming blood, that which represents life in animals. Thus, even as the categories of what humans can eat are expanded, so are the rules governing eating.

Lest we think that the rules apply only to the taking of the life of other creatures, the story of Noah continues immediately: "Noah, the tiller of soil, was the first to plant a vineyard. He drank of the wine and became drunk, and he uncovered himself within his tent" (Gen. 9:20–21).

No life is taken to produce wine and yet wine is a potent representative of the complexity of food and drink. Wine is outstanding; both in the pleasurable feeling it can give to the drinker and to the persistent and pervasive problems it can create for those who drink too much. Through wine we are to sanctify the Sabbath day and to celebrate our weddings. We are told "No rejoicing before God is possible except with wine" (Talmud, *Pesahim* 109a). Yet the loss of self-respect in drunkenness is portrayed beginning with Noah and continuing in every Jewish teaching on food.

> We have been taught that R. Meir said: The tree whose fruit Adam ate was a vine, for nothing brings as much woe to humans as wine. [Talmud, *Sanhedrin* 70a]

> As wine enters each and every part of a human's body, it grows lax, and his mind is confused. Once wine enters, reason leaves. [Midrash, *Numbers Rabbah* 10:8]

> When Noah began planting, Satan came by, stationed himself before him, and asked, "What are you planting?" Noah: "A vineyard." Satan: "What is its nature?" Noah: "Its fruit, whether fresh or dried, is sweet, and from it wine is made, which gladdens a person's heart."

Satan: "Would you like the two of us, me and you, to plant it together?" Noah: "Very well."

What did Satan do? He brought a ewe lamb and slaughtered it over the vine; then he brought a lion, which he likewise slaughtered over the vine; then a monkey, which he also slaughtered over the vine; and finally a pig, which he again slaughtered over the vine. And with the blood dripping from them, he watered the vineyard.

The charade was Satan's way of saying that when a person drinks one cup of wine, he acts like a ewe lamb, humble and meek. When she drinks two, she becomes as mighty as a lion and proceeds to brag extravagantly, saying, "Who is like me?" When he drinks three or four cups, he becomes like a monkey, hopping about, dancing, giggling, and uttering obscenities in public, without realizing what he is doing. Finally, when she becomes blind drunk, she is like a pig; wallowing in mire and coming to rest among refuse. [*Midrash Tanhuma, Noah* 13]

Food plays many roles in the stories of the Torah. Abraham and Sarah employ food as an expression of hospitality. Jacob uses a pot of lentils to buy the birthright from his hungry brother, Esau. Food is central to the plot of the Joseph story, for food brings Joseph to power and brings his brothers to Egypt. When Joseph reveals himself to his brothers, breaking bread together is depicted as a social setting. The stories of the patriarchs are filled with feasts and famines.

Food occupies a pivotal role in the story of the Jewish people after they leave Egypt. The Israelites complain that they do not have enough to eat or drink. God sometimes provides for them and at other times is angered by their constant complaining. Near the beginning of their desert travels they are given manna from heaven. This mysterious food, provided daily by God, is meant to fill all of their food needs. Yet later on (in Num. 11), the Israelites express unhappiness despite having the manna.

The riffraff in their midst felt a gluttonous craving; and then the Israelites wept and said, "If only we had meat to eat! We remember the fish that we used to eat free in Egypt, the cucumbers, the melons, the leeks, the onions and the garlic. Now our gullets are shriveled. There is nothing at all! Nothing but this manna to look to!" . . . Then the Lord said to Moses, "The Lord will give you meat to eat and you shall eat. You shall not eat one day, nor two, not even five days or ten or twenty, but a whole month, until it comes out of your nostrils and becomes loathsome to you. For you have rejected the Lord who is among you, by whining before God and saying, 'Oh why did we ever leave Egypt!' . . ." A wind from the Lord started up, swept quail from the sea and strewed them over the camp, about a day's journey on this side and about a day's journey on that side, all around the camp, and some two cubits deep on the ground. The people set to gathering quail all that day and night and all the next day—even he who gathered least had ten *homers*. . . . The meat was still between their teeth, nor yet chewed, when the anger of the Lord blazed forth against the people and the Lord struck the people with a very severe plague. [Num. 11: 4–6, 16, 18–20, and 31–33]

Perhaps this is a tale about the confusion that comes from thinking you want one thing when really you want something else. In a fashion, God re-creates the Garden of Eden in the desert. God supplies the Israelites' needs through the manna. No hard work is required to obtain this food; no struggle with nature; no vulnerability to weather conditions. God provides manna, the perfect food, but perhaps the people want something else. They say they want food, but it seems they want love and reassurance.

God's consistent support of them in the desert through the manna is seemingly insufficient. Perhaps they know that God can withdraw love and punish them out of anger. Perhaps they are afraid of the unknown future that lies before them, or they feel overwhelmed by all the choices ahead of them as a newly freed people.

The people complain about what they have, the manna, but when they get what they want, the quails, it sickens them. Even in ancient times, food represented the twin complexities of need and want. Two themes are evoked by food and eating. The first is the issue of nourishment. When we eat, we often seek nourishment that goes beyond our bodies' basic needs. Sometimes this comes in the form of physical cravings, as when we are "addicted" to particular foods. At other times eating becomes a substitute for some emotional nourishment we lack. In this case, we may equate food with love, or in moments of anxiety or loss we may eat in the hope of "feeling better."

The second issue, often related, has to do with body and appearance. Our society places an enormous emphasis on how we appear to others. At the same time, many of us have a distorted sense of our own bodies. In an experiment, women were asked to close their eyes and place their hands to show how wide they believed their hips to be. Most indicated their hips to be wider than they really were. We all know people who are not fat by any objective standard, but who think of themselves as fat and diet constantly to lose weight.

Judaism postulates that we can approach food and eating in a spiritual way.

In the midrash cited in the first chapter, the creation of human beings was compared to the striking of coins. As coins are struck, each is produced in the same image. When God creates people, each is created in God's image, yet each one is unique. This midrash is a basic affirmation of every body. No body can be more Godlike than any other. One could even say that this body is the one that has been given to me by God. In a sense, this is similar to saying that some people are overweight because of a genetic disposition, not because they cannot control their eating. For superficial features, plastic surgery can make some difference. When it comes to how tall or short you are, however, these things cannot be significantly changed at all. Thinking of your body as a gift from God is a good beginning, though clearly for those born with disabilities there are difficult burdens that accompany that gift.

Still, this gift, this body, is given into our care and—like Hillel, who considered it a *mitzvah* (precept) to bathe in the bathhouse—we are responsible for striving for a healthy body because our body is the image of God. According to some rabbinic authorities, an understanding of the verse *venishmarteim me'od l'nafshoteichem*, "for your own sake, therefore, be most careful" (Deut. 4:15), is broader than avoiding harmful situations. It also implies not doing things that are clearly detrimental to our health. For these authorities, alcoholism, cigarette smoking, and overeating fall into this category.

"He who does good to his own self is a person of mercy" (Prov. 11:17), as may be inferred from what Hillel the Elder once said. After bidding farewell to his disciples, he kept walking along with them. His disciples asked him, "Master, where are you going?" He replied, "To do a good turn to a guest in my house." They said, "Every day you seem to have a guest." He replied, "Is not my poor soul a guest in my body—here today and tomorrow here no longer?" [Midrash, *Leviticus Rabbah* 34:4]

And whatever he eats or drinks . . . his intention will be to keep his body and limbs healthy. . . . he will eat what is healthy, whether it is bitter or sweet. His practice will be to have his intention that his body be healthy and strong so his soul will be fit and able to know God. For it is not possible to understand and become wise in Torah and mitzvot when you are hungry or sickly or when one of your limbs hurts. [*Orchot Tzaddikim*, Gate 5, p. 39]

The impulse that we have to nourish ourselves through food is a good one, reflecting God's desire that we feel cherished. (Thanks to Joyce Krensky for this insight.) Thus we see food equals love not because we are sick but because it reflects a measure of truth. There is an emotional quality to eating. Food gives pleasure. (By the same token, hunger is also a gift from God, for it promotes self-preservation and impels us to action.)

In the world-to-come a person will be asked to give an account for that which, being excellent to eat, she gazed at and did not eat. [Jerusalem Talmud, *Kiddushin*, end]

[You should realize that] God created the food that is before you, and God gives it its existence and puts within it its taste and nourishing qualities. And God gives to a person the desire to eat and also his sense of taste, whereby the food tastes good. *[Menorat Zahav]*

Food, however, cannot replace love. There may be an uncontrolled desire to attain through food that which it cannot ultimately provide. Clearly, then, a healthy approach to eating is rooted in a healthy body and a healthy psyche. Thus eating can be transformed into a spiritual exercise.

A healthy/spiritual approach to food is rooted in three areas of traditional teachings: *berakhot,* "blessings"; *kashrut,* "dietary laws"; and *seudah,* "food as celebration and pleasure." Taken together, they make the everyday act of eating an essential part of a spiritual path.

## Berakhot

The rabbis created the basic liturgical formula of the *berakhah,* the "blessing," from the Great Assembly. Its standard wording is: *Barukh atah Adonai eloheinu melekh ha-olam . . . ,* "Praised are You Eternal our God source of the universe . . . ," followed by a specific attribute, "who created the fruit of trees" or "who brought forth bread from the earth." There are many specific *berakhot,* but they all begin with this formula. A *berakhah* is to be said before partaking of food. There are *berakhot* for fruit, vegetables, bread, cake, wine, and a catchall formulation for everything else. Saying a *berakhah* is meant to bring us to awareness. For the rabbis, the first level is awareness of God.

> Our rabbis have taught: It is forbidden for a person to enjoy anything of this world without a *berakhah.* . . . R. Levi contrasted two texts. It is written, "The earth is the Lord's and the fullness thereof" (Psalm 24:1) and it is also written, "The heavens are the heavens of God, but the earth God has given to human beings!" (Psalm 115:16). There is no contradiction: in the one case it is before a blessing has been said, in the other case after. [Talmud, *Berakhot* 35a]

The rabbis begin with a notion that God as creator has made this world and all that it contains. Whoever eats without saying a blessing is like someone who robs from the Holy One. This notion conveys an important statement about God and about humans. Despite all our strivings, our sustenance is only partly the result of our own endeavor. Ultimately everything comes from God. We are little more than tenant farmers on this planet. Our spiritual awareness begins when we sense that we have received this gift from the Creator of all life.

The *berakhah* before eating brings us another awareness, too. The act of eating is meant to be one of pleasure and enjoyment. We should savor our food rather than just devour it. The Baal Shem Tov taught: "When you eat and take pleasure in the taste and sweetness of the food, bear in mind that it is God who has placed into the food its taste and sweetness. You will, then, truly serve God by your eating." On this level, we should make ourselves aware of the pleasurable nature of eating.

We should likewise be aware of food as a necessary source of health and sustenance. Without food we could not live—this is a fact that we may easily take for granted. The Rebbe of Mikolayeve taught:

> Eat and drink because you are commanded to safeguard your health, as it is said: "For your *own* sake, therefore be most careful" (Deut. 4:15). Such eating is a pious deed. But to eat merely to satisfy a craving is a form of transgression. [Louis Newman, *Hasidic Anthology*, p. 86]

This also brings to awareness the fact that there are many people in this world who cannot take their next meal for granted. They suffer not a lack of awareness, only a lack of food. In the past, the tradition encouraged us to share our meals with the poor. In an immediate sense, this is not often practical today. We could, however, accept the suggestion of the Reshit Hochmah:

> In a place where poor people are not to be found, what can a person do . . . ? It is possible to say that you should estimate what the cost of the meal for a poor person would have been, and put that amount aside for charity before you eat. [*Sh'ar ha-Kedushah* 15:64]

All in all, the spiritual awareness of the meaning of food that is contained in the berakhah enables us to nourish our souls as we nourish our bodies.

> The essential advice on how to deal with food lust is that when you eat you should be aware of what you are doing; then it ceases to be just an animal action. The lust for food is intact if you allow your mind and all your senses to be immersed in eating until you forget what you are doing. Then eating is like an animal's action. [*Emunat Tzadikkim*, p. 78]

Eating is intended to be a purposeful act. While animals eat out of instinct, we eat out of awareness of all that the act of eating entails. We are to remember all that brought this food to the plate. The Jerusalem Talmud (*Hallah* 1) says: "Before you eat your piece of bread, remember that ten *mitzvot* [commandments] have been performed in preparing it for your consumption: it was not sown on Shabbat or the Sabbatical year; it was not plowed then either; the ox's mouth was not tied while he worked in the field; the grower has not gathered the left-over and forgotten sheaves; he has not reaped the corners of his fields; he has given the tithes to the priest and Levite; he has given the second tithe and the tithe to the poor; and his wife separated a piece of dough for the priest."

### KAVANAH

Rabbi Zalman Schachter-Shalomi offers a contemporary *kavanah*:
When you eat your bowl of corn flakes, devote at least a few seconds to "seeing" the corn—how it grows, with the tassels hanging down; and how the wind sweeps across the cornfield, blowing pollen from one side to the other and making the plants fertile. When you watch this in your imagination, and carry the process from the planted seed up to the present moment in which you are chewing the corn flakes, you see how your eating is connected with the whole fertility dance of the plant world. If we

don't become a conscious part of the process, what right have we
to eat the corn flakes?

That sense of being part of the universe rather than being apart from
it leads to one final level of awareness.

> The Baal Shem Tov taught: When you take a fruit or any other
> food in your hand and recite the blessing "Praised are You, O God"
> with intention, your mentioning the holy name awakens the spark of
> divine life by which the fruit was originally created. Everything was
> created by the power of the holy name. Since an element is awakened
> when it comes into contact with a similar element, the blessing awak-
> ens the element of divine life in the fruit, the element that is the food
> of the soul. This applies to all the permitted and kosher foods, since
> God commanded us to uplift them from a material existence to a
> spiritual existence. [*Keter Shem Tov*, p. 43]

> The will of the Creator, then, is to "enliven every living thing" by
> means of eating. So I have to eat in holiness and purity, for I am
> doing God's will by eating. And when you think this way, then
> you can accomplish the spiritual purpose of eating by lifting up the
> holy sparks to their source. . . . And you should realize that it is God
> who has brought you to this hunger and thirst. For the hunger is
> from God. [*Mazkeret Shem ha-Gedolim*, p. 79]

If sparks of holiness are found everywhere in the world and we are to
work toward restoring the wholeness of the divine, then the act of eating becomes in and of itself a holy act. By eating with this level of consciousness we are helping in the process of *tikkun*, "repairing" the
world. We can transform hunger and thirst into a hunger and thirst for
the experience of the holy.

There are different *berakhot* for the various categories of food and
drink.

**Over bread and meals**    *Barukh atah Adonai eloheinu melekh ha-
olam ha-motzi lehem min ha-aretz.* "Praised are You, Eternal One

our God, source of the universe, who brings forth bread from the earth."

From time immemorial, bread was the central food of meals. Meals would begin with the "breaking" of bread and the recital of this blessing. The blessing over bread, the *motzi,* therefore represents all foods eaten at a meal, so no other blessings are necessary.

**Over fruit**    *Barukh . . . ha-olam borei peri ha-etz.* "Praised . . . of the universe, who creates the fruit of the trees."

**Over vegetables**    *Barukh . . . ha-olam borei peri ha-adamah.* "Praised . . . of the universe, who creates the fruit of the earth."

**Over wine or grapes**    *Barukh . . . ha-olam borei peri ha-gafen.* "Praised . . . of the universe, who creates the fruit of the vine."

Apparently, because of wine's ritual use, it requires its own *berakhah.* The grape is also an exception to the *berakhah* for fruit.

**Over cake**    *Barukh . . . ha-olam borei minai mezonot.* "Praised . . . of the universe, who creates various kinds of food."

**Over other foods, such as cheese or meat**    *Barukh . . . . ha-olam she-hakol niheyeh bidvoro.* "Praised . . . of the universe, by whose word all things come into being."

While it is customary to use these traditional *berakhot,* the issue of nontraditional liturgy has been debated since the time of the Talmud.

> R. Meir said: Even if one merely sees a loaf of bread and says, "Blessed be the One who created this bread; how beautiful is this bread!"—that is the same as a blessing over it. But R. Yose said: A person who changes the formula the sages have fixed for blessings has not discharged her or his duty. [Tosefta, *Berakhot* 4:4–5]

For those who struggle with the traditional language for its use of gender in referring to God or because of its notions of a transcendent

God, a groundbreaking work is *The Book of Blessings,* by Marcia Falk (Harper San Francisco, 1996).

While we have focused on the *berakhot* before eating that encourage us to eat with awareness, there are also *berakhot* to be recited after eating.

1. *Birkat ha-mazon,* the Grace after Meals, consists of four long *berakhot* as well as additional liturgy. It is recited after meals, traditionally after any bread is eaten. Because it is lengthy, a number of abridged versions and short contemporary alternatives exist.

2. *Al ha-mihyah,* which is an abridged form of the themes of *birkat ha-mazon* recited after eating cake, wine, or fruits associated with the land of Israel, e.g., grapes, figs, dates, olives, and pomegranates (see Deut. 8:8).

3. *Borei nefashot,* literally, "who creates living beings." This blessing is recited over all food not covered above. It is also used if you don't have the text for the above blessings. This blessing, like its longer cousins, expresses gratitude for the sustenance just received from God.

*Barukh . . . ha-olam borei nefashot rabot ve-hesronan al kol mah she-bara le-hayyot bahem nefesh kol hai barukh hai ha-olamim.* "Praised . . . of the universe, who creates innumerable living beings and all that they need to sustain each and every life. Praised is the One who is the Life of the universe."

*Berakhot* as pointers to spiritual awareness exist in other forms in the tradition. (In their long form, they are also a basic component of Jewish liturgy. See "*Avodah:* The Path of Prayer," pp. 176–205). As we noted above, they are a prelude to whatever *mitzvah* they describe. They serve to call our attention to the act that we are about to perform. One category of *berakhot,* including washing the hands in the morning, lighting Sabbath candles, and so on, is known as *birkhot ha-mitzvah,* "blessings recited before performing a commandment." Another category is *birkhot ha-nehenin,* "blessings related to the enjoyment of our senses." In addition to the blessings related to eating and taste, there are also blessings for smell, sight, sound, and touch. There are blessings for smelling fragrant spices or seeing a rainbow or hearing thunder or putting on a new piece of clothing. All of these blessings are to remind us not to take the simple wonders of life for granted.

Since awareness comes not only through our five senses, but also from what we encounter in the events of our lives, the blessing *sheheheyanu* is recited when we do something for the first time or when we participate in special occasions. A new home, a new fruit, a first-time reading from the Torah, are all occasions for this blessing. It reads:

*Barukh . . . ha-olam sheheheyanu ve-kimanu ve-higiyanu lazman ha-zeh.* "Praised . . . of the universe who has kept us alive and sustained us and enabled us to reach this moment."

There are even *berakhot* to be recited upon hearing news. *Ha-tov u-mativ,* "who is good and does good," is said upon hearing glad tidings. *Dayan ha-emet,* "the true Judge," is said when hearing bad news, including the news of a death. As creator of the universe, God creates both the beautiful sunset and the devastating earthquake. Being aware of the holy does not mean that we miraculously escape the horrendous. Being aware means being conscious of everything that life holds in store. Being aware of God means being aware of the One "who forms light and darkness, establishes peace and creates destruction" (Isa. 45:7).

## Kashrut

*Kashrut* refers to the laws and customs regulating which foods and under what circumstances permitted foods may be consumed according to the Jewish tradition. The original source for these laws is found in the Torah, for example in Leviticus 11. The Torah tells us which categories of food are permitted and which are prohibited. The tradition also tells us how animals should be slaughtered and prohibits the eating of milk and meat together.

In summary: All vegetables and fruit are kosher and have no restrictions upon their consumption. There are permitted and forbidden animals, birds, and fish. Cow, sheep, goat, chicken, turkey, and fish with fins and scales are kosher. Pig, birds of prey, lobster, shrimp, and crab are not kosher. Also reptiles, insects, and creepy-crawly things in general are not kosher. To be kosher, permitted animals (not including fish) must be slaughtered in a ritual way. The additional prohibition of eating milk and meat together prohibits not only cheeseburgers but also even eating milk and meat foods at the same meal. Around these basic rules, many other customs and restrictions have developed that serve to help prevent our violating these rules accidentally.

Many questions surround this ancient system of food rules. While *kashrut* is clearly intended to regulate our eating, the logic behind the system is hardly apparent. Unlike vegetarianism, the permitted and forbidden foods of *kashrut* seem almost arbitrary. Today, some Jews observe *kashrut* simply because they believe God commanded it. Others follow these laws because this is the way the Jewish people have eaten for hundreds of years. Yet the question remains—what is the purpose of these laws?

The Torah does give us an answer to that question in Lev. 11:44: "For I the Lord am your God: you shall sanctify yourselves and be holy, for I am holy." Thus *kashrut* involves holiness. Through *kashrut,* we are to be holy just as God is holy. *Kadosh* is the biblical word for "holy." In ancient Israel, *kadosh,* "holiness," was a term that was applied to God. Departing from other ancient Middle Eastern civilizations, the Torah teaches that nothing in this world is intrinsically holy. There are no sacred trees or rivers. Only God is holy. All other holiness is derived from God or is ascribed by God to some thing.

> The source of holiness is assigned to God alone. Holiness is the extension of his nature; it is the agency of his will. If certain things are termed holy—such as the land (Canaan), person (priest), place (sanctuary), or time (holy day)—they are so by virtue of divine dispensation. [Jacob Milgrom, *Leviticus,* p. 730]

Created in God's image, we strive to emulate God's holiness, and *kashrut* is one means to do this. As we have already seen, the rabbis' understanding of God's holiness is related to how we act in the world— "just as God is merciful so should you be merciful." *Kashrut* is, then, a specific ethical teaching. Professor Jacob Milgrom, a Bible scholar, suggests that the biblical dietary laws are part of a larger structure that calls upon Jews to increase holiness in the world. The world can be divided into *kadosh,* the "holy," and *hol,* the "common" or "ordinary." The task of the Jew is to expand holiness by transforming the common into the holy.

Specifically, *kashrut* is a holy and ethical way of eating with a basic goal of teaching a reverence for life. This is accomplished through the various laws of food consumption. (1) The criteria of chewing cud or fins and scales limits greatly what kinds of animals can be eaten. The slaughtering of these animals is done in a way that very quickly brings about unconsciousness and death. (2) Milk, which is a symbol of life and nurturance, cannot be eaten together with meat, which is an image of death. While recognizing that death exists, we try to keep the two realms separate. (3) There is a prohibition against consuming blood, which is seen as representing the life force of living creatures. In ancient times the blood was spilled on the sacrificial altar or buried. Today, kosher meat is salted to draw out the blood.

These practices are intended to remind us that the taking of the life of animals for food is a concession to us by God; it is not a human right. Animals are also God's creatures. When we eat meat, we must do so within a context that reveres life.

"*Kashrut,* then, is a kind of spiritual ecology, manifesting a deep, subliminal process which Mircea Eliade termed 'religious nostalgia,' the universal desire of people to 'live in the world as when it came from the Creator's hands, fresh, pure and strong' " (Samuel Weintraub in *Reconstructionist* 77[2], winter 1991, pp. 12–14).

The eating of animals seems, somehow, to place us at one remove from that ideal condition. It is obvious that animals do not simply exist for our pleasure, so the consumption of flesh is a compromise. It should not separate us from our quality of mercy, as the following story suggests:

A calf was being taken to be slaughtered. Just then Rabbi Judah the Prince (known simply as Rabbi) was seated in front of the Babylonians' house of study in Sepphoria. The calf broke away, hid its head under Rabbi's skirts, and lowed pitifully, as though pleading, "Save me." "Go," said Rabbi. "For this you were created."

Then it was said in heaven, "Since he has no pity, let suffering come upon him now."

And they [the sufferings] departed because of another incident: One day Rabbi's maidservant was sweeping the house. Seeing some young weasels lying there, she was about to sweep them away. "Let them be," he said to her, "for it is written, 'And God's tender mercies are over all God's works' " (Psalm 145:9).

Then it was said in heaven, "Since he is compassionate, let Us be compassionate to him." [Talmud, *Bava Metzia* 84b]

Finally, *kashrut* is a discipline. *Kashrut* establishes limitations on what and when we can eat. A sense of limitation on the self can be a powerful acknowledgment of the existence of God.

*The basic laws of* kashrut   As mentioned, only certain animals are kosher. The Torah permits eating animals with split hoofs that chew their cud: cattle, sheep, goats, and deer. Most domestic birds are permitted, including chickens, turkeys, ducks, and geese. Fish with fins and scales are permitted, such as bass, bluefish, carp, cod, flounder, fluke, haddock, halibut, herring, mackerel, pike, red snapper, salmon, sardines, trout, tuna, and whitefish. All fruits and vegetables are kosher. Animals and birds must be slaughtered in a ritual manner called *shehitah*. The person who is trained to perform this correctly is known as a *shoheit*. The basic method is severing the trachea and esophagus in one swift motion with a very sharp knife. This is reputed to be a relatively painless way to kill an animal. Kosher animals cannot be stunned or shot (nor for that matter be found dead of natural causes in the woods). Only this manner of ritual slaughter makes the meat kosher. (Fish are not ritually slaughtered and can be caught in the usual manner.)

The Torah's prohibition against seething a kid in its mother's milk has been interpreted to mean that milk and meat may not be eaten together. This has created three food categories: meat *(fleishik or besari)*, including all meat and fowl; dairy *(milchik or halavi)*, including milk and foods derived from milk, like cheese, butter, and yogurt; and everything not specifically placed in the above two categories *(pareve)*, including fruits, vegetables, most drinks, and most pasta. Fish is also defined as *pareve*. One can eat *pareve* food with either milk or meat, but one cannot eat milk and meat together at the same meal. It is customary to wait after eating meat before eating dairy. There are a number of different customs in this regard based on the practice of different Jewish communities. For instance Jews of Eastern European descent wait six hours, while German Jews wait three hours. Some communities wait only one hour. The separation of meat and milk led to the practice of having two sets of dishes, silverware, pots and pans, etc.: one for milk and one for meat.

Those who observe *kashrut* soon discover that neither liberal nor strict observance precludes a great variety. No matter how strict one's observance may be, rest assured that there is someone in the Jewish world who will refuse to eat in your home, claiming that their measure of piety is still stricter. Some areas of choice include:

*Processed foods*   It is fairly simple to keep kosher with respect to unprocessed foods. You can buy fresh fruit anywhere and fresh meat from a kosher butcher. (Many people will buy fresh fish at any fish store. Some will only buy at a kosher fish market out of concern that the knife used to cut your kosher fish may have just been used to cut a nonkosher fish and particles of the previous fish may still be on the knife.) Processed foods, however, are more complicated. Some people will only buy products that have a label indicating rabbinical supervision, such as the *OU*. This certifies the processed food is kosher.

*Rabbinical supervision*   There are many organizations and rabbis that give rabbinical supervision to food. Besides the *OU*, the *kof-k* and the *OK* are two other labels used by prominent organizations. There is no centralized clearinghouse for all these different rabbinical supervisions, though many use the letter *K* in some form or another. Check with your rabbi if you have a question about a product's *kashrut* supervision.

*Ingredients*   Others will read the ingredients on the package to see if all the ingredients seem kosher. The concern here basically lies in three areas. (1) There may be an ingredient which is so minute it is not listed in the package, e.g., lard to grease the machines. (2) The same company may also make nonkosher products and not be careful enough when switching from one production line to another. (3) The manufacturer might run out of one ingredient and substitute another, e.g., a meat tomato sauce for a marinara. For some people the complexity of the processing makes a difference. They will use milk without rabbinical supervision (since milk is simply processed), but they will only eat cookies with rabbinical supervision because any of the above concerns could be applicable. It is important to remember that nothing is foolproof. Rabbinical supervision does not mean that a rabbi is standing there all day watching Nabisco make Oreo cookies. In most plants there are occasional inspections. There is no absolute guarantee against a piece of a worker's ham sandwich falling into the cookie vat. It is only a question of where the reasonable line is to be drawn and how cautious you want to be.

If you are reading ingredients, here are some things to look for:

- Shortening, glycerides, stearates. These could be either animal or vegetable if not specified.
- Whey, lactose, lactic acid, sodium caseinate. These may be milk derivatives; products that contain them should not be eaten with meat. For instance, many breads contain dairy ingredients that pose a problem for your hot dog roll. Most magarines are also dairy.

*Other decision points*   Cheeses are an interesting *kashrut* conundrum. Almost all cheeses are made with rennet, which comes from the stomach of cows. Orthodox opinion is that kosher cheese needs to be made from rennet taken from kosher animals. A Conservative opinion says that rennet is no longer a food substance but rather a chemical. Chemicals fall outside the boundaries of *kashrut* laws. The Conservative opinion is based on the logic that if rennet were still a food, then even from a kosher animal it would be a mixture of milk and meat. But since rennet is a chemical, all domestically produced hard cheeses are kosher. The Orthodox view argues that the standards for meat and milk are different than for kosher and nonkosher products and therefore all cheeses need rabbinical supervision to certify that the rennet comes from a kosher animal. (A similar dispute exists about gelatin, which is made from the bones of animals. Has gelatin become a chemical or does it retain the classification of "animal"?)

There is also an argument about the status of swordfish and sturgeon, because they have scales only at one stage of their lives. Orthodox opinion is that they do not meet the criterion of fins and scales; Conservative opinion is that they do.

*Kosher wine*    The concern about wine is not so much that someone will put liquid lard into the wine. Ancillary to the laws of *kashrut* is a category of foods that are forbidden because they may have been used in idol worship. Such things are forbidden for Jews to use even after the idol-worshiping ritual is over. In ancient times wine libations to the gods were common. Kosher wine exists to eliminate the possibility that the wine was once used in an idolatrous ceremony. There is also a traditional prohibiting of any wine handled by non-Jews as a means to discourage socializing and intermarriage. Even today there are some people who will not drink wine if it has been touched (poured) by a non-Jew, even if the wine was originally kosher. How then do non-Jewish waiters pour wine at Jewish wedding feasts? Some kosher wine is boiled after its production is completed, and thereby halakhically it no longer has the status of wine. This may explain why some kosher wine doesn't taste like wine either!

*Glatt kosher*    Glatt kosher literally means "smooth" kosher. After an animal is slaughtered, its lungs are checked for lesions. If the animal would have died on its own because of these lesions in the not-too-distant future, then the animal is not considered kosher. Glatt kosher raises the standards of what lesions fall into the nonkosher-making category and requires "smoother" lungs. This stringency has only become widely observed in the last twenty-five years. Glatt kosher has come to mean "extra kosher" and has been incorrectly applied to kosher chickens (the issue of lesions on the lungs does not apply to chickens) and even to "glatt kosher pizza."

*Lettuce*    A more recent issue has arisen regarding lettuce. While all vegetables are kosher, eating the little bugs sometimes found in lettuce is forbidden. The standards of how big the little bugs can be has risen to such an extent that some people won't eat lettuce no matter how carefully washed or will only eat hydroponically grown lettuce. This concern has spread to other vegetables. Others ignore this concern by pointing out that such vegetables have been eaten since time immemorial.

*Halav yisrael*    Not as popular yet among the traditional crowd is "Jewish milk," which stems from the concern that milk from non-kosher animals could be mixed in with cow milk. *Halav yisrael* is milk produced by Jews who consciously avoid any such practices.

*Hindquarters*    Because of the prohibition against eating the sciatic nerve (see Gen. 32:33), kosher meat from the hindquarters of animals is not generally available. It is very difficult to remove the nerve and most butchers do not have this skill. Among Jewish communities of Middle Eastern origin, however, the hindquarters are available from kosher butchers.

*Blood*    As mentioned, blood is seen as a symbol of life. Therefore, the consuming of blood is prohibited. Meat is salted to draw out as much of the blood as possible. Usually the butcher does this. For those who want to avoid salt, broiling meat also draws out the blood and thus eliminates the requirement for salting.

The desire to avoid blood applies to a blood spot found in an egg. Therefore, eggs are cracked open and checked before being used. Since unless otherwise indicated eggs sold in the United States are not fertilized, only the blood spot, and not the whole egg, must be discarded.

Since the blood in liver is difficult to remove, the regular salting of kosher meat is not seen as effective. Therefore, kosher liver is always broiled.

*New* kashrut *practices: vegetarianism*   A growing number of people are opting for vegetarianism for health, ecological, or moral reasons. According to the Bible, of course, there was a time when all human beings were vegetarians. In a practical sense, vegetarianism greatly simplifies the laws surrounding *kashrut*. There are no issues regarding the mixing of milk and meat. Nor is there a problem with nonkosher food, since all nonmeats are kosher. Of course, one still needs to check the labels of processed food for ingredients derived from meat. Since *kashrut* considers fish as *pareve* and nonmeat, some Jewish vegetarians will eat fish but not animals. Still others will eat meat on Shabbat or other festive occasions because traditionally meat is part of festive meals. Others have not become strict vegetarians but have cut down their consumption of meat. They use the *kashrut* categories to create a scale with animal meat at the bottom, then birds (e.g., chicken) next, and finally fish. (According to the Talmud, birds are really *pareve,* but in practice they are considered meat.)

*Eco-kashrut*   Zalman Schachter-Shalomi coined the phrase "eco-*kashrut*." Eco-*kashrut* suggests that we apply new principles to the ancient practice of *kashrut*. It shares the assumption with traditional *kashrut* that what we eat makes a difference to our spiritual lives. According to eco-*kashrut,* modern methods of food production have created new categories of unkosher foods. While there is no specific set of guidelines for eco-*kashrut,* its proponents have raised such questions as: Is food grown with pesticides kosher? Are chickens raised in densely packed coops that may violate the law by causing pain to animals (*tza'-ar baalei hayyim)* kosher? Are grapes harvested by underpaid workers kosher? Are products that are overpackaged kosher? Eco-*kashrut* adherents express spiritual awareness regarding exploitation of workers, ecology, health, and cruelty to animals, all of which have sources in the Jewish tradition.

*Creating a* kashrut *practice*   In establishing a personal practice for *kashrut,* there are two major concerns: what you will do in your home and what you will do outside your home.

In your home, practice could range from:

- No pig
- No pig or shellfish
- Above plus only kosher meat
- Above plus not eating milk and meat together
- Above plus checking the ingredients of processed food
- Above plus two sets of dishes, pots, and silverware
- Above plus only using food with kosher supervision

Similar choices need to be made in eating outside the home, whether in a restaurant or at a friend's house. Except where paper plates and plastic utensils are available, one difference is that you have to assume that plates and utensils are not kosher. Otherwise, the normal range of options includes:

- No pig or shellfish
- No meat
- No cooked foods (e.g., eating salads)
- Cooked foods whose ingredients seem okay, e.g., pasta with marinara sauce
- Eating only in kosher restaurants

These options do not include all the possibilities, and people may create varying standards for eating at home and eating outside the home. The desire to socialize and enjoy restaurants has meant that even many Jews who observe some form of *kashrut* will eat in restaurants with some restricting practices. Some make exceptions to their general practice out of respect for parents and other relatives, for example, by eating Thanksgiving dinner in a grandparent's nonkosher home.

### Food as Social Intercourse

Food is also a means for people to have social interaction. Part of the enjoyment derived from eating comes from eating with others. This is reflected ritually in the *birkat ha-mazon*, the Grace after Meals. If three or more people have eaten together, an introductory formula is added to the regular blessings. This formula, called *zimun,* is an "invitation" by one person (as leader) to the others at the table to join in reciting blessings to praise God. The idea is that a fellowship has been created (even if it is just a transitory fellowship) when people break bread together. A shared meal, then, has an additional sacred character.

### Words of Torah

If three have eaten at the same table and words of Torah were spoken, it is as if they had eaten at the table of God. [*Ethics of Our Ancestors* 3:3]

"Words of Torah" does not necessarily imply talk of Judaism and its teachings, rather that the table conversation has been "good speech." In the previous chapter, we talked about *lashon ha-ra,* literally "evil speech." Gossip and slander, words that destroy, are not words of Torah. All other speech, no matter how trivial or casual, is, in this context, "words of Torah."

Meals are also offerings made for celebratory occasions. On Shabbat and festivals, part of our celebration consists of good foods, special foods, and drink. Traditionally, Jews saved their best foods for Shabbat.

A special category of meals is known as *seudat mitzvah,* literally "a *mitzvah* meal." The feast following a wedding is one example. It is not just a party, but a part of the wedding ritual itself. Specifically, as we will see when we discuss weddings, it fulfills our obligation to rejoice with the bride and groom. The meal served at a *brit milah* (circumcision) has the same kind of ritual character. There is also a tradition that, upon completing a course of study, a *seudat mitzvah* is held in celebration. All these meals are sacred in character, probably meant to be similar to the experience of eating the meat of sacrifices brought to the Temple in Jerusalem in ancient times. Even as we party and have a good time, we bring a higher spiritual awareness to a sacred occasion.

## Practice

It is a challenge to eat with awareness amid busy schedules and business lunches. Even the ritual does not always help. Sometimes, like eating, the practice of *kashrut* and the saying of *berakhot* become rote matters.

My practice is to pause for a few seconds in silence, then recite the *berakhah* or its equivalent, and then eat the first bite of food slowly and with consciousness. Paying attention to just the first bite is a good beginning. It also echoes the tradition that the first fruits of the harvest were seen as having a special status. (They were offered up in the Temple as part of the sacrificial system in ancient times.) Like many people, though, when I am in a hurry, I sometimes eat food even before it and I have reached the table. To help me avoid this trap, I try to ritually wash my hands before I eat a meal as a way to prepare my spirit. (I do that even if I am not eating bread, which is when washing is traditionally required.) Another way of slowing down to raise consciousness might be achieved through a conscious setting of the table.

Reciting even the short form of the after-eating blessings is a way to honor the food, the preparation of the food, and the experience of eating before rushing off to the next activity. It is also another transition point calling us to awareness.

> Through eating one dish and one meal a week (or a Shabbat meal) with true kavanah for the sake of heaven, and to lift up the animal powers of your soul to God, you raise up spiritually all the food and meals you ate that week. [Rabbi Tzadok ha-Cohen, *P'ri Tzaddik*]

> "A wooden altar three cubits high . . . and he said unto me: 'This is the table that is before the Lord' " (Ez. 41:22). Why does the verse begin by calling it an altar and end by calling it a table? Because, as R. Yohanan and R. Eleazar both said, as long as the Temple stood, the altar made expiation for Israel, but now a person's table makes expiation for her. [Talmud, *Berakhot* 54b–55a]

Our goal then is to come to the table with a sense that this is a table set before God. What should it mean that our dining tables have taken the place of the sacrificial altar in the Temple? Certainly, that our eating should feel as holy as the sacred process of eating the meat of those Temple sacrifices. For the worshiper in the Temple, such sacred feasts must have felt as though they were eating in the very Presence of God. We can easily imagine the sense of holiness experienced by the elders who, after the revelation at Sinai, ascended the mountain with Moses and saw a vision of God in the context of a meal—"they beheld God and they ate and drank" (Exod. 24:11).

Sadly—with pre-cooked foods, microwaves, takeout and home delivery—many of us hardly touch our food before consuming it, let alone physically prepare it or reflect on its origin in divine love and wisdom. [Samuel Weintraub in *Reconstructionist* 77(2), winter 1991, pp. 12–14]

It may also be that our tables are like altars when we offer up on them healthy eating instead of overeating. Just as the animals offered in the Temple had to be from the right category and also needed to be without blemish, so should our foods be "unblemished." We can offer up food at our tables that does not blemish our bodies. Perhaps at our tables we want to sacrifice our gluttony, our behaving like animals who eat only out of instinct. We surely forget that we are created in the Divine image when we "stuff our faces."

Instead, this is the table set before Adonai. Eating is an opportunity to open ourselves to the holy. By opening our mouths, we open our selves to that potential. Eating can be dangerous. Our vulnerabilities and insecurities are exposed and yet at the same time it is an opportunity. The pleasure from food is to be enjoyed, not avoided in an asceticism that would in effect deny this gift from God.

*Ta'amu u're'u ki tov Adonai,* "Taste and see how good God is" (Psalm 34:9).

# THE END OF THE DAY

At the end of the day, we return home to pass the evening hours before going to bed. We spend time relaxing and doing household chores. If we live with others, this is our principal time to reconnect with them. The spiritual challenge is to leave behind the stresses of the workday to make room for a heightened awareness in all our evening interactions.

*KAVANAH*

Upon reaching your doorway, pause and look at or kiss the mezuzah on your doorpost and say:

Let me rejoice in my return to the warmth of my home. This day, as all workdays, was filled with a mixture of accomplishments and missteps. If I can, let me leave the anxieties and problems of the day ensconced in my briefcase. If I am struggling with a major issue at work, let me reflect upon it in a manner that leads to clarity rather than overwhelming anxiety. Let me share it with those who love me in an open and honest manner so that I may be nurtured by them. Let me not displace that anxiety on the people with whom I share the intimate aspects of my life. Let this be a homecoming to all that I treasure.

Returning home at the end of the day bespeaks what home can represent: a comfortable and safe environment, a place to relax, and for many, a setting for the significant relationships of our lives. Yet each of us has our own life situation. Some people work at home or work nights. Many people live alone. Relaxation takes place outside the home, as well; and not only in the evenings, but at other times such as weekends and holidays. This chapter will focus on two aspects of homecoming: relaxation and bringing your day to an end. Issues surrounding relationships with loved ones, children, and friends are discussed in Part Four of this book.

## Relaxation

After a long day at work, what many people desire the most when they cross their home's threshold is minimal stimulation. They want a mindless activity—to read a light book or magazine or to watch an insignificant television program. In their attempt to "forget" the day, many try to create enough static in the mind to drown out the voices from the day. They may turn on the television as soon as they walk in the house just to have the sound. This could be a warning sign that they are working too hard or that their life is unsatisfying.

But mindless relaxation is a serious misunderstanding of what the mind really needs. To be numb is, in effect, to go to sleep the minute you come home, to make the evening an extended sleepwalking in preparation for going to bed. The search for mindlessness is part of a larger pattern of putting life on hold. "I'm too tired tonight" (every night that is) is one part of a litany that includes "Thank God it's Friday" and "I'll do that when I'm financially secure." Such delaying tactics are little more than postponements in the hope that "tomorrow will be better."

The truth is, all that we have is *this* moment. It is a precious commodity because it will never come again in this lifetime. To live with awareness is to live every moment. This does not necessarily mean spending the evening reading James Joyce or only engaging in philosophical discourses with family and friends.

Relaxing with awareness is not about highbrow versus lowbrow culture. Nor is it about scheduling each minute of our leisure time. Awareness simply means being present in the moment. If God is in everything, then there is holiness in classical music as well as in the latest musical craze: holiness in Shakespeare's sonnets and in the latest Victorian romance novel. Holiness is everywhere, even in the laugh track of a silly television comedy. Awareness is learning to appreciate things for what they are. This leads us to a more conscious selection of those activities that bring us pleasure rather than just those with which we try to drown out the world.

Relaxing may mean taking off our work clothes. Those clothes reflect our need to be concerned about how a boss or client looks at us during our work lives. At night, we can luxuriate in being just who we are. This is our opportunity to please ourselves and those with whom we share the intimacy and casualness of our homes.

In our leisure time, we can also make sure that we are taking care of ourselves. Exercise and other forms of attention to the body are essential for our continued health. We can make time for spiritual activities that are hard to fit into a busy workday. Whether we choose to study Torah, engage in prayer, write in a journal, or meditate, this time allows us to nourish our souls. Both our bodies and our souls need exercise if they are to stay in shape instead of becoming flabby from lack of use.

### Saying Good Night to the Day

There are two strands within the Jewish tradition concerning sleep. One view is that you should sleep as little as possible in order to spend as much time as possible in Torah study and prayer. The other view stresses the importance of sleep to rest the body for the coming day. Rabbi Yitzhak Isaac of Komarna said:

> When people want to serve God with *devekut* [devotion] and Divine light, and with joy and desire, they must have their minds clear and bright and undimmed, and their body vigorous. And if they are awake more than they should be, their vitality will decline and the mind will become dulled. My holy father [Rabbi Alexander Sander] said to those who were making every effort to perfect themselves to the fullest and hardly sleeping, that it would be better to sleep the whole day and be a human being for the two hours they were awake,

rather than stay awake all the time and be a horse for ten hours, dully carrying the yoke. [*Ateret Tiferet*, p. 37, #49]

Therefore, some would say before going to sleep that their intention in sleeping was to renew their strength in order to worship God.

Just as there are traditional rituals for waking up, so is there a traditional ritual for going to bed: *Keriat shema al ha-mitah*, "the reciting of the Shema in bed." Even though the Shema prayer ("Hear O Israel, Adonai our God, Adonai is One") is recited as part of the *ma'ariv,* the evening service, it is traditionally said again at bedtime, along with its accompanying first paragraph. There is also a *berakhah* that is said: *Ha-mapeil hevlei sheinah al einai,* "who makes the weight of sleep to fall upon my eyes." Over time, a number of additional prayers have been added to this ritual to ask for God's protection while we sleep. The general notion was that being asleep meant being vulnerable. Nighttime was dangerous. It was a time when demons and the forces of evil were at their most powerful. Today this may seem primitive, yet even now night can be scary for adults as well as children. In the additional prayers of the traditional *Keriat shema al ha-mitah*, we ask to be surrounded on each side by an angel while the *Shekhinah*, God's Presence, hovers over us. We all want to feel protected and tucked in our beds. Thankfulness for the blessings of the day is another appropriate theme that can be expressed through the liturgy or in our own words.

---

KERIAT SHEMA AL HA-MITAH

The following is a version of the *Keriat shema al ha-mitah* adapted from the *Reconstructionist Daily Prayer book:*

Blessed are you, Eternal One, our God, the sovereign of all worlds, who makes the weight of sleep to fall upon my eyes, and slumber on my eyelids. May it be your will, Eternal Guardian, my God, and God of my ancestors, that you help me to lie down in peace, and to arise in peace, and do not let my thoughts make me afraid, nor my bad dreams, nor my preoccupations. May my bed be safely guarded in your Presence, and may you give light to my eyes lest I should sleep without awakening, for you are giver of the light of living to the pupil of the eye. Blessed are you, Eternal Lamp, who gives light to the world in all its glory.

Hear O Israel, Adonai our God, Adonai is One!

Blessed be the glory of the Sovereign Name forever.

And you must love The One your God, with all your heart, with every breath, with all you have. Take these words that I command you now to heart. Teach them intently to your children; speak them when sitting in your house and walking on the road, when lying down and getting up. Bind them as a sign upon your hand, and keep them visible before your eyes. Write them on the doorposts of your house and on your gates.

Let our divine protector's pleasure be upon us, and the labor of our hands, make it secure, the labor of our hands ensure!

Help us to lie down, Dear One, our God, in peace, and let us rise again, our sovereign, to life. Spread over us the shelter of your peace. Decree for us a worthy daily lot, and redeem us for the sake of your great name, protecting us, removing from our midst all enmity, disease, and violence, all suffering and hunger, and enfold us in the wings of your protection. For you are our redeeming guardian. Truly, a sovereign, gracious, and compassionate God are you. Please guard us when we go forth and when we return, ensuring life and peace, both now and always.

I lie down, I sleep, and I awake, knowing the Eternal One is my support.

Thankfulness for the blessings of the day and soul-searching *(heshbon ha-nefesh)* are also appropriate themes at bedtime.

Every night before going to bed [Rabbi Levi Yitzhak of Berditchev] searched his actions of the day and went over them carefully. He considered them so closely, with such a fine-tooth comb, that he always found faults in everything he did. And he did *teshuvah* [repentance], saying, "Levi Yitzhak won't do any of these things again!" Then he would say aloud, "But Levi Yitzhak—didn't you say the same thing last night?" And he would answer himself, "Yes. But yesterday I wasn't telling the truth; now I am!" [*Zichron l'Rishonim*, p. 96]

The *Mishneh Berurah* comments as follows on the ritual of *Keriat shema*:

It is written in holy books that before people go to sleep at night it is proper for them to examine the deeds that they performed during the entire day. If they discover that they transgressed they should confess to it and accept upon themselves not to do it again. The common sins especially, such as flattery, lying, mocking, tale bearing and also the sin of neglecting Torah study need thorough probing. It is also fitting for people to forgive everyone who sinned against them and distressed them. [*Shulhan Arukh, Orah Hayyim* 239:9]

One possible custom is to do a short review each night and, perhaps on Thursday night, do a more complete review. This process of review, if done in a way that allows us to examine what we have done and to obtain clarity on our motivations, can help bring closure on one day even as we prepare for the next. If the *heshbon ha-nefesh* can be done in a positive and healing manner, it could also lead to a peaceful night's sleep. An honest evaluation should not be accompanied with harsh self-criticism. We need to accept our own limitations even as we strive to change. Similarly, we try to be forgiving of those who have hurt us by accepting their limitations. If we have wronged someone, making a commitment to set it right the next day is also part of this process.

Things tend to feel worse at night when we are tired and overwhelmed with the struggles of the day. The value of a nighttime ritual is that it sets a limit on our dwelling on the day. The introductory prayer to *Keriat shema al ha-mitah* reads as follows:

> Behold, I now forgive whoever has provoked my anger or annoyance, whoever has done wrong to me, whether to my body or my spirit, or to my honor, or to all that may belong to me, whether willingly, or inadvertently, or by design, whether by speech or deed—let no one suffer punishment on my account.

We can construct a more complete model of *heshbon ha-nefesh* based on the structure set out in the book *Heshbon ha-Nefesh*, by Rabbi Mendel of Satanow (published in 1845). His system involves choosing thirteen *middot,* "character traits." During the course of one week, we focus on one trait, e.g., *hoda'ah,* "gratitude" or "joy." Over the course of a year, we spend a total of four weeks working on a specific trait. As mentioned in the first chapter, we begin each day by reciting the summary statement of the trait to bring it to our consciousness. At the end of the day, most commonly in the few minutes before we go to sleep, we review the day and see how well we did regarding that trait. We may want to keep a diary in which we jot down what happened that day in terms of that trait. Underlying this practice is a belief that by focusing on these traits we will improve our character through an increased awareness. Also, by taking one trait a time, we are less likely to be overwhelmed. At the end of the year, we can review the year and change or refine our selection of traits.

If you would like to try this practice, you should first consider which of the thirteen characteristics you want to choose. You will see from my list that some of these traits overlap. This is my own selection with accompanying summary statements. Feel free to create your own. (For more about *musar,* "character development," see *Climbing Jacob's Ladder,* by Alan Morinis.)

- *Hoda'ah*—gratitude, joy. We are born with all we need for life, the gifts of heart, mind, hands, and senses. Remember to enjoy the blessings of the world.
- *Metinut*—deliberation, mindfulness. We can approach each mo-

ment either unconsciously in a form of slumber or awake to its potential. Be mindful of what you say and do before you open your mouth or hand.

- *Nedivut*—generosity, openhandedness. Generosity comes from a willingness to be connected to others and thus be vulnerable. Give because an open heart is a better place to live than in a heart that counts and weighs each penny.
- *Zerizut*—zeal. We often put off doing things out of insecurity or dislike. Zeal encourages us to do them now and not waste all the energy involved in putting them off to tomorrow.
- *Emet*—truth. Facing the truth means telling the truth even when it is easier to lie. Facing the truth means acknowledging who we are, including our faults.
- *Tzedek*—righteousness. We are to live by the principle that what is hateful to you, you should not do to others. In the face of injustice, we are to rally to the cause of justice. We should not be silent.
- *Histapkut*—simplicity. What do I need and what is unnecessary? *Histapkut* challenges me to examine whether what I own or want to own overwhelms my ability to be clear about what is really important.
- *Savlanut*—patience. We are to respond with patience to the world, especially to the other equally flawed human beings in our lives. We come to understand that anger, even on the rare occasions when necessary, only breaks and never heals.
- *Hanun ve-rahum*—forgiveness and mercy. When we are willing to forgive both for our sake and for the other person, everyone is able to move on. We need to resist the impulse to rate everyone on a criticism scale.
- *Anivut*—modesty, correct perspective. All of us are created in the image of God. When we really remember that no one is intrinsically better than or even different from us, then we can strive to learn from everyone.
- *Ratzon*—openness. When we live with openness rather than fear, we allow for the possibility of change and growth. Let our initial response be "yes" rather than "no."
- *Betahon*—trust, optimism. If we believe that change is possible

then we can see the possibilities inherent in each new day. With *be-tahon* we see every glass as half full rather than half empty.

- *Menuhat nefesh*—calmness. When faced with a setback that you have no control over, do not make things worse by useless worrying. Instead, focus on the present moment, whether it is joyous or difficult, rather than become lost in the stories spun by our insecure selves.

---

KAVANAH

Safe and sound, I lie down and sleep, for You alone, O Lord, keep me secure (Psalm 4:9).

Or:

I place my spirit in Your care, when I wake as when I sleep, God is with me; I shall not fear, body and spirit in Your keep (last lines of *Adon Olam* prayer).

# SHABBAT: A DAY FOR
# WALKING SOFTLY THROUGH
# THE WORLD

Shabbat is the central ritual of Jewish life. Its centrality lies in its origin as an intrinsic part of creation. While the festivals mark moments in Jewish history or moments in the relationship of God to the Jewish people, Shabbat exists in the very weave of the universe. According to the Torah, God created the world in six days and then rested on the seventh, not out of Divine weariness, but as a model for us to imitate. Created in God's image, we are called upon to create the world for six days of the week and to rest on the seventh. This establishes the deep rhythm of our world; the rhythm of a week. We are meant to endlessly repeat that week, attempting to finish the work of creation. Yet we come full stop at the seventh day, known as Shabbat, which literally means "to cease," "to rest."

Shabbat enables us to gain perspective, to reflect on what we have done, and to notice what still needs to be done. For Shabbat is first of all a haven from the week. Especially in our modern world, it reminds us to stop worrying about our accomplishments, about "getting somewhere" or about "being someone." Shabbat shows that meaning in our lives lies not in what we have accomplished but in being part of the universe. It provides both time and opportunity to rediscover ourselves.

Shabbat is also a reflection of the way the world should be, a pointing in the direction of all that still needs to be created. Shabbat is, in the rabbis' words, *me'ain olam haba*, "a taste of the world to come," a sketch of a world of messianic peace. In this way, Shabbat reminds us of why we are here: to be partners with God in the creation of the world.

Shabbat's rest is physical, restoring the body as does a night's sleep. It is spiritual in that it gives us time to reconnect with the spirit found in friends, community, nature, and the Holy One. By giving us a chance to look at ourselves and our lives, Shabbat encourages us to find our true direction. Looking at the world through messianic glasses allows us to see a vision of the world as it should be and thus calls us to renew our efforts to make the weekdays and Shabbat become more and more alike.

## A Day for Recycling the Soul

Every religion faces the challenge of how to relate to the mundane world, the world filled with the trivial and the tempting. In the mundane world, the ego cries at its loudest, Feed me—with power, with food, with money and possessions, with all the desires and lusts that make the everyday a place of beauty and ugliness. In the hurly-burly *tohu u-vohu,* "chaos of the world," the spiritual often can't be heard over the din. Some religions urge people to withdraw from the world, others urge an ascetic approach, while still others create a religious elite to serve as models for the rest of us. Faced with the challenges of the mundane and the corruption of *hol,* the "everyday," Judaism challenges us to remain in the world, grappling with life and its complexities. But it balances that immersion in the workday world with a retreat from that world every seventh day. One-seventh of our lives, we are called to the practice of Shabbat, a key aspect of the spiritual discipline of Jewish life.

Shabbat is to be unlike the other days of the week. Not because *hol,* the "ordinary," is evil, but because we are normally caught up in the demands of those days to work, to earn a living, to succeed, to participate in the act of creation. If we lived our lives only in that way, particularly in the work ethic of our times, we would too easily lose our way in the ever-faster pace of the superhighways of modernity.

In that first week of creation, after each day except the second, God said, "and behold it was good." The midrash asks: Why does it not say at the end of the second day, "and behold it was good," as it does with all the other days of creation? Rabbi Hanina answers: "Because on that day division was created" (see *Genesis Rabbah* 4:6). To make heaven and earth, the separation of the waters was necessary, but that brought divisiveness into the world. According to another midrash, the story of Adam and Eve took place on the afternoon of the sixth day. The week of creation thus ended with disappointment, conflict, and expulsion. God needed Shabbat to rest and reflect on all that had been created before the second week would begin. Divisiveness and disappointment are conditions of the days of *hol*.

Amid the worldliness of Judaism, Shabbat is *me-ein olam haba*, "a taste of otherworldliness." It takes us back to the first few hours of human existence when humans and nature coexisted in harmony in the Garden of Eden. On Shabbat, we do not struggle to overcome the curse "By the sweat of your brow shall you get bread to eat" (Gen. 3:19). Our food, as in the garden, is prepared for us in advance. We do not work on Shabbat—we are back in the garden, where work and earning a living was not necessary. Renouncing our mastery of the world, we live again as partners with all creatures.

Shabbat gives us back the world's most precious commodity: time. We have nowhere to go and nothing to do. We can just be. We can think. Reflect. Search our innermost selves to remember the essentials of life. Time to be with others and in community. Time to be with the Holy One. Time to be with one's self, to remember who you are and whom you want to be.

The harmony of Shabbat points not just to the past of the Garden of Eden, but to the messianic future when the world will be one, a world where it is always Shabbat. Recycling our souls, we also allow the world to recycle and heal itself from the wounds we inflict upon it during the weekdays of creating. Both by resting on Shabbat and by refraining from work, we create the one thing allowed to be fashioned this day—Shabbat. Though the story of Genesis tells us that Shabbat is in the weave of the universe, we need to actualize it in our lives if it is to be real for us. This we do by sanctifying the day. It is a paradox in the Jewish tradition. Shabbat is Shabbat even without the Jewish people. It certainly existed long before Abraham. It is unlike the Jewish holidays in that way. If no Jew anywhere observed Passover, then Passover would not exist. Passover needs Jews to sanctify it and thereby give it reality. Shabbat exists even if no Jew observes it, and yet, paradoxically, we are called upon to sanctify it every week. Without us, Shabbat is lacking its partner. Without us, Shabbat is lacking those who could make the healing of the world happen. Without us, Shabbat is lacking those who could work toward fulfilling the messianic vision inherent in the day.

### What Is Work?

It is often noted that Shabbat is the only "ritual" in the Ten Commandments. The rest of the commandments speak either of our relationship to God or of ethical and moral principles. Yet, as the time to reexamine our relationship to the universe, Shabbat is ritual on its most mythic level—the level where we find meaning for our lives.

The Torah tells us to rest on Shabbat. But to define rest, we must first define work. The rabbis defined work as *melakhah mahshevet,* "creative enterprise."

> The *melakhah* which is forbidden on the Sabbath is conceived as the execution of an intelligent purpose by the practical skill of man. Or, more generally, production, creation, transforming an object for human purposes; but *not* physical exertion. Even if you tired yourself out the whole day, as long as you have *produced* nothing within the meaning of melakhah; as long as your activity has not been a constructive exercise of your intelligence, you have performed no melakhah. On the other hand, if you have engendered, without the slightest exertion, even the smallest change in an object for human purposes, then you have profaned the Sabbath, flouted God, and undermined your calling as a Jew. Your physical power belongs to your animal nature; it is with your technical skill which serves your spirit that you master the world—and it is with this that, as a human being, you should subject yourself to God on the Sabbath. [R. Samson Raphael Hirsch, *Horeb*]

It is not physical exertion but rather the engagement in creative processes linked with physical efforts that defines work. The work of creation is the human task, but on Shabbat we must cease from that goal and rest and reflect.

The rabbis developed very specific details of the law in order to flesh out the general principles of the Torah. For Shabbat, they used as the model for a creative enterprise the building of the *mishkan,* the sanctuary in the desert. God said to Moses, "Let them make Me a sanctuary, and I will dwell in their midst" (Exod. 25:8). No act could be holier, and therefore more creative, than constructing a dwelling place here on earth for God's Presence. Having found the *model* creative act, the rabbis then made a list of activities involved in making the *mishkan* and used these as the basic categories to define *melakhah,* "work."

In the rabbinic development of Shabbat, there were always two elements, reflected in the differing versions of the Ten Commandments. In Exod. 20:8 it says, *Zakhor,* "Remember," the Sabbath day. In Deut. 5:12 it says, *Shamor,* "Observe," the Sabbath day. If *Shamor* (observe) focuses on the negative, that is, ceasing from work, *Zakhor* (remember) focuses on the positive—sanctifying the Sabbath day. For the rabbis, Shabbat was a time to be sanctified through *oneg,* "pleasurable things." People were to engage in physical pleasures such as good food, wine, and sex; and spiritual pleasures such as praying, studying, and singing. This was especially true in the past, when work was only a matter of making a living, a job rather than a career, something done for food rather than fulfillment. Shabbat became a time to spend on the finer things of life. Even today, when many of us find satisfaction in our work or our careers, Shabbat frees us from the everyday responsibilities and routines and allows us to focus on the pleasures of life and on its spiritual dimension. Deadlines become irrelevant, the ticking of clocks fades away—no meetings and no list of "to do's." What remains is a sense of the eternity of the world and its Creator, and of our place in that scheme as both creature and creator of the world.

## Traditions: Preparing for Shabbat

Shabbat's status as the completion of the week is reflected in the way Jews refer to the days of the week. Rather than by a name, each day is known by a number, beginning with Sunday as "the first day." The week leads up to the seventh day, which has a name—Shabbat. Traditionally, the best of everything was set aside for Shabbat. The best food was kept until then, the best tablecloth, the best serving utensils, etc. This was both to honor Shabbat and to make it a truly pleasurable and "rich" day.

The whole week moves toward a climax on Shabbat. Even as we save the best food for Shabbat, we can try to put aside some spiritual dainties to taste on Shabbat: a book to read, a conversation with a good friend or lover, a text to study, a physical pleasure to linger over, an aspect of nature to be appreciated.

Beginning on Saturday afternoon of the week before, and continuing on Monday and Thursday mornings, we begin to read the Torah portion that is fully read on Shabbat. We read the first *aliyah* (section of the Torah portion) on each of those days. The week itself is referred to by the name of the coming Shabbat's Torah portion. In this way, the Torah portion becomes part of the cycle of Shabbat and the week. Traditionally, Jews were supposed to review the Torah portion twice in the original Hebrew and once in translation each week. Others would study a seventh of the portion each day, completing the whole portion on Shabbat. You may find it helpful to make the Torah portion part of your week. Read at least one verse of the next week's Torah portion each day.

Each day at the end of morning services we recite a psalm for the day. On Wednesdays, we begin to anticipate the coming Shabbat in the liturgy. We add to the end of Psalm 94, the first two verses of Psalm 95. These verses, which begin with the words *lekhu neranenah*, are the first lines of the Friday night service, the Kabbalat Shabbat. In the midst of the week, when we stand furthest both from Shabbat past and Shabbat future, we look forward with eager anticipation to the coming Shabbat when we will be reciting these lines.

### Erev Shabbat

Preparations intensify on Friday as we engage in shopping, cooking, and cleaning to make everything ready for Shabbat. Many people buy flowers to grace the Shabbat table. Friday is referred to as *erev Shabbat,* the "eve of Shabbat."

**Kavanah:** *double manna*   The first observance of Shabbat by the Jewish people occurred even before Israel heard the sixth commandment at Mount Sinai. When the Israelites were wandering in the desert, they were fed by manna that miraculously fell from heaven every morning. On Fridays a double portion of manna fell and the Israelites were instructed to save some manna for Shabbat. They were also told that no manna would fall on Shabbat so no one should bother to go out to collect it. (Of course, there were some people who went that first Shabbat to check out if manna had fallen.) This double portion of manna has been given as the symbolic reason that today we have two *hallot* on our Shabbat table (see below).

The double portion of manna can also be seen as the *kavanah* approach to Fridays as *erev Shabbat.* Just as the manna collected on Friday served as the food for Shabbat, so should our preparations be a gathering of what we need for our Shabbat celebration. Try to do some aspect of the preparation for Shabbat on Friday even if it is only shopping for the *hallot* or setting the Shabbat table. The physical preparation should not be delegated. Spiritual preparation does not mean being devoid of the physical. As busy as a Friday can be, strive for a feeling of anticipation or at least relief at the end of a workweek.

Like the doubling of the manna, we also should double whatever our preparations have been for Shabbat. For example, if we have been reading one verse from the week's Torah portion we should now read two. If we give to beggars on the street, then give double on Fridays (or if we have not given during the week, then specifically give on Fridays).

*The transition*   How do we shift from one mode of experience—the workweek of creation—to the holiness of Shabbat? The rituals of Friday night itself are meant to aid us in that transition. Even the moments before Shabbat are part of that transition. As Shabbat approaches, we try to create a ritual of transition. In a traditional home that might involve turning on the oven or the electric lights to be left on for Shabbat.

This is also accomplished by setting the table or preparing the Shabbat candlesticks by removing old wax and putting in new candles. Traditionally, you empty your pockets because you don't carry things outside on Shabbat. It can also be a way to mark the change from the week, just as putting aside your briefcase or daily planner shows that Shabbat is not part of the world of work. A wallet, office keys, coins, a pen put away in a drawer are ways to leave the week behind as we make the transition to Shabbat.

Taking the loose change and giving it to *tzedakah* by depositing it in a *pushka,* "a collection container," before Shabbat became a tradition because money is not used or even touched on Shabbat. It is also an ironic acknowledgment that our Shabbat is only partly real; the rest is a dream. For despite our resting on Shabbat, the world does not get to rest. Despite our enjoyment of good food, there are those in the world who have no food. In the Garden of Eden, our food was just there waiting to be plucked. We try to reenter the garden on Shabbat, but it is only a partial return. We may not prepare our food on Shabbat, but then we do have to prepare it before Shabbat. Manna no longer falls from heaven. We need to work at it. We can only make Shabbat as gardenlike as possible in an imperfect world. Similarly, before we begin Shabbat, we acknowledge the imperfection of the world—a world of poverty and oppression—by giving to *tzedakah*. Finally, by giving *tzedakah,* we are opening our hearts to others, which in turn readies our hearts to be open to the spirit of Shabbat.

Finally, while preparing our homes and surroundings, we prepare ourselves. This internal process also has an external dimension. We shower before Shabbat. In this way we not only wash away the "sweat of our brow" of the workweek, we also freshen and renew our bodies for Shabbat. There is a tradition among Jewish mystics to immerse in the *mikvah,* the "ritual bath," each week before Shabbat. Take a moment in the shower to experience the warmth and the sensuous feel of the water as it washes over your body. Remind yourself that this shower has an additional purpose beyond the other showers of the week. With it, we move from the ordinary week to the spirit of Shabbat, a time when the body is not to be left behind. The time in the shower can also be used to prepare our spirit for Shabbat. Try to "wash away" anything from the week that you don't want to take into Shabbat—anger, despair, or stress. Feel those emotions wash away as you leave them aside for Shabbat. Now we clothe our bodies for Shabbat. Traditionally, our best clothes were worn on Shabbat, so there was a marked difference between dress for Shabbat and for weekday. Nowadays, since many people wear their "dress-up" clothes all week, in some communities it has become the custom to dress informally for Shabbat. A few people have a special garment reserved for Shabbat even if it is only a special *kippah,* "skullcap."

## Friday Night

The central motif of Friday night, expressed through its rituals, is the welcoming of Shabbat. We sanctify the day as we gather with friends or family to eat a meal. Often in our busy world this is the only time all week that a family sits down and eats a meal together.

Shabbat begins at sundown on Friday nights. Since the rabbis wanted to make sure no one accidentally continued working past the sundown deadline, they created a margin for error by setting Shabbat's initiating ritual eighteen minutes *before* sundown. This was also done because of the rabbis' desire to expand the precious day as much as possible by adding to both its beginning and, as we shall see, to its ending.

**Hadlakat ha-neirot,** *lighting the candles*    Candle lighting marks the beginning of Shabbat. Since lighting fire on Shabbat was prohibited, a candle or lamp was lit before Shabbat began so that its light would last as long as possible on Friday nights. The Shabbat candles, however, have more than a practical purpose. Their fire symbolizes the warmth and joy Shabbat can bring to those who welcome her, and their light symbolizes the enlightenment that can come to those who stop for a day of rest. This is one of the few *mitzvot* traditionally performed by women, who were seen as the upholders of the home and family. Women would use the moment of candle lighting to pray for good health and fortune for their family. Here is a traditional women's prayer at candle lighting:

O God of Your people Israel: You are holy and You made the Sabbath and the people of Israel holy. You have called upon us to honor the Sabbath with light, with joy, and with peace. As a king and queen give love to one another—as a bride and her bridegroom—so have we kindled these two lights for love of your daughter, the Sabbath day. Almighty God, grant me and all my loved ones a chance to truly rest on this Sabbath day. May the light of the candles drive out from among us the spirit of anger, the spirit of harm. Send Your blessings to my children that they may walk in the ways of Your Torah Your light. May You ever be their God and mine, O Lord, my Creator and my Redeemer. Amen. [Translated from the Yiddish by Arthur Green, in *The First Jewish Catalog*]

It is customary to light two candles, perhaps symbolic of the two versions of the Shabbat commandment in the Ten Commandments (one found in Exodus and the other in Deuteronomy). The candles are also said to symbolize the different parts of ourselves—the disunity and disharmony that exist in the everyday world, which now are being drawn together by the lighting of the two candles. Some people light one additional candle for each member of the household above the number two (e.g., three candles for one parent with two children).

Many people have the custom of holding out their hands and then drawing them in to cover their eyes. Some repeat this gesture of "drawing in" a number of times. Shabbat begins in darkness—a world without light, but then we open our eyes to its light. Anytime we make a rapid transition from darkness to light our eyes are first dazzled by the light. We symbolically create Shabbat's brilliant radiance by moving from darkness to light. We follow this with an open-armed gesture of welcome as we draw into ourselves the light and warmth of Shabbat.

The origin of this custom may be related to a halakhic concern. In general, we say a blessing for a *mitzvah* before we actually do the *mitzvah*. In this case there was concern that if the blessing were said it would initiate the beginning of Shabbat, and thereby prohibit the lighting of the candles (since it is forbidden to start a fire on Shabbat). Therefore, we first light the candles and then we cover our eyes. After we recite the blessing, the light of the candles is "revealed" to us.

*Saying the blessing*   *Barukh atah Adonai eloheinu melekh ha'olam asher kidshanu be-mitzvotav ve-tzivanu le-hadlik ner shel Shabbat.* "Praised are You, Eternal One, our God, source of the universe, who has made us holy through the *mitzvot* and commanded us to kindle the Sabbath lights."

While their eyes are still covered, some meditate or add their own prayer. It is customary to wish anyone present a *"Shabbat shalom"* after the candle lighting (see "Shabbat Salutations" below).

Once the candles are lit, Shabbat has begun and its splendor and peace descend on the household. In some synagogues candle lighting precedes the Friday night services. Similarly, some people light candles immediately before their Friday night meal whether or not this is the traditional time for candle lighting. In this view, Shabbat "officially" begins for them when the ritual candle lighting is performed.

## Kabbalat Shabbat

The Friday night service is different from the evening weekday service and has its own name, Kabbalat Shabbat, "the welcoming of the Shabbat." The service begins with six psalms, representing the six days of the week, followed by the hymn "Lekha Dodi," "Come My Beloved." This hymn, usually sung, calls upon us to rise and greet the Sabbath Queen. Kabbalat Shabbat helps us make the transformation from weekday to Shabbat. This service is a relatively recent addition to Jewish liturgy, composed by the mystics of Safed in Israel in the sixteenth century. This part of the service is followed by *ma'ariv,* the evening service. In the *amidah,* the "standing prayer," the central blessing takes for its theme creation and Shabbat.

*The* kavanah *and imagery of Kabbalat Shabbat*   The mystics saw our task in the world as bringing together the scattered divine sparks (see "After the Words: God," pp. 490–91). One image they used was the uniting of the masculine and feminine aspects of the Godhead. Shabbat was described as feminine, as the bride whose arrival is to be greeted with affection and enthusiasm. For the mystics, Kabbalat Shabbat was the way to welcome the Shabbat bride into the world. Their Shabbat-welcoming custom was to go out into the fields around Safed to show their eagerness to greet her. As a remnant of that custom, we still turn toward the door for the last stanza of "Lekha Dodi" and bow twice in a sign of welcome to the arriving Shabbat. All of our preparation leads up to this moment when Shabbat is welcomed into our lives. We stand cleansed and wearing fresh clothes, our hearts opened by the act of giving to *tzedakah,* our bodies having basked in the light of the Shabbat candles, eagerly taking Shabbat into our souls. It is through this act of welcoming that we can really enter into the unique quality of the world of Shabbat.

The image of the mystics' journey to greet Shabbat can also be a model to us to go out into the world on Shabbat. This going-out would mean to really *see* the world on Shabbat rather than view it as we often do during the week, as if from a window of a passing train.

*Shabbat salutations*    It is customary to greet people on Shabbat by saying (Yiddish) *Gut Shabbos!,* "a good Shabbos!" or (Hebrew) *Shabbat shalom,* "a peaceful Shabbat!"

## The Friday Evening Meal

"Shalom Aleichem," "Peace Be unto You," is the traditional hymn sung at the Friday night table. We welcome the Sabbath by greeting the angels who accompany the Sabbath. It is also a call for *shalom,* "peace," to come into our homes.

*Blessing the children*    It is customary for parents to bless their children on Friday night. A number of customs are observed as to when this is done—at candle lighting, upon returning from the synagogue, or before reciting *kiddush.* The traditional blessing is:

For a girl: *Yesimekh elohim kesarah rivkah rahel ve-le'ah.* "May God make you like Sarah, Rebecca, Rachel, and Leah."

For a boy: *Yesimekha elohim ke'efrayim ve-khimnasheh.* "May God make you like Ephraim and Menasheh."

Some parents place their hands on the child's head and recite the priestly blessing or their own prayers for their children.

The Priestly Blessing:

*Yeverekha Adonai veyishmerekha. Ya'er Adonai panav elekha vihuneka. Yisa Adonai panav elekha veyasem lekha shalom.* "May God bless you and keep you. May God's Presence shine on you and be gracious to you. May God's Presence rise toward you and give you peace."

Some families have expanded on this custom by having the children bless their parents and siblings.

Traditionally, at this moment, men sang or recited "Eshet Chayil," "A Woman of Valor," to their wives. These verses from Prov. 31:10–31 praise a woman's many virtues. Actually, this custom originated with the mystics who regarded these verses as a reference to the *Shekhinah*, the feminine aspect of God. Many people nowadays no longer recite "Eshet Chayil" since its recitation reinforces stereotypical roles for women. A closer reading of the text of Proverbs, however, actually portrays an image of a woman accomplished at many things. For some this too is problematic for its presentation of a "superwoman" stereotype. Some have attempted to remove the one-sidedness of the custom, which is its inherent problem, by including an equivalent paragraph recited by the wife in honor of her husband. There is no standard text for this but some use Psalm 112.

*Blessing significant others*    Shabbat is a time when the Divine energy flows into the world, when we can feel God's blessings and the blessings of this world, God's creation, as well. Building on the tradition of "Eshet Chayil" on Friday night, some people have begun to express words of blessing to their spouses and loved ones. To offer blessings is both an expression of appreciation for the gift of someone's presence in your life and a way of verbalizing good wishes and hopes for that person. Often we are too busy during the week to express such feelings and can too easily take for granted the significant others in our lives.

**Kiddush:** *sanctifying the day*    *Kiddush,* from the word for "holiness," is the prayer recited over a full cup of wine or grape juice. It consists of a recitation of the verses in Genesis that describe Shabbat, followed by blessings over the wine and a blessing stating that God has given us the Shabbat for us to sanctify. While on some metaphysical level Shabbat exists without us, it is up to us to celebrate and consecrate and thus make holy this day. *Kiddush* is a statement of our intent to sanctify this day. We make *kiddush* over wine because wine is a symbol of rejoicing. The roundness of the grape and the fullness of the cup symbolize the completeness that Shabbat brings and the hope that our cups are running over with the bounty of the day.

While any wineglass can be used, many people have a cup designated for *kiddush*. The most traditional medium used for making *kiddush* cups is silver, though recently ceramic *kiddush* cups have also become common.

The cup is raised during *kiddush*. Some people stand for the recital of *kiddush;* others sit. The person making *kiddush* says it on behalf of everyone present, who respond with *amen* at the end of the blessings. According to tradition, grape juice can always be substituted for wine, which is helpful for those for whom alcohol is problematic. It is customary to cover the *hallot* (plural of *hallah*) during the recital of *kiddush*.

**Washing before the** hallah    *Hallah* is a special braided loaf associated with Shabbat. Before *hallah* is eaten (or, for that matter, before partaking of any bread), there is a custom of ritually washing our hands. In ancient times, the early rabbis were very strict regarding matters of purity and impurity. Most of these regulations have been suspended since the destruction of the Temple in Jerusalem. However, it is still traditional to wash before eating bread as a symbolic purification. In this manner our table and eating are a symbolic reflection of the sacred quality of the priests and the altar in the Temple. While this washing is still observed by traditional Jews whenever bread is eaten, others wash ritually only on Shabbat and other special occasions.

Ritual washing begins with the filling of a pitcher or glass with water. Take the pitcher in one hand and pour water over the fingers of the other hand. Then reverse hands and pour the water over the unwashed hand. Some people do this up to three times over each hand. After the washing, recite the blessing:

*Barukh atah Adonai eloheinu melekh ha'olam asher kidshanu be-mitzvotav ve-tzivanu al netilat yadayim.* "Praised are You, Eternal One, our God, source of the universe who has made us holy through the commandments and commanded us concerning the washing of hands."

Dry your hands with a towel. Since the washing is preparatory to eating the bread, it is customary not to talk between the washing and the *motzi.*

---

### KAVANAH

We ritually cleanse our hands—those appendages that are so characteristically human and with which we create all during the week. Slowly dry them while reciting the blessing. Sit in silence as others wash. Meditate on the meaning of Shabbat, of our enjoyment of and gratitude for the Shabbat table filled with good food and good company. The notion that our Shabbat table is a symbolic altar encourages us to focus on eating as a sacred activity. Shabbat's pace allows us to be aware of our eating more easily than during the hectic week.

---

**The** motzi, *blessing the* **hallah**    It is customary to use two loaves of *hallah,* termed *lehem mishneh,* at Shabbat meals. The common explanation is that it is a reminder of the double portion of manna that fell on Fridays to miraculously feed the Israelites during the forty years wandering in the desert.

The *hallot* are covered, sometimes with specially decorated cloths. One explanation for covering the *hallot* relates to the order of the various Shabbat rituals. Since precedence is given to the wine and *kiddush,* we cover the *hallot* so that they won't "realize" that they are our second priority. Being sensitive to a loaf of bread implies that we should be sensitive toward the other people gathered at our table.

It can also suggest a level of sensitivity toward the inanimate aspects of our world.

Another explanation is provided in a parable:

> A mortal king . . . had two servants whom he loved with perfect love. To one he gave a measure of wheat, and to the other he gave a measure of wheat; to one a bundle of flax, and to the other a bundle of flax. What did the clever one of the two do? He took the wheat and made it into fine flour by sifting the grain and grinding it. Then he kneaded the dough and baked it, set the loaf of bread on the table, spread the napkin over the bread, and left it to await the coming of the king.
>
> But the foolish one of the two did nothing at all. After a while the king came into his house and said to the two servants: My sons, bring me what I gave you. One brought out the table with the loaf of bread baked of fine flour on it and with the napkin spread over the bread. The other brought out his wheat in a basket with a bundle of flax over the wheat grains.
>
> What a shame! What a disgrace!
>
> So, too, when the Holy One gave the Torah to Israel, God gave it as wheat to be turned into fine flour and as flax to be turned into cloth for garments. [*Tanna de-Bei Eliyahu Zuta*, ch. 2]

On Shabbat, it is the raw Torah that we are to turn into bread and cloth. Our creative challenge shifts from the natural world to the world of the spirit. We are to be creative, not in the development of the earth, but rather in the development of ourselves. Our inner world is to be created and transformed on Shabbat. The *hallah* and its cover on our Shabbat table point to all the human enterprises of the past week that have gone into the creation of this moment. At the same time, they also point beyond, to the transformative character of Shabbat.

Now that the time has come to say the blessing, we uncover the *hallah*:

*Barukh atah Adonai eloheinu melekh ha'olam ha-motzi lehem min ha-aretz.* "Praised are You, Eternal One, our God, source of the universe, who brings forth bread from the earth."

Slice the *hallah* and distribute a piece to everyone. It is customary to sprinkle a little salt on it. Salt was used in the sacrificial rites in the Temple. Since the destruction of the Temple, our tables have become "altars" and our use of salt symbolizes this transference. Some tear the *hallah* instead of slicing it because of the symbolism. Just as the altar was built without any iron tools (iron connoting war and violence), so too, at our table we do not use a knife to cut the *hallah*.

**The meal and zemirot**    A traditional Friday evening meal generally consists of chicken soup and chicken, but the menu is not fixed. The point is to save the best that we can serve for the Sabbath.

Singing at the table on Friday night after the meal is a time-honored custom. Song affords both physical and spiritual pleasure, and singing together enhances companionship. We sing praises of Shabbat as well as of God. Some have the custom of singing Israeli and Hasidic melodies, while others sing the traditional Shabbat table songs called *zemirot*. These *zemirot* can be found in almost any *Siddur* (prayer book) and also in small booklets that contain both the *zemirot* and the Grace after Meals (see below). Such booklets are called bentschers, from the Yiddish word for "bless." There are also many songbooks that contain *zemirot* and the Grace after Meals, as well as contemporary Jewish songs. These include *Book of Songs and Blessings* (National United Jewish Appeal, 1980); *B'kol Echad: In One Voice*, edited by Jeffrey Shiovitz (United Synagogue of Conservative Judaism, 1986); *NCSY Bencher* (National Conference of Synagogue Youth, 1993); and *Kol Haneshamah: Songs and Grace after Meals* (Reconstructionist Press, 1993).

**Birkat ha-mazon**    It is traditional to say *birkat ha-mazon,* the Grace after Meals, upon finishing any meal in which bread is eaten. Even among those who do not practice this at every meal, many take the time to recite it after meals on Shabbat and other special occasions. There is a fairly standard melody for this prayer. There are also contemporary alternate versions of the text.

Taking the time to sing *zemirot* and say the Grace after Meals reminds us that the mood of Friday night should be contemplative and slow. We should immerse ourselves into the relaxing atmosphere of Shabbat as we would immerse ourselves in a warm tub. Time slows down and joy seeps in.

## Shabbat Morning

Shabbat morning provides us more opportunities for expanding our spiritual awareness. There isn't the usual morning rush at home to get up and out. Everything moves at a more leisurely and relaxed pace. Traditionally, nothing is eaten before morning services on Shabbat, but some people prepare a special breakfast that differs from their normal breakfast. For example, we allow our children to eat the sugared cereals that are not allowed in our house on weekdays. A friend chooses a special pastry each week for his Shabbat breakfast.

*Synagogue/shul*    The Shabbat morning service is the highlight of the weekly liturgy. It includes both prayers and the weekly reading of the Torah portion. It is also the setting for the communal celebration of life cycle events, especially the bar/bat mitzvah. As Jews gather together each Shabbat, the communities they create form the heart and soul of the Jewish people. The morning service itself has a central theme, the revelation of Torah, which is emphasized by the *amidah* (the central or "standing" prayer), as well as by the practice of reading the weekly portion.

*On the weekly Torah cycle*    Each week, we read from the Torah in a cycle that takes us from Genesis and creation to Deuteronomy and the death of Moses. The stories of our ancestors, Abraham and Sarah, Joseph and his brothers, Moses and the Israelites, are all heard by us once each year. Similarly, the Torah's laws, from the Ten Commandments to those of leprous houses and that of not placing a stumbling block before the blind to the details of the sacrificial cult, are regularly placed before us. The building plans of the sanctuary and the warnings and promises of Deuteronomy all come before us in an unending weekly parade. The sublime and the problematic are all here in their unexpurgated version.

The Torah is read out loud in public, just as it was read to our ancestors long before there were printing presses. We read it from a scroll that is punctiliously handwritten in its original Hebrew form, without vowels or punctuation. The reader chants the words using an ancient system of cantillation. As we listen, or follow along in printed versions of the text, our awareness is heightened to the fact that our ancestors have engaged with this text, wrestled with it, and lived with it and by it for thousands of years.

By establishing the weekly cycle of reading the Torah, the rabbis wanted to ensure that Torah would remain accessible to all Jews, not just to kings or priests or rabbis. This access and interaction with Torah is a basic notion in Judaism (for more see the "Torah: Path of Study, pp. 139–75). The public reading on Shabbat, often accompanied with a *d'var torah,* a "word of Torah," a sermon or a discussion, is a prime way this engagement with Torah occurs.

Following morning services, it is customary to have a *kiddush* in shul. Making *kiddush* on Shabbat morning is only a custom and therefore lacks the sanctification *berakhah* of Friday night's *kiddush.* Since it is only a custom, we may make *kiddush* over liquor as well as wine. On Shabbat morning, the term *kiddush* has taken on an additional meaning in the context of the synagogue. It often involves providing cake or more traditionally gefilte fish, herring, and kichel to all those who attended services. Each synagogue has its own custom of what is served. Individual members or families often sponsor the *kiddush,* either by bringing the food or paying for it. This is usually done to mark an occasion: a new job, a birthday, the birth of a grandchild, and so on. In most synagogues, one person leads the *kiddush* while everyone else holds their own cup of wine, grape juice, etc. The etiquette is to wait until the *kiddush* is made communally before eating.

In many synagogues, *kiddush* over wine is immediately followed by the *motzi,* the blessing over *hallah,* which then enables everyone to enjoy the *kiddush* food. *Kiddush* encourages people to linger after services and spend social time together. It is also an opportunity for newcomers to meet synagogue members. Some synagogues are friendlier than others. Some have lots of newcomers weekly; for others a newcomer is rare. While as a stranger you want to feel welcomed, it is good advice to make the extra effort to go up to people and introduce yourself. An easy way to start is by introducing yourself to the rabbi. Since she or he has an official position, this may feel more comfortable than approaching a random stranger. Hopefully, the rabbi responds in a friendly manner (it's part of the job!). Besides, you are already on a first-name basis, since every rabbi's first name is Rabbi!

## Shabbat Lunch

Traditionally, part of the *oneg* (pleasurable aspect) of Shabbat is having three meals rather than only two meals, which were normal on weekdays in ancient times. Lunch is the second of these meals. Its ritual nature is similar in some ways to Friday night dinner. It begins with another *kiddush,* the washing of the hands, and *motzi.* The menu is not as standardized as the Friday night chicken dinner. Some people have *chulent* for lunch. *Chulent* is a stew made of meat, potatoes, and beans. (There are a number of traditions regarding its ingredients, but the preceding is the most common list.) The ingredients are put into a pot before Shabbat and are cooked either on the stove or in the oven until Shabbat lunch. This makes for an extraordinarily delicious or extraordinarily fatty and heavy dish, depending on your point of view. Some explain the origin of the Shabbat afternoon nap as merely an aftereffect of *chulent,* which makes any strenuous movement impossible. The real origins of *chulent,* of course, lie in the prohibition of cooking on Shabbat. *Chulent* is a dish that survives continuous cooking, thus creating a way to have hot food for Shabbat lunch.

Each of the three meals of Shabbat has its traditional *zemirot,* "songs," to be sung at the table, though, as on Friday night, other nontraditional songs may be sung as well. The meal concludes with *birkat ha-mazon,* the Grace after Meals.

## Shabbat Afternoon

Shabbat afternoon begins as a time to relax, study, sleep, take a walk, play with your children, or chat with friends.

The day starts to draw to a close with *minhah,* the afternoon prayer service. This is a short service distinguished by two features. First, we read the beginning of the coming week's Torah portion. This makes a statement that no sooner do we finish one part of Torah than we are eager to begin the next; it also points to the coming week and the conclusion of this week. Since a bar or bat mitzvah can be celebrated any time the Torah is read, some people have a bar or bat mitzvah at *minhah* (see pp. 345–52). The second distinguishing feature is the theme of the *amidah*, which concentrates on the unity of God and the future redemption of Israel. Thus the liturgy looks toward a future time when every day will be like Shabbat. The mood expressed in the musical *nusah*, the mode for chanting the *minhah*, is one of sadness and longing. We are sad because we know the specialness of Shabbat is departing and we long for a messianic world when it will always be Shabbat.

**Seudah shelishit (shalah shoodis)**   The third meal of Shabbat (hence *seudah*, "meal," and *shelishit*, "third") is eaten late in the afternoon. In the synagogue it fills the time between the afternoon and evening service. It is a light meal (herring is a traditional feature). During the meal, *zemirot* are sung, usually to quieter melodies reflecting the meditative mood of this time. Between Passover and Shavuot, the custom is to study *Pirkei Avot* (translated as *Ethics of Our Ancestors*) at this time of day. This text, which contains short aphorisms or teachings by the talmudic rabbis, is found in many prayer books.

**Ma'ariv *and* havdalah**   Just as at its beginning, the rabbis added to the ending time of Shabbat for two reasons. The first related to a question about when a day is over. Twilight is an ambiguous time. Is it part of the preceding day or the beginning of night and thus the next calendar day? To prevent any desecration of Shabbat, twilight Saturday night was treated as part of Shabbat. Secondly, this adding-on was an expression of the love of the rabbis for Shabbat and their desire to make it last as long as possible. Therefore, traditionally, Shabbat does not conclude until forty-two minutes after sunset. (This makes it exactly an hour after the candle-lighting time. There are some people who follow an extra strict tradition and wait seventy-two minutes after sunset.)

Shabbat is concluded with the recital of the prayer called *havdalah* (which literally means "to differentiate"). As a ritual it differentiates holy from ordinary time by marking the end of Shabbat and the beginning of the new week. Besides prayers of praise, the ritual includes blessings over wine, spices, and fire.

We use spices to compensate for our sense of loss over Shabbat's departure. According to tradition, on Shabbat we are given a *neshamah yeteirah*, "an extra soul," that leaves us at the moment of *havdalah*. We are spiritually faint as that extra soul leaves and the spices help to restore us. Others say the spices are symbolic of the fragrant aroma of the Garden of Eden and the messianic world yet to come. Shabbat is a foretaste, or more accurately a foresmell, of the world to come, and the spices help the scent of Shabbat linger into the week.

For fire, a special multiwicked candle is usually used. (It should be torchlike according to the *halakhah*). By lighting a candle, an act forbidden during Shabbat, we are demonstrating that Shabbat is over. As the blessing over the candle is recited, the custom is to raise our hands and look at the flame through our fingers or look at our fingers (some say fingertips or fingernails) by the light of the candle. The symbolism of this part of *havdalah* has a number of interpretations. The use of fire is a widespread symbol of human creativity and power (as, for example, in the myth of Prometheus). We also look at our hands during the blessing since they are the principal tools of human creation. This blessing marks the return to the regular activity and creating of the six "workdays." Others note that we begin and end Shabbat in the same way: with our hands and with light. On Friday night, we draw in the warmth of Shabbat with our hands. On Saturday night, we watch Shabbat slip away through our fingers. On Friday night, we light two Shabbat candles. On Saturday night, we light one candle made up of multiple wicks. Thus, we begin Shabbat with the dualities of this world represented by the two candles. We end Shabbat with the two candles merged into one candle representing the unity, wholeness, and peace of Shabbat that we hope to take with us into the week. This oneness exists without losing our individual diversity represented by the candle with its multiple wicks and yet single flame.

For the *havdalah* ritual, you need a cup of wine, spices (cloves are often used), and a *havdalah* candle. Some people have a *havdalah* set or at least a spice box that they use for *havdalah*. Some people fill the wine cup to the brim, symbolizing our sense of the abundant blessing of Shabbat. If no *havdalah* candle is available, two regular candles can be used and their wicks brought together when the blessing is said. In fact, any light source, even an electric light, can be used in a pinch.

After reciting *havdalah*, we drink from the wine. Some pour some of the wine into a plate and then extinguish the candle in it. Others extinguish the candle right in the wine cup. Still others just blow the candle out. Everyone wishes one another "a good week" in Hebrew *(Shavua Tov)* or in Yiddish *(A guteh vakh)*.

A number of traditional songs are associated with *havdalah*, including "Eliyahu Ha-navi," "Shavua Tov," and "Ha-mavdil." The first is a song about Elijah the prophet, who, according to Jewish legend, is the herald of the messiah. Even as we end Shabbat, we long for a time filled with its messianic peace. Recently it has become popular to sing about Miriam the prophet, as well.

---

*KAVANAH*

At this moment, at *havdalah*, the order of creation is reversed. We move back from Shabbat, the seventh day, to the creation of humans on the sixth day (symbolized by the words of *havdalah*) to the fruit trees and the vines (symbolized by the wine) to the sweet-smelling grasses (symbolized by the spices). Finally, back at the beginning, we come to the light, that first point of creation.

It is to this light that we raise our hands, those appendages that separate us from animals—our hands, the signs of human creativity. With our hands, at this moment we draw the world away from *tohu u-vohu*, "primordial chaos." We do not allow a complete reversal of creation. As we look through our fingers, light and darkness are once more separated as we imitate God's first act of creation. The order of creation is not fully reversed, but rather moves forward as both the world and we start a new week of creation.

## Melave Malka

There is a custom in some traditional circles to hold a *melave malka* on Saturday night. *Melave malka* means "accompanying the queen," and refers to our desire to accompany the Sabbath Queen as she leaves on Saturday night just as we welcomed her on Friday night. It reflects our reluctance to let her go. It is similar to a *seudah shelishit,* with lots of singing, some food, and maybe some teaching.

## Shabbat *Halakhah:* Ceasing from Work

As mentioned, the rabbis derived the categories of work prohibited on Shabbat from the different tasks involved in making the *mishkan,* the "sanctuary" built in the desert. These thirty-nine categories, ranging from planting to writing, are called *av melachot,* "major categories of types of work." Other activities are forbidden on Shabbat if they seem similar to the *av melachot,* even if they are activities not specified in the Torah as having been employed in the building of the desert sanctuary. These analogously prohibited activities are called *toledot.* The laws related to Shabbat have been explicated and codified in great detail over the centuries. When something new is invented, the leading rabbinic scholars of the day discuss whether it is permitted or forbidden. Thus there was a discussion as to whether electricity should be forbidden on Shabbat, since electricity is similar to fire. This led to an analysis of the nature of fire and the elements that render it forbidden for use on Shabbat. Is fire combustion? Is it the giving off of heat or the giving of light? Does electricity involve combustion? And so forth. In the end the rabbinic authorities decided that despite some differences between the nature of fire and electricity, electricity is forbidden.

The details of the laws of work on Shabbat are too extensive and complex to give a full summary here. However, let me mention some of the more prevalent activities that are affected by the traditional categories. This will also explain why traditional Jews act in certain "confusing" ways on Shabbat.

*Cooking and lighting*    Cooking is forbidden on Shabbat. Therefore, all food to be eaten on Shabbat needs to be cooked beforehand. However, it is permissible to warm food that has already been cooked. This leads to the following complications: Since lighting a fire is also forbidden on Shabbat, you cannot turn on your stove or oven on Shabbat. Therefore it needs to be turned on before Shabbat begins and left on for the duration of Shabbat. It is not a simple accomplishment to warm food over a period of time without burning it. This has led to the *blekh* and *chulent*. A *blekh* is a piece of tin laid over the top of the stove, that allows you to leave only one burner on and yet have a warming surface for a number of pots. Best of all, a *blekh* makes the heat indirect, lessening the chance of burning the food. *Chulent* is the stew composed of meat, potatoes, and beans that cooks either in the oven or on top beginning before Shabbat and continuing until lunchtime (see above).

Particular care needs to be taken with liquids, since even if previously cooked they can boil again, and some authorities would regard this as cooking rather than warming and, thus, forbidden. This is particularly true if soup is removed from heat, becomes cold, and then is placed again on the heat. Boiling water for tea or coffee is considered cooking and thus forbidden unless a kettle is left on the flame/*blekh* for the whole Shabbat period.

Since lighting a fire is forbidden, turning on and off lights, ovens, and cars are also forbidden. Some people will put some of their lights on an electric timer to turn them on and off at designated times.

*Carrying*    Carrying in the public domain (most simply defined as outside of a building) is forbidden, whether it is carrying a suitcase or a set of keys. Since an enclosed area is treated as a private domain, some communities have strung wires around the whole town, creating an *eruv,* the Jewish legal concept that a separate area, no matter how large, even a city, can be made into a "private" area. Within the *eruv,* Jews are permitted to carry items such as prayer books, prayer shawls, infants, and so on.

*Writing and the spirit of Shabbat*    Another common activity prohibited on Shabbat is writing.

Needless to say, spending the day at your workplace, even if it does not involve a specific violation of Shabbat laws, is forbidden. However, there are lots of other things you could do on Shabbat that would not be forbidden under any of the thirty-nine categories. For example, while it is forbidden to carry a handkerchief in the public domain, you could move all the books in your library up two flights of stairs in your house. The rabbis believed it was important to define as clearly as possible what is forbidden, because they wanted to keep people from accidentally violating Shabbat. Yet they knew that there was no way to establish principles without loopholes. They therefore created two other kinds of forbidden activities, *shvut* and *muktzah*. *Shvut* (from the same root as the word *Shabbat*) can be most easily defined by a Yiddish word, *Shabbosdik,* that is, things that are not in the spirit of Shabbat, even if technically they might be permissible. Thus lugging three dozen boxes of books upstairs, while technically permissible, is not in the spirit of Shabbat. *Muktzah,* includes those objects which you should not handle or move on Shabbat. You should not move them because they might lead you to do something forbidden. For example, you pick up a pen (which is not a technical violation) and, forgetting it's Shabbat, you write a letter, which is prohibited. Better give up the pen altogether, the rabbis reasoned. Another category of *muktzah* includes objects that have no use on Shabbat. For example, since you cannot buy or sell on Shabbat, money has no value and therefore is *muktzah*. Both of these principles serve to prevent you from violating the spirit of Shabbat by "building a fence" around the actual laws of Shabbat.

The above is a brief and simplified conceptual framework of the Shabbat laws. Each item discussed is much more complex than we have presented here. For a number of other contemporary ways to approach these laws, see below.

### Where to Begin?

Shabbat is both a central ritual in Judaism and also among the most demanding of traditional practices. After all, it asks you to change your life every seven days. For those just beginning a Shabbat observance, here are two suggestions that you may find helpful. First, take on or try out pieces of Shabbat observance. Go one step at a time. Give yourself and the ritual a chance. You will need to try each new part of the ritual for a while before you stop feeling self-conscious. Second, begin defining *your* notion of Shabbat. Your definition might include (a) a day of rest from your job without a commitment to refrain from the halakhic definition of work; (b) a commitment not only to stay home from your job, but also not to do any errands or chores; (c) a day of relaxation involving no jobs or errands, which might include going to the movies, a drive in the country, or devoting time to your hobby of painting (even though these leisure activities might involve "violations" of traditional Shabbat laws); or (d) a day with no work but which allows for errands as long as they are done as a family. For contemporary families, Shabbat may be the only set time to be together all week. One family I know has a rule that anything done on Friday nights is okay—even homework or job-related work—as long as it is done at home. All of the above, and lots of other variations, are practiced by Jews today.

Another factor you need to determine is how much of the Shabbat period should be observed. Some Jews observe Shabbat only on Friday nights, leaving Saturday indistinguishable from Sunday. Others will go to synagogue Shabbat morning, but go shopping in the afternoon. While some will observe Shabbat until its official ending time, others will end the day when they feel it should be over.

If you are a Shabbat "beginner," it is a good idea to try to get an invitation to the home of a "veteran" for a Friday night dinner. Alternatively, your local synagogue may have a communal Friday night dinner. Shabbat can be a difficult ritual to celebrate alone. Find friends to celebrate it with even if they are also novices.

Each of the denominations upholds the primacy of Shabbat, though they have different approaches to Shabbat observance. The Orthodox movement upholds the traditional laws. The Conservative movement decided to allow people to drive to synagogue on Shabbat, arguing that it is better for people to drive and attend services then not drive and stay home. They have also allowed the use of electricity on Shabbat to the extent of turning lights on and off. In every other way, they encourage the observance of the traditions of Shabbat. The Reform movement leaves decisions about Shabbat practice to the individual. At the same time, it encourages the observance of Shabbat rituals and the making of Shabbat into a special day (see *Gates of Shabbat: A Guide for Observing Shabbat,* by Mark Shapiro [Central Conference of American Rabbis, 1991], for three models of Reform observance). Reconstructionism, in keeping with its focus on community, often develops congregational norms for Shabbat observance, emphasizing the spirit of Shabbat rather than the specific prohibitions.

Some useful books for learning how to do Shabbat home rituals (with accompanying tapes) are *Gates of Shabbat,* by Mark Shapiro (see above); and *The Shabbat Seder,* by Ron Wolfson (Federation of Men's Clubs, 1986).

## A Spiritual Shabbat Orientation

Beyond the specific rituals and practices lies the question of how we orient ourselves for Shabbat, a time of rest and renewal, a time for pleasure and the growth of the spirit. The tradition tells us that on Shabbat we are given an extra soul, a *neshamah yeteirah*. One understanding of this notion is that Shabbat enables us to have more of a sense of soulfulness. This can be created in a number of simple ways.

For one thing, our pace on Shabbat can be different from that of the week. Setting aside work, commitments, and responsibilities, there is no reason not to take a leisurely pace on Shabbat. Traditionally, it is forbidden to run on Shabbat. It is too worklike. Slow down. Walk. Have a leisurely breakfast. Spend time with those in your life with whom you are mostly passing ships during the week.

It is particularly helpful to begin Shabbat with a different pace. Often because of Shabbat preparation, the time before Shabbat begins can be hectic, getting everything ready to meet this last deadline of the week. As Shabbat starts, change your pace. When walking to synagogue (even if from the parking lot to the synagogue's door), stroll rather than walking briskly. One Hasidic rebbe was known to circle the synagogue seven times on Friday night before entering to prepare himself for the onset of Shabbat.

Slowing our pace can also help as we strive to be more aware— aware of the world, of the people in our lives, of ourselves. Ultimately it can bring an awareness of all the gifts that God has given to each of us. Being mindful of God's gifts can lead to a mindfulness about the Presence of God, thus bringing us to a place where we fulfill the verse *Shiviti YHVH le-negdi tamid,* "I have placed God before me always" (Psalm 16:8).

Make Shabbat different by what you do. Reserve some special things that you only do on Shabbat. Let your conversation be different on Shabbat. Do not talk about weekday matters, especially work-related things. Do not use Shabbat to plan for things that are to happen during the week. Do not let the stress and obligations of the week creep into Shabbat, whether in thought or in speech.

The tradition's emphasis on the restrictions for Shabbat is a recognition of how difficult it can be to withstand the pressures of work. Deadlines can come up in work that tempt us to make exceptions and suspend our Shabbat for this week. Only a firm commitment can create the space for an ongoing Shabbat practice. In creating the space for Shabbat, include all the things you *need* to do, such as running errands, paying bills, fixing the broken door, straightening the house, etc., as activities to be avoided even if they don't violate the traditional categories of work.

Instead, some of us use Shabbat as a time to reflect on ourselves, to do a *heshbon ha-nefesh,* "self-examination" (see the previous chapter). Review the week for how well you did on your goals for the coming week; that is, work on yourself, not on the world. Others try to focus on the spiritual by studying the Torah portion or other Jewish texts, meditating, or singing.

Shabbat is a time for simplicity, but not asceticism. Fasting is forbidden on Shabbat. The physical world is not denied; rather, it is to be savored. We are to enjoy good food and wine. The tradition encourages couples to have sex on Friday night. Yet Shabbat discourages the acquiring of material things.

We turn inward on Shabbat. Accordingly, some people don't answer the phone or read their mail or e-mail, just so the world intrudes less on their lives.

If we try, we can cultivate the *neshamah yeteirah,* that extra measure of soulfulness, which is at the heart of the Shabbat experience.

## Toward a New Definition of Shabbat

One final way to define Shabbat is to perceive it as a statement about our relationship with the world, with creation, and thus with the environment. At the beginning of this chapter, we talked about Shabbat as part of the weave of the universe. God asks us to rest on the seventh day, to cease from creating. Shabbat becomes a time to reflect on our creation and our world, a time to pause before we go hurtling on. The world can and must change, but it also needs to rest. For six days, we are meant to have an impact on the world. We strive to complete the creation left uncompleted by God in the first six days of creation. On the seventh day, we rest and rediscover our connection with the rest of the world. For it is said: "But the seventh day is a Sabbath of the Lord your God: you shall not do any work—you, your son or your daughter, your male or female slave, *your ox or your ass, or any of your cattle. . . .*" (Deut. 5:14).

The animals are to rest. If during the week we are the masters of the world or at least its movers and shakers, on Shabbat we are all part of creation. On Friday night we celebrate Shabbat as the climax of creation. In the Shabbat morning's liturgy, we declare that we observe Shabbat because God took us out of Egypt. Having once been freed, we strive to bring freedom to all people and to the whole world. Finally, on Shabbat afternoon, we move toward the messianic world of *atah ehad,* "You are One," Israel is one, we are all part of the Oneness of the world. We return to the garden, which we are to *shamor,* "watch" (Gen. 2:15), just as we are to *shamor,* "watch" Shabbat. The world and all its parts are in harmony once again, not at war, not competing, not striving. As it was, so shall it be again, with the lion lying down with the lamb. Therefore, even your animals are to rest on Shabbat.

Of course, we can no longer bring our technological world fully to a rest. Our homes and apartments still need heat, our refrigerators need cooling, and our rooms need light. However, the *halakhah* is very sensitive to these issues. It differentiates between those actions that cause a direct change in the environment from those that cause only an indirect change. These halakhic distinctions, as minute and even insignificant as they seem, can help us to create new models to enable us to leave our environment as untouched as possible during Shabbat.

New principles may lead us to depart at times from custom or even *halakhah*. The traditional food of Shabbat is chicken on Friday nights, and in many homes a *chulent* with meat for lunch. If Shabbat is to partake of the world to come, perhaps we should aspire to the vegetarianism of the Garden of Eden. Even if we continue to eat meat during the week, might we be vegetarians on Shabbat? This is not to advocate eating only raw fruit during Shabbat. Shabbat is still a day of joy and pleasure, not asceticism. Therefore, as in the traditional *halakhah,* we would still advocate the cooking and preparing of food before Shabbat begins. Certainly to cook food is to change our environment, but we must recognize that we live in an imperfect world. We acknowledge the complexity of that imperfection and our role in it as well by continuing to cook but doing so before Shabbat begins. Perhaps, by being vegetarians and not cooking on Shabbat, we show how we strive for the ideal of a world in harmony and balance with all its elements.

Using this environmental orientation might lead us to create a different hierarchy of values from the traditional *halakhah*. For example, painting a picture might seem less of a violation of Shabbat than using a sewing machine that runs by electricity. On the other hand, some of the traditional halakhic hierarchies are useful in thinking about Shabbat observance. For example, in terms of travel, a car is certainly forbidden. Riding a bicycle is only forbidden because of the concern that if it breaks down you will try to fix it.

More difficult for those who uphold the traditional *halakhah* is the issue of the use of fuel and electricity. Since lighting fire is forbidden on Shabbat, we are told by traditional authorities to turn on whatever lights, stove, etc., we want to use before Shabbat begins and leave them on for all of Shabbat. (Some people use timers to turn lights on and off on a preset basis.) The tradition obviously does not suggest sitting in darkness and eating only cold food in joyless celebration of this special day. Yet leaving lights on for the whole duration of Shabbat, or even having a timer shut them off after a lengthy period, is not energy-efficient. If we think ecology is very important, it would seem to call for a departure from tradition, including the turning off and on of lights and the stove during Shabbat. These and other traditional halakhic definitions may aid us in reformulating new categories of forbidden activity on Shabbat.

Earlier, we discussed the concept of *muktzah*, those objects that you are not supposed to move or handle on Shabbat, such as money, pens, or a hammer. These objects are in general used for actions forbidden on Shabbat. There is another category of *muktzah*, which includes objects from the natural world, such as sticks and stones. There is a traditional explanation related to the issue of preparation for why objects that are not human-made are "inherently" *muktzah* and thus in their own category. One way to view this tradition of *muktzah* is that it calls on us to leave our world, particularly the natural world, as untouched as possible on Shabbat. To leave the rock where it is, to burn as little fuel as possible by not driving, to be conscious of our use of electricity, to not write on paper—all this lets the earth rest. It expresses our desire to pass through this day leaving as few human footprints as possible marking our passage in the sands of the natural world. On Shabbat, instead of trying to leave our mark on the world, we attempt to leave it as unmarked as humanly possible. We ask ourselves how much we can make this world, on this day, mirror the world to be, the world of perfect harmony between humans, animals, and plants—and the Holy One.

Emphasizing this aspect of Shabbat in many ways reinforces the meaning of the traditional Shabbat laws. When we avoid lighting fires, driving our cars, or shopping, we decrease our usage of our planet's natural resources. When we go for a walk, spend time with community and friends, wait for the stars to come out, or even just know when sunset is, we are in better touch with the natural cycles of the world. Shabbat is a day to stand in awe of the Creator and Her Creation, calling on us not just to rest, but also to live a simpler life. It is a time not just to step away from the "rat race," but also from a consumer culture with its visions of unlimited acquisition. As we rest, our tired world rests. We all stand a little closer to a garden, a place of nakedness rather than possessions, a place of being rather than owning.

Part Two

# THE
# THREE PATHS

# TORAH:
# THE PATH OF STUDY

Ben Bag Bag said: Turn it [the Torah] this way and that way because everything is in it. Pore over it; grow old and gray over it. Do not budge from it. You can have no better guide for living than it. [*Ethics of Our Ancestors* 5:24]

If one word is the most essential word in Judaism, it is the word *Torah*. It literally means "teaching," but through the centuries, it has developed many dimensions of meanings. *Torah* can refer to the Five Books of Moses—Genesis to Deuteronomy—or, alternatively, to the whole Bible. *Torah* can also refer to the handwritten parchment scroll containing the Five Books of Moses. In its broadest application, *Torah* connotes all of Jewish tradition, encompassing all Jewish learning, both written and oral. As such, Torah is a process, not a static object.

In part, the path of Torah is an intellectual enterprise. We use our intellect to acquire knowledge about how to act as Jews. Torah is the rituals, customs, and beliefs of those who are committed to the Jewish tradition. Yet Torah cannot be conceived of as a body of knowledge to be mastered. There is no graduation ceremony, no time when you have fulfilled your obligation to study Torah. Basic skills and knowledge aside, Judaism even affirms that the ultimate purpose of Torah study is the study of Torah itself.

We might say that Torah study is an intellectual endeavor with a spiritual purpose. When practiced in this way, it is described as *torah lishmah,* "Torah studied for its own sake." This kind of Torah study leads us to contemplate or even encounter the Divine.

Engaging in Torah study may be an encounter with the Divine, but it is also an encounter with the Jewish people. For three thousand years Jews have recorded in Torah the struggle to live in the light and awareness that comes from encountering the Holy One. In Torah study, we hear thousands of Jewish voices. Today we also hear the faint echo of women's voices—too often unrecorded in the past. As we engage in Torah we join this conversation—a sort of giant "chat room" of the Jewish people—helping to create the Jewish future even as we link ourselves to the past.

The rabbis state:

> These are the activities whose income people can enjoy in this world but whose principal remains undiminished for them in the world-to-come: honoring father and mother, deeds of loving-kindness, making peace between two people. *Talmud torah ke-neged kulam,* "the study of torah, however, equals all of these put together." [Talmud, *Peah* 1:1]

How can Torah study be the equivalent of so many important *mitzvot*? Because Torah study leads to them. Study of Torah should lead to acting in honest and caring ways. Study of Torah should lead to sincere prayer. Study of Torah should bring meaning to our lives. When the rabbis say, *Hafokh bah ve-hafokh bah dekhola bah,* "Turn it [the Torah] this way and that way because everything is in it" (*Ethics of Our Ancestors* 5:24), they mean that the Torah is all-inclusive and it requires real effort on our part, looking at Torah this way and that way, to discover its meaning. The study of Torah from many perspectives, the rabbis suggest, is a process that can bring us to a moment of understanding or revelation. By examining different perspectives we can find the particular one that opens for each of us the "allness" of Torah. Simultaneously, the process drives home the understanding that there are multiple truths contained within the Torah, not one simple truth. Seeing the multiple truths brings us to an understanding that "everything is in it."

## Is the Torah True?

Jewish tradition holds that the Torah served as God's blueprint for the world; and, likewise, that the Torah has a particular role with the Jewish people. The Torah states, and the ancient rabbis affirm, that the Torah was given to the Jewish people at Mount Sinai by God. Torah is described as God's precious gift to us. Torah is also the laying-out of the covenant between God and the Jewish people. In effect, God says, "I have taken you out of slavery in the land of Egypt to be My people. I, God, will be in relationship to you to reward and protect you; and you, the people, need to fulfill the laws as I set them down in the Torah." Thus, Torah is the contract listing all the specifics in the partnership agreement between God and Israel.

The authority of Torah is based on the fact that it is the word of God as spoken or given to the Jewish people at Mount Sinai. This notion is known by the term *torah mi-sinai*, "Torah from Sinai." The traditional view is that God gave the entire Torah (the Five Books of Moses) to Moses at Mount Sinai. Therefore, every word of the Torah is the word of God. The Torah has Divine authority and its teachings are unchanging and infallible.

In fact, according to the ancient rabbis, not one but *two* aspects of Torah were given at Mount Sinai: *torah she-bikhtav,* the "written Torah," and *torah she-be'al peh,* the "oral Torah." The written Torah is, of course, the Five Books of Moses (called the Humash in Hebrew, from the word for "five"). The oral Torah consists of explanatory teachings that illuminate the written Torah. These were handed down orally for many generations until they were finally written down, first in the Mishnah (the "Repetition"), then, more fully, in the Gemara (the "Completion"). Together, the Mishnah and the Gemara are collectively known as the Talmud (the "Study" or "Learning").

On the surface, it would seem that having the word of God spelled out in the written Torah would be sufficient, but it was clear to the rabbis that there were many laws and rituals not fully explicated in the written Torah—for example, the details of the wedding ceremony. Yet such laws and customs must have existed alongside the written Torah for a long and indeterminate time. Therefore, there had to be oral traditions. The rabbis averred that this spoken tradition (the oral Torah) must also derive from God's words with Moses on Sinai, therefore it too has Divine authority. The authority of rabbinic Judaism lies upon this claim of Divine authorship for both Torahs.

Even before modern times, more complex understandings of the notion of *torah mi-sinai* existed. Examining the biblical account, it seems clear that God had planned to reveal only the Ten Commandments directly to the Jewish people at Sinai. Yet when God began to speak, the people fled and said to Moses: "you speak to us . . . let not God speak to us, lest we die" (Exod. 20:16). According to one midrash, God spoke only the first two commandments before the people fled. Whatever was heard directly by the people at Sinai, the Ten Commandments and all the rest of Torah were recorded by Moses. While some of the ancient sages viewed Moses as simply a faithful scribe taking dictation from God, others wondered about the human element that Moses' role interposed between God and the Torah as written. This question poignantly underlies the rabbinic discussion of who wrote the last verses of Deuteronomy, the verses that describe the death of Moses. One opinion is that Joshua, Moses' successor, wrote those verses. The other opinion is that a weeping Moses himself wrote those verses before his death (Talmud, *Bava Batra* 15a; *Menahot* 30a).

It is a rabbinic principle that the Torah speaks in the language of humans, meaning it was composed so it could be understood by the people of its time. This has allowed some commentators to argue against a literal understanding or to advocate a belief in an evolving understanding of the text. One example is the account of the creation of the world. While some understand the text literally to mean that the world was created in six days, others say that the text is a mythic account of creation. The Torah was not going to speak about dinosaurs or evolution long before humans were aware of them. Similarly, to the ancients, the story of Joshua telling the sun to stand still made (miraculous) sense. We now know that the earth revolves around the sun, not the other way around. But, for the text to say that the earth stood still would have been incomprehensible to the people of biblical times. So the

Torah text, while of Divine origin, is a text of its time, reflecting the ancient Israelites' understanding of their world. This is widely accepted in the case of the factual material, but for some commentators it is also true theologically. The sages read anthropomorphic references to God, e.g., God's outstretched arm, as metaphor. Some commentators believe that such expressions as *God became angry* or *God went down upon the mountain* are also only metaphorical descriptions of a Being who neither angers nor moves.

Maimonides, an important medieval commentator, believed that as humans we cannot describe God. He also believed that some of the practices in the Torah were intended only for our biblical ancestors with their more "primitive" understanding of the world. Such practices as animal sacrifice are in the Torah because they were common in the ancient world. As Judaism developed, however, people evolved more sophisticated understandings of how to worship God—for example, substituting prayer for sacrifice. For Maimonides, then, even in terms of practice and law there was an evolutionary nature to the Torah. It was a text that was written both for a specific time period and for eternity.

All Jewish authorities agree that the biblical books included in the sections called Prophets and Writings (books other than the Five Books of Moses) have a different status. They were not given to Moses at Sinai and are not regarded as a source of Jewish law. However, they are believed to be the word of God, since they were either spoken by a prophet such as Jeremiah or were written by someone divinely inspired such as King David (the traditional author of the Psalms).

Challenges to the traditional notions of Torah have arisen throughout Jewish history. In particular, the authority of the oral Torah was disputed by various sects including the Sadducees (about the first century C.E.) and the Karaites (beginning in the eighth century C.E.). While upholding the sanctity of the biblical text, these sects denied the Divine authority of the oral Torah. They maintained that the oral tradition was an invention of the rabbis of the talmudic period. This critique is echoed in the works of many contemporary scholars of Judaism, who find a major shift in Jewish practice from the biblical period to the rabbinic period. They doubt that the oral tradition recorded in the Talmud reflects an unbroken chain leading back to the Revelation at Sinai.

An even more fundamental challenge to the traditional notion of Torah as the word of God emerged from biblical criticism. This new approach to Bible study developed beginning in the nineteenth century. It posited that a careful reading of the text of the Five Books of Moses shows that different authors wrote it in different time periods. Critical Bible scholars point to parallel or contradictory passages as well as linguistic studies as evidence for this theory. While biblical criticism took a number of approaches to the scientific study of the biblical text, one main approach was the documentary hypothesis. The documentary hypothesis claims that a number of sources can be identified within the text of the Five Books of Moses. These are often identified as "P," the priestly source; "D," the Deuteronomic source; "J," which uses *YHVH* as the name of God; and "E" for *elohim,* a different name of God. While there is no consensus among Bible scholars about which verses are from which source or the approximate dates of each source, Bible scholars do agree on the main ideas of the documentary theory.

Clearly, biblical criticism is incompatible with a belief that the Torah is the word of God revealed to Moses at Sinai. Orthodox Judaism therefore denies the validity of modern biblical criticism. It maintains as a matter of faith that the biblical text has one author, who is God. The text as we have it has been carefully preserved from biblical times and is thus the authentic word of God. Orthodox scholars point out that many of the contradictions and parallel accounts were also noted by traditional Torah commentators in rabbinic and medieval times. A broad answer to those contradictions is based on the rabbinic notion that since this text is the word of God, every word has meaning. Rather than a parallel account being redundant (or evidence of two sources), the second account is in the text to teach a new aspect of a particular law. The rabbis carefully read the biblical text using this principle to derive or find biblical support for Jewish law. A somewhat similar approach was used to harmonize narrative texts in the Torah. The ancient rabbis also employed principles that helped to obviate some of the problems in the biblical text. One is *ein mukdam u-me-uhar ba-torah,* "there is no before or after in the Torah," meaning that the biblical account of events is not chronological.

Outside the Orthodox world, the basic principles of biblical criticism are accepted by all other Jewish religious branches. For modern Bible scholars the evidence seems compelling and overwhelming that our text has multiple origins and was stitched together at one or more points in history.

## Is Torah Binding?

This raises some very difficult questions for non-Orthodox Jews. If the Torah is not the word of God, does it have any authority to bind us to its laws? What happens to *halakhah*, Jewish law? What happens to the concept of *torah mi-sinai*, that the Torah was given at Sinai? What about the covenant? What should our relationship to the Torah be?

Liberal Jews have struggled with these questions, arriving at answers that range from assigning a binding legal character to the Torah text all the way to assigning it a nonlegal character. There are a wide variety of views regarding Torah and the nature of Jewish law. Those who still believe the Torah is a sacred document fall into three constellations of reasoning. The first two believe that the Torah is holy because it is a divinely inspired document. For one group of thinkers that means it is a series of attempts to put in writing a human response to actual encounters with the Divine. The second group hold that the Torah is mythically true. It does not really matter whether 600,000-plus people stood at Mount Sinai and heard God speak. The myth of the Revelation at Sinai and of the sacred quality of Torah is "true" on a different level from ordinary factual truth. The third group believes the Torah is sacred because it has been made so by the Jewish people through the course of many centuries. By treating it as sacred text, studying it and living it, the Jewish people have in fact transformed it into a sacred text. Each of these approaches allows for change, since they all acknowledge the human element involved in creating the text. Many Jews also make room for ongoing revelations in the belief that the human-divine encounter is continuous.

## Interpretation

All Jews agree on one fact: the Torah is subject to human interpretation. Moreover, it can be interpreted on many levels. One traditional formulation for biblical interpretation is known by the acronym *PaRDeS* (literally, "Paradise"), formed by the first letters of four methods, *pshat, remez, derash,* and *sod.* Simply speaking, *pshat* is the plain meaning of the text; *remez* is an allegorical reading; *derash* is a homiletic reading, and *sod* is an esoteric, mystical reading. These are not four separate schools of interpretation, rather a progression of methods of interpretation. Whether you believe the Torah is word for word the dictation of God or is a human recording of a striving to be holy, the text remains sacred, even as its meanings can be exposed by many methods and on many levels.

Both traditional and contemporary Bible scholars strive to explicate the *pshat,* the "plain" meaning of the text. The rabbinic tradition was also heavily engaged in *derash,* the homiletic "interpreting" of the text. There is also a genre of rabbinic literature known as *midrash,* from the same root as *derash.* Midrash is filled with stories and homilies (called midrashim) that enlarge upon the biblical narrative and draw lessons from the text. Midrash is found interspersed with legal material in the Talmud and among the works of many traditional commentators on the Torah. The process of creating midrash is very much alive today. Recently, both psychology and feminism have given rise to contemporary midrashim. Whether in books, sermons, or discussions of Torah, engaging in the midrashic process is an essential way Jews approach this sacred text. It is a process open to anyone, for a midrash may come as much from a careful reading of the text or from your own insight as from knowledge. For many, this attempt to understand the text includes a commitment to struggle with difficult passages in Torah. While committed to struggling with, rather than simply dismissing, such passages, it is not an attempt to find a pious understanding of the text. Abraham or any of the biblical characters can have acted immorally. Even God's actions or biblical attitudes ensconced in legal sections can be rejected. However, the engagement in the struggle both to understand the text and to explore its possible meaning in our lives is the basis for the activity of *talmud torah,* "the study of Torah," especially in regard to the Torah text.

Less common methods of studying the text are *remez* and *sod.* *Remez,* the allegorical method, was used in the Middle Ages by commentators with a philosophical orientation. In this reading, the biblical characters stood for virtues or philosophic principles like truth. In a somewhat similar fashion, in the mystical reading of the text *(sod),* biblical characters became aspects of the Divine (e.g., Abraham represented *hesed,* the aspect of "loving-kindness"). But the mystical reading of the text was more complex than the allegorical. As its name, *sod* (secret), implies, there is a belief that there are secret meanings to be uncovered in the text. It was easy to believe that God was not just talking about mundane matters when the text was describing in great detail, for instance, the building of the sanctuary in the desert. For those attempting a mystical reading, the challenge was to uncover those secret meanings. Various methods were used by different schools of mystics to uncover the meanings. One such method is *gematria,* a system that assigns a numerical value to every Hebrew letter. In *gematria,* words with the same numerical value can be associated together, even if on the surface they seem to be unconnected. At times, the numerical value of a word itself becomes a teaching about the word. For example, the word *Torah* has a numerical value of 611. The commentators teach that the numerical value should really be 613 since that is the traditional number of *mitzvot,* "commandments," in the Torah. Why, then, 611? Because God spoke the first two commandments to the people at Sinai, therefore only 611 commandments were conveyed via Moses to the people. Since we have the verse "the Torah as commanded to us by Moses," Torah's numerical value is only 611.

### Mitzvot and Halakhah

For the rabbis, the interpretation of Torah is the basis for *halakhah,* Jewish law. While it is clear in the biblical texts that there are things we should and should not do, the Torah does not lay out an overall system. That system came much later and is based on the tradition of 613 commandments, an oral law, and the authority of a group of legal rabbinic scholars acting as ongoing interpreters and decision makers. *Halakhah,* from the root meaning "to go," describes the rabbis' notion of the right way to "walk" through the world. *Halakhah* sets forth in very specific detail how we should behave in the world.

The halakhic system includes four categories. The first category is *mitzvot d'oraita,* the 613 biblical commandments. These *mitzvot* and many of the details about their performance are derived from a careful reading of the Torah text and the teachings of the oral Torah. Beyond the *mitzvot* that are in the Torah, there are those established by the rabbis of the talmudic period. The second category is called *mitzvot de-rabbanan,* "commandments of the rabbis." An example is lighting Hanukkah candles. The third category is that of *takkanot,* "enactments." (They can also be referred to as *gezerot,* "decrees.") These are laws established by the rabbis on their own authority, in a manner vaguely akin to laws enacted by a legislature. Unlike *mitzvot de-rabbanan,* which are often related to the biblical text, *takkanot* are enactments established to better uphold the *halakhah.* Sometimes these create a "fence around the Torah" to better protect a person from making a mistake. One famous *takkanah* is that of Rabbenu Gershom, a rabbinic authority from the early Middle Ages, who decreed a ban on polygamy despite the example of the multiple wives of the patriarchs in Genesis. Although he could not ban polygamy, he believed it was destructive to the social order, so he issued a *takkanah.*

Finally, the fourth category is *minhagim,* "customs," such as breaking a glass at the end of the wedding ceremony. In premodern times, there existed more variation in custom from one community to the next than exists today. One area that has still encouraged differences is the embrace of *humrot,* "stringencies," in the last few decades. Beyond what is required by Jewish law, there have always existed *humrot,* stringencies and extra restrictions that individuals have taken upon themselves. These have ranged from additional fast days to being extra strict with keeping kosher, glatt kosher (see "Eating and Food," pp. 66–93). Most often in the past, these were the practices of individuals or of small intentional communities. In the last few decades, as part of an intensifying of observance within the Orthodox community, a number of these *humrot* have become widespread. Thus glatt kosher has become the standard rather than a stringency in much of the Orthodox community. The *humrot* that have gained increasing acceptance have been in certain areas related to food, women, and (yes) wine (the last really having to do with whether non-Jews are permitted to handle kosher wine at any stage in its growing or making). They have not involved other areas that evoked *humrot* in the past, such as ascetic practices like fasting. The spread of *humrot* within Orthodoxy has been both praised as a sign of increasing commitment and condemned as self-righteous one-upmanship.

What practices are rabbinic commandments, *takkanot,* or customs is not always clear. In fact, in terms of actual practice, all these categories are basically treated equally. As an overarching system, *halakhah* is seen as the correct path to living a complete Jewish life. Therefore its adherents strive to fulfill all of it, without making a distinction among the various categories of commandment or custom.

When questions about practice arise, they are taken to a rabbi who decides what should be done in that particular circumstance. There is a whole body of literature known as *shaylot u'teshuvot,* "questions and answers" (commonly called *responsa*). Rabbinic authorities will look at the literature of earlier rabbis to see if there is a precedent for how to decide the particular question before them. While any rabbi can make halakhic decisions, more difficult questions are relegated to the leading masters of the rabbinic tradition of that generation. This mastery is not established in any formal way. There is no election or supreme court. Rather it is demonstrated over time that this individual through his writings, teachings, and halakhic decisions is one of the masters of a particular generation. (This person is known as a *poseik,* one who "decides," as distinguished from an ordinary rabbi.)

Finally, fundamental to the rabbinic system of *halakhah* as it developed is the notion that *halakhah* is based on the word of God as expressed in the written and oral Torah. Therefore, *halakhah* cannot be changed in any significant way by later human interpreters of the Torah. The unchanging and divine origin of *halakhah* is the core of Orthodox Judaism's approach to it.

Even what a faithful student was someday to ask his teacher, the Holy One uttered to Moses at that time. [*Midrash Tanhuma, Ki Tissa* 60]

This statement can be understood to express the most conservative notion of the tradition, that is, all of it was spoken by God to Moses and nothing new can ever be said of it by any future student. Yet other rabbinic texts point to a more complex understanding of the nature of *halakhah* and tradition.

For example, in regard to the debate between the School of Hillel and the School of Shammai, there are a number of sources that speak of a pluralistic notion of the truth. There appears to have been such a gap between these two schools that it was as though they had two different Torahs. For three years they argued over who was right, until a heavenly voice proclaimed: "Both these and those are the words of the living God" (see Talmud, *Sanhedrin* 88b; *Eruvin* 13b). There is, then, a notion that even though one school said permitted and one said forbidden—which logically cannot both be true—there is a deeper notion of truth, whereby both their opinions are the words of God.

The following text suggests *halakhah* can develop and change:

On that day Rabbi Eliezer (ben Hyrcanus) brought forward every imaginable argument, but the sages did not accept any of them. Finally he said to them, "If the *halakhah* agrees with me, let this carob tree prove it!" Sure enough, the carob tree was uprooted [and replanted] a hundred cubits away from its place. "No proof can be brought from a carob tree," they retorted.

Again he said to them, "If the *halakhah* agrees with me, let the stream of water prove it." Sure enough, the stream of water flowed backward. "No proof can be brought from a channel of water," they rejoined.

Again he urged, "If the *halakhah* agrees with me, let the walls of the house of study prove it!" Sure enough, the walls tilted as if to fall. But R. Joshua rebuked the walls, saying, "When disciples of the wise are engaged in a halakhic dispute, what right have you to interfere?"

Hence, in deference to R. Joshua they did not fall, and in deference to R. Eliezer they did not resume their upright position; they are still standing aslant.

Again R. Eliezer said to the sages, "If the *halakhah* agrees with me, let it be proved from heaven!" Sure enough, a divine voice cried out, "Why do you dispute R. Eliezer, with whom the *halakhah* always agrees?" But R. Joshua stood up and protested, "*Lo bashamayim heh*, 'It [the Torah] is not in heaven' (Deut. 29:12). We pay no attention to a divine voice, because long ago, at Mount Sinai, You wrote in the Torah, 'After the majority must one incline' (Exod. 23:2)."

R. Nathan met [the prophet] Elijah and asked him, "What did the Holy One do in that moment?" Elijah: "God laughed [with joy], saying, 'My children have defeated Me, My children have defeated Me.' " [Talmud, *Bava Metzia* 59a–b]

This remarkable text teaches that "the truth" is as decided by the majority of the rabbis. It is not decided by one who can demonstrate spiritual greatness by causing miracles to happen. It is not even decided by one who can have God, source of the Torah, proclaim the correctness of his interpretation. It is rather decided by the fallible and human decision making of rabbinic scholars. After the Revelation at Sinai, the Torah was given to these scholars. God, as it were, relinquished God's authority over Torah. Perhaps, then, the postscript of the story, when Elijah the eternal prophet reveals what happened in heaven, suggests that God rejoices at the rabbis' appropriation of the Torah as theirs. As a parent, God is happy that God's children have grown up and have taken responsibility for the Torah.

How changed Torah can be and yet still be authentic is reflected in one more story from the Talmud:

When Moses ascended on high [at Mount Sinai], he found the Holy One affixing crowns to letters. [Certain letters in the Torah scroll have marks above them called crowns.] Moses asked, "Lord of the universe, who stays your hand?" [I.e., is there anything lacking in

Torah so that additions are necessary?] God replied, "At the end of many generations there will arise a person, Akiva ben Joseph by name, who will infer heaps and heaps of laws from each *tittle* on these crowns." "Lord of the universe," said Moses, "permit me to see him." God replied, "Turn around." Moses went and sat down behind eight rows [of R. Akiva's disciples, and listened to their discourses on law]. Not being able to follow what they were saying, he was so distressed that he grew faint. But when they came to a certain subject and the disciples asked R. Akiva, "Master, where did you learn this?" and R. Akiva replied, "It is a law given to Moses at Sinai," Moses was reassured. [Talmud, *Menahot* 29b]

Since, in fact, no one including Akiva has derived any laws from the crowns on the Torah letters, this tale has gone out of its way to make a point. Akiva, perhaps the greatest master of the talmudic period, is teaching a class. Moses sitting in that class cannot understand anything of what is going on. Clearly, the rabbinic tradition as exemplified by Akiva is vastly different from that of Moses. This is despite the claim that Moses received both the written and oral Torah at Sinai and that no student would ever say anything not already revealed at Sinai. Moses is lost and very upset until Akiva states that the authority for a particular law is that it was given to Moses at Sinai. Instead of jumping up and calling Akiva a liar, since Moses has not heard of anything in Akiva's discourse, Moses is reassured by Akiva's "lie." Why? Because by that statement Akiva has placed himself in the tradition of the Torah of Sinai. Akiva is not advocating a new Torah, but rather is teaching Torah as he understands it both as a tradition handed down beginning with Moses and as understood by its contemporary teachers. Akiva's Torah is a dynamic one.

The sages in the school of R. Ishmael taught: "As a hammer may shatter rock" (Jer. 23:29). Just as a hammer that strikes a rock may shatter it into many fragments, so may a verse [encountering the scrutiny of a keen mind] yield many meanings. [Talmud, *Sanhedrin* 34a]

As we have already seen, modern biblical scholarship has undercut the notion of the Torah text as the literal word of God. Talmudic scholarship has also challenged the traditional notion of the oral law. Recent scholarship has challenged the notion of *halakhah* by suggesting that attributions of statements to Rabbi Akiva and others are not authentic. What, then, should our relation to Torah and *halakhah* be? If it is not the word of God, should it have any authority? As we said earlier, for non-Orthodox Jews the Torah still is sacred text because it is a reflection of the encounter between God and Israel, between the Divine and the human. Whether mythically true, divinely inspired, or simply an attempt to record what we, the Jewish people, have understood from that encounter, the Torah is sacred for us as Jews living today. Yet what about the *halakhah* that is based on the Torah? For Conservative Judaism, such law is still binding because the Jewish people have accepted it as binding for centuries. While the law can change, that change should happen slowly in light of the wisdom and value inherent in Jewish practices we have inherited from our ancestors. Modern rabbis are the inheritors of authority and can make changes, so the Conservative movement has created a unique body of rabbis, the Law Committee of the Rabbinical Assembly, that can make decisions or more frequently set out legitimate options for practice by Conservative Jews. For Reconstructionist Judaism, each generation of Jews is called upon to "reconstruct" Judaism for its own time. This reconstruction takes the Jewish past and Jewish ritual very seriously, even as it may reinterpret its meaning for the present moment. Reconstructionism is more open to change than Conservative Judaism and has rejected certain concepts as "unreconstructible," particularly the notion of Jews as the Chosen People. Reconstructionism believes that Jewish communities are empowered to make decisions on what their practice will be. For Reform Judaism, some of the ritual laws and practices of the Torah are antiquated and obsolete, while others are relevant and potential religious practices for today. It remains to the individual Jew to decide which to observe. In Reform belief, observance of the *mitzvot* is based on personal autonomy.

## *Mitzvot* as Spiritual Practice

Whatever opinion we follow concerning *halakhah,* the question remains, Why do we need the *mitzvot,* especially those that concern rituals? It seems clear that ethical norms are necessary, but how can the animals we eat or whether we observe all the prohibitions of Shabbat make any difference? Even if we accept the notion that the Torah is God's word, it is still hard to imagine that any God worth believing in cares whether you write on Shabbat or only eat meat bought from a kosher butcher!

> "As for God, God's word is purifying" (Psalm 18:31). Rav said: Precepts were given only so that mortals might be purified by them. For of what concern can it be to the Holy One whether, in [preparing meat] a person slaughters an animal at the windpipe or at the gullet? Or of what concern is it to God whether a person eats animals that are unclean or animals that are clean? Hence, precepts were given only so that mortals might be purified by them. [Midrash, *Genesis Rabbah* 44:1; *Tanhuma, Shemini,* 8]

Traditional answers, like the comment of Rav above, assert that we should observe the *mitzvot,* first of all, because God commanded us to do so; they are an essential part of the *brit,* the "covenant," between God and the Jewish people. Our part of the covenant is to fulfill the *mitzvot,* while God's part is to care for us and protect us. Second, we must fulfill the commandments to be righteous, "purified" Jews. The goal in life is to be ethical and religious and *halakhah* is the path. Third, as Rabbi Hananiah ben Akashia said, "The Holy One, desiring to bestow upon Israel abundant merit, made Torah and precepts abundant for them" (Talmud, *Makkot* 23b). The *mitzvot* then are an opportunity for Israel to gain merit. The reward for this merit is usually ascribed to the next world. Those who keep the *mitzvot* are rewarded with a portion in heaven and/or in the world to come (see pp. 458–59).

While these answers still speak to some Jews, for many others they are inadequate for a number of reasons. As we have seen, the notion that Torah is the actual words of God has been undermined by modern biblical scholarship. In the modern period, there has also been a de-emphasis in the importance of the belief in life after death. If we no longer feel commanded and are less concerned with afterlife, why per-form the *mitzvot,* particularly those that are ritual? Can't someone be a good person without ritual? Can't someone feel the Presence of God without all the trappings of institutionalized religion—synagogue, liturgy, rules, and rabbis?

There are those who argue that *halakhah* and *mitzvot* are the Jewish way to be ethical, to interact with God and to maintain the identity of the Jewish people. Therefore, even many of the rituals are worth doing. One contemporary teacher, Rabbi Saul Berman, maintains that the rituals in fact include an ethical component and the details are not arbi-trary but rather point to the ethical meaning of the ritual. My own view is that rituals are part of a spiritual practice intended to heighten our awareness of the Divine.

> R. Aha said in the name of R. Isaac: It is written, "In all that is to be observed, guard your heart, for in each such observance are the wellsprings of life" (Prov. 4:23). Be observant with regard to all that is prescribed for you in Torah, for you do not know out of which pre-cept life issues for you.
>
> In this regard, R. Abba bar Kahana said: Scripture puts the easiest of commandments on the same level as the most difficult of ob-servances. The easiest of commandments—letting a mother bird go (Deut. 22:6–7, driving off the mother bird before taking her young); and the most difficult of commandments—honoring your father and mother. And with regard to each, it is written, "That your days may be long." [Jerusalem Talmud, *Peah* 1:1, 14d]

A number of statements in the Talmud echo the above by warning us not to differentiate between the major and minor *mitzvot.* This suggests that all the *mitzvot* are part of a spiritual practice. While not murdering and lighting Hanukkah candles may not be of the same importance morally or otherwise, they are both part of the larger spiritual disci-pline known as Judaism. This view sees *halakhah* not as law but as path, a way to travel with awareness through life. Since all *mitzvot* call for awareness and remind us of the Holy One, any one can create for us a transformative experience. As the first text states, "you do not know out of which precept life issues for you." Will it be kissing the mezuzah or helping a poor person that will give your life meaning? As the second text reiterates, a *mitzvah* easily accomplished, driving away the mother bird before taking her eggs, is equal to a *mitzvah* that we all struggle with, honoring our parents.

> Ben Azzai said: Run to perform even a minor precept as a major one, and flee from transgression, for one good deed leads to another, and one transgression leads to another. The recompense for doing a good deed is another good deed [to be done], and the recompense for a transgression is another transgression. [*Ethics of Our Ancestors* 4:2]

Ben Azzai suggests that *halakhah,* as a spiritual path, is a self-reinforcing discipline. As you do one *mitzvah* and come to a place of awareness, then you will desire and be able to do more *mitzvot* and build a practice that gives an overall structure to your life. Rather than getting a reward here on earth or a future reward in heaven, the reward for a *mitzvah* is the ability to do another *mitzvah,* just as the punishment for a misdeed is to become further stuck in the world of misdeeds, confusion, and unawareness.

> "The spirit of a human being is the lamp of the Lord" (Prov. 20:27). The Holy One said: Let My Lamp be in your hand, and your lamp will be in My hand. What is the Holy One's lamp? The Torah, of which it is said, "The commandment is a lamp, and Torah is light" (Prov. 6:23). What is implied by "The commandment is a lamp"? That people who perform a commandment are accounted as if they had kindled a lamp before the Holy One, and thereby they quicken their own spirit, which is called a "lamp," as in the verse "The spirit of a human being is the lamp of the Lord." [Midrash, *Exodus Rabbah* 36:3]

## *Hiyyuv* versus *Kavanah:* Obligation versus Intention

The notion of *hiyyuv,* "obligation," is an important one in the traditional halakhic system. Defining exactly what needs to be done to fulfill an obligation certainly enables observant Jews to know when a *mitzvah* has been performed correctly. Yet it also runs the risk of what has been called "*yotze*ism," a focus more on whether an obligation has been performed exactly than on whether it has acquired meaning or purpose for the person fulfilling it. Upon reflection, it is apparent that the notion of being *yotze,* of having fulfilled the *mitzvah* perfectly, is not an absolutely necessary component even of a system with obligatory *mitzvot.* After all, there are a number of *mitzvot* that do not fit easily into the rabbinic system because they defy quantification. "Loving your neighbor" has no time limitation, nor can love be easily defined. There are a number of similar "emotional" *mitzvot,* which make it difficult to define how and when you are *yotze,* in fulfillment of your obligation.

Perfection is not the issue. There can be an obligation to do a *mitzvah,* but most of the details can be left to you. Thus, in answer to one who asks how much *matzah* should be eaten at the Passover Seder, the most logical answer is that the question is misdirected. Eat some *matzah.* If you like *matzah,* eat a lot; if not, eat a little. In contemporary Jewish life, it may be best to focus not on how but on why a particular *mitzvah* should be performed.

A major tension within the rabbinic system of *mitzvot* is the question of *kavanah. Kavanah* most simply means "intention." Must we think about what we are doing when we perform a *mitzvah* or is the act itself the most crucial component? Certainly, everyone agrees that ideally you should be aware and focused, but living in a less than ideal world, what is the highest priority? There is also the issue of motive. Is it permissible to perform *mitzvot* for ulterior motives, such as to receive a reward from God or to have people admire you?

Precepts do not need to be performed with deliberate intention.
[Talmud, *Rosh ha-Shanah* 28b]

R. Nahman bar Isaac said: A transgression performed with a good motive is better than a precept performed for an ulterior motive. R. Judah said in the name of Rav: People should always occupy themselves with Torah and its precepts, even if it be for an ulterior motive, for out of occupying themselves with them for an ulterior motive, they will come to occupy themselves with them for the right motive. [Talmud, *Nazir* 23b]

These two texts represent the opinion that the actual doing of the *mitzvah* is what is essential. Rabbi Judah suggests that doing a *mitzvah* for an ulterior reason not only means that we perform the *mitzvah*, but that the performance will lead to further *mitzvot* not done for ulterior purposes. We will also come to comprehend from the spiritual growth emanating from *mitzvot* that ulterior motives are inconsequential and that doing a *mitzvah* is its own reward. On the other hand, the opinion of Rabbi Nahman suggests that it is better to sin out of a good motive than to do a *mitzvah* with an ulterior motive. While this may be hyperbole, it still conveys strong disapproval of doing *mitzvot* for ulterior motives.

Contrariwise, there are also texts that stress the need for intention:

The one who performs numerous precepts and the one who performs only a few have equal merit, provided the heart is directed toward Heaven. [Talmud, *Berakhot* 5b]

The Holy One requires the heart, for Scripture says, "The Lord looks at what is in the heart." [1 Sam. 16:7; Talmud, *Sanhedrin* 106b]

While officially the *halakhah* seems to come down on the side that *mitzvot* require *kavanah*, the reality is otherwise. If all you were thinking about while lighting the Hanukkah candles was what presents you were getting, you still have fulfilled the obligation by lighting the Hanukkah candles. The act as defined by *halakhah* becomes the way to be *yotze*, to fulfill the obligation. The issue of *kavanah* was a more difficult issue for the traditional halakhic system with *mitzvot* that did not require an act. Can you fulfill the *mitzvah* of prayer by saying words even if you are not paying attention to what you are saying? After all, no matter what you are thinking, in the end the Hanukkah candles are lit. Is saying the words the equivalent of lighting or does prayer by its very nature require attention, *kavanah,* for it to be an "action." In practice, even in regard to prayer, *kavanah,* while encouraged, was not required with one exception—the recital of the Shema.

One could speculate that having adopted a system of *mitzvot* and being *yotze,* ultimately the rabbis of talmudic times had to drop the requirement of *kavanah* to fulfill a *mitzvah* as too difficult. Performing *mitzvot* could have become like filming a movie—take number seventy-three on candle lighting—if every time your mind wandered you had to do it over again. Staying focused for a few minutes, never mind for more than an hour, at a service is no easy task for our busy minds. If the average person was going to be able to succeed at all in the halakhic system, what was needed were relatively simple and tangible requirements for fulfilling the *mitzvot.* On the other hand, without *kavanah,* the danger existed that *mitzvot* could become rote ritual divorced from their spiritual meaning. Then *halakhah* would be like trying to earn a merit badge by gaining enough *mitzvah* points to qualify from the Great Scoutmaster in the sky.

For our lives, we can imagine a system that does not focus on being *yotze,* yet which still appreciates the importance of actually performing *mitzvot.* Something happens in the doing that is different from the thinking. This would be a system without obligation and sin, which still holds that a spiritual life requires both practice and discipline. Shabbat cannot be much of a spiritual practice if observed only once in six months. Nor can prayer be a spiritual discipline if you only pray when you are moved to do it. Therefore there will be times to do a *mitzvah* despite your lack of interest or *kavanah,* because, like any discipline, you need to practice on a regular basis. This is true even as you strive to make this a practice of the heart—a practice of opening the heart, of awareness of the moment and of the Holy. It is *kavanah,* the intention of the heart and mind, which gives these precepts meaning.

## A Spiritual Observance

What is required in such a spiritual system of Torah observance?

### 1. *An attitude of readiness*

"Verily, the word is very nigh unto you, when it is in your mouth and in your heart to do it" (Deut. 30:14). R. Isaac said: When is it nigh unto you? When readiness to do it is in your mouth as well as in your heart. [Talmud, *Eruvin* 54a]

R. Joshua ben Korhah said: A person should always be as alert as possible to perform a *mitzvah*. [Talmud, *Nazir* 23b]

As stated in the beginning of this chapter, the best way to study is *torah lishmah*, "Torah for its own sake." There should be no ulterior motive. Therefore, the sages of the Talmud made a point of practicing occupations other than that of rabbi, to avoid using the Torah "as a spade to hoe with," that is, a means of earning a livelihood.

R. Meir said: They who occupy themselves with Torah for its own sake acquire many blessings. More; the entire world is under obligation to them. They are called [God's] companion, [God's] beloved, those who love God who is everywhere, those who love their fellow human beings, those who gladden God who is everywhere, those who gladden others. The Torah clothes them with humility and fear of God, and fits them to be virtuous and devout, upright and faithful. It keeps them far from sin and draws them near to the doing of good deeds. People are aided by their counsel, sagacity, understanding and strength. It gives them a regal appearance, a manner that commands respect, and the capacity to be searching in judgment. Secret meanings of the Torah are revealed to them, and they become a fountain that never ceases and a stream that gathers strength. With it, they are modest, long-suffering, and forgiving of personal slight. The Torah makes them great and exalts them above all God's works. [*Ethics of Our Ancestors* 6:1]

This rather extraordinary and perhaps somewhat hyperbolic list of that which awaits the one who studies Torah for its own sake reflects both the spiritual nature of Torah study and its purpose.

It is easy to get carried away with yourself while studying Torah. This is true even if you have no ambition to be a sage. There is a kind of intellectual gamesmanship that many of us play. It goes something like this: Let us see who makes the smartest comment. Who can quote other related sources, thereby demonstrating greater knowledge? Who can impress the teacher? This kind of game is never good for the soul, but is particularly jarring in Torah study, which is both a spiritual and an intellectual endeavor.

Again, the ideal is *torah lishmah,* the study of Torah *for its own sake.* When you make the study of Torah a priority in your life, it is for the sake of enlightenment and for the sake of encountering the Divine.

## 2. An attitude of joy

> R. Isaac said: The Torah teaches you a rule of good conduct, namely, that when people perform a precept, they should do so with a cheerful heart. [Midrash, *Leviticus Rabbah* 34:8]

> "The writing was the writing of God, graven *(harut)* upon the Tablets" (Exod. 32:16). Read not *harut,* "graven," but *herut,* "freedom," for no one is truly free until they occupy themselves with the study of Torah. [*Ethics of Our Ancestors* 6:2]

The view reflected in these sources is that the reason to study Torah is for its spiritual and emotional benefits. The study of Torah brings us a sense of freedom, a kind of release from anxieties. How? Every day we face choices about matters big and small. Often, we are unsure about how to respond to those choices. As humans we also face difficult moments in our lives, moments of great pain and loss. By sharing the accumulated wisdom of the Jewish people, Torah study gives us a clearer perspective on life. This process may not tell us whether to continue in a particular romantic relationship or whether to stay at a job. Torah is not a Ouija board. What it can do is help shape the values that we bring to our decision making. It can help us face the hard times in our lives with stories about how others have dealt with similar issues. Torah also gives us perspective by reminding us that each of us is only one person among billions. This is not to say our particular crisis is insignificant, but the connections that study makes can put it in a context larger than the world of our self. Finally, Torah and its call for awareness in the moment can help us see more clearly what is going on. There will be losses and difficult decisions in life. These need to be faced and not denied. However, worrying about them is unnecessary and only increases the pain and confusion. By striving for a truthful understanding of the moment, Torah can bring us a kind of joy and a freedom from anxieties.

### 3. Getting started

Shammai said: Make your study of Torah a regular practice. Hillel said: Do not say, "I will study when I have leisure." Perhaps you will never have leisure. [*Ethics of Our Ancestors* 3:7; 2:4]

Many people find it difficult to start a regular practice of Torah study. It seems a bit overwhelming, especially to those who come to the practice as adults. How can we begin to study Torah, when the amount to learn seems so vast? We start with a recognition that *talmud torah* is a lifelong process, so we must bring patience to it. That patience should be reflected in a meditative style of learning that allows time for us to ponder the meaning of a verse or section before rushing on to the next verse or section. Our goal is to engage the text, not just to accumulate knowledge. As with all learning, we should never fear to pose questions. As the great sage Hillel said: "A bashful person is not apt to learn" (*Ethics of Our Ancestors* 2:5). In other words, whether we begin studying Torah as children or as adults, the process is the same. Consider Rabbi Akiva:

It is said: Up to the age of forty, he had not studied a thing. R. Akiva said to himself: "I will go and study at least one section of Torah." He went directly to a schoolhouse, and he and his son began reading from a child's tablet. R. Akiva took hold of one end of the tablet, and his son of the other end. The teacher wrote down *alef* and *bet* for him, and he learned them; *alef* to *tav*, and he learned them; the book of Leviticus, and he learned it. He went on studying until he learned the whole Torah. [Talmud, *Ketubbot* 62b]

As with any discipline, each of us must discover what will help establish our routine. Clearly, a first step is to find a text that is accessible and yet feels rich with meaning. Do not be discouraged by a false start; if one text does not appeal, try another. The texts described below are some that can be fruitfully studied even by those with limited backgrounds. Give both the text and yourself a chance. Be willing to leave some parts of the text that you may not understand. It will not matter as long as most of the text can be understood. Parts of any text may also seem boring or technical or offensive. Everything does not have to be interesting; skip any boring material. On the other hand, try to struggle with any offensive section while understanding that some parts of the tradition, particularly ancient texts, may remain offensive despite our best efforts. It can be useful to have someone more knowledgeable as a reference—a teacher or a study partner—especially to reassure you that you haven't gone off in completely the wrong direction in interpreting the text.

Besides the choice of a text, the format for study is equally important. How do you best learn? What routine will assist you in making study a regular activity? Questions to consider include: Do you have enough self-discipline to study on your own? Would a study partner help create the routine because of the commitment to the other person? Is studying a little bit every day the best mode, or would setting aside a one-hour block of time every week or every other week work best for you? How do you set aside time that will be relatively inviolable? What time of day? Over lunch, in the morning, late at night, on weekends?

A word about *hevruta*, "studying with a peer": *hevruta* is a traditional method of study, particularly of Talmud, in a yeshiva. For example, you and your study partner would sit in a large room, the *beit midrash* (literally, "the house of study") in a yeshiva. You would prepare a specific part of the Talmud by taking turns reading a line of text out loud and then explaining and discussing it. Afterward, your Talmud teacher would lecture in class on that selection. Your study partner would be someone on much the same level of knowledge as you are. *Hevruta* study has value not because it is traditional, but because it reflects the notion that two people at the same level of knowledge can teach each other and together decode a text. Often people feel the texts of Judaism are closed to them without a teacher. There is, of course, some truth to that, especially with difficult texts. Yet Judaism has a fundamental belief that the Torah text is accessible to anyone, and one of the best ways to make it yours is through *hevruta* study. It is said, "People do not fully understand words of Torah until they have stumbled over them" (Talmud, *Gittin* 43a).

### 4. Regarding Torah as a never-ending process

R. Eliezer said: If all seas were ink, all reeds quills, heaven and earth scrolls, and all people scribes, they would not suffice to write down the amount of Torah I have learned, even though I abstracted no more than a person might take by dipping a painting stick in the sea. So too did Rabbi Joshua say. . . .

R. Akiva said: As for me, I am in no position to say what my teachers [R. Eliezer and Joshua] said. For, in fact, my teachers did abstract something, while I have abstracted no more than one who smells [the fragrance of] an *etrog*—one who smells it benefits, while the *etrog* itself is not diminished. [Midrash, *Song of Songs Rabbah* 1:3, 1]

There is no end to the vast library of Jewish texts. It is our own reading of and into these texts that has kept both them and the Jewish people vibrant. There are of course many worthwhile books about Judaism in all its aspects. Ask a rabbi or someone who is knowledgeable to recommend secondary literature in any aspect of Judaism in which you are interested. One good source is *The Schocken Guide to Jewish Books,* edited by Barry Holtz (Schocken, 1992).

In this regard, there is particular value in studying classic Jewish texts. Not only are these the original sources, but your study of these texts gives you the opportunity to arrive at your own understanding of the text unmediated by others' impressions or biases. In the list below, I have focused on classical Jewish texts, but there are new Jewish texts being written all the time. These reflect the contemporary moment as well as the voices of those not often included in the past, especially women. Any work of substance and meaning can be treated as text and considered "Torah" for the sake of study. "Text study" simply means that the text is read carefully, paying attention to each word or sentence. I have also omitted literature, poetry, drama, and the like, though you will find easy access to them in any synagogue library. If you wish to know more about the traditional texts discussed in "Texts" below, an excellent guide is another work edited by Barry Holtz, entitled *Back to the Sources: Reading the Classic Jewish Texts* (Summit, 1984).

### 5. Most of all to love Torah

Hour after hour, words of Torah are loved as much by those who study them as when they first made their acquaintance with them. [Talmud, *Eruvin* 54b]

"Attend and hear, O Israel: this day you have become the people of the Lord your God" (Deut. 27:9). Was it on this day that the Torah was given to Israel? Was not this day in fact forty years after the Torah was given? However, the verse intends to teach you that, to those who study Torah, it is beloved every day as the day when it was given from Mount Sinai. [Talmud, *Berakhot* 63b]

### Texts

*The Torah*    The best place to begin studying is with the Bible, the central text of Judaism. The Bible is a good starting point because it is in many ways the most accessible of the traditional texts, being an important component of Western culture. Your course of study might be following along in the Torah reading cycle by studying each week's Torah portion (see "The Torah in the Synagogue," pp. 170–75).

The standard Jewish Bible translation is *The Holy Scriptures*, published by the Jewish Publication Society of America (JPSA). JPSA has recently issued a five-volume commentary on the Humash (the Five Books of Moses) that combines current biblical scholarship with traditional Jewish commentaries on the text. It is a very useful guide to understanding the basic meaning of the words and their ancient Middle Eastern context. In addition, the Conservative, Orthodox, and Reform movements have issued one-volume commentaries on the Humash. These are less imposing than a five-volume work, but still useful.

*The Talmud*   For centuries Jewish study has focused on the Talmud. It is the sole curriculum of most yeshivot, academies of higher Jewish learning. (Bible is often studied only informally in yeshivot.) Through the ages, Talmud was studied as the written version of the oral law handed down from teacher to student since Sinai. It is also a record of the discussions of several generations of sages and rabbis over a period of five hundred years. It is composed of two parts: the Mishnah and the Gemara. The Mishnah, a brief compilation of practice and ideas, was edited by Rabbi Judah ha-Nasi around 200 C.E. The Gemara is a loose and lengthy commentary on the Mishnah composed between 200 and 500 C.E. The Gemara often seems to have been written in a stream of consciousness. It jumps from topic to topic, connected only by association and not necessarily by theme. There are actually two Gemaras— the one composed in the land of Israel (called the Jerusalem Talmud) and the larger and much more frequently studied Babylonian Talmud.

The Talmud contains legal material, comments on the Torah, theological speculations, stories about the rabbis, and much more. It is not a code of law, though Jewish law is in large part derived from its discussions. It is not an easy book to study because it is an ancient work that employs a style and logic foreign to the modern ear. It is also not organized in a systematic manner; and its discussions often begin with an assumption of a fair amount of knowledge on the part of the student. There are two ways that you can begin to study Talmud in English. The first is to study excerpts to give you a flavor of what it is like. The second is to jump right in with the understanding that you have to experience a certain quantity of Talmud before it becomes fully coherent. Certainly the second approach requires a teacher or at least a study partner. For those without a local teacher there are increasing opportunities for long-distance learning via the Web.

The Talmud is divided into tractates that are broadly topically based. Soncino Press has translated the Talmud in its entirety (this translation is also available on CD-ROM). More useful are the individual volumes in translation with extensive notes, either by Artscroll Press or by Adin Steinsaltz published by Random House. (Neither series yet covers the entire Talmud.) Another good approach is *The Talmud for Beginners* (vols. 1 and 2), by Judith Abrams, which takes you step by step through a section of Talmud. Many beginners start with the tractate *Berakhot*, "Blessings," both because it deals with familiar liturgical matters and because it is one of the easiest tractates to understand.

Mention should also be made of *Pirkei Avot*, or *Ethics of Our Ancestors*. This is a collection of pithy statements ascribed to various rabbis and sages of the Talmud. There are many modern commentaries on *Pirkei Avot*. As with any collection of sayings, some are profound, some obvious, some unclear, and some contradictory. The text can be found in many prayer books, since there is a custom of studying *Pirkei Avot* on Shabbat afternoon for the weeks between Passover and Shavuot.

*Midrash*    *Midrash* is broadly defined as the process of commenting on the biblical text from a homiletic perspective. A midrash is an individual commentary or exposition. However, *midrash* or its synonym, *aggadah*, "legend," actually includes a whole range of material, including legends, theology, law, and comments on the biblical characters. Midrash can be found in the Talmud but also exists in separate works. The best-known collection is *Midrash Rabbah*, which is a midrashic commentary on the Torah. This is available in English translation. A number of other books of midrash have also been translated. By far the best way to enter the world of midrash is through *Sefer Ha-Aggadah*, a collection of sources edited by Hayim Bialik and Yehoshua Ravnitzky. The topical arrangement allows the student to see the rich variety found in the rabbinic midrashic literature. Originally published in Hebrew, it has been translated by William Braude under the title *The Book of Legends* (Schocken, 1992). Another extraordinary collection of midrash is *Legends of the Jews*, by Louis Ginzberg (Jewish Publication Society,

1913). He weaves the midrash into a narrative that gives the reader a flavor for the midrashic variety. His extensive footnotes point the reader to his sources, but his work does not give you the opportunity to read the original sources yourself.

*Traditional Bible commentaries*   Beginning in the Middle Ages, many commentaries were written on the Torah. The classic commentary is that of RaSHI (Rabbi Solomon ben Isaac, 1040–1105), who tries to explain the plain meaning of the text even as he draws upon midrashic literature. A number of translations of RaSHI exist. A more difficult commentary, also available in English, is by Nahmanides, also known as the RaMBaN. Nahmanides (Rabbi Moses ben Nahman, 1194–1270) has fewer comments than RaSHI, but his comments are longer. He interprets the text on many levels, including *sod,* mystical interpretations.

RaSHI and RaMBaN, together with Abraham ibn Ezra, are the primary traditional commentators on the Torah. They, as well as some other commentators, are included in a work called *Mikraot Gedolot* (literally, the "Great Scriptures"), which is available in many Hebrew editions.

When studying these commentaries you will inevitably find some that don't make sense. These are premodern texts, with a style and an approach very different from our own. One very useful path into the world of traditional Bible commentators is the work of Nehama Leibowitz (beginning with *Studies in Bereshit,* published by the Jewish Agency, 1972). In six volumes, she covers each portion of the Torah, focusing on themes as they are treated by a wide variety of traditional commentaries. She has translated these commentaries, and her selection allows you to focus on the richness of this literature.

**Halakhah,** *Jewish law*   Beginning in the Middle Ages, a number of codes of Jewish law were published. These abstracted talmudic material and combined it with other rabbinic literature to set out the laws and customs of Judaism in plain language. Codes are arranged by subject matter, allowing readers to more easily find specific information they may be seeking. The classic code of Jewish law is the *Shulhan*

*Arukh* (literally, the "Arranged Table"), first published in the sixteenth century. It has never been fully translated. A translation of one section of the *Shulhan Arukh* is in progress. It is called the *Mishneh Berurah,* after a commentary written by the Hafetz Hayyim (1838–1933), a leading rabbinic scholar. His commentary is on the first of four volumes of the *Shulhan Arukh,* which is the volume that covers liturgy and Shabbat and holidays. This edition provides both the text of the *Shulhan Arukh* and the commentary of the *Mishneh Berurah* in Hebrew and English.

An even better place to begin studying codes is with the *Mishneh Torah,* compiled by Maimonides. Although earlier and therefore surpassed in authority by the *Shulhan Arukh,* Maimonides' work is the most accessible code because of his organization and clarity of language. There is a vocalized Hebrew edition, and most of the text has been translated into English. The first volume, *The Book of Knowledge,* focuses on fundamental principles of Judaism and such topics as ethics and repentance. The second volume, *The Book of Adoration,* focuses on prayer. Both are rich and accessible in English texts (Feldheim, 1981; other volumes are available in the Yale Judaica Series).

*Other texts*    Among other traditional texts, one can consider studying the *Siddur,* the prayer book; works of Jewish philosophy; Kabbalah or Jewish mysticism (the classic work of medieval Jewish mysticism, the *Zohar,* has been translated into English, but it is incomprehensible to anyone without a background in its ornate symbolism—it is best to begin with general collections of texts on Kabbalah); and Hasidism, a more modern form of Kabbalistic thinking. Many good collections of texts in all these areas are available in both English and vocalized Hebrew.

---

A *KAVANAH* FOR TORAH STUDY

With constancy, if not consistency, You, God, have loved Your people Israel. Torah and *mitzvot,* teaching and ways of acting, beliefs and being You have given us. Therefore *be-shakveinu u-vekumeinu,* in our ups and downs, in our lying down and our rising, in all the moments of the cycles of our lives, we speak and think of You. For the Torah is our *orekh yamim,* it is what lengthens our days by giving them meaning, it lengthens our days by stretching them so that they are attached to what comes before and after. For Torah is our life, and we are called to meditate on it day and night, night and day. Praised are You who has asked of Israel that we occupy our lives in Torah.

## The Torah in the Synagogue

The Torah, in its basic meaning, refers to the Five Books of Moses (in Hebrew, the Humash). The five books are Bereishit (Genesis), Shemot (Exodus), Va-Yikra (Leviticus), Be-midbar (Numbers), and Devarim (Deuteronomy). The Hebrew names are taken from the first significant word of the book; the names we commonly use indicate a major theme of each book. The Humash is divided into fifty-four portions. Each book is also divided into chapters and verses; for example, we refer to Exodus 15:20. This division is adopted from Christian divisions, which is why the chapters sometimes seem at odds with the Hebrew weekly portions.

> It is to a book, the Book, that we owe our survival—that Book which we use, not by accident, in the very form in which it has existed for millennia: it is the only book of antiquity that is still in living use as a scroll. The learning of this Book became an affair of the people, filling the bounds of Jewish life, completely. [Franz Rosenzwieg, *On Jewish Learning,* p. 95]

While the term *Humash* refers to a printed book, the phrase *sefer torah* refers to the Torah scroll. The text of the Torah is handwritten by a scribe on parchment according to very specific rules. The parchment is attached to rollers to facilitate its use. The scroll is then covered both to protect it and to honor it. It is placed into the ark *(aron kodesh)* on the eastern wall of the synagogue and is the point of orientation for our prayers. The *sefer torah* is removed from the ark to be read as part of the service. The *sefer torah* is the holiest object in Judaism and is treated as such. It is not touched directly by our hands and traditionally is kissed by first touching it either with a prayer shawl or a prayer book and then kissing the object as a gesture of respect and affection. Traditionally, a *sefer torah* cannot be sold for any reason except to ransom a kidnapped Jew, that is, to save a life.

**The Torah service** The *mitzvah* of *talmud torah* calls us to study Torah, with a class, a study partner, or on our own. Yet the study of Torah has also been institutionalized as part of Jewish liturgy. Each Shabbat we read the Torah portion of the week. According to the tradition, Ezra instituted reading the Torah on Monday and Thursday mornings to ensure that we would hear the Torah read at least every three days. The Torah service is not a class, but a public reading. We are to listen to the words and thereby reengage ourselves with Torah. Its purpose is to keep Torah present in our lives.

The Shabbat Torah service has developed over time and has existed in a number of forms. Today, the Torah is read from the beginning of Genesis to the end of Deuteronomy over the course of one year. Thus each week and Shabbat is associated with one Torah portion or *parsha*. (Depending on details of the Jewish calendar, there are usually some weeks when two portions are read to facilitate the completion of the whole Torah each year.) There are, however, two major variations in how this yearly cycle is carried out. The more traditional pattern is to read all of the Torah during the course of the year. Many liberal congregations read only a portion of the weekly cycle. This is done to allow greater focus on the section being read as well as to shorten the overall length of the service. Some congregations that read only part of the portion follow a triennial cycle, reading a third of each weekly portion each year. Over three years they read the whole Torah.

Either before or after the reading there is usually a *d'var torah*, literally, "a word of Torah," a sermon given about the Torah portion. Some congregations have a Torah discussion or Torah study instead of a sermon. This can make the study/teaching aspect of the Torah service explicit rather than just implicit.

There are two things going on during the Torah service. First, the

Torah is chanted by the reader according to an ancient cantillation system called *trop*. Second, designated people are called up to the Torah to stand by the reader; this is known as an *aliyah* (plural: *aliyot*), which literally means "going up." (It is the same word used to denote settling in Israel.) To be called to the Torah is described in the spatial term of ascension because it is considered an honor. This notion is reflected in the architecture of synagogues. The reading table is often on a raised platform so that you physically go up to the Torah. (In older synagogues, the Torah reading table was usually located in the center, rather than up in front as in most modern synagogues. This conveyed the notion that the Torah was in the midst of the congregation.) In talmudic times those called up for an *aliyah* read their own section from the Torah. However, when it became clear that not everyone could do this, to avoid embarrassment an official Torah reader read on behalf of all those receiving an *aliyah*.

**What to do if you have an** aliyah   If you would like an *aliyah,* you can ask an usher if there are any available. Or you might be approached and offered one. It is considered an honor and so the polite response is to say yes, but it is always permissible to decline. The procedure for an *aliyah* is the same whether on a weekday or Shabbat. You will be told you have a specific *aliyah,* for example the fifth. In Orthodox and in some Conservative synagogues, the first two *aliyot* fall into a special category. The first is reserved for *kohanim,* people who trace their lineage back to the priestly caste of the ancient Israelite cult. The second is reserved for those of Levitical descent. Everybody not in the first two categories is an Israelite and can be called for the rest of the *aliyot*. Unfortunately for non–Hebrew speakers, the number of the *aliyah* may only be announced in Hebrew. If this is the case, you can ask for help from the usher. Also, most Bibles have the *aliyot* and their numbers marked in the text. Many synagogues will also announce the *aliyah* in English and/or announce in English the name of the person being called to this *aliyah*.

In Orthodox synagogues, the custom is to wear a *tallit* (prayer shawl) for an *aliyah* even if you normally do not wear one (Orthodox practice is to wear a *tallit* only after marriage, not after bar mitzvah).

Usually all men in Conservative synagogues are wearing a *tallit* already. Customs vary whether women wear a *tallit* both in general and for an *aliyah*. When called, you go up to the place where the Torah is being read. The *gabbai*, the person who stands beside the Torah reading table and calls people up, may ask you for your Hebrew name. Your Hebrew name includes the names of your parents. For example, *Moshe ben Meir ve-Rahel,* "Moshe the son of Meyer and Rachel." You stand to the right of the Torah reader. In Orthodox synagogues only men are called to the Torah and your Hebrew name is "so and so the son of your father" (your mother is unmentioned).

The Torah reader will point to the place in the scroll. It is customary for you to kiss the Torah, using the corner of your *tallit* or prayer book and then bringing the *tallit* or prayer book to your lips. You then chant or say the *berakhah*, the blessing before the Torah reading. It is often reproduced in large print and placed next to the Torah scroll. In many prayer books, the *berakhah* is printed in both Hebrew and in transliteration. After reciting the blessing, hold on to the right side of the Torah roller while the reader chants the Torah selection. When she or he is finished, some people kiss the Torah again. You recite the *berakhah* after the Torah reading. If you want a *mi-sheberakh* or *eil maleh* prayer (see glossary, pp. 174–75) recited, you may request it at this point. It is the custom to remain for the next *aliyah* to express a reluctance to leave the Torah. Usually you move to the side and follow the reading silently. After the person who received the next *aliyah* recites the blessing following the Torah reading, you return to your seat. People you pass may congratulate you by shaking your hand. A traditional congratulation is *yasher koah* or *yishar kohakha* (to a female, *yishar kokhekh*), "May your strength increase."

---

### A *KAVANAH* FOR AN *ALIYAH*

Since our purpose is to develop a spiritual sensibility in our every action, when it comes to something as important as an *aliyah*, you may wish to prepare yourself by reciting a *kavanah* such as the following:

As I come for my *aliyah*, let me feel connected to Torah and all that it represents. Let me hear the echoes of generations of Jews discussing and debating the meaning of Your words. Let me not flee from the truths found in Torah as the Israelites fled from Sinai. Open my heart and mind to hear the Voice of Sinai found in Torah. Let me grasp it as a tree of life as Torah gives meaning to my life. Let it renew my days as I return once again to You.

As mentioned, the Torah is read not just on Shabbat morning. Every week it is read on Shabbat afternoon during the *minhah* (afternoon) service as well as Mondays and Thursdays during the *shaharit* (morning) services. Starting on Shabbat afternoon, we read the first selection of next week's portion and repeat it again on Monday and Thursday. There are only three *aliyot* at these Torah services.

The Torah is also read on holidays. The Torah reading is not from that week's portion but rather is a selection about the festival. The number of *aliyot* changes based on the sanctity of the day. For Rosh Hodesh, the new month, and *hol ha-moed,* the intermediate days of Pesah and Sukkot, we have four *aliyot*. For the three pilgrimage festivals (Sukkot, Pesah, and Shavuot) and for Rosh ha-Shanah we have five *aliyot*. On Yom Kippur, we have six *aliyot,* and on Shabbat we have seven.

### GLOSSARY OF TORAH SERVICE TERMS

*aliyah*—a summons to go up and stand by the reader while the Torah is being read.

*aron kodesh*—the ark (literally the holy ark) that holds the Torah scrolls.

*atarah, keter*—two synonyms for the crown, often made of silver, that fits over each roller.

*bimah*—the reading table.

*eil maleh*—a memorial prayer to honor the deceased relative of a person who had an *aliyah*.

*etz hayyim*—the wooden roller, literally the tree of life, a reference to the phrase chanted as the scroll is returned to the ark: "It [the Torah] is a tree of life to those who grasp it" (Prov. 3:18).

*gabbai*—a person who stands to the side of the *bimah*, corrects the reader, and calls people up for an *aliyah*.

*gellilah*—the dressing of the scroll after it is lifted; literally, "rolling the scroll together."

*hagbah*—the lifting of the scroll after the reading.

*mapah*—the cloth that covers the reading table.

*mi-sheberakh*—a prayer said for the person having an *aliyah*. It can be for their general well-being, for someone who is ill, to name a baby, etc.

*parokhet*—a curtain that covers the ark.

*rimonim*—a decorative piece, often made of silver, that goes over the top of each roller.

*wimpel*—in some communities, a long wrapper used to bind the scroll tightly. (Most communities use a piece of cloth tied or secured with buckles.)

*yad*—the pointer used by the reader to follow the text without touching it directly; literally, "hand."

# AVODAH:
# THE PATH OF PRAYER

The world rests on three things: Torah, *avodah,* and *gemilut hesed:* the study of Torah, worship, and deeds of loving-kindness. [*Ethics of Our Ancestors* 1:2]

*A*vodah is commonly understood as worship. It is often referred to as *avodah she-be-lev,* the "worship of the heart." Yet for many people, whether they grew up practicing Judaism or are coming to it for the first time, prayer is often the most difficult ritual. While Shabbat has an innate appeal as a day of rest, and holiday customs can be fun, prayer confronts us with questions: Why pray? What do we believe about God? Can God hear and answer our prayers? If we don't believe in God, is there any reason to pray? Why are we saying a fixed liturgy rather than spontaneous prayers? These questions are often particularly difficult because we have been raised in a secular world with its skeptical stance. Even Jews who attend services regularly may struggle with these questions.

For many Jews, attending synagogue services is an act of communal solidarity. Going to synagogue on Shabbat is the "best" way to identify with the Jewish community. Talking over *kiddush* with others who make up your Jewish community, people you probably don't see during the week, is a crucial part of the synagogue experience for Jews. Without denying that aspect of the experience, the question remains, especially for those standing on the outside and wondering whether to come in, what is prayer all about?

In different periods of Jewish history, other questions have been posed. In the past, the notion of a God who could hear and answer prayer was not "unbelievable." But for those who believed in a God who could answer prayers, questions arose about what was inappropriate to ask from God. The ancient rabbis, for example, developed a notion of "praying in vain," which basically meant praying to ask God to miraculously change something that had already happened. Thus, while it was perfectly appropriate and possibly efficacious to pray for the gender of a baby before conception, it was a "prayer in vain" to beseech that the gender of the baby should change once it had been established. The belief in prayer's potential to change the future as well as its limitations on changing the already existing present raised a number of philosophical questions for traditional theologians. How can God know the future if our prayer can change it? (To answer that God knows we will pray only begs the question.) If God is omnipotent, why couldn't God change the sex of a baby?

Sometimes the concerns go deeper. Can prayer change anything? Is there a Being who can hear our prayers and respond to them? Isn't it kind of cheesy to ask for things from God, to pray for a new bike or a red sports car for Hanukkah? If most people only pray when they are in the proverbial foxhole, isn't prayer just wishful thinking seeking some magical way to get out of a dire circumstance?

While the question of what is God will be dealt with more fully in the last chapter of this book, it is useful to speak of God either as immanent or transcendent. To say that God is transcendent means that God is a Being that is separate from us. Many traditional views of God posit a transcendent God. These range from the traditional notion of a transcendent God who rewards and punishes to a Being or Force that acts in a caring fashion in the universe. To say that God is immanent means that God is inside us rather than separate from us. If God is the good inside us, then the Godliness inside us can act in a caring fashion.

Some recent studies suggest that ill people who have a group of people praying on their behalf do better physically than ill people who don't. The web of the universe is complex. Cause and effect may not explain everything. It may well be that having people express good wishes/prayers on our behalf can affect the cosmos and us in ways that we cannot yet clearly understand. This possibility of making a difference for the good can be called God. Whether God is the caring impulse inherent in every human being or God is a Being or Force that can act in a caring manner when called upon, the universe responds to our actions—including our prayers.

There are still prayers that are in vain. God, as it were, always answers, but sometimes the answer is no. But prayer and the response it calls forth are part of the "physics" of our spiritual universe—to every action of prayer there is a reaction.

## Kinds of Jewish Prayer

It is important to understand that prayer was never just about asking for things. *Bakasha,* "asking for things," is only a minor element in the totality of Jewish liturgy. In fact, on Shabbat, prayers of *bakasha* are removed from the liturgy, since Shabbat is meant to be a day of rest and contemplation, not of worry about what you do not have. In weekday services, the liturgy consists of three types of prayer: *shevah* (praise), *bakasha* (asking), and *hoda'ah* (gratitude). It is customary to view the progression of liturgy as reflecting the progress of a person approaching a king with a request. First you would praise the king, then make your request, and finally express your gratitude. This metaphor of God as king is explicit in Jewish liturgy and the most common way of referring to God. Earthly court protocol may have influenced much of the overall structure of the liturgy, as well as specific customs such as bowing.

In general, praise rather than request is the dominant theme of Jewish liturgy. Praising God can bring us to a recognition of our human finiteness in comparison to God. It makes us aware that the world does not end and begin with ourselves. When we praise God as the creator of the world we also remember that God has given us the gift of all the wonders of creation. Most especially, we can remember that God has given us the most precious gift of all—the gift of life. Finally, engaging in the act of prayer reminds us that despite our limitations and foibles,

God desires to be in relationship with us. Prayer can help lead the worshiper to move beyond the self to a sense of standing before the presence of the Holy One. The metaphor of a kingly court is not the only one possible in this understanding. Praise can lead to prayer as the experience of the Divine Presence, however that Presence is imaged or experienced. This awareness then leads to a thankfulness for the experience of God's Presence, the feeling of being cared for or loved by God, and an increased appreciation for the blessings of our lives.

Yet the purpose of prayer is not totally encapsulated by an explanation of these three types of prayer. For the mystics, prayer had the capacity to move the worshiper beyond praise, request, or thankfulness to a literal experience of the Divine. For Hasidism in the eighteenth century, prayer was the central religious path, often replacing the traditional notion of Torah study as the primary path of the religious Jew. Hasidism saw prayer as the means to achieve the goal of religious life: *devekut*, "cleaving to God."

Another approach to prayer is based on a typology of Jewish mysticism that posits the existence of four worlds that bridge from the materiality of this world to the spirituality of the Godhead. (This typology is in part an attempt to answer how an infinite spiritual being, God, could have created a finite material world.) This approach, as set forth in contemporary language by Rabbi Zalman Schachter-Shalomi, sees the morning liturgy as a progression from the material to the spiritual. We begin with the morning blessings that focus on the body and continue with the psalms that give voice to the world of emotions. We continue with the Shema, which states the principle of God's oneness, reflecting the world of the intellect. Finally, we come to the *amidah*, during which we stand before the Presence, striving to enter the world of spirituality.

The act of prayer itself and its forms can be understood to have a variety of purposes, each of which can be found in the traditional liturgy, and some of which move beyond that liturgy to the contemplation of God. Different schools of Jewish thought emphasized different aspects of the prayer experience. Eventually, Jewish tradition favored fixed liturgy over spontaneous prayer, and communal prayer in a *minyan*, "quorum of ten," over individual prayer.

## The Prayer Services

Since before talmudic times, Jews have been called upon to pray three times a day. These services are *shaharit* (morning), *minhah* (afternoon), and *ma'ariv* (evening, though Jews of Sephardic origin call the evening service *arvit*). On Shabbat and festivals an extra service called *musaf* ("additional") is added to the morning prayers.

Yet the origins of the liturgy are not clear. It is striking that despite being "one of the pillars of the world," prayer is not one of the *mitzvot* in the Torah. Most rabbinic authorities believe prayer is only a rabbinic *mitzvah*. Why?

Perhaps it is because *avodah* originally referred to the sacrificial system rather than to prayer. In fact, some Bible scholars question whether there was any liturgy accompanying the sacrifices in the First Temple. Whatever prayers we do have in the biblical text are simply the spontaneous prayers of individuals, such as Moses' prayer to heal Miriam, his sister. It would seem that the Torah sets out in detail the rituals related to bringing sacrifices and has apparently no notion of liturgy.

Liturgy as we know it seems to come about only during the late Second Temple period, in the last century before the common era. Even the rabbinic texts, which generally like to maintain the antiquity of the forms of rabbinic Judaism, acknowledge the late development of Jewish liturgy. For example the Talmud tells us that one sage, Shimon ha-Pekuli, set in order the central prayer of Jewish liturgy, the *amidah*. The significance of prayer was accelerated by the destruction of the Second Temple in 70 C.E., which eliminated sacrifices as a manner of divine worship. The rabbis explicitly designed the daily liturgy as a substitution for sacrifices. Synagogues, which had coexisted with the Second Temple in its last years, now became the focus of public religious life. The rabbis of the Talmud established all the basic elements of the service, though Jewish liturgy would continue to grow in an unabated process from their time to ours.

In the Talmud there is a discussion concerning the origin of the services. One opinion held that the prayers paralleled the sacrifices in the Temple. There were daily morning and afternoon sacrifices as well as an additional sacrifice on Shabbat and holidays. Since there were no daily nighttime sacrifices, the evening prayer service originally had a status different from the other services—it was not obligatory. The other opinion held that the patriarchs instituted the three daily services. Abraham instituted the morning service, Isaac the afternoon, and Jacob the evening. In this schema there is no character that introduces *musaf,* the additional service. While the Talmud likes to place the origin of Jewish liturgy back in the historic past, one still wonders how the Talmud understood this tradition. For after all, it tells us that saintly Abraham did not pray the afternoon or evening services. One also wonders what prayers the patriarchs might have uttered, since, as we have seen, it is only in talmudic times that the *amidah* was composed. Perhaps the talmudic tradition is meant to suggest that the impulse to pray has always existed and beginning with the patriarchs there was a regularity to the expression of prayer even if the words of prayer were still fluid.

### Fixed Liturgy

The coexistent strands of fixed and fluid liturgy continued for some time in liturgical practice. Even as the rabbis of the Talmud formulated the *amidah,* using the traditional *berakhah* formula (see "Eating and Food," pp. 66–93), the specific wording of the liturgy remained for the most part fluid. This was due in large part to the lack of prayer books in the pre-Gutenberg world. Thus even as the rabbis created and set the theme of a particular *berakhah,* they left the wording up to the person leading services. Since most people did not have the text of the liturgy in front of them, they would listen to the leader composing the *berakhah* on its requisite theme and then answer *Amen,* "So be it." The liturgy was much shorter than it is today. Over time the liturgy became ever more fixed. The services became longer, especially the morning service and those of festivals. Yet creativity and the introduction of new liturgy continued for over a thousand years after the talmudic period. From the end of the Middle Ages until the nineteenth century, however, little new material was added. In the twentieth century there was a contraction of the liturgy, even in traditional circles. (The rejection of many of the additions to the standard liturgy is an exception to the trend toward stringency in many Orthodox circles.) However, today in all the liberal movements there have been both changes and deletions of traditional liturgy as well as the addition of new liturgy.

Even as the liturgy became more and more fixed, the tradition remained concerned that the tension between *keva* and *kavanah* be maintained. *Keva* is the "fixed" liturgy; *kavanah* is the "intention" of the worshiper. In the last chapter, I discussed the rabbinic debate about whether fulfilling a *mitzvah* requires intention. This is a particular problem with regard to prayer. While in the end *kavanah* is not required, it is still very much desired, especially when it comes to prayer. After all, what is the point of praying if you are paying no attention to the words and their meaning!

If *kavanah* is so important, why is Jewish prayer so focused on a fixed liturgy that tells you what to say and when to say it? After all, isn't spontaneous prayer by its very nature a prayer with *kavanah*? On one level the answer may lie with the broad trend within the tradition to set out ever more specifically what needs to be done to fulfill the *mitzvot*. If it is a *mitzvah* to pray, then what do I need to say to fulfill my obligation? Yet there may also be an insight into the nature of prayer that is operative here. It is clear that a fixed liturgy runs the risk of a rote recital of the prayers. Yet however appealing spontaneous prayer may be, the tradition is concerned that without a regular prayer practice we will never come to spontaneous prayer or come to it only very rarely. There is an art to prayer. It is not something that comes easily, even to those who have no doubts about the existence of God. It is a practice like any other. It needs to be done on a regular basis if we are to become skilled at it, just as learning to play an instrument requires frequent rather than spontaneous practice, and physical exercise needs to be done on an ongoing and regular basis to obtain the health benefits. If prayer is not part of a regular practice, it will end up on the list that many of us keep: the things we want to do that we somehow never seem to get around to doing.

Prayer, then, is a practice that requires just that—practice. It does not work very well if you pray only once in a while. It may not work very well if you pray only once a week on Shabbat. Yet the more frequently we pray the more we run the risk of prayer becoming a rote ritual. You have probably seen people who are "speed daveners," those who say the words at the speed of light while checking their watch for the time and waving hello to an acquaintance who has just entered the room. How to avoid prayer as rote?

## Reconceiving Prayer

One place to begin is to reconceive of prayer as a discipline rather than an obligation. Prayer as obligation can lead too easily to speed-davening just to get it done. Prayer as discipline acknowledges that there will be times when the act of prayer has no real meaning to the worshiper. Yet it is still important to pray in order to maintain the discipline of prayer. The difference, then, is that you have not fulfilled an obligation in this rote prayer. You understand that this act of prayer was unsuccessful, but it is important to keep on praying to increase your prayer skills. It also lays the groundwork for the future potential of your prayer experience. Being unsuccessful is a goad to try harder next time rather than being satisfied with having fulfilled the *mitzvah* in a system that sees prayer as an obligation.

Another element in creating a vibrant prayer life is to reacquire the ability to pray in our own words. While there are some places in the traditional liturgy that allow for personal prayers, basically Jewish liturgy has become fixed and formal. A number of years ago, a group from my synagogue met a few times a year with a group from a church. We ate together and then engaged in a Black-Jewish dialogue. At our first meeting, before we ate, the minister offered a prayer that spoke about the coming together of diverse communities to talk with each other. All I could think of doing was saying the *motzi*, the traditional blessing over bread. I had never "made up" a prayer. Or similarly, at a conference about religion and healing, a nun gave examples of prayers she said with ill patients. They were beautiful and also reflected the particular circumstance of the patient. The rabbi on the same panel spoke about two traditional prayers for healing which are formulaic and therefore do not reflect the patient's particular circumstance, e.g., he is about to be operated on or she just received a bad prognosis. The paucity of our tradition was striking. We limit the outpouring of our hearts when we feel bound to use only the fixed liturgy. Told to put aside our prayer books and just speak from the heart, most of us feel embarrassed and tongue-tied. Along with the treasures and tradition of our liturgy we need to add our own words if prayer is to become a practice rather than an obligation.

## How to Pray

There is a particular style to Jewish prayer that is derived from Hannah. Hannah (whose story is found at the beginning of the First Book of Samuel) is childless and she goes to the sanctuary to pray for a child.

> R. Hamnuna said: How many important rulings may be derived from the verses about Hannah at prayer (1 Sam. 1:10ff). "Now Hannah, she spoke with her heart"—hence, they who say the *Tefillah* must direct their full hearts to the prayer; "only her lips moved"—hence, they who say the *Tefillah* are to do it clearly with their lips; "but her voice could not be heard"—hence it is forbidden to raise one's voice in the *Tefillah*. . . . [Talmud, *Berakhot* 31a]

The traditional style of prayer then is to articulate the words, not to say or read them silently. The words should be said loudly enough so the worshiper can hear them but not so loudly as to disturb the person next to you. The "silent" *amidah* is not really silent at all; rather it is said to oneself, in distinction to when the *amidah* is chanted out loud by the person leading services.

It is ironic that the basic style of Jewish prayer should be modeled on the practice of a woman, Hannah, and yet, according to traditional *halakhah*, women are not obligated to observe the *mitzvah* of prayer, which also means that they cannot lead services!

Another part of the style of Jewish prayer, often practiced, is shuckling. This refers to moving the upper body back and forth during prayer. The origin of the practice is uncertain, but it is commonly associated with Eastern European Jewry. Both articulating the words and moving back and forth provide a physical dimension to the act of prayer.

## Making Prayer a Daily Practice

The three daily services create a framework for the creation of a daily practice of prayer. Upon rising in the morning, prayer can be both a way to give thanks for the new day and a spiritual preparation for that day. Similarly, praying at the end of the day can be a thanksgiving for the blessings of the day just past as well as an opportunity for a reflection upon the experience of the day. It can also serve as a way to come to a calm place, making the transition to sleep easier. *Minhah*, the afternoon prayer, is less obvious in its purpose. It is not tied to any natural phenomenon such as sunrise and sunset. It is the shortest service of the day, since it lacks the Shema and its blessings. Each service then has its own character.

**Shaharit:** *a morning practice*    The challenge of *shaharit* is that it is the longest daily service and yet for many this is the most pressured time of the day. How much time you have to devote to a *shaharit* will naturally affect how many prayers you can say. You will also need to weigh how much of the traditional liturgy you want to include as well as being aware of what are the central elements of the traditional liturgy.

Some models:

1. In the "Dawning" chapter (pp. 3–21), several prayers are mentioned that are said on waking up, each of which takes less than a minute. This is all some people will have time for.

2. In that chapter we discussed the *birkhot ha-shahar*, the morning blessings that can serve as a morning liturgy. This first part of the service contains many of the elements of the rest of the service in concise form. Blessings, the Shema, Torah study are all found in the first few pages of the prayer book. This then could serve as a basis for a *shaharit* of five to ten minutes.

3. You can find a verse, a phrase, a psalm, or a song that speaks to you and that becomes your mantra repeated over and over for your *shaharit*.

4. You can do an abbreviated version of the traditional liturgy, such as Psalm 145 *(ashrei)*, a short version of the blessings before and after

the Shema including the Shema and its first paragraph, the *amidah,* or a shortened version thereof. (A traditional version of an abbreviated *amidah* can be found in *Siddur Sim Shalom,* edited by Jules Harlow [Rabbinical Assembly, 1985], pp. 228–31.) Conclude with *aleinu* or some other closing liturgy. This would take approximately fifteen minutes.

There is another factor to take into account. You may want to give yourself some time to make the transition into prayer. It is not easy just to jump in without any "warm-up." This could consist of sitting in silence, singing a *nigun* (a wordless melody), chanting, studying, or reciting some liturgy. (Part of the reason that *shaharit* service is so long is that a preliminary section was added as preparation, but then over time that "preparation" became part of the core of the service. Then a new preliminary service was added and served its function until it too became part of the core, etc.) Similarly, you might not want to rush immediately away, rather you might want to sit in your devotional mood, letting it sink in before going off to the hustle and bustle of the day. This would add to the "length" of your prayer service.

A very nice collection of Jewish prayers, including nonstandard ones, is *A Language of Faith,* edited by Nahum Glatzer (Schocken, 1947).

**Minhah**    The challenge of *minhah* is to carve out some time in the middle of the day. The traditional liturgy could be said in ten minutes, so it is not so much a question of length as it is of stopping work in order to pray. Yet it would seem that the busier our workday and the faster the pace of our lives, the more beneficial would be a break, not for coffee or a snack but to breathe. Or to reflect on the questions: Who are we and who do we want to be? Perhaps then the Shema is not recited in *minhah* because it is too much to ask amid the business of the day to come to a sense of God's Oneness and thus the Divine unity that underlies the world. The fragmented nature of our work—forty-five-minute meetings, production deadlines, multiple memos, various clients or patients—seems to point in the opposite direction. *Minhah* then asks only for a pause to reflect, to remember what is important and what is ultimately extraneous—to return to our real selves, who

want to be caring and helpful to others even as much as we want to succeed and earn a living.

The challenge of *minhah* is to find what will allow us to do that.
What liturgy will bring us back to clearer awareness? Where can we go
for a few minutes of uninterrupted time? Our office? Outdoors? The
bathroom?

**Ma'ariv**   The evening service has both the Shema and *amidah* but is
still much shorter than *shaharit,* since it lacks the morning service's preliminary psalms. The traditional liturgy could be said in fifteen minutes. Or, as with the other services, you can construct your own *ma'ariv*
with or without elements of the traditional service. You may want
to directly connect it with going to bed (see "The End of the Day,"
pp. 94–102). Like *shaharit,* the evening service includes the theme of
the transition from light to darkness. It also includes a request that we
lie down in peace as our day draws to a close. If, in the morning, we are
awakening to and preparing for the new day, then in *ma'ariv,* even as
we reflect back on the day, we are bringing ourselves to a place of calm
and peace in order to have a restful sleep.

## Prayer Practices

Whether one is meditating or praying the traditional liturgy, it can be
helpful to the experience to have a set place at home for your spiritual
practice. Ideally, this would be a space set aside for it; at least it should
have some visible decoration to help create a devotional atmosphere.
Even if it is simply a chair that you also use for reading or watching TV,
coming to the same place for your daily prayer practice at home can
still help in creating a prayerful experience.

There is a tradition of using wall plaques as a devotional focus. One
form is a *mizrah,* from the word meaning "east." Since the tradition
is to face east toward Jerusalem while praying, such a plaque reminds
us which is the correct way to face. Another form is a *shiviti* plaque,
whose name is taken from the first word of the verse "I have placed
God before me always" (Psalm. 16:8). A centerpiece of the *shiviti* is the

name of God. Both kinds of plaques are often artistically rendered, sometimes in paper-cuts (there are examples at the beginning of each part in this book). Today they are found in some traditional synagogues, and they may also be adopted as a devotional focus at home.

The garments of prayer also can be a devotional aid. They are discussed toward the end of this chapter.

## Praying in a *Minyan*

Jewish prayer classically takes place in a *minyan,* a quorum of ten or more Jews. Despite prayer's being an intensely personal experience, we do it in a group. This communal setting is emphasized by the fact that almost all of the prayers use plural forms rather than singular. Perhaps to be able to pray we need to move beyond the walls of our self. An awareness of the others around us can lead to an awareness both of the Other and of our shared humanity. In the presence of others we are more likely to acknowledge our shortcomings as human beings. Likewise, in the presence of others we are enabled to move beyond disappointment in or condemnation of our self to an outpouring of the heart that longs for a change.

Thus, praying in a *minyan* serves as a setting for our own prayer. Sometimes this can be literally true. We have all been in services that have seemed rote or uninspired, or in which we cannot keep up with the pace of the prayers being recited. Or sometimes our mood seems at variance with that of the community; for example, they are joyous and celebratory and we are contemplative or even sad. In these cases, the service can become the setting for our own prayer. We do not need to be always on the same page literally or emotionally with the congregation. Having a group of people praying in the background can help create a prayerful environment. We can join again with the congregation at the central prayers such as the Shema or when they are singing (it is hard to pray when others are singing) or when we are ready. No matter how uninspired the service may seem to us, our own experience is very much in our hands.

## Prayer as a Way of Being

As mentioned, it is striking that prayer is not a *mitzvah* according to most rabbinic authorities. One could say that there is no *mitzvah* to pray because none is necessary, prayer is a natural impulse. Or because prayer is beyond the system of *mitzvot*, it is not something to be done only at specific times and with specific words. Rather, prayer is a way of being.

> How many Tefillahs is one required to utter every day? Our masters taught: One is to utter no more than the three Tefillahs which the fathers of the world ordained. David came and specified the times: "Evening, morn, and noon" (Psalm 55:18). Hence, one is not permitted to utter more than three Tefillahs a day. However, R. Yohanan said: Oh that one could continue to pray the entire day! [*Midrash Tanhuma, Mi-ketz, 9*; Talmud, *Berakhot* 31a]

> "As for me, let my prayer be unto You, O Lord, in an acceptable time." For everything the Holy One set a time and a season, as is said, "There is a time for experience" (Eccles. 8:6)—except for prayer. Whenever people pray, they are answered. Why is there no set time for prayer? Were a person to know the time when, if they pray, they will be answered, they would leave off other times and pray only then. Accordingly, the Holy One said: For this reason I do not let you know when you will be answered, so that you will be willing to pray at all times, as is said, "Put your trust in God at all times" (Psalm 62:9). [*Aggadah Bereishit* 77]

To live a prayerful life is to live a life of devotion. It is to carry with you an attitude toward the unfolding of your life. To always be praying is to live with an awareness of the true reality of nature.

"For prayer is not the shutting of one's eyes to reality. It is the glimmer, the intimation, the daring which leads to the transcending of reality" (Jakob Petuchowski). Prayer leads us to an understanding of our limitations and our frailty as well as our capacity for goodness and greatness. As we pray, we become aware of all that lies beyond the self, of the mountains and valleys of the psalmist, of the play of light and dark in the daily cycle of our world, of the birds and all the other creatures singing praise to God, and finally of all of creation. As we achieve the correct perspective of being only a small dot in a vast universe, we can feel alone. Moments of prayer in our busy lives become opportunities for self-reflection. Most often when we do that, when we gaze in the mirror of truth, not only do we see that we are only an insignificant dot in the universe, but the countenance staring back at us is an ugly one. We see all the bruises and warts on our faces earned in our lives. It is the portrait of Dorian Gray that we see rather than the prettified self we like to think we present to the outside world. Some commentators understand the word for prayer, *mitpalel,* with its reflexive grammatical form, to mean "judge oneself." Prayer prevents us from being carried away with ourselves. Yet even as we gain true perspective and a truer sense of ourselves, we are not meant to berate ourselves for our failures. Nor are we meant to feel insignificant or that in the scope of the universe whatever we do or whatever happens to us is insignificant. Nor is the goal to achieve an equanimity that leads you to feel nothing matters. Nor to come to a realization that all life is just a passing breath, as in the imagery of Kohelet, Ecclesiastes. For as small and as fallible as we are, as we encounter God in prayer we are reminded that we are created in the image of God. This means that each person is unique and each of us is called to act in Godly, that is, holy, ways.

The Hasidic master Isaacher Baer of Zlochow taught on Gen. 44:18 the following. At first, when a person wishes to pray, he thinks of God's greatness and says to himself: "Who am I, a mere flawed mortal to pray before the great and exalted God." But upon further reflection, he realizes that there is no place absent of God and therefore he too is part of the Divine. We are all created in the Divine image. With this understanding the person will now be able to pray with great enthusiasm.

Prayer becomes the expression of and evidence for our relationship to God. It is an affirmation that we are never alone, we always stand in relationship to the Holy One, who loves us with an everlasting love.

Prayer reminds us that God the Creator is everywhere in the universe, including, most importantly, in ourselves. To live a prayerful life is to see the image of God in every person we see, to see the everyday blessings of a blue sky and a green tree. In fact, it is to see the many blessings of our lives even as we don't ignore the curses and the suffering that is inevitably our fate.

Standing on an empty beach, we look back across the sand stretching as far as the eye can see. Lost from our sight is not what lies beyond the horizon, but rather the millions of grains of sand lying at our feet. All those millions make up this sandy vista, but we only perceive the mass whole. A life of prayer is to make us aware of the millions of moments that together make up the sandy beach of our individual lives. As small as each of us is in the vista of the universe, as fleeting as this moment is, this moment and myself are integral parts of the tapestry of existence. The challenge of prayer is even harder than we think. It is not only to pray three times a day in a *minyan,* it is to be prayerful at every moment of the day. To know before Whom you stand, and to act and react to the world in a holy way.

If prayer is pure and untainted, surely that holy breath that rises from your lips will join with the breath of heaven that is always flowing into you from above. Thus our masters have taught the verse: "Every breath shall praise God": with every single breath that you breathe, God is praised. As the breath leaves you, it ascends to God, and then it returns to you from above. Thus that part of God which is within you is reunited with its source. [From the Hasidic work *Keter Shem Tov,* as adapted in *Your Word Is Fire,* by Arthur Green and Barry Holtz]

---

A *KAVANAH* FOR PRAYER

Teach me my God, a blessing, a prayer
On the mystery of a withered leaf
On ripened fruit so fair
On the freedom to see, to sense,
To breathe, to know, to hope, to despair.
Teach my lips a blessing, a hymn of praise
As each morning and night

You renew Your days,
Lest my days be as the one before
Lest routine set my ways.
[Leah Goldberg, translated by Pnina Peli]

## A Brief Guide to Jewish Liturgy

There are a number of components in Jewish liturgy. Broadly they fall into three categories.

1. Prayers from the Bible. Most of these are from the Book of Psalms. In addition, the best-known piece of Jewish liturgy, the Shema prayer, is composed of three selections from the Torah.

2. Prayers composed by the rabbis of the Talmud. The *amidah*, the central prayer of every Jewish service, was composed in the rabbinic period. The Talmudic rabbis employed the form of the *berakhah*, the blessing, which is an essential element in the liturgy. The final wording of the rabbinic liturgy was only established in the early Middle Ages.

3. Beginning in the rabbinic period and continuing until the end of the Middle Ages, liturgical poetry was composed and added to the services. Known as *piyyut* (plural: *piyyutim*), these poems often developed around themes from the festival cycle. Thousands were written. Some were adopted only by a local community, though certain of them became widely accepted as standard parts of the liturgy. This was especially true of the expansion of the High Holiday liturgy, where some of our most famous prayers are *piyyutim*, for example, the *u-netanah tokef* prayer. In the modern period, with the printing of the prayer book and the increased standardization of the liturgy, *piyyutim* that were used only locally mainly disappeared, and in general *piyyut* was de-emphasized, since the poetry was often difficult to understand.

*The* berakhah    The talmudic rabbis inherited the basic *berakhah* formula. A *berakhah* for the rabbis needed to include the words *barukh atah Adonai eloheinu melekh ha-olam*, "Praised are You, Eternal One, our God, Ruler of the universe." There are a number of types of *berakhot*. (1) There are short forms said before eating, such as the blessing over bread, which begins with the *berakhah* formula and continues *ha-motzi lehem min ha-aretz,* "who brings forth bread from the earth" (see the chapter "Eating and Food," pp. 66–93, for further examples). (2) A short form said before doing a *mitzvah.* It adds the following to the opening formula: *asher kidshanu be-mitzvotav ve-tzivanu,* "who has made us holy through the commandments and commanded us." This is followed by reference to the particular *mitzvah,* such as lighting the Hanukkah candles. (3) The long form of a *berakhah,* which is usually the length of a paragraph but which can occasionally be longer. This form is a key underlying structure in Jewish liturgy. The long-form *berakhot* begin with the opening formula *barukh atah Adonai eloheinu melekh ha-olam* and continue by setting out a theme. One example is the *berakhah* at the beginning of the evening service, which talks about God as the bringer of light and darkness and night and day and celebrates God and God's creation. This long-form *berakhah* then concludes with part of the *berakhah* formula, *barukh atah Adonai,* "Praised are You, Eternal One," followed by a few words that recapitulate the theme of this liturgical unit. Thus this long form is framed by parts of the basic *berakhah* formula. These long-form *berakhot* were the basic building blocks of rabbinic liturgy. Thus, the evening service is composed of two such *berakhot* preceding the Shema, two following the Shema, and then the *amidah.* The *amidah* itself is a series of such paragraph *berakhot,* each one on a different theme. The *amidah* is also known as the *shemoneh esreh,* literally "eighteen," which was the number of blessings that made up this prayer group. (Later, a nineteenth was added, but the name had become traditional by that time and was not altered.)

Recognizing the formula *barukh atah Adonai eloheinu melekh ha-olam,* followed after some lines of liturgy by the formula *barukh atah Adonai,* alerts you to the beginning and the end of a unit of liturgy. There is one complication. When there is a series of blessings that make up a larger liturgical unit, the opening *berakhah* formula is not repeated each time but rather is "assumed," though the concluding *berakhah* formula is always present. Thus only the first *berakhah* preceding the Shema opens with the *berakhah* formula. The second *berakhah* opens with the words *ahavat olam,* "with eternal love," though it does conclude with the concluding blessing formula of *barukh atah Adonai,* with the summary of the theme of this second *berakhah,* that is, *ohev amo yisrael,* "who loves God's people Israel." This is similarly true of the *amidah,* where only the first blessing opens with the *berakhah* formula, the rest beginning with their themes but including the concluding *berakhah* formula.

***An additional word on the*** amidah    The *amidah* is the central prayer of Jewish liturgy. Every "service" contains an *amidah.* The *amidah* begins with three blessings of praise and concludes with three blessings of thankfulness. The middle section changes according to the occasion. During the week the middle consists of thirteen blessings of request that range from healing or wisdom to a restoration of the people to the land of Israel. On Shabbat and festivals, the middle section consists of a single blessing on the theme of the day. (The Rosh ha-Shanah *musaf* is exceptional in having three central blessings for a total of nine overall.) The *musaf* service is an additional *amidah* said on Shabbat and festivals.

Traditionally, when there is a *minyan,* the *amidah* is said silently and then repeated aloud by the service leader in every service except for the evening service. (This difference reflects the original optional status of the evening service.) During the repetition in the third blessing, the *kedushah* is recited. This is a prayer recited responsively based on verses quoted from the prophets. The *kedushah,* reciting *kaddish,* and reading from the Torah are among the elements of the service that are omitted when praying alone or without a *minyan.* In some congregations, there is no silent *amidah;* instead, the congregation recites the *amidah* aloud. In other congregations the first part of the *amidah* and the *kedushah* are recited together out loud and then everyone continues silently to the end of the prayer.

The *amidah* has a kind of choreography: it is traditional to bow four times while reciting it. The bowing is done at the beginning and end of the first *berakhah* of the *amidah.* Bend your knees at *barukh,* "praised are," and then bend over from the waist at *atah,* "you." Straighten up at the word *Adonai,* "God." This is done the same way in the next-to-last *berakhah* of the *amidah*. We bow on the words *modim anahnu lakh*, "we thank you," at the beginning of the *berakhah*, and again on *barukh atah* at the end of the *berakhah*.

This manner of bowing is done at a number of other places in the liturgy. The two most common are during the call to pray *(barekhu)* which opens the main part of the *shaharit* and evening service and in the *aleinu* prayer which concludes every service. (We bow during the line *va-anahnu kor'im u-mishtahavim u-modim*, "We bend our knee and bow and acknowledge.")

Why bow? One understanding is that we are acting out the metaphor of God as king. As we approach the king we bow in obeisance before God's majesty and power. Another understanding sees the bowing as admitting that a world exists outside of ourselves. It acknowledges our own limitations. In support of this second interpretation is our custom of returning to an erect position when saying God's name. If the purpose of bowing is to bow before the king, then we should be bowing specifically at the mention of God. Instead, we stand erect, for we are not supposed to be fawning servants before the Almighty; rather we are to understand clearly that we are human beings, small specks in the universe which nonetheless carry a divine spark. We are humbled by our deficiencies and yet we stand facing the Holy One, for God desires partners in the work of creation.

*Other prayers* Berakhot include most of the essential elements of the liturgy. Other important prayers are the *aleinu* prayer at the conclusion of all services and the *kaddish*. The *kaddish* prayer, one of the few prayers recited in Aramaic, the common language of Jews in talmudic times, is a praise of God. It exists in a number of versions, the best-known of which is the mourner's *kaddish*. Though it does not speak about death, it is the widespread custom to recite this prayer after the death of an immediate relative (see p. 449). The *kaddish* is also used as a marker to conclude a large section of the service or to mark the imminent conclusion of a full service. As the former, the *kaddish* exists in a *hatzi kaddish*, "half *kaddish*," version. As the latter, the *kaddish* exists in its *kaddish shalem*, "full *kaddish*," version.

## An Outline of a Shabbat Morning Service

1. *Birkhot ha-shahar,* the morning blessings. This is a series of blessings related to awakening to the day. (For a fuller description see the first chapter of this book.)

2. *Pesukei de-zimra,* verses of praise. These are a number of Psalms or collected verses from Psalms, meant to be a preparation, a warm-up, for the main part of the service.

3. The Shema and its *berakhot.* This is the "Hear, O Israel" prayer, preceded and followed by blessings.

   a. *Barekhu,* "let us bless," an opening call to join in prayer.

   b. *Yotzer,* "creator of light," the first blessing, which is about God as creator and the daily renewal of the world.

   c. *Ahavah rabbah,* "with great love," the second blessing, whose theme is God's love for us as expressed through the gift of Torah.

   d. The Shema, "Hear, O Israel." This consists of three paragraphs from the Torah: Deut. 6:4–9, Deut. 11:13–21, and Num. 15: 37–41.

   e. *Emet ve-yatziv,* "your teaching is true and enduring," the blessing after the Shema that describes God as redeemer.

4. *Amidah,* the "standing" prayer, consisting of seven blessings.

   a. *Avot,* the "ancestors," focusing on the theme of the patriarchs' and matriarchs' relation to God.

   b. *Gevurot,* God's "power," focusing on the theme of how God's power is manifested in the world. Traditionally, this includes the belief in the resurrection of the dead. Reform and Reconstructionist prayer books change this blessing to focus on God as the source of life.

   c. *Kedushat ha-shem,* "God's holiness." This section includes the *kedushah* described above.

   d. *Kedushat ha-yom,* "the sanctity of the day." This central blessing focuses on the holiness of Shabbat or the festival as appropriate. On Shabbat, this blessing is different in each of the four services of the day.

   e. *Avodah,* "worship." This asks that our prayers be acceptable to God.

f. *Hoda'ah,* "thanksgiving." We are thankful for all the blessings of life. (In this blessing we bow twice as described above.)

g. *Birkat ha-shalom,* "prayer for peace."

The *amidah* is followed by a time for personal meditation. One of the rabbis of the Talmud composed a meditation, *elohai nitzor,* that is included in the prayer book as a beautiful model of a personal meditation, and also for recitation by those who are unprepared to offer their own meditation. It is often recited automatically, showing how the spontaneous prayer used as an example for others has instead become standard liturgy, obscuring this as a moment for spontaneous prayer.

When Shabbat coincides with a festival, Hallel, "Praise," is recited. This is a collection of Psalms (113–118) praising God. Otherwise the service continues with the second major part of Shabbat morning: the Torah reading.

5. The Torah reading begins with the singing of a number of verses that precede the taking of the Torah scroll out of the ark. The Torah is then carried through the congregation and brought to the reader's table. People are honored with *aliyot,* being called up to the Torah, which is then read to its cantillation. (For more details see "Torah: The Path of Study," pp. 139–75). After the Torah is read, it is lifted up and then wrapped. The reading from the Torah is followed by a chanted reading from the prophets, called the *haftarah.* (The *haftarah* is read from a printed book rather than a scroll.) The rabbis chose selections from the prophets based on the theme of each week's Torah reading. After the Torah service, the scroll is returned to its place in the ark.

6. In more traditional synagogues, the Torah reading is followed by *musaf,* the additional service. It is another *amidah* whose theme is the animal sacrifices in the Temple of Jerusalem. Many liberal synagogues, which do not believe in praying for the restoration of the sacrificial cult, have eliminated *musaf.* In either case, the service ends with a number of songs, the *aleinu* prayer, and the mourner's *kaddish.*

For more information, a good book to read is *Entering Jewish Prayer* by Reuven Hammer (Schocken, 1995).

## Garments of Prayer

A *kippah,* "skullcap" (*yarmulka* in Yiddish), was traditionally worn all the time by a man. This custom is still observed in the Orthodox community. In liberal communities it has become the custom in most synagogues for men to wear a *kippah* during prayer services. In some Reform synagogues the wearing of a *kippah* is optional. In the last few years some women have begun to wear a *kippah* in liberal synagogues (traditional women have long worn some form of head covering when attending the synagogue). The *kippah* is commonly understood as a reminder that there is "someone," i.e., God, above us.

There are also two ritual objects that are worn during prayer, specifically during *shaharit,* the morning service. The *tallit* is a prayer shawl. It is a rectangular piece of cloth with four corners. At each corner there are fringes tied in a specific manner. These *tzitzit,* "fringes," transform the garment into a *tallit.*

*The* **tallit**   Traditionally, the *tallit* was made of wool or linen. It was worn during morning services by men after they were married. Among liberal communities, the practice is for males to wear a *tallit* following their bar mitzvah. Some women also wear a *tallit* after their bat mitzvah. The *tallit* may be any combination of colors, but until recently it was most commonly white with black stripes. In modern times blue stripes have become common. Blue and white, the colors associated with the State of Israel and its flag, actually originated as the "Jewish colors" because of the *tallit.* In Numbers we find the source for *tzitzit* and *tallit:*

> The Lord spoke to Moses as follows: Speak to the Israelite people and instruct them to make for themselves fringes on the corners of their garments throughout the ages; let them attach a cord of blue to the fringe at each corner. That shall be your fringe; look at it and recall all the commandments of the Lord and observe them, so that you do not follow your heart and eyes in your lustful urge. [Num. 15:37–39]

The rabbinic tradition understood these verses to mean that you should put fringes, *tzitzit*, on any garment that had four corners. Specifically, they developed the notion of wearing a four-cornered fringed garment during prayer (though this idea is not in the biblical text). They also posited the notion of the *tallit katan*, the small *tallit* that is a four-cornered undershirt with *tzitzit*, which is still worn by Orthodox Jews. Originally, one of the fringes at each corner of the *tallit* was dyed blue, hence the blue-and-white color. According to the tradition, this blue dye had to be made from a particular snail found in the Mediterranean. Sometime after the destruction of the Second Temple in 70 C.E., the identity of the snail was lost (or perhaps the snail population had been so diminished by the dye trade that it was impossible to find enough snails of this type), and so it was decided to forgo the use of blue in the fringes. (In the eighteenth century, a Hasidic rebbe, Rabbi Gershon Henikh of Radzhin, claimed to have discovered the correct way to make the dye. His followers as well as a few others use blue fringes.)

In the late twentieth century, there began to be a greater diversity of materials and colors used in the cloth of the *tallit*. Weavers began producing *tallitot* (plural of *tallit*), making these new styles readily available. Different hues and even rainbow stripes became adopted by worshipers even in traditional communities, though the more conservative styles still predominate. As women began wearing *tallitot*, some experimented with departing from the traditional form of the *tallit* in order to distinguish between a man's and a woman's *tallit*. Yet all these variations shared having four corners and having the *tzitzit* tied in the traditional manner.

*Symbolism of the* tallit    The *tallit* helps the worshiper create an environment conducive to prayer just by marking the time to worship in a physical way. At times it conveys a sense of being enveloped in the surrounding divine, while at other times it simply encloses us, helping us focus on praying. It is for the latter reason that some people cover the top and sides of their head with a large *tallit* to block out any distractions.

It was traditional to think of the color blue in the *tallit* as a royal blue meant to remind us of God's kingship. In addition, the numerical value of the letters *(gematria)* of the word *tzitzit* is 600, which combined with the eight strings and five knots on each fringe adds up to 613, the traditional number of *mitzvot* in the Torah. Here, too, the symbolism is meant as a kind of focus, making us aware of the relationship between prayer and service to God.

The *tallit* is also known traditionally by its most important feature as the *arba kanfot*, "the four corners." A Hasid asked the Kotzker Rebbe what he should do, since he did not have a *tallit*. The Rebbe answered: Wrap yourself in the four corners of the world and then begin to pray.

*How to put on a* tallit   Most *tallitot* have an *atarah*, literally "a crown." This is an extra border of material often decorated with words or a special design. It also signifies the top of the *tallit*. This part of the *tallit* should rest on the back of your neck with the design facing out. To put on a *tallit*, hold it spread out in front of you and say the blessing for donning a *tallit*. Then wrap it around your shoulders as though you were putting on a cape. A scarf-shaped *tallit* will hang down your front from your shoulders as it rests on the back of your neck. A larger-size *tallit* may require you to take the ends hanging in front and fold them up so some of the shawl is doubled up on your shoulders and yet it still hangs down over your front. Some people wrap the *tallit* around their heads after saying the blessing and before resting it on their shoulders.

The *tallit* is only worn during morning services (except on Yom Kippur, when it is worn all day, and Tisha be-Av, when it is worn only in the afternoon). In many congregations, the person leading the afternoon service wears a *tallit*. In some congregations the leader wears it during the evening service as well.

### HOW TO TIE THE KNOTS

A set of *tzitzit*, or "fringes," can be purchased at a Jewish bookstore or on the Internet. Each set should be divided into four groups composed of one long string and three short strings. Take one group, line up all the strings at one end, and then fold in half, giving you eight strings. Thread the strings through the corner hole of the *tallit*. Seven should be approximately the same length, with one much longer. This eighth string, called the *shammash* or "guardian" (like the extra candle on the Hanukkah menorah), is used to wind around the others. Now, taking four strings in one hand and four in the other, make a double knot. The knot should be at the edge of the garment. Then wrap the long string around the other seven strings seven times. Try to begin and end the wrapping at the same spot so you have exactly seven wrappings. Make a double knot as before. Wrap the long string eight times around the others followed by a double knot. Then eleven times, double knot, thirteen times, and a double knot.

## Tefillin

Bind them as a sign on your hand and let them serve as a symbol on your forehead. [Deut. 6:8; see also Deut. 11:18, Exod. 13:16, 19]

This verse was traditionally understood not as a metaphor, but rather literally—that words of Torah should be bound upon the hand and head of the worshiper. *Tefillin* (literally, "prayer objects," but usually translated by the Greek-derived word *phylacteries*) are two little boxes, each containing four selections from the Torah. *Tefillin* are worn during morning services every weekday. The boxes have leather straps, which are used to attach one of the boxes to the arm and the other to the head.

The inside of the *tefillin* consists of four selections from the Torah, all of which mention *tefillin*. Two of these are also part of the Shema prayer. The verses are Exod. 13:1–10 and 13:11–16, and Deut. 6:4–9 and 11:13–21. They are written on parchment by a scribe, like the insert in the mezuzah and like the Torah scroll. In the *tefillin* of the hand they are on one parchment. In the *tefillin* of the head each passage is written on its own scroll and each scroll is in its own compartment.

Wearing *tefillin* is an ancient practice whose purpose is not made explicit. Certainly it can be a way to focus while praying. Putting the *tefillin* on the arm facing the heart and on your head is a way to bring hand, heart, and mind together. Similarly, it can be understood as a commitment to worship God with hand (deed), heart (intention), and mind (intellect).

***Putting on* tefillin**   Putting on *tefillin* is a little complicated and is best done following someone's example. The basic order is to put on the *tefillin* of the hand *(tefillin shel yad),* then the *tefillin* of the head *(tefillin shel rosh),* and then finish the wrapping of the straps around your fingers. When taking the *tefillin* off, you reverse the order.

1. Take the *tefillin* of the hand out of the bag in which it is stored. To facilitate this, it is customary to always put this *tefillin* on the left side of the bag. Unwrap the straps and remove the cover, if it has one.

2. Slip the *tefillin* up your forearm until it rests on top of the muscle. The tradition is to put the *tefillin* on your left arm, though someone who is a lefty, according to most halakhic authorities, wears *tefillin* on the right arm. The side with the straps should be closest to your body. The knot should be next to the box *(bayit)* of the *tefillin.* Then recite the *berakhah* (blessing). Tighten the strap by pulling on it through its loop. Wind it once around your upper arm to help keep the *tefillin* in place.

3. Wrap the strap clockwise seven times around your arm between your elbow and wrist. The black side of the strap should be visible. Then wrap the strap once around your palm, beginning with the outside of your hand. Wrap the remainder around the middle of your hand (palm). Finish by tucking the end under the wound strap (on the inside palm side of your hand).

4. Take the *tefillin* of the head out of the bag and unwind its strap and remove any cover. Holding the box in your hand, place it on your head. Its front edge should rest on your hairline (or where your hairline once was!). It should also be centered between your eyes. The back knot should rest on the nape of your neck at the back of your head. Then recite the blessing. Tighten the *tefillin* slightly by pulling down on

the straps on your head. The two loose straps that come from the knot should cross your shoulders and hang down over your chest to the waist. Some people tuck them through their belt to make sure that the black side remains facing out during services.

5. Release the strap on your hand and unwind it, leaving in place the first coil from your wrist to palm. Wrap it around your middle finger three times (twice between knuckle and hand, once above the knuckle). As you do each of these wrappings, recite the following verses: "And I will espouse you forever; I will espouse you with righteousness and justice, and with goodness and mercy. And I will espouse you with faithfulness; then you shall be devoted to the Lord" (Hosea 2:21–22). Then wrap the strap under the ring finger and over the hand, forming a V. Then wrap a strap between the other two (forming the Hebrew letter *shin*) and wrap any extra around this middle coil and finish by tucking the end under the strap (on the inner palm side).

To take *tefillin* off, basically do everything in reverse order. Unwind the straps on your hand and temporarily wrap it all around the middle of the hand. Then take off the *tefillin* of the head. Put on its cover and wrap the strap around the box. There is no prescribed way to do this wrapping. Put it back on the right side of the bag. Then unwrap the *tefillin* of the hand, remove it, cover it, and wrap it up and put it in the bag.

*A few pointers*    *Tefillin* are put on after putting on a *tallit* and taken off before taking off a *tallit*.

Nothing can be between your skin and the *tefillin*. Therefore, you need to roll up your sleeve and remove your watch from that hand.

Sephardic Jews have slightly different customs in regard to *tefillin*; for instance, they wrap the straps around the arm in a counterclockwise manner.

Sometimes people put a cover over the *tefillin* of the hand during services. While the *tefillin* of the head is supposed to be a "sign" and therefore visible to everyone, that of the hand can be covered even with a sleeve.

*Tefillin* are not worn on Shabbat or festivals, which are themselves a "sign" or reminder of the holy. There is a variety of customs about wearing *tefillin* during *hol ha-moed,* the intermediate days of Sukkot and Passover. Some do not wear them, some do, and some do but do not recite the blessings over them. If worn, they are removed after the *amidah* of *shaharit.* On Rosh Hodesh, *tefillin* are worn as usual but are removed before *musaf.*

*Tefillin* should be checked periodically by a scribe to make sure the writing hasn't faded, etc. Some people have them checked twice in seven years.

*Buying* tefillin    *Tefillin* are not inexpensive. Those that seem too cheap probably have Torah inscriptions that are mechanically reproduced instead of being handwritten by a scribe. According to traditional *halakhah,* only handwritten texts are "kosher." *Tefillin* themselves are made from the skin of a kosher animal. The boxes should be square with sharp corners. Deluxe *tefillin* are typically made out of a single piece of leather. When buying the *tefillin* you should have the straps adjusted to fit your head and check for any other necessary adjustments. There are variations in customs that dictate whether the knot at the back of the head should resemble the Hebrew letter *daled* or *heh.*

*Symbolism*    The manner in which the *tefillin* are wrapped spells out one of God's names: *Shaddai.* The letter *shin* is formed on the hand, The letters *daled* and *yood* are formed on the fingers or the *daled* is the knot on the nape of the neck and the *yood* is formed by the knot that is next to the box on the hand. The *shin* also appears on the box of the *tefillin* of the head. It is unusual, since it has four prongs rather than the usual three prongs. One interpretation is that is how the letter was written on the tablets of the Ten Commandments, which according to one tradition were incised all the way through the tablet so that they could be read from either side. Thus the four prongs create a regular *shin* in a "negative" image in the three spaces between them.

## A *KAVANAH* OF FOCUS AND CONNECTION

Before putting on a *tallit:*

"Wrap yourself in light as a garment, stretch out the heavens like a curtain" (Psalm 104:2). I gather myself to pray, drawing together my scattered attention in order to focus. I look for the light within me and in so doing I find that my individual self is connected to the universe stretched out before me.

While putting on *tefillin:*

I bring together my heart and my mind in order to help make the activities of this day ones of holiness. As I wrap the *tefillin* seven times on my arm, I pause at the appropriate number corresponding to the day of the week, thus reminding myself of the uniqueness of this day. Wrapping the *tefillin* on my weak hand reminds me that it is not strength or power, but rather the aligning of heart, mind, and deed that brings together the letters of God's name.

# GEMILUT HESED: THE PATH
# OF LOVING-KINDNESS

The world rests on three things: Torah, *avodah*, and *gemilut hesed*—
the study of Torah, worship, and deeds of loving-kindness. [*Ethics of
Our Ancestors* 1:2]

If Torah is meant to give us insights on how to act, and if worship
and prayer are meant to cultivate a certain attitude toward living in
the world, then *gemilut hesed* is about acting in the world. It is the actual doing of good deeds. It is how we interact with other people, which
is the ultimate test of whether we have assimilated the Torah that we
have learned and have meant the prayers that we uttered. While we
might study Torah or pray by ourselves (though the tradition encourages learning with a teacher and praying in a *minyan*), doing deeds of
loving-kindness by necessity involves dealing with the other people in
our lives. The ideal religious type in Judaism does not withdraw from
the world to become a hermit. Rather, just as God is believed (traditionally) to act in the world, so are we to strive to be caring and ethical
individuals.

How do we know this? The very beginning of the story of the Jewish
people starting with Abraham conveys to us the importance of acting in
the world according to the principle of caring. Abraham is told by God
to go forth to the land that God will show him. God promises Abraham, "I will make of you a great nation . . . and you shall be a blessing . . . and all the families of the earth shall bless themselves by you"
(Gen. 12:2–3). What that means is made clear in Genesis 18, when God
is about to destroy the wicked cities of Sodom and Gomorrah. God

says: "Shall I hide from Abraham what I am about to do, since Abraham is to become a great and populous nation and all the nations of the earth are to bless themselves by him? For I have singled him out, that he may instruct his children and his posterity to keep the way of the Lord by doing what is just and right, in order that the Lord may bring about for Abraham what God has promised him" (Gen. 18:17–19). Abraham is to instruct his children in *derekh Adonai,* the "way of the Lord." The way of the Lord consists of doing *tzedakah u-mishpat,* what is "just and right." We are created in the image of God not only because there is something holy within each human being, but because we are intended to act as God acts. The rabbis say: "Just as God is kind so should you be kind; just as God is merciful so should you be merciful; just as God is holy so should you be holy" (Talmud, *Shabbat* 133b).

This is the meaning of God's words at the beginning of Abraham's story. Go forth on the journey of your life and of the story of the Jewish people. If you remember to walk with justice and mercy, then you will not only be blessed, but you will become a blessing to all those you meet, for they will feel blessed by an encounter with you. Abraham immediately puts into practice this ideal by challenging God over whether the planned destruction of Sodom and Gomorrah is just and right.

The word *tzedek* or *tzedakah* encapsulates what is envisioned as the "way of the Lord." *Tzedakah* is commonly understood to mean "charity," which is helping the poor. Yet the two words *mishpat* (justice) and *tzedek* form a phrase meaning "righteousness and justice" in the sense of doing the right thing. While we are supposed to care for all human beings (and in fact all of God's creation), we are not to act merely out of caring but also out of a sense of justice and righteousness. All people deserve to have enough food to eat, clothes to wear, and so on. It is not our caring that should impel us to help bring this about, rather it should be our sense of social justice.

Yet the phrase used in our opening quotation is *gemilut hesed,* "deeds of loving-kindness," not *tzedakah,* "charity." Why? Because ultimately an even holier way is to act out of loving-kindness, that is, to go beyond what is required by justice. To act out of loving-kindness is to identify with other people, to feel for them, to want to help them or ease their burden even if simple justice would not require it. To act out of loving-kindness is to understand we are all lost in a broken world, yet together we can improve the journey of life. *Gemilut hesed* means to care even when it is "not deserved." It also means to understand that we all need deeds of loving-kindness to be done for us, not just the "poor."

> Our masters taught: Loving-kindness is greater than charity in three ways. Charity is done with one's money, while loving-kindness may be done with one's money or with one's person. Charity is given only to the poor, while loving-kindness may be given both to the poor and to the rich. Charity is given only to the living, while loving-kindness may be shown to both the living and the dead. [Talmud, *Sukkah* 49b]

This caring is reflected in another principle: *arevut,* a sense of "responsibility" toward others, derived from the verse "You shall not stand idly by the blood of your neighbor" (Lev. 19:16). We encountered this verse in the chapter on speech. It is a call to intervene in the face of injustice.

> Whence is it derived that if one sees her neighbor drowning in the sea, being dragged by an animal, or being waylaid by robbers— whence is it derived that she is obligated to save him? From: You shall not stand idly by the blood of your neighbor. [Talmud, *Sanhedrin* 73a]

American law does not hold a person liable for criminal prosecution for not attempting to save a drowning person. We may be critical of such a person, but no law was broken. Judaism, however, commands us to intervene, not to remain silent. We must try to save the drowning person if we can.

*Kol yisrael areivin zeh ba-zeh,* "All Israel is responsible one for the other," is an oft-quoted principle based on the traditional understanding of "You shall not stand idly by the blood of your neighbor." In the contemporary world that sense of responsibility has expanded to include not just all Jews, but the whole planet and all that is contained in creation.

## Tzedakah

R. Assi said: Charity equals in importance all the other precepts combined. [Talmud, *Bava Batra* 9a]

If, however, there is a needy person among you, one of your kinsmen in any of your settlements in the land that the Lord your God is giving you, do not harden your heart and shut your hand against your needy kinsman. Rather, you must open your hand and lend her sufficient for whatever she needs. [Deut. 15:7–8]

We are commanded to respond to those in need with an open hand. According to *halakhah*, we are to give a tithe—ten percent—of what we own to *tzedakah* annually. Anything less is considered ungenerous. You are allowed to give up to a fifth of your wealth, which is considered extra generous. While you cannot possibly support all those in need, the tradition lists priorities in terms of proximity. Thus your relatives should be your first priority, then the poor of your city, and so on in an ever-widening circle of concern. One strand in the tradition emphasizes the priority of the poor in the land of Israel over other poor.

The highest form of *tzedakah* is to help the needy to stand on their own two feet—for example, start their own business. Instead of sustaining the needy persons, this creates an opportunity to transform their lives by enabling them to leave a life of poverty behind.

Short of that, giving *tzedakah* should be governed by being attentive to the needs of the poor. First and foremost is to try to diminish the demeaning aspect of needing assistance in order to live. One way this can be accomplished is by giving anonymously so that the donor and the recipient do not know each other. This helps avoid the embarrassment of the recipient. Certainly if the giving is face-to-face, the recipient should be treated as another image of God. To give *tzedakah* in an ungracious manner undercuts what *tzedakah* is trying to accomplish. To treat the poor with anger, disgust, or even obvious pity diminishes their humanity (and yours as well). We are all equal as people, even if we are not financially equal.

Sensitivity to the poor extends to trying to pay attention to what they need, not just what you want to give. But that is not always simple. It comes down to cases—What does this particular poor person expect and what is his or her previous history?

Our masters taught: "[You must open your hand and lend] sufficient for her need" (Deut. 15:8). This implies that you are enjoined to maintain her, but you are not enjoined to make her rich; "in that which she wants" (ibid.) includes even a horse to ride on and a slave to run before her. It is related about Hillel the Elder that, for a certain poor person who was of a good family, he bought a horse to ride on and a slave to run before him. When on one occasion he could not find a slave to run before the person, he himself ran before him a distance of three miles. [Talmud, *Keritot* 67b]

A poor person came [for sustenance] before R. Nehemiah, who asked, "What do your usual meals consist of?" He answered, "Fat meat and aged wine." R. Nehemiah: "Will you join me and make do with a dish of lentils?" The poor person made do with lentils at R. Nehemiah's table, and then died. R. Nehemiah said, "Alas for this person: Nehemiah killed him!" . . . On the other hand, [the person himself was to blame]—he should not have coddled himself to such an extent. [Ibid.]

The second story encourages a concern for the requirements of the poor, while suggesting they should not have unrealistic expectations that become a burden on the community. Similarly, not every commentator thinks the Hillel story has to be taken as a directive on how we should act—it may be an extreme case. Yet it does suggest that we should take into account the emotional as well as the physical needs of the poor. Being poor is a dehumanizing experience that damages a person's sense of self-worth. Every time people ask for a handout can be a reminder that they are failures as breadwinners. The tradition teaches that even if we have no money to give to the person asking for help, we should respond in a caring way. This is a particular challenge to those of us living in cities where we may be confronted with homeless beggars daily. Do we try to pass by quickly so as to avoid them? If we are not giving, do we answer them? Even if we do respond by saying "Sorry, I can't help," do we avoid meeting their eyes?

Of course a much greater challenge is determining whether it is the right thing to do to give to particular street beggars. Are they fakes? Will they use the money for drugs? The tradition was very aware of fakes and had a naive belief that those who pretended to be poor would in the end become poor. For instance:

> If one is neither lame, nor blind, nor halt, but pretends to be like one of them, she will not die in her old age before she actually becomes one of them, as it is said, "He that searches for evil, it shall come unto him" (Prov. 11:27). [Jerusalem Talmud, *Peah* 8:5, 21b]

Despite this awareness, the tradition stated that if people ask for food, you should give them assistance. On the other hand if they ask for clothes, you could check out the situation first. This distinction is based on the sense that food is a need that should be immediately met, even though that means you will sometimes be giving to someone who is undeserving. On the other hand, while clothes are necessary, you are allowed enough time to determine whether the person is in actual need.

*Spiritual application*    How to apply these traditions to our contemporary situation is not clear. One could argue that the tradition did not foresee having such a large concentration of homeless in cities. For one thing, the number of poor and homeless can be overwhelming. Also, unlike in a small town or village, you do not know these poor people personally, making it much harder to determine the facts of their situation.

Nevertheless, the tradition certainly would require dealing with them in a humane way even if you will not be giving them assistance. All too often we respond, instead, out of guilt, frustration, annoyance, or all three.

Here are three personal accounts. I used to give money to a particular homeless person I encountered nearly daily. After a while I felt annoyed by this "obligation" and took to crossing the street to avoid him if possible. Then one day I decided to stop giving him money. Eventually, he asked me if he had done anything wrong to explain why I was angry at him. This only made me more confused about my own emotions and made me avoid him at all costs.

As a rabbi of an urban congregation, I would be approached by people walking in off the street to ask for money on an average of once a week. Often they would promise to pay the money back, going so far as to ask for an envelope with the synagogue's address. I never received one such envelope. I now fervently wish that when I give out money the recipients do *not* say anything about repayment.

On another hand, at a memorial service at my synagogue, a relative of the deceased rose to speak. While mourning the deceased, who had led a tragic life, he said: "I could empathize, since I also have had a hard life and one time I was helped through a difficult time by your rabbi giving me some money."

These and other experiences led me to reflect on my own feelings about giving *tzedakah* and about the recipients. Why was I bothered by my sense of obligation to the homeless person in the first story? Why could I not overcome my embarrassment to answer his question about what he had done wrong? Was I just being cheap? Was I bothered by a certain sense of entitlement? Was I worried that the money was being used for liquor or drugs? Did I simply want to be able to walk down the street and not have to deal with a whole bunch of questions and moral decisions?

Even when I was giving out *tzedakah* on behalf of the synagogue and it should have been simpler because it was not my money, it was still complicated. I think I did not want to hear about repayment because I did not want to say to myself, "Here is another liar." I felt my sense of humanity corrupted. I was becoming overly cynical.

Yet, the third story sharply reminded me that you never know what effect your deeds will have. Even as I felt good about hearing of the impact that one act of *tzedakah* had had, I learned another important lesson. This person would have been helped just as much if I had never heard that from him. The *tzedakah* was for him, not for me. My giving should be unrelated to any validation by the recipient.

What all three stories together taught me is that I needed to be aware of my personal issues related to the giving of *tzedakah*. I needed to remind myself constantly that each recipient is another image of God, not a member of a category of people known as homeless or poor. I am not God, so I can never be certain who is worthy and who is a fraud. I must give without that certainty and without knowing the impact of my giving. My challenge is to be helpful to each person I meet and to watch my own responses in order to better remain in a place of openheartedness.

Consider these two talmudic stories.

It is related of Nahum of Gamzo that he was blind in both eyes, stumped in both hands, and crippled in both legs; his entire body was covered with boils. The legs of his bed stood in four basins of water to prevent ants from crawling all over him. Once, when his bed was in a house about to collapse, his disciples proposed first removing the bed and then clearing the furniture out of the house, but he said to them, "My children, remove the furniture first and then remove my bed, for you may be sure that so long as I am in the house it will not collapse." So they cleared out the furniture, then removed his bed, and in the next instant the house collapsed. His disciples asked, "Master, since you are so perfectly righteous, why has all this [affliction] come upon you?" He replied, "My children, I invoked it upon myself. Once I was journeying to my father-in-law and had with me three heavily laden asses, one with food, and another with drink and the third with all kinds of delicacies. A poor man appeared and stopped in front of me on the road, saying, 'Master, give me something to sustain me.' I replied, 'Wait until I unload the ass.' I had barely managed to unload the ass when the man died [of hunger]. I then threw myself over him and said, 'Let these eyes of mine which had no pity upon your eyes be blinded, let these hands of mine which had no pity upon your hands be stumped, let these legs of mine which had no pity upon your legs be crippled!' Nor could my soul rest thereafter, until I added, 'Let my whole body be covered with boils.' " [Talmud, *Taanit* 21a]

R. Yohanan and Resh Lakish went down to bathe in the public baths of Tiberias. When a poor person met them and said to them, "Earn merit by giving me something," they replied, "After we come out, we shall earn merit through you." When they did come out, they found him dead. So they said, "Since we did not earn merit by attending to him in his life, let us attend to him in his death." As they were washing his corpse [in preparation for burial], they found a bag containing six hundred dinars suspended from his neck. So [relieved of the feelings of guilt] they said, "Blessed be God who has chosen the sages and even their [hasty] words. Did not R. Abbahu state in the name of R. Eliezer, 'We ought to be grateful to imposters, since but for imposters among the poor, if anyone begged alms from a person and that person refused, he would immediately be punished.' " [Midrash, *Leviticus Rabbah* 34:10]

You just never know. We live in a world of uncertainty. How then should we deal with those begging for help? You may choose to give a little bit to everyone who asks. Or you may choose to give to one or two people consistently, thus participating in the giving of *tzedakah* without being overwhelmed by numbers. This also allows you to have a relationship of sorts with particular people. It could be seen as based on the principle of giving precedence to the poor of your city over the needy of other cities. Or you could use a different narrowing category, such as giving money only on particular days, as on Friday in preparation for Shabbat.

Some people feel that they are doing what is best when they buy food for the poor, thereby eliminating their concern about giving money and not being sure how it will be spent. A variation is to give out a coupon that can be redeemed for groceries at a local supermarket or food at a fast-food restaurant. And, of course, when you choose not to give, the tradition reminds us to decline in a way that is respectful, remembering that everyone is created in the image of God.

Shammai said: Receive all people with a cheerful countenance. What does this mean? It means that if a person presents the most precious gifts in the world to another person, but with a sullen and downcast countenance, Scripture regards that person as though she presented nothing at all to the other person. On the other hand, a person who receives everyone with a cheerful countenance, even if she gives them nothing—Scripture accounts it to her as though she had presented them with the most precious gifts in the world. [*Ethics of Our Ancestors* 1:15; *Avot de-Rabbi Natan* 13]

**Tzedakah tatzil mi-mavet,** *charity saves from death*    The tradition considers *tzedakah* a critical component of Jewish ethics.

R. Judah used to say: Ten strong things have been created in the world. The [rock of the] mountain is hard, but iron cleaves it. Iron is hard, but fire softens it. Fire is powerful, but water quenches it. Water is heavy, but clouds bear it. Clouds are thick, but wind scatters them. Wind is strong, but a body resists it. The body is strong, but fear crushes it. Fear is powerful, but wine banishes it. Wine is strong, but sleep works it off. Death is stronger than all, yet charity delivers from death, as it is written, "Charity saves from death" (Prov. 10:2). [Talmud, *Bava Batra* 10a]

What can it mean to say that "charity saves from death"? In a short story entitled "Charity" by Hugh Nissenson, the author portrays a poor Jewish immigrant family on the Lower East Side. Despite their poverty, the father brings a beggar home every Friday night for Shabbat. The young son resents the imposition of these beggars. One week the mother becomes ill and is rushed to the hospital. The son, alone with his father, can't believe that his father still brings home a beggar for that Shabbat. In a late-night conversation the boy says to his father that he feels confident that his mother will be fine. When the father asks why, the son replies that he knows this from the father, who is constantly saying, "Charity saves from death."

His father angrily replies, "Is that what you think a *mitzvah* [commandment] is? A bribe offered to the Almighty?"

"But you said so," the boy insists. "You said that charity saves from death."

The father answers, looking at the poor guest, "No, not Mama, him."

For the father this notion that charity saves from death is simple and direct. If you feed a hungry person, you save that person from starving. The father is also rejecting some cosmic scorecard notion; that is, if you do enough good deeds, then you can collect from God at an opportune moment. Yet, while certainly the recipient of *tzedakah* can be literally saved from death, something greater is conveyed by that expression. The Midrash emphasizes that *tzedakah* is more powerful than even death. It is a misunderstanding to think that *tzedakah* can end death in the world. Rather the Midrash is positing that in the face of all the harsh realities of the world, death being the ultimate harsh reality, *tzedakah* does change the world. *Tzedakah* can make a difference. In making a difference, it changes the life of the giver as well as that of the recipient. The giver too is engaged in an act of life. This is true even when life is not literally hanging in the balance. Every act of *tzedakah* is an act of life in the face of death. It is a moment of caring, of healing, of openheartedness, and most simply of connection between two human beings.

R. Joshua taught: More than what a householder does for the poor person, the poor person does for the householder. [Midrash, *Leviticus Rabbah* 34:9]

*Tzedakah* also saves one other from death: God. If we believe that God acts through human beings and/or that God wants us to repair the world from its brokenness, then we need to give *tzedakah* so that God or Holiness does not "die" from this world.

R. Judah son of R. Simeon said: The poor person sits and complains, saying, "How am I different from So-and-so? Yet she sits in her own house, while I sit here; she sleeps in her own house on her own bed, while I sleep on the bare ground." So you come forward and give her something. Then, as you live, I [God] will deem it as though you had made peace between her and Me. [Midrash, *Leviticus Rabbah* 34:16; *Yalkut, Isa.* #496]

In this teaching, we are called to make this world a better place on behalf of God. Every poor person is a critique of the notion of God's goodness. We can make a difference. *Tzedakah* can fill lives with hope rather than despair.

*Extraordinary* tzedakah  While the tradition establishes an appropriate range of giving as described above, there are many stories of unlimited generosity:

> Abba the Cupper used to receive daily greetings from the academy on high. What was the special merit of Abba the Cupper? When he let blood, he had a discreet place outside [his office] where the client would put in a few coins. Whoever had money would put it there; but he who had none would sit before Abba the Cupper without feeling embarrassed. Whenever a disciple of the wise came to consult him, he would accept no fee from him, and after the disciple stood up to leave, Abba would give him a few coins and say to him, "Go and get yourself well."
>
> One day, Abbaye sent two disciples to Abba in order to test him. They came to his house, and he had them sit down, gave them food and drink, and in the evening spread woolen mattresses for them [to sleep on]. In the morning, the two disciples rolled up the mattresses and brought them to the marketplace. When Abba the Cupper came to the marketplace and found the two, they said to him, "Sir, will you estimate how much they are worth?" He replied, "So-and-so much." The two: "Surely they are worth more?" Abba: "This is what I paid for some like them." Then they said to him, "They are yours—we took them away from you."
>
> Then they asked him, "Please tell us what you supposed we were up to?" He replied, "I said to myself: Perhaps you needed money to redeem captives and were too embarrassed to say so to me." The two: "Now, sir, take back what is yours." Abba: "From the moment I missed them, I put them out of my mind by considering them assigned to charity." [Talmud, *Taanit* 21b-22a]

*Creating a* tzedakah *giving practice*  For a successful practice you need to set a charitable goal for the year and create some organized system of regular giving. Such a practice will involve responding to requests for money as well as taking the initiative in finding worthwhile charities. We are requested to give money to people on the street and to the numerous organizational requests that come in the mail. Some of the dilemma regarding giving to homeless people was discussed above. Thinking through to whom and how much you will give on the street is helpful. Reflecting on your experience can change your future practice. Similarly, you need to evaluate to which appeals you will respond. Most if not all the mail appeals are for worthy causes. Will you give a small gift to all those that have any interest to you or will you select out a smaller number for large donations? Are you on the lookout through newspaper articles, etc., for new organizations that are doing work that seems especially worthwhile?

Some people stack up the requests and then make all the decisions at once, especially at the end of the tax year. Others find that writing all your *tzedakah* checks in the last weeks of December (in the United States) is too much of a sudden bite out of your budget. They find it better to give throughout the year and then calculate at the end of the year how much more they have to give to meet their charitable goal. Some make a point of giving each month as they pay bills.

A *pushka* is a container like a piggy bank for the collection of small donations to *tzedakah*. Having one prominently placed in your home is both a statement of your values and a convenient reminder to give. Some people have a *pushka* from a particular organization such as the blue-and-white box of the Jewish National Fund. Others have a generic *pushka* and decide periodically to whom the money collected should go. *Pushkas* come in a variety of styles and mediums and contemporary Judaic craftspeople have created some beautiful new designs. Some people have a regular time for putting money in the *pushka*. One such time is on Friday afternoon before Shabbat. People will empty their change (traditionally money is not used on Shabbat and part of the preparation for Shabbat is emptying your pockets) into the *pushka*. Other traditional times to give are at the end of weekday daily services in the synagogue. There are certain Jewish holidays that are particularly associated with the giving of *tzedakah*. These include Yom Kippur (another good deed cannot hurt before the Day of Judgment); Purim, because a line in the scroll of Esther refers to gifts to the poor; and

Passover, because the tradition recognizes that kosher-for-Passover food can be expensive and an additional burden on the poor (this *tzedakah* is known as *ma'ot hittin*, money for bread or *matzah*).

More broadly, there is a tradition that at moments of joy and celebration such as weddings, the less fortunate are remembered. A number of decades ago a new organization called Mazon was formed based on that tradition. Mazon encourages people to donate three percent of the cost of the food at their *simha* (celebration) to Mazon, which in turn gives grants to food relief projects across North America. Their address is 1990 S. Bundy Dr., Suite 260, Los Angeles, CA 90025-5232.

### Acts of Loving-kindness

R. Hama son of R. Hanina said: "After the Lord your God shall you walk" (Deut. 13:5). But is it possible for a human being to walk right behind the Presence? Has it not already been said, "The Lord your God is a devouring fire" (Deut. 4:24)? Yes, but what the verse means is that you are to follow the ways of the Holy One. God clothed the naked: "The Lord God made for Adam and for his wife garments of skin, and clothed them" (Gen. 3:21). So should you clothe the naked. The Holy One visited the sick: "The Lord appeared unto him [Abraham] in the terebinths of Mamre" (Gen. 18:1). So should you visit the sick. The Holy One buried the dead: "God buried [Moses] in the valley" (Deut. 34:6). So should you bury the dead. [Talmud, *Sotah* 14a]

Ultimately an attitude of responsibility and caring needs to be translated into deeds. God is portrayed as modeling for us how we are to act. Visiting the sick, clothing the naked, burying the dead, comforting the mourner, and providing hospitality are among the general categories of deeds of loving-kindness. They share in common a concern for people in need who can benefit from a caring response.

*Cultivating a practice of* gemilut hesed  There are numerous occasions for practicing *gemilut hesed*, "deeds of loving-kindness." It can be the basis for how we interact with all the people in our lives. We begin by trying to be attentive to what we say and do and how that affects others. We broaden that concern to be attentive to how other people in our lives are treating each other. Do we let someone in our workplace be the butt of everyone's humor or be treated unfairly by coworkers? Are we complicit in our silence? Often the hardest places to stand up for what is right and just are not in the public arena but in our jobs, communities, and families. The circle of *gemilut hesed* must eventually be enlarged to include those in the world, whether nearby or across the globe, who need support or assistance. No one can support every worthy cause in the world; therefore choose one or a few that speak most directly to you, and become involved beyond just writing a check.

Recently I felt my own lack of direct involvement in *gemilut hesed* beyond donating money and what I did professionally as a rabbi. I heard about a national program to improve the literacy of students in public schools. It involved volunteering for an hour a week to read with a third-grader. It appealed to me because I thought that here was a simple but potentially effective way to have an impact on a major problem in our society—a growing gap in the educational skills required to get good jobs in an increasingly information-based economy. I have often felt discouraged from engaging in social justice on an issue like homelessness, which seemed if not unsolvable at least without an obvious solution. The Jewish Community Center in Manhattan was the local coordinator for the Jewish community of this program. I volunteered and encouraged members of my congregation to volunteer. I began going to the local public school every Wednesday morning at eleven a.m. to read with my assigned student, Nicholas. The first day I met him, I was shyer than he was. He seemed completely comfortable with this tall stranger reading with him week after week.

Truth be told, there were days I felt too busy to go, but I still went. There were moments when I hoped for some obvious breakthrough, some epiphany like Nicholas bringing in *War and Peace* to read, but of course nothing like that happened. I never knew for sure, never had proof that what I did made a difference. I learned that doing a good deed means acting without knowing the results of that action. It is the definition of doing a *mitzvah lishmah,* "a good deed for its own sake." There is no heavenly chorus proclaiming your virtue on high. And so I went each week all year. Why? It comes down to a word that modern Jews don't like to use very much, *emunah*, "faith."

The Hebrew word *emunah* has an interesting origin. In the Bible, we are told that the Israelites, after leaving Egypt and even before reaching Sinai, were attacked by Amalek. In Jewish tradition Amalek has come to symbolize everything in the world that stands in opposition to the Divine, the holy, and basic goodness. In a surprise attack, Amalek strikes down the weary stragglers bringing up the rear of the Israelite march. In response, Joshua leads the Israelite army in a counterattack. Moses stands on a hill overlooking the fighting, holding a staff raised in both hands. When the staff is raised the Israelites are victorious, but as Moses gets tired his hands and the staff droop and the Israelite army starts losing. Then two people stand on either side of Moses supporting his hands. The Hebrew text reads *va-yehi yadav emunah ad bo ha-shemesh,* "and his hands were *emunah* until sunset." *Emunah* clearly doesn't mean "faith" here, but rather "steady," with a steadiness resting on the support of others. From this specific physical meaning in the Bible, *emunah* then comes to mean a steadiness, an assurance based on support, hence a faith, an ability to rely on one another. When you have faith, you are not alone.

We live in a world that is filled with many who are tired and straggling, falling ever further behind the progress of society. Weighed down by poverty and discrimination, and with the deck stacked against them, they are easy prey for Amalek, the enemy of our common humanity. How do we fight Amalek? By standing by the side of those who are struggling and supporting them, helping them hold up their hands as they stretch to reach for all that they can be. Our hands joined with theirs will be enough so that they are *emunah*, feeling supported and secure in the faith, the *emunah*, that the future still remains open, that they are still on a journey that can lead to a promised land, that all is not lost by the time that they have finished third grade.

In the end I went every Wednesday at eleven a.m. to spend an hour with Nicholas. I had *emunah* that this was the most significant insignificant-seeming activity that I did all year. I also came to a new understanding of the concept of a *mitzvah*. A *mitzvah* is not an obligation but a privilege and an opportunity to make a difference.

We are taught: The reason Adam was created alone in the world is to teach you that whoever destroys a single soul, Scripture imputes it to him as though he had destroyed the entire world; and whoever keeps alive a single soul, Scripture imputes it to him as though he had preserved the entire world. [Talmud, *Sanhedrin* 37a]

What we do makes a difference. Perhaps it is not as big a difference as we would like. Sometimes it may not even make any difference to the one we intended to help. But, *it always makes a difference to us*. We need to cultivate an open heart and a generous hand for our own spiritual well-being and be ready to help when those qualities might make a difference to those in need of an act of *gemilut hesed*.

### Tikkun Olam

R. Dostai son of R. Yannai preached: Pause and consider that the way of the Holy One is not like the way of flesh and blood. How does flesh and blood act? If a person brings a substantial present to the king, it may or may not be accepted; and even if it is accepted, it remains doubtful whether the person will be admitted into the king's presence. Not so with the Holy One. A person who gives but a small coin to a beggar is deemed worthy of being admitted to behold the Presence, as it is written, "I shall behold Your face through charity" (Psalm 17:15). [Talmud, *Bava Batra* 10a]

Ultimately, *gemilut hesed,* an attitude of caring response, becomes an integral part of a striving for *tikkun olam*, "a repairing of the world." Our responsibility is to bring the world a step closer to a place of peace, bounty, and happiness for all. The concept of *tikkun olam*, adapted from the Kabbalists, sees us living in a shattered world. The world is littered with broken hopes and shattered dreams. We all live in exile from each other and most of all from ourselves. Acts of *tzedakah,* of caring concern, of social justice, help move the cosmos a little closer to a perfected world. This is our challenge. To recognize ourselves in the other. To respond with caring. To remember those in need who are not directly in our line of sight. To champion the oppressed without demonizing the oppressor.

A life of Torah or of prayer is not enough. A life of caring is necessary. Torah can help infuse difficult decisions with wisdom. Prayer can help remind us that we are on a spiritual path, and can give us strength to engage in the struggle for justice. However, neither can change the world. Only deeds of loving-kindness can help bring about God's vision for the world.

R. Eleazar said: People who execute charity and justice are as though they have filled the entire world, all of it, with loving-kindness, as is said, "When one loves charity and justice, the earth is full of the loving-kindness of the Lord" (Psalm 33:5). [Talmud, *Sukkah* 49b]

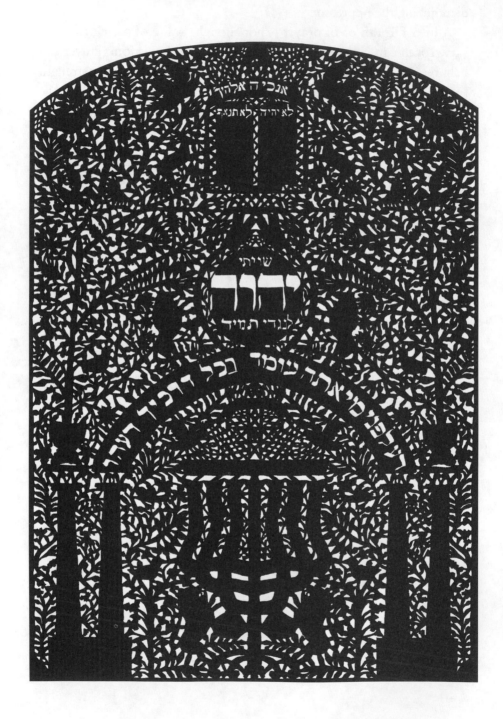

Part Three

# LIVING
# THROUGH
# THE YEAR:
# THE FESTIVALS

# THE FESTIVALS

In our lives, we are all ceaseless time-travelers as we move from moment to moment, event to event . . . yet time whizzes by until suddenly we approach our end of days.

The Jewish people, perhaps because we have done so much traveling in space, have developed a map for traveling in time. Called the "festival cycle," this map has its origin in the Torah and has continued to develop and change even in our era. The special days of the festival cycle are not random moments scattered over the year, but purposeful occurrences that draw their power from multiple sources—the natural world and its seasons, myth, religious traditions, folk customs, and decisive historical events in the life of our people. As such, the festivals operate on several levels at one and the same time, and hence can serve as a guide for travelers moving through the several dimensions of existence. One can also say that the festivals act as lodgings for travelers making their way through the year. These festival inns are special accommodations not solely for rest or retreat from the world, but also places to halt and take our bearings to make sure we are traveling and not just going around in circles. These are inns not for sleeping but rather awakening from obliviousness. The cycle comes to remind us both of eternal nature and its order, and the ever-recurring history of an eternal people. Even more fundamentally, the festival cycle causes us to focus on how our human life cycle parallels that of the natural and historical cycles of this world. The festivals bring us into contact with the great human themes of food, shelter, and security; birth, growth, and death; freedom and responsibility; the earthly and transcendent.

It is part of the richness of the festival cycle that any one holiday can mean different things to different people. Each of us will find that some holidays will speak more clearly than others at different times in our lives; however, each also provides a sustaining continuity to our lives as we celebrate it once again. [From *The Jewish Holidays*]


A number of years ago I wrote a book entitled *The Jewish Holidays: A Guide and Commentary* (Harper and Row, 1985). Space limitations alone would prevent me from including everything I covered in that large volume. I encourage you to read that book if you want a fuller guide to the practice and meaning of the holidays. Yet no guide to Judaism as a spiritual practice could be complete without reference to the Jewish holidays. Our focus here is on the spiritual messages of the holidays and how you can approach the sacred through this elegant map of the spirit.

# THE JEWISH CALENDAR

The Jewish calendar is basically a lunar calendar, with each month being approximately twenty-nine and one-half days long. As this is calculated, some months have twenty-nine and some have thirty days. Rosh Hodesh is a minor holiday that marks the beginning of each new month, as Shabbat marks the end of each week.

Since the lunar year is approximately eleven days shorter than the solar year, the Jewish calendar is constantly adjusted to keep holidays in their correct seasons. This is done by adding a "leap" month (Adar Sheni, the "second" Adar) on a regular basis. Without this adjustment, for example, Pesah eventually would occur in the winter and lose its connection to spring. The difference between the lunar and solar calendars explains why Jewish holidays vary in their dates on the secular Gregorian calendar, so that Pesah can shift from the beginning to the end of April from year to year.

Most Jewish holidays can be characterized as *yom tov,* "festival." This means that in many ways they are similar to Shabbat. Work is prohibited, candles are lit, and *kiddush* is recited. Rosh ha-Shanah, Yom Kippur, the first day(s) of Sukkot, Shemini Atzeret and Simhat Torah, and the first and last day(s) of Pesah and Shavuot are in this category. There are some major differences in regard to the prohibitions of Shabbat and festivals. Certain kinds of work needed to prepare food are permitted during festivals. Thus, using fire (lit from an existing fire), cooking, and carrying are all generally permitted. However, all the other categories of work are prohibited on festivals.

Pesah and Sukkot are distinguished by intermediate days between their beginning and their end. These are called *hol ha-moed,* "normal days of the holiday." Work restrictions generally do not apply. However, the holiday customs still apply. Eating *matzah* during Pesah and taking meals in the *sukkah* and waving the four species during Sukkot continue being observed during these otherwise "normal" days. In addition, Sukkot has its own unique structure as a holiday. Its last day, Hoshana Rabbah, while having its own special rituals, is not a final festival day. The observance of Shemini Atzeret and Simhat Torah, which immediately follows, serves as the end of Sukkot even though it is an independent festival.

The festival calendar differs in Israel and in the Diaspora. In Second Temple times, the calculation of holiday dates depended on the testimony of eyewitnesses before the high court in Jerusalem as to when the new month began. Following the decision, a variety of methods were used to carry the official dates to the Diaspora. As the Diaspora became more far-flung, it became impossible to communicate with Diaspora communities in a timely fashion. To eliminate any doubt, the rabbis established *yom tov sheni shel galuyot,* "the second festival day of the Diaspora." Thus, in the Diaspora, there are two festival days at the beginning and end of Pesah, making Pesah eight days rather than the seven prescribed in the Bible. Similarly, Shavuot and Shemini Atzeret/Simhat Torah are two days instead of one. Sukkot also begins with two festival days. Rosh ha-Shanah was also observed for two days in the Diaspora, but Yom Kippur remained one day because of the necessity of fasting. In Israel, the extra days of the festivals were not observed. (Rosh ha-Shanah is observed for two days in Israel for other reasons.) The institution of the "second day" continued even after the calendar was regularized for both Israel and the Diaspora. In modern times the Reform and Reconstructionist movements have mostly eliminated the second day, and some Reform congregations only observe one day of Rosh ha-Shanah. Practice varies among Conservative synagogues. For a good explanation of Conservative practice, see *Conservative Judaism* 24, no. 2 (winter 1970).

# PESAH/PASSOVER

Pesah commemorates the Exodus from Egypt and marks the real beginning of the covenant between God and the Jewish people. Over and over, the Torah reminds us that the covenant rests on the fact that God "took us out of the land of Egypt."

Pesah's most striking feature revolves around food. We are forbidden to eat any bread during the holiday. Instead, we are commanded to eat special bread, *matzah*, that is unleavened. Bread that is allowed to rise (leavened), which is perfectly "kosher" all during the year, may not be eaten or even owned during Pesah. This has led to intensive rules about what is permitted and forbidden during Pesah as well as requiring an extensive spring cleaning to remove any trace of *hametz*, leavened bread, from our homes.

The major ritual of Pesah is the Seder, a meal that involves symbolic foods and the reading of the Haggadah. This recital, with its accompanying rituals, is intended to enable us to "relive" the experience of the Exodus from Egypt. We are not just to remember the events of the past, we are to see this experience as though we personally were slaves in Egypt and were redeemed. It is a remarkably ambitious notion. Through the eating of foods that symbolize the bitterness of slavery and the joy of freedom, we are to ingest these experiences. Through a retelling of the story, we are to reappropriate this ancient tale not just as the experience of our people but as our own individual experience. We are provoked by the text and the rituals to question, for in questioning what is, we begin the journey to freedom. All this is in order for us to understand that the struggle against slavery and for freedom is an

eternal one, until a time when everyone in the world will reside in a vision called Jerusalem, city of peace.

## Getting Ready

Perhaps Pesah requires the most extensive preparation because so does
liberation. Lest we think that slavery only comes in some obvious form
of chains and Pharaohs, Pesah asks us to see the most common element
of our life, bread, as enslavement. It suggests that while slavery can be
found everywhere and in everything, perhaps most of all it is found in
the routine of the everyday. Slavery can be found in the rote repetition
of activities that leads us to sleepwalk through existence. Instead, Pesah
calls us to reexamine our daily routine by making us change our most
basic element, bread, the staff of life. Nothing is to be accepted as is;
rather, all is to be held up for examination and reflection. This process
is not meant as a rejection of who we are and what we do; rather it is to
lead to a renewal of our daily lives. After all, once Pesah is over, we go
back to eating bread. Our goal is not to reject bread but to renew our
priorities, to provide a greater appreciation for what we have and to remind us of all that we have yet to accomplish. We begin the cycle of the
festival year with a holiday that comes to shake us out of our smugness
and to remind us that the God of Israel calls us to work for the liberation of all people, including ourselves.

The first stage of Pesah preparation involves the removal of *hametz,*
"leaven." Traditionally, all leavened bread (grain) and leavening agents
(yeast) are strictly forbidden on Pesah. This prohibition involves even
owning *hametz,* thereby necessitating the removal of all *hametz* from
the household. As in other aspects of our spiritual lives, we need to develop a personal practice in regard to removing *hametz.* I have found it
helpful to begin with the idea that removing *hametz* should help us
focus on the themes of slavery and liberation. Since *hametz* is the food
we eat all year long, it is strange to turn it into a great evil for one week
a year.

There are two strands of thinking regarding the evil of *hametz.* One
sees something intrinsically wrong with *hametz* and focuses on the difference between *hametz* and *matzah. Hametz* is dough that has been

allowed to rise, that has been "puffed up." *Hametz* then is seen as symbolic of pride, that which leads to an exaggerated sense of self. Passover is a call to return to a simpler sense of self, one that is not artificially inflated. In the context of the Passover story, it reminds us that Pharaoh was filled with a hubris that led to destruction. Instead of being like Pharaoh, who thought of himself as a god, we are to remember that there are things more powerful than any Pharaoh or than ourselves. The force of nature represented by the plagues is one. The power of resistance to injustice as represented by the midwives is another. Finally, God as redeemer represents all that is beyond us that brings about positive change in the world. Thus, in this view, the purpose of the removal of *hametz* is to bring us to a clearer sense of self and place in the world. We can be significant players in the world—as were the midwives and Moses—but we should always remember our limitations and our mortality and not become Pharaohs.

Another strand focuses on the fermenting nature of yeast. *Hametz* is that which stirs things up. In traditional terms, *hametz* is symbolic of the *yetzer ha-ra,* "the evil inclination." The evil inclination is what encourages the worst aspects of ourselves—our fears, our hardheartedness, and our lust. It is that which makes us act less generously and openheartedly toward others as well as that which makes us think negatively about ourselves. Those moments when we look deep inside and see only flaws and failures are the times when the evil inclination is at its most powerful. Getting rid of *hametz* then is an attempt to quiet the evil inclination and to see with clarity who we really are. Of course, we are deeply flawed, but we also try to be good people. The Passover story demonstrates how the evil inclination can lead to a dead end. We can see how every bad step took Pharaoh deeper toward destruction. His life is an example of the self-destructiveness of the evil inclination unchecked. By contrast, Moses grows up in the palace, yet discovers his place with the oppressed. He fashions a life of growing awareness. He turns aside to notice the burning bush and sees that it remains unconsumed. Though he yearns to flee from responsibility, in the end he accepts the burden of leadership.

Most of all, the Pesah story is a story of change. The mighty power of Egypt is humbled. An enslaved people are freed. Once a year, we remember that real change is possible. Having reached that understanding during Passover, we can return to the regular world by eating *hametz*. Hopefully we will emerge with a clearer sense of self, a vision of purpose, and the knowledge that change is within our grasp.

There is another strand in the tradition that does not consider *hametz* as evil. It asks, Why is something permissible fifty-one weeks a year suddenly prohibited? Why are we not only forbidden to eat *hametz* but even to possess it? The answer may be that we are prohibited from owning *hametz* to remind us that slavery lies among our possessions. The things we possess often possess us. *Hametz* may represent the way possessions lead to servitude. Are we working in order to acquire the necessities we need to live or in order to support ourselves in a style we covet? Is acquiring the only way we can measure our success? What do we really want, and is it reflected in or distorted by what we have? The prohibition of *hametz* asks us to reexamine not only our expensive electronic equipment, summer homes, and mammoth gas-guzzling vehicles, but our most basic possession, our food. By asking that we not just refrain from eating *hametz* but also diligently remove it from our homes, the tradition tells us that slavery cannot be successfully put aside for a week. It is too easy just to hide it away; rather we must remove it from our homes, from our lives. We must be freed from all the things that we think we possess, but which in fact possess us.

Taking something like *hametz* that is normally permitted, making it evil, and prohibiting it, causes us to question our basic assumptions about the certainties in our lives. Passover's symbols are complex. The *haroset*, the dip for the bitter herbs, reminds us of the mortar that joined the bricks of slavery, yet its purpose is to sweeten the bitterness of *maror*. *Matzah*, the central symbol of Passover, is both the bread of freedom eaten by the Israelites rushing to leave Egypt and also the "bread of affliction," the cheap but filling food given to slaves in Egypt. The rabbis remarked that the Hebrew words *hametz* and *matzah* were very similar. Closing a little space in the letter *heh* in *matzah* would make the letters identical. Pesah shows us that little separates the prohibited from the permitted, the slave from the free. From this we are to understand how easy it is to slip from freedom to slavery, and how important it is for us to seek freedom and guard it vigilantly.

We are to strive for freedom not only for ourselves but for all people everywhere. The Torah states, "You shall not oppress a stranger, for you know the feelings of the stranger, having yourself been strangers in the land of Egypt" (Exod. 23:9). And "You shall not abhor an Egyptian because you were a stranger in his land" (Deut. 23:8). We are exhorted to remember the experience of slavery in Egypt. That remembering is freedom's permanent clarion call. We are not to treat anyone as a stranger, for we ourselves were strangers. We know how easy it is to de-personalize the stranger, to be tempted to treat the stranger as less than us. Even the Egyptians who enslaved us are created in the image of God. Nevertheless, the Egyptian is not to be oppressed. Why not? Are we supposed to forgive and forget? It is rather that to continue to hate the Egyptian would mean to be enslaved by that hatred. We would be stuck to each other in a way that allows neither of us to move on. We need to move on without hate, a sense of martyrdom, or moral superiority. Pesah reminds us to use our lesson of freedom wisely: by ensuring freedom for all. From Egypt, we go forth carrying only *matzah* and a desire for freedom.

## Physical Preparation

Traditional Jews prepare for Passover by disposing of all *hametz*. This includes bread, pasta, crackers, etc. Even products that contain such ingredients, such as liquor and many processed foods, are forbidden. This usually means getting rid of most regular food, so it requires a thorough cleaning of the home. The laws of *kashrut* require special Passover dishes, silverware, pots and pans, and so on. Some people use Pesah as an opportunity to bring unopened boxes of *hametz* to a local food pantry. Many people wind down their purchases of *hametz* a few weeks before the holiday. If you have too much *hametz* to get rid of, there is a practice called *mehirat hametz*, "the selling of *hametz*," in which *hametz* is sold to a non-Jew (usually only for the period of the holiday). This "sale" is often arranged through a rabbi. Whether sold or not, it is a good idea to put away *hametz* in order to prevent any accidental eating of non-Passover food. I put masking tape on any kitchen cabinet that contains either non-Pesah foods or ordinary dishes.

Foods that are specifically kosher for Passover usually contain a note on their label. Some foods—including coffee, tea, sugar, eggs, meat, fish, fresh fruits, and vegetables—do not require such a label. Some people also abstain from eating *kitniyot,* "legumes"—this category includes beans, peas, lentils, rice, millet, sesame and sunflower seeds, and corn.

In addition to special dishes and utensils, those who keep the laws of *kashrut* can kasher (make kosher) some ordinary utensils for use on Passover. Refrigerators are washed. Ovens are rendered usable by allowing them to sit unused for twenty-four hours, by thoroughly cleaning them with oven cleaner, or by setting them to their highest temperature for an hour (self-cleaning ovens can simply be set to their cleaning cycle). Oven racks are cleaned with steel wool. The stovetop is kashered by turning the burners on (fifteen minutes on a gas stove, five minutes on an electric stove). Microwave ovens are kashered by leaving them unused, washing them, and boiling water inside them until the oven fills with steam. According to liberal opinion, dishwashers (after twenty-four hours of nonuse) are kashered simply by cycling them empty of dishes. Metal sinks are kashered by pouring boiling water on them (porcelain or enamel sinks require the same treatment but can be used during Pesah only with a sink liner at the bottom).

## Spiritual Preparation

I begin preparing for Passover by focusing on using up as much food as possible. Here is an opportunity to get rid of things I am never going to eat. The gradual emptying of the freezer, the food cabinets, and the refrigerator constantly reminds me of the approach of the holiday. It also makes me aware of my consumption of food in a different way than the rest of the year does. During the year I want to make sure I have enough to eat for my family without making frequent runs to the supermarket. Before Pesah, it feels like I am playing a card game. In order to win I have to get rid of all my cards, but only at the right moment. As my food supplies dwindle, I realize that this is an opportunity to begin again. At times, I realize that various kinds of products are unnecessary and I can get by with fewer boxes in my cabinets. It reminds me to strive for a simpler though not spartan lifestyle.

Other vital preparations include deciding whom to invite for the Seder (or deciding whose Seder invitation to accept) and planning meals for the Passover holiday. Both of these have spiritual dimensions, as well. For example, the number of products available for Passover have so expanded in variety in the last few years that almost all ordinary foods can be duplicated on Passover. But there should remain some special food dimension to the holiday, and I find myself struggling with how to maintain that special quality. My children, however, hate restrictions on food and dislike the poor quality of many kosher-for-Passover products. How to juggle my spiritual needs without depriving them is an ongoing challenge.

Of course, many people complain about feeling burdened by all the cleaning and changing of food and dishes that Passover entails. It is easy to maintain that Passover/freedom is not supposed to come easily, but it seems wrong that people should dread the holiday of freedom as a burden. I deal with this tension by sticking to the vital essentials and not viewing Passover as a time for spring cleaning. It is probably not necessary to clear out the mess in your garage (at least not now).

### Bedikat Hametz

The night before the Seder is the traditional time for the ceremony of *bedikat hametz,* the "search for *hametz.*" Since this is a final symbolic check, there should be little *hametz* to be found. Many people hide bread crumbs or pieces of bread around the house and challenge the children to find them. In the old days, the search was conducted by the light of a candle, using a feather to brush the stray *hametz* into a wooden spoon. To replicate the feel of the "old days," *bedikat hametz* kits (candle, feather, and spoon) are available in many Jewish bookstores and on the Internet. Of course, flashlights and mini-vacuums work equally well. Any *hametz* collected is set aside to be burned the next morning. A formula is then recited in which we declare the *hametz* null and void and renounce any ownership of it. (The text for the blessing before the search and the nullification after is found in almost any Haggadah.)

The time of *bedikat hametz* is also an opportunity to become aware of the *hametz* in your life. If *hametz* is that which puffs you up or is more broadly the evil inclination, then we should spend some time this night reflecting on the *hametz* that lies hidden inside us. If *hametz* is a symbol of the ways we have enslaved ourselves, then pondering its removal might help us see ways to free ourselves. The search for *hametz* is traditionally done in silence, allowing for this kind of reflection to take place.

The next morning we burn whatever *hametz* we discovered and whatever remains after breakfast. The burning is followed by a version of the formula of nullification *(bittul hametz)* as recited the previous night. The rest of the day is spent preparing for the Seder. The tradition is not to eat *matzah* on the day before Pesah in order to make its eating at the Seder special. For the same reason, some people will not eat *matzah* for a week or more before Pesah.

## The Seder

Passover officially begins with the Seder. *Seder* means "order," for the evening has an order of rituals and text. This order is found at the beginning of the Haggadah, the "telling." The central focus is, of course, the story of the Exodus. This the Haggadah asks us not just to remember, but to experience as our own story. As the Haggadah says, "In every generation, each individual should feel personally redeemed from Egypt." The Haggadah creates that experience in two ways: The first way is through taste. We consume the experience by eating foods like the bitter herbs that remind us of slavery or the *matzah* that reminds us of freedom. The second way is through the raising of questions. We are not simply to recount the events of the Exodus. We are provoked to question the story anew each year—by wondering at the strange customs of the Seder, by contemplating the four classic questions of the Haggadah, and by studying the text itself. The text purposely makes puzzling statements. For example, near the beginning of the Seder, in the paragraph that starts *ha lahma anya,* "this is the bread of affliction," we recite: "This year we are slaves, next year we will be free." If Passover is a celebration of our liberation, why then do we begin with a statement that denies that liberation?

Children are particularly encouraged to ask questions, because, as the Haggadah states, we are fulfilling the *mitzvah* of telling the story to the next generation, the next link of the chain of the Jewish people. However, we are all meant to question. Why? Because questioning reflects an engagement with the story, even when, like the "wicked child," you express some skepticism or critique. More important, questioning in and of itself is a mark of freedom. Maimonides says: "If he has no child, then let his wife ask him [the Four Questions]; if he has no wife, then let one person ask the other even if they are all sages. If he is alone, then he asks himself 'Why is this night different?' "

The elements of the Seder and all its essentials—*matzah,* wine or grape juice, vegetables for *karpas* (a symbol of spring), salt water (a symbol of the bitter tears of slavery), *maror* (bitter herbs—horseradish or romaine lettuce), *haroset* (a mixture of apples, nuts, and wine, symbolizing the mortar we used as slaves in Egypt), *beytzah* (the roasted egg, symbolizing the festival sacrifice), and *zeroa* (the roasted shankbone of a lamb, symbolizing the Pesah sacrifice)—are spelled out in the Haggadah, along with instructions on how to organize them on the Seder plate. Each person at the Seder should receive a copy of the Haggadah. Sometimes, pillows are provided for reclining (reclining while eating was a mark of a free person in ancient times; slaves ate while standing).

In addition to the Seder plate and its symbols, a cup of wine is poured for Elijah. According to legend, Elijah—the prophet who has become a symbol of hope for our messianic future—visits every Seder on Passover. Toward the end of the Seder we open the door for Elijah. More recently, some Jews have added a Miriam's cup, a cup of water to symbolize the well of water that, according to the Midrash, accompanied the Israelites through the desert because of the merit of Miriam. While Elijah is a symbol of the future redemption, Miriam is a symbol of the ongoing hope and striving for that redemption.

*Matzah* is a special focus. Though many varieties are available, it is traditional to use plain *matzah* at the Seder. Some people use *shemurah matzah,* "guarded *matzah,*" that is, *matzah* that is watched from the moment of harvest to ensure there is no contact with water. (Regular *matzah* is watched only from when the grain is ground.) The *matzah* is displayed covered on the table alongside the Seder plate.

There are a number of elements to balance at a Seder.

*1. Who is present?*  Are there a lot of children? Of what age? No children? Do the participants have similar Jewish backgrounds? Are non-Jews participating? If the population is diverse, you can either seek to satisfy everyone or else focus on particular groups at certain points in the evening. For instance, you might focus on the children before the meal and on the adults after the meal.

*2. Leadership and involvement*  You may wish to have someone leading or pacing the evening. It is also important to involve as many people as you can. At some Seders, everyone takes turns reading the text. At others, people are asked ahead of time to prepare one particular section. Planning ahead is especially important if the Haggadah you have chosen offers supplementary readings or commentary.

*3. Choosing a Haggadah*  There are many Haggadot available, with more being published each year. Some have a particular orientation—for children, for feminists, for secular Jews, etc. Each of the liberal denominations has produced a Haggadah (Joy Levitt and I edited one entitled *A Night of Questions,* published by the Jewish Reconstructionist Federation). In choosing a Haggadah for your Seder, consider: Should everyone at your Seder have the same version? If so, do you want a Haggadah with a particular orientation? Do you want a simple, straightforward Haggadah, or one that has lots of commentary and optional readings? Do you want one that contains only the traditional text or a mixture of traditional and contemporary? One way to choose is to compare the Haggadot in a bookstore. If a lot of reading will be done in English, make sure the translation is appealing. Also, reading the introduction will generally tell you the orientation of a particular Haggadah.

Running a Seder can be a challenge. The Seder is the one time of the year that we recite a major piece of liturgy without the benefit of clergy. After all, it takes place in our homes rather than in the synagogue. So decide on your goals for the evening and prepare ahead of time. Know the Haggadah text you will be using. Read its introduction. Familiarize yourself with the flow of the evening. Have some idea of timing. Know that you cannot possibly accommodate everyone all the time at a Seder.

To forestall the proverbial question "When do we eat?" you may wish to serve vegetable crudités with dips for *karpas*—this takes the edge off everyone's hunger.

One important thing to remember: you really cannot "do it wrong." The goal of the Seder is to engage the participants in telling the story of and reexperiencing the slavery and freedom. So if you tell the story and perform the major rituals, you will have fulfilled the traditional requirements for the night.

***Why is this night different?*** Why is this night different? How can it be different, if each year we observe the same rituals of Passover? It's all a question of attitude and awareness.

Pesah is the beginning. Its place at the start of the festival cycle represents the place it is to hold in our lives. It is a moment of liberation, of starting over. We go back to the basics—just flour and water. *Matzah* is a life unadorned. During the year, we become distracted by desires, by pain, by defeats, and even by victories. We become *hametz*tesized. Pesah brings us back to the starting point and says you are only *matzah*, plain and simple. You are neither great nor terrible. Just when you might think that your choices have become narrow or nonexistent, Pesah proclaims the possibility of freedom. We begin by returning to our simplest selves to prepare for the journey of the year to come. For the rest of the year, our choices and our deeds should be infused with the experience of the Exodus—a striving for freedom for everyone.

## A *KAVANAH* FOR THE FESTIVAL CYCLE

The famous four children of the Seder show us how we can come to appreciate what we have without ignoring the pain and loss that is part of life. The Haggadah starts with the wise child, seeing each of the types of children as simpler. In this *kavanah*, I propose a somewhat different model, growing ever deeper as we move from wise to wicked to simple, until we finally reach the child who does not ask. This may be a good *kavanah* to focus us as Passover comes to an end.

When we are the wise child, we know what is. We look at the world and see it as teeming with blessings, a garden filled with delights for the senses. We see humans created not to be alone but rather blessed with relationships of friendship and love, with the gift of eternity and *naches* (gratification) through children. We are wise enough not to take the blessings of the world for granted.

When we are the wicked child, we have a critical view of the world. Without denying the blessings, we see that all of life is not blessings. God is both *oseh shalom u-borei et ha-ra*, "the maker of peace and the creator of evil" (or, as in the version we have in the *Siddur, borei et ha-kol*, "the creator of all things"). All of it is part of life, both peace and discord, both wholeness and shattering.

When we are the simple child, we see both the good and the evil. We respond neither with anger nor with despair to human fate. Instead, we affirm all of life by saying amen to the world. A sense of blessing comes from accepting the world in all its parts. We do not seek to deny human experience with all its complexities. We understand that the key to life and feeling blessed is to be aware of all that life has to offer. It is in an aware response that life is fully lived.

When we are the child who does not know how to ask, we remain silent. We are silent first of all because in that silence we can hear the rhythm of the world, the beating of the heart, and the voice that goes forth every day from Sinai calling to all those lost and wandering in the deserts of our own creation.

However, we are also silent because we understand the limits of what can be known. Bernie Glassman, a Zen teacher, writes:

Yet, we still want to know. In some way we can't help it—we're human. As part of being human, we believe that the reason we're not happy or not successful is that somewhere in the world there is a piece of knowledge we haven't acquired yet. If we can find it with the help of the right book, the right religion, the right teacher, or the right job, we'll be happy and successful. [Bernie Glassman, *Bearing Witness*]

Instead, we have come to a place where the questions no longer matter. Coming to a place of unknowing, we are freed from a striving for that which cannot be attained. Instead, we can focus on living a life that is fully alive to every moment—whatever that moment may bring. Freed from striving for "wisdom," we can focus on bringing peace and healing to the world. This is a life aware of all the blessings filling the world and most of all aware of *the* blessing—the gift of life itself.

God says: I will pour out for you blessings without end,
Until your lips tire from saying: Enough! [Mal. 3:10]

# THE OMER

The period between Pesah and Shavuot is called the Omer, "sheaf."
The Torah says:

> From the day after the Sabbath, the day that you bring the sheaf
> (*omer*) of wave-offering, you shall keep count until seven full weeks
> have elapsed: you shall count fifty days until the day after the seventh
> week, then you shall bring an offering of new grain to the Lord. [Lev.
> 23: 15–16]

This verse was understood to mean that the first sheaf of the new
grain was brought to the Temple on the second day of Pesah. We are
then told to count seven weeks (forty-nine days). On the fiftieth day, we
are to bring loaves of bread made from the new grain as part of the
holiday celebration of Shavuot.

After the Temple was destroyed, the agricultural rituals were no
longer practiced. Therefore, the ritual of counting the days and weeks
between Passover and Shavuot itself became the focus of this period. In
fact, this time period is also known as *sefirah*, "the counting," which is
shorthand for *sefirat ha-Omer*, "the counting of the Omer."

### Preparing for Sinai

The Omer is a spiritual preparation for receiving the Torah on Shavuot.
It is a time when we are challenged to discover what is new in Torah. A
Hasidic teaching suggests that the Torah is given anew each year. The

next seven weeks determine whether we are ready to receive this new Torah on Shavuot. During the Omer period, we need to focus internally, allowing our lives to parallel the story of the Israelites as they journey through the desert. The Promised Land seems far away, the unknown seems not just challenging but terrifying. The past, despite its problems and disappointments, becomes more attractive because it is familiar. We long to return to Egypt, forgetting the "slavery" and remembering only the good food (as the Bible says, "the leeks and cucumbers") that sustained us in slavery.

How do we create guidelines and principles to serve as our moral compass in our wanderings? The counting of the Omer challenges us to make our days count. Rabbi Everett Gendler teaches that the verse *limnot yameinu kein hoda* (Psalm 90:12) means "make our days count by saying yes to each one of them." If we can create a practice of awareness of each day, then hopefully we can carry that practice beyond Shavuot to every day of the year.

The Jewish mystics fit the counting of the Omer into their larger system of belief. They linked the seven weeks with the seven lower *sefirot*. In this context, the *sefirot* refer to the different aspects of the Godhead. The seven *sefirot* are: *hesed* (loving-kindness); *gevurah* (structure); *tiferet* (truth); *netzah* (endurance); *hod* (humility); *yesod* (construction); and *malkhut* (presence). (The translations given do not convey the full meaning of these *sefirot*; in fact, the meanings differ in different schools of Jewish mystical teaching.)

Not only was each week linked with one *sefirah*, but each day of the week was also linked with a *sefirah*. Thus the first week is associated with the *sefirah* of *hesed*/loving-kindness. The first day is linked to *hesed* combined with *hesed*. The second day is *gevurah* combined with *hesed*, and so on. For the Kabbalists, this period was a time to focus on these different aspects of God as preparation for the day after seven weeks of seven days. The fiftieth day is thus symbolic of perfection and appropriately is the day when God reveals both the Torah and God's Presence to the Israelites assembled at Mount Sinai. Thus the Omer becomes a mystical preparation for the moment of Sinai. Recently, this connection of the *sefirot* to the counting of the Omer has been adapted in a new way. In addition to reflecting aspects of the Godhead, the *se-*

*firot* reflect aspects of the human personality. This is what is meant when the Bible says we are created in the image of God and that we are to act as God acts. Thus the linking of the seven weeks to the seven *sefirot* creates a specific structure related to significant personality traits. In one understanding of the *sefirot, hesed* and *gevurah* are opposites that come to a synthesis in *tiferet*. I would like to suggest that rather than being opposites, they are complementary. Thus all of the *sefirot* are necessary aspects of humanity. Accordingly, a way to think of the *sefirot* is as follows.

### Omer and the *Sefirot:* A *Kavanah* for the Seven Weeks

**Hesed,** *loving-kindness or love*    We begin with love, for that is how creation begins. God created the world as an act of love for human beings. Humans create new human beings through love.

In this first week of the Omer, we reflect on *hesed*/love. When is it easy for us to offer love? When is it difficult? How can we be generous? When are we not? Are there dangers both to ourselves and to those we love from too much love? Is there a stifling aspect to our love? An encouraging of codependency? Are there things that prevent us from being loving? Are there things that compel us to be loving? What should *hesed* mean for us?

**Gevurah,** *structure*    *Gevurah* is also known as *din,* "judgment." I think of this *sefirah* as *"limitations."* Love is free-flowing and yet it needs a container, a structure to hold it. Without limits, love can be overwhelming, leaving no space for the object of that love. *Gevurah* then has an aspect of respect/*kavod*. Unlike love, respect intrinsically recognizes the worth of the other. *Gevurah* is discipline. It is knowing that not only children need structure. *Gevurah* involves contraction of self to leave space for others. It calls for focus in place of the boundless nature of *hesed*.

Do we set limits easily or find it difficult to do? If setting limits is easy, is it too easy? When can we say yes? If setting limits is hard, when can we say no? We need both *hesed* and *gevurah* to be able to open our hands, arms, and hearts, and yet know when to set limits both for our-selves and for others.

**Tiferet,** *compassion* Tiferet, "compassion," is also known as *emet,* "truth." *Tiferet* blends and harmonizes *hesed* and *gevurah*. Herein lies the compassionate heart. *Tiferet* enables us to feel compassion toward people by perceiving their totality—their strengths and their weaknesses—and accepting them. The same is true regarding our-selves. *Tiferet* is compassionate acceptance. It is often translated as "beauty," because when we see with truth we find beauty in all things. Shammai and Hillel debated what to say to a bride on her wedding day. Shammai held for the truth: if she is beautiful, say so, if not, de-scribe her as she is. Hillel held that every bride is beautiful. Beauty is not some objective standard; it can be found in all things. *Tiferet,* which is the heart, perceives the beauty in all things. This is *tiferet,* the heart of compassion.

What kind of person or situation evokes our compassion? What kind of person or situation evokes our annoyance or antipathy? What can we learn about our own issues and limitations by reflecting on these contrasts? What inhibits our compassion? Is our compassion tinged with patronizing condescension? Can we be compassionate even with ourselves?

The next three *sefirot*—*netzah, hod,* and *yesod*—are also seen as a unit.

**Netzah,** *endurance* The qualities of endurance, fortitude, determina-tion, certitude, energy, and commitment are associated with *netzah*. While often translated as "victory," *netzah* really has more to do with achievement. It is the *sefirah* of creativity. Like *hesed*, its energy flows outward. As the *sefirah* of creativity, it has no limits and boundaries. It is the *sefirah* that reminds us that we are powerful, we are "little lower than angels."

When do we feel energetic and empowered? When do we feel the opposite? When do our creative juices flow? When do we feel stuck, indecisive?

**Hod,** *humility*   The qualities of humility, yielding, modesty, patience, planning, calm, forgiveness, and compromise are associated with *hod*. *Hod* focuses the energy of *netzah*. It takes creativity and actualizes it in reality. It reminds us that we are not always right, and there are times when change and compromise may be necessary. Our sense of humility comes from a recognition of the limitations of our power. True, we are little lower than angels; yet we are also dust and ashes. We are imperfect and mortal, no matter how powerful we seem. *Hod* can also be connected with *hoda'ah,* "gratitude." Unlike the striving associated with *netzah,* in *hod* we experience gratitude for the blessings that we have.

When are we impatient? Can we accept our limitations without self-flagellation? Can we drop our defenses enough to admit our flaws and become vulnerable? How can we be aware and thankful for the gifts and blessings that we have?

**Yesod,** *construction*   *Yesod* is associated with the qualities of bonding, connection, and foundation. It is traditionally associated with the generativity of the sexual organs. *Yesod* brings together all the *sefirot* that came before. It specifically takes the pair of *netzah* and *hod*— creativity and planning, determination and patience—and combines them to create the foundation for what will be. It also adds to *netzah* and *hod* the element of connection. Connecting to others is essential for human beings. At creation we are told, *lo tov heyot ha'adam l'vado,* "it is not good for a human being to be alone." Thus, amid our creativity and planning, our connections to one another should not be lost. *Yesod* is about building relationships based on *hesed, gevurah,* and *tiferet.* By urging the connection to others, *yesod* moves us closer to unity, which is the energy underlying the system of *sefirot.*

How can we bring together *netzah* and *hod* to build balanced lives? Which kinds of relationships come easily to us and which do not? Do we work on building and maintaining those relationships or just expect them to flourish on their own?

**Malkhut,** *presence*   *Malkhut* is often translated as "sovereignty," as in *melekh,* "ruler." I have translated it as "presence" because this *sefi-*

rah is associated with God's indwelling Presence or the immanence, known as *Shekhinah*. In Kabbalah, the *Shekhinah* is the feminine aspect of God. As the last *sefirah*, *malkhut* is considered the most accessible, the closest to our human world. If we live with a constant awareness of God's Presence, our beings are transformed. We become a presence ourselves, being openhearted but not overwhelming; compassionate, able to hold both assurance and doubt simultaneously, and yet comfortably and constructively building a future. *Malkhut* is the challenge to act in ways that imitate God. In that way, *malkhut* echoes its traditional aspect of sovereignty. Just as God is *melekh*, "ruler" of the world, so we too have an aspect of sovereignty.

Paradoxically, another understanding of *malkhut* is a sovereignty that comes from not being in control. When we give up the notion of control, we can stop striving to reach that mirage that is always out of reach. As mortals we can never control our fate, but we may achieve an aspect of *malkhut* by controlling our reactions to life's unfolding. Though we cannot stop suffering or death, we can make choices about how we respond.

## Customs of the Omer

Traditionally, the Omer period is a time of mourning. The most common explanation is that we are mourning the thousands of students of the talmudic sage Rabbi Akiva who died in a plague. In time, the reasons for mourning expanded to include other tragedies in Jewish history that occurred during this time of the year, such as the massacres of Jews during the Crusades. Therefore, it became customary not to hold weddings or other celebratory events, and not to cut the hair (a traditional sign of mourning) during the Omer.

The lack of clarity in the origin of the mourning led to a number of customs about when the mourning should be observed. Some observe it from Passover to Lag B'omer (the thirty-third day of the Omer), others from the first day of Iyyar until Shavuot. Some regard the whole time period from Pesah to Shavuot as a period of mourning. Because of its uncertain origin and meaning, liberal communities have increasingly disregarded mourning practices entirely.

*Lag B'omer*    The thirty-third day (Hebrew: *lag*) in the Omer is a minor holiday. According to tradition, the plague either stopped for a day or ceased completely on this day. Lag B'omer is celebrated with picnics and outdoor activities, especially in Israel.

*Pirkei Avot*    It is a custom to study one chapter of *Pirkei Avot* (*Ethics of Our Ancestors*) each week during the Omer. There are five chapters in this tractate of the Mishnah, each containing short ethical teachings by the rabbinic sages. To facilitate its study during the afternoon service on the six Shabbatot from Pesah to Shavuot, a sixth chapter was added in the prayer book. The study of *Pirkei Avot* and its many commentaries is seen as an appropriate preparation for Shavuot, particularly since the sixth chapter is all about Torah.

## Modern Holidays of the Omer

Three modern holidays fall during the counting of the Omer: Yom ha-Shoah, "Holocaust Memorial Day" (Nisan 27); Yom ha-Atzma'ut, "Israel Independence Day" (Iyyar 5); and Yom Yerushalayim, "Jerusalem Day" (Iyyar 28). Various liturgies for Holocaust Memorial Day have recently emerged, but in the main these holidays are marked by Jewish communal gatherings, replete with speeches by public figures or scholars. This is in part because they were established by the Israeli government rather than by religious authorities. Even more important, especially in regard to Israel Independence Day and Jerusalem Day, the theological meaning of these holidays is only slowly emerging. It will probably take time for spiritual practices to emerge. Yom Yerushalayim, celebrating the reunification of Jerusalem during the Six-Day War, is primarily observed in Israel.

*Yom ha-Shoah*    Yom ha-Shoah commemorations often include the lighting of six candles in memory of the six million who perished during the Holocaust and also the recital of the memorial prayer *(eil maleh)* and *kaddish*. Some people light a yellow *yahrzeit* (memorial) candle. But neither synagogue nor home rituals are set.

The theological challenge of Yom ha-Shoah is stark. How could the

Holocaust have happened? What does it say about the human capacity for evil? Most of all, where was God during the Holocaust? For most people, the traditional response that the Jewish people were punished for their sins is in itself blasphemous. Yet the Holocaust only sharpens the question that has existed from the beginning of time: Why do the innocent suffer? How can you explain the death of one child, never mind one million children? My own response to the issue of suffering is discussed below in the section on Yom Kippur. Whatever one's theological answers, Yom ha-Shoah stands in sharp contrast to Pesah. There is no outstretched hand striking the Nazis with ten plagues. The promise of the Haggadah that in each generation God will save us from our enemies seems patently false. How quickly have we moved from joyous liberation to catastrophic destruction!

Yom ha-Shoah is a time to reflect on what was and in that remembering recommit to not letting it happen again. Let me share with you two notions of commemoration that give space for that reflection. Under the leadership of the Jewish Community Center in Manhattan, many synagogues have joined for an all-night program in which volunteers read from a list of names of those who perished in the Holocaust. Only a small percentage of the six million names can be read during the eight hours of the reading, but the vigil provides a way to grasp the significance of individual deaths as well as the overwhelming magnitude of the Holocaust.

The second commemoration is based on the medieval Kabbalistic custom of *tzom shtikah,* "a fast of silence" rather than a fast from eating. In response to the unspeakable nature of the Holocaust, we cease from speaking. In the silence, we reflect upon the silence of those years—the silence of God and the silence of the world. In my community, on the evening of Yom ha-Shoah, we enter the sanctuary in silence and receive a text for the service, but we participate in silence. The service is read, chanted, and sung to us on a tape. The service is made up of readings, songs, and some of the traditional liturgy rewritten to challenge rather than affirm God's goodness. It thus follows the example of some medieval *piyyutim,* liturgical poetry responding to persecutions in their times. The service concludes with the memorial prayer and *kaddish.* The community leaves in silence.

***Yom ha-Atzma'ut, Israel Independence Day***    Yom ha-Atzma'ut also lacks home customs or special liturgy. Some communities recite Hallel and have a Torah reading for the day. Parades and cultural events also mark the holiday. In Israel, this is a national holiday. As we develop new conceptions of our relationship to the State of Israel, an underlying theology will be the foundation for practices for Yom ha-Atzma'ut. For one suggested theology, see "Israel: Toward a Torah of Zion," pp. 467–74.

# SHAVUOT

The holiday of Shavuot marks the giving of the Torah at Sinai. Actually, the biblical texts never refer to its historical context. Rather it is described as an agricultural holiday during which the first fruits of the new growing season were brought as offerings in the Temple. Shavuot means "weeks"; its name derives from the fact that it falls on the fiftieth day, the climax of the seven weeks of counting the Omer. Over time, the agricultural nature of the holiday faded and the connection with the Revelation at Sinai became the central focus of the holiday.

Perhaps because of its origins in agriculture, Shavuot has a paucity of rituals as compared to Pesah or Sukkot. Some have suggested that the experience of Sinai cannot be re-created. The image of God descending upon the mountain amid the horns and noises, the people gathered below, and the act of revelation itself are almost beyond human experience. Even the Israelites, who gathered at Sinai, fled the Presence of God, asking Moses to listen and relate God's words to them. Perhaps, then, it is appropriate that there are few rituals for Shavuot. Perhaps, too, all we need is the Torah itself. On Shavuot, we engage in Torah. We literally embrace it by holding the scroll. We hear the words of Torah (specifically the description of Sinai) read to us as part of Shavuot services. We need no symbol of Torah, for we have the Torah itself.

In another sense, the moment of Revelation at Sinai is not an event that only happened in the past. Rather Sinai, the giving and receiving of Torah, is an ongoing experience. God's voice calls from Sinai every day.

The Torah is given every day. The difference between Passover and Shavuot is that the Exodus is over, while revelation continues. Thus Sinai needs fulfillment, not reexperiencing; enactment, not reenactment. Sinai is part of the dynamic of our lives. Our task is to hear anew and renew the Torah each day. *Any* time a person studies Torah with devotion and holiness is a *zeman matan Torah,* "moment of the giving of the Torah." As the rabbis said: "Anything any student in any age will say was already given to Moses at Sinai." This means anything we add to the Torah is considered part of what was originally transmitted to Moses. Revelation of the Torah began at Sinai and has never ceased.

How are we to hear the voice of Sinai? One possibility is suggested by the puzzling verse describing the experience at Sinai: "and all the people saw the sounds" (Exod. 20:15). What does it mean that the people *saw* rather than heard the sounds? Imagine a deaf person entering a room filled with music and dancing people. At first it might seem that the dancers are crazy. Yet, with some awareness, even a deaf person can realize that the people are dancing to music.

It might be said that we are all deaf when it comes to the voice of Sinai. The first step is to realize that the music is playing; that is, that God is calling us. Looking at the world that way, we can at least see the *effects* of that voice, in such things as nature and acts of lovingkindness. Perhaps, by seeing the sounds, we may eventually come to hear them, too (based on the *Degel Mahaneh Efraim*).

For more on the Torah and its meaning, see pp. 139–75.

### The Reading of Ruth

Among Ashkenazic Jews, it is customary to read the Book of Ruth as part of Shavuot services. The reason most commonly given is that Ruth's voluntary acceptance of Judaism is like our acceptance of the Torah at Sinai. The book also recalls the agricultural setting of the biblical Shavuot.

## *Tikkun leil Shavuot:* All-Night Study Vigil

Studying Torah the entire night of Shavuot is a Kabbalistic custom that has been increasingly observed. The mystical background and the order of study ordained by the Kabbalists have been dropped. Instead, study normally focuses on texts chosen specially for the occasion. The all-night study is sometimes attributed to a midrash that says the Israelites slept late that morning until awoken by Moses. To demonstrate our love for and eagerness to get Torah, we stay up all night. The custom is to follow the all-night study with a sunrise service.

Other lesser customs for Shavuot include eating dairy foods such as blintzes and decorating the synagogue with greens.

# THE THREE WEEKS
# AND TISHA BE-AV

The period called the Three Weeks begins with the fast of the seventeenth day of Tammuz, when the Babylonians breached the walls of Jerusalem. It concludes with the fast of the ninth of Av, known as Tisha be-Av. It is traditionally a time of mourning. According to tradition, both the destruction of the First Temple by the Babylonians in 586 B.C.E. and that of the Second Temple by the Romans in 70 C.E. occurred on the ninth day of the month of Av. After the First Temple fell, Jews were sent into exile in Babylonia. Following the destruction of the Second Temple, Jews were exiled from their land and scattered through the world in what has been known ever since as the Diaspora.

In days past, and for a minority of Jews today, the days of mourning were accompanied by hope for the restoration of all we have lost: the rebuilding of the Temple, the reinstitution of the sacrificial cult, the return of the Davidic dynasty, and the regathering of all Jews in the Promised Land.

## Exile and Diaspora

*Exile* and *Diaspora* are distinct terms. *Exile* emphasizes a state of alienation—from our land and from God. In Bible and Talmud, the Promised Land is vouchsafed to the people as long as they are loyal to the covenant. Exile is the result when God punishes the Jewish people for its sins. *Diaspora* emphasizes the dispersal of the Jews to other lands. Still negative, it does not have the theological connotations of punishment and alienation, which is why this term has become more widespread in modern times.

Sometimes, Jews felt part of the surrounding world and the hope for a return to Israel seemed a distant dream. At other times, particularly facing persecutions, that hope must have felt like a fervent imperative. At still other times, this vision of the future seemed so ideal that it was linked to the notion of a messianic period when each Jew would sit under a fig tree at peace in the land of Israel.

In the daily liturgy and at particular moments such as the Three Weeks, Jews express the wish for the restoration of all that was— Temple, nation, and land. Yet, for many contemporary Jews, the idea of restoration is problematic. Rebuilding the Temple and reinstituting sacrifices is no longer a goal for the vast majority of Jews. It goes without saying that the current political situation makes it impossible to destroy the mosque that sits on the Temple site, but in fact most elements of the Temple service are actually distasteful to modern Jewish thought. The ancient priesthood was hereditary and hierarchical and excluded women from its ranks. And we shrink from the idea that sacrificing animals and sprinkling their blood on the altar are the best means to atone for sin. Few Jews today would prefer a Davidic king to democracy and Diaspora Jews resist the idea that authentic Jewish life can only be restored if all Jews return to the Promised Land.

Questions of state and land have also been challenged by the founding of the State of Israel in 1948. That hope—central to the Three Weeks and repeated daily in the liturgy—has been fulfilled, at least partially. In light of the existence of a Jewish presence in the Promised Land, should we continue our practice of mourning during the Three Weeks? Many have argued that we should not. Though the dream of centuries has not been perfectly realized, many Jews believe we should now celebrate the achievements of the Zionist dream.

My approach is more metaphorical. While we should cease mourning for a destroyed Jerusalem and celebrate the astounding turn of events that brought about the modern state, we should recognize that we are still in exile. We live in an unredeemed world. Exile continues in an existentialist sense and all Jews—in Israel and in the Diaspora—are in exile. In this way, all human beings are in exile. Therefore, it seems appropriate to cease mourning for ancient and outmoded forms while acknowledging that we live in an unredeemed world.

One possibility is to stop observing the mourning practices of the Three Weeks with one important exception: its concluding fast day. The fast day of the ninth of Av (Tisha be-Av) would still be observed because the destruction of the Temple and the beginning of the exile, which Tisha be-Av commemorates, still have mythic meaning. They reflect our reality of brokenness and alienation. Actually we have been in exile from the moment we left the Garden of Eden. We were in exile in our many Egypts and while we wandered in the deserts of this world. All of this happened to us and continues to happen to us. Our feeling of God's abandonment is not only a memory, but an ongoing experience despite the existence of the State of Israel.

This new paradigm requires a new understanding of Tisha be-Av that reflects its place in the festival cycle. We have stood at Sinai and received the Torah. But no sooner do we hear God's commandments to have no other gods and make no graven images than we make a golden calf to worship. The Golden Calf is *the* sin in the Torah. It is the ultimate symbol of estrangement, alienation, and disappointment. The glory of Shavuot is past; Tisha be-Av reminds us that we remain wanderers in the wilderness. Tisha be-Av represents the dark night of the exile. As such, it is linked to all the catastrophes in Jewish history, including the expulsion of the Jews from Spain in 1492. It is the low point in the Jewish year.

### Laws and Customs of the Three Weeks and Tisha be-Av

The period begins with the minor fast day of the seventeenth of Tammuz. It is customary not to hold weddings or other joyous events during the Three Weeks. The cutting of hair is forbidden. Beginning with the first day of Av, the mourning practices intensify. Swimming and washing clothes are prohibited; eating meat is permitted only on Shabbat.

Tisha be-Av is a full fast day (like Yom Kippur), beginning at sunset. (For all the other fast days in the Jewish calendar, there is no fasting at night. The fast begins with sunrise.) As on Yom Kippur, eating, drinking, sex, and wearing leather are all prohibited. Uniquely, since Torah study is a joyous activity, it is expressly prohibited on Tisha be-Av. We are only permitted to study those sections of the Bible or the Talmud that talk about the destruction of Jerusalem.

We behave as mourners on Tisha be-Av. We sit on the floor or on low chairs while the Book of Lamentations is chanted as part of the evening service. For this service, we use candlelight or dimmed lights. In general, the musical modes for the day are sorrowful. There are special liturgical poems, called *kinot,* recited at both the evening and morning services. These poems recall the destruction of the Temple or other tragedies in Jewish history. Just like mourners before a funeral, we refrain from wearing *tallit* and *tefillin* for the morning service. As recovering mourners, we become more hopeful by the time of the afternoon service. *Tallit* and *tefillin* are worn and we add a paragraph of consolation to the *amidah.* Tisha be-Av ends on a somber but positive note. On the Shabbatot following Tisha be-Av, we read special prophetic readings of consolation. We look forward to the reconciliation promised by the High Holidays.

# HIGH HOLIDAYS:
# ROSH HA-SHANAH AND
# YOM KIPPUR

Rosh ha-Shanah (the New Year) and Yom Kippur (the Day of Atonement) are known as the High Holidays, a time that centers more on the synagogue and the community than on the home. These days and the time surrounding them are a solemn period for reflection and repentance. Yom Kippur, in particular, is called a day of judgment. The notion that God tallies our virtues and sins from the past year is expressed in the image of a God who inscribes the fate of each person in a heavenly book during this period. One does not have to believe either literally or metaphorically that we are being inscribed in a book of life and death to see the High Holidays as both an opportunity and a challenge. This is a period when we are encouraged to engage in *teshuvah,* "repentance." *Teshuvah* literally means "turn" or "return." The process of *teshuvah* is one of turning toward God, that which represents the holy and the good. The High Holidays have a particular structure that encourages this process of change, of turning.

Recognizing that this is not easily accomplished, the rabbis extended the process back from Yom Kippur, the Day of Atonement, to Rosh ha-Shanah to Elul—the month leading up to the High Holidays. During Elul, we blow the shofar at the end of every weekday morning service, thereby announcing that the High Holidays are coming. We also recite Psalm 27 at the end of morning and evening services. The Saturday before Rosh ha-Shanah, *selichot* services are held usually around midnight. *Selichot* are special penitential prayers that focus on the themes of repentance and forgiveness. (In some communities, *selichot* are recited every morning until Rosh ha-Shanah.) All of these preparatory customs recognize that the process of change needs time and work and cannot be accomplished even in the intense format of the one day of Yom Kippur.

## Preparing

One starting point is the rabbinic teaching about the name of the month, Elul. The four Hebrew letters that make up the name are understood as an abbreviation for the phrase from the Song of Songs (6:3), *ani le-dodi ve-dodi li,* "I am my beloved's and my beloved is mine." This phrase suggests an ideal image for our relationship with God. The rabbis understood the Song of Songs as the love song between God and Israel. After the estrangement represented by the Three Weeks, we long for each other as lovers do.

Our most basic desire is to feel not alone in the universe. We all want to feel wanted, loved, appreciated, and understood by those around us. We are often disappointed as those we care for most fail or seem to fail to love and support us. The High Holidays remind us that there is One who always cares, who responds to each of the beings in the world with *hesed,* "loving-kindness," the Holy One. The work of Elul is to recapture a sense of being in relationship with God. It is also to recapture a sense of self-worth based on being cherished by the Holy One. If we can achieve a sense of that relationship, then we can examine our inner selves unafraid of what we will discover. Free from that concern, we can really look at what we have done this past year—where we have hurt others and ourselves, where we did not live up to our own expectations, or where we had too high an expectation. Having gained clarity, we may be able to move on to change, to struggle with that which can be improved, to repair the relationships that we had damaged in the past year.

## Rosh ha-Shanah

Rosh ha-Shanah is the Jewish New Year. It conveys the hope for change and renewal, that things do not have to be as they were. We can begin again. This may be why Rosh ha-Shanah precedes Yom Kippur, though you might expect that first we would ask for forgiveness for the past and only then begin the New Year. Instead, we first enter the New Year with its promise of change. Rosh ha-Shanah says the new is right here before us. This promise supports us as we struggle with the past and with the nagging feeling that nothing ever changes. Though these may be our thirtieth or fiftieth High Holidays, many of us are still dealing with the same issues that we struggled with last year or ten years ago. Rosh ha-Shanah says that change is possible. The Torah readings speak of pregnancy in old age and a slaughter knife halted in mid-descent. The possibilities of the future lie stretched out before us.

Rosh ha-Shanah is observed for two days (one day in many Reform congregations), mainly in a lengthy synagogue liturgy. During the liturgy, the shofar, or ram's horn, is blown. We are not specifically told why we sound the shofar during services. Some understand it as a clarion call to awake from living life as a slumberer and engage with all that life has to offer. For others, it is a sound beyond words, the cry of our souls seeking healing or seeking a response from heaven. For still others it evokes echoes of the Jewish people who have heard that call down through the centuries back to the moment of Sinai. Perhaps too it echoes forward to the sound of the shofar that will announce the messianic era.

The themes of Rosh ha-Shanah are set out in a unique *musaf* or "additional" service. The *amidah* for this *musaf* has three central blessings called *malkhuyot, zikhronot,* and *shofarot. Malkhuyot* focuses on God as king, *zikhronot* on God who remembers all deeds and rewards and punishes the righteous and the wicked, and *shofarot* on the shofar as a symbol of the Revelation at Sinai and the future messianic redemption. For Franz Rosenzwieg, the German philosopher, these sections reflect the three major themes underlying Judaism: creation, revelation, and redemption. Thus, *malkhuyot* represents God as creator of the world, *zikhronot* describes the God who reveals the Torah and who expects us to live by its laws, and *shofarot* relates to the future redemption. The same three themes can also serve as challenges to us personally. Our humanity can be defined by our ability to act *(malkhuyot),* to remember and think *(zikhronot),* and to communicate *(shofarot).*

The dominant motif of Rosh ha-Shanah is God as *melekh*, "ruler," but usually translated as "king." The tendency to ascribe male qualities to God is, of course, unnecessary and undermines the place of women in Judaism. But this is just a matter of translation and adaptation. More troubling, a king is a hierarchical ruler with absolute power. Is that how we want to describe God? Do we believe in a sovereign who rewards and punishes his subjects? Yet the metaphor and the theology of God as absolute ruler is clearly central to Rosh ha-Shanah (and prevalent in all Jewish liturgy).

The value of such a conception of God as sovereign is to remind us that we are not. Modernity once fostered a notion that human beings can cure all diseases and solve all of our problems. That notion was shattered in the twentieth century by the Holocaust and the threat of nuclear war. Still, modernity stresses the primacy of the individual, while Rosh ha-Shanah reminds us that there is something larger—God. God, not human beings, created the world. We are but a small piece in this vast universe. The real truth, as we all know, is that destiny is not in our hands.

Rosh ha-Shanah also reminds us that we have considerable influence on the course of our lives. God created the universe, but we have the choice whether to become its destroyers or to become co-creators with God. We are created in the Divine image, which means we partake of an aspect of *melekh*, of ruler. Human free will is a miracle, given to the world; it is not part of the natural order. It is God's greatest gift to us and God's most terrifying demand of us.

We need to choose. God says: "I set before you life and death, choose life." This means that *choosing is life*. As long as we are engaged in choosing we are alive. The tradition teaches that everything is in the hands of God, except we have free choice. In this way we are like royalty. Rosh ha-Shanah's message is both humbling and empowering—we are not a *melekh* or a god but we do shape our destiny and the destiny of all with whom we interact.

## A *KAVANAH* FOR A NEW YEAR

We stand once again on the brink of a New Year. The air is redolent of opportunity. Rosh ha-Shanah is a call to change, a crying out for hope even in the bleakest landscapes. In response, the people of Israel stir in their sleep, aroused by dreams carried by the music and memories of this season. But then they turn over, pulling the blankets of the familiar more tightly around themselves, hoping to once again fall back asleep. We blow the shofar, that eerie and ancient sound that called our ancestors to battle and to prayer. We blow it over and over again to stir our souls, or in the words of Maimonides about the shofar call: "Sleepers, awake from your sleep. Slumberers, rouse yourselves from your slumber. Search your deeds and return to and remember your Creator."

God still calls to us humans as in the garden: *Ayeka?*, "Where are you?"

The only unknown is which of us will respond: *Hineni!*, "Here am I!"

**Rosh ha-Shanah customs**   It is customary to wish people a happy New Year by saying *le-shanah tovah u-metukah tikateivu,* "may you be inscribed for a good and sweet year." This expression echoes the image of God recording our fate in the book of life. Many people also send New Year cards with similar wishes. At Rosh ha-Shanah meals, we also dip apples and/or *hallah* in honey while saying: "May it be Your will to renew us for a year that is good and sweet."

The custom known as *tashlikh,* "sending," involves throwing bread into a flowing body of water (an ocean or a stream), thus symbolically casting our sins away. This ritual is performed on the afternoon of the first day of Rosh ha-Shanah (or on the second day, if the first day is a Sabbath). Many synagogues organize groups of members, making this a nice opportunity to socialize. There is no real liturgy for *tashlikh.*

## Yom Kippur, the Day of Atonement

Yom Kippur is a day of soul searching. We focus on ourselves, and yet Yom Kippur is incomplete if we do not also focus on our relationships and responsibilities to others. Yom Kippur is also known as Yom ha-Din, "Day of Judgment." The liturgy is replete with images of our being judged by the Chief Justice of the universe. According to tradition, sentence is passed on Yom Kippur: God determines who shall live and who shall die. Central to the Yom Kippur liturgy is the frequent recitation of the confessional in which we list a whole variety of sins for which we are asking forgiveness. It is striking that this list of sins does not contain ritual sins. We do not ask for forgiveness for not attending synagogue regularly or not keeping Shabbat. Instead, we confess for transgressions against the community and transgressions of our hearts. More striking still, the confessional is in the plural, yet it is clear that none of us has committed all these sins. Why should we confess even to transgressions of which we are innocent?

First, the plural form reminds us that we are part of a community—simultaneously our congregation and the people of Israel. We are responsible for one another, not just for ourselves alone. On Yom Kippur, we stand together as a community of sinners; not some righteous and some wicked. All of us recite the same list of sins; no one's list is shorter than anyone else's. Together we seek forgiveness and strive for change. Second, it is only as a community that we can effect the social changes necessary to better all our lives. Our concern on Yom Kippur is not just for the self. Toward the end of the day, after spending so much time looking inward, we read the Book of Jonah. Jonah, called by God to save the city of Nineveh, flees the responsibility of carrying out God's word. When at last this reluctant prophet reaches Nineveh and prophesizes the city's doom, people repent and God relents. Instead of being happy that he has succeeded, the only prophet in the Bible that anyone ever really listened to, Jonah is unhappy. For Jonah was never worried that he might fail, but rather that he might succeed. He just did not care about the people of Nineveh or their fate. In the end, sitting outside town, he swelters in the sun until God causes a sheltering plant to miraculously grow over him. Jonah is briefly happy until the plant dies. God asks him if he is deeply grieved about this single plant and Jonah says, "Yes, so deeply that I want to die." God responds: "And should not I care about Nineveh, that great city, in which there are more than a hundred and twenty thousand persons . . . and many beasts as well?" (Jonah 4:9,11). God is disappointed in Jonah. For despite everything that has happened, Jonah *just doesn't get it*. His concern lies only with himself. We read his story to remind us that even as we spend hours looking inward, examining who we are, we cannot forget to look at the world around us. Yom Kippur does not focus entirely on how we act toward God.

*The theology of Yom Kippur*    There is for me a larger problem in the traditional theology of Yom Kippur as set out in our liturgy. It was brought home to me when I visited a congregant in the hospital before the High Holidays. She had a serious illness, though it was not yet life-threatening. *Yet* is a big word in such a sentence. She asked me: How am I to deal with the High Holiday liturgy when the notion of life and death hanging in the balance is not an abstract concept but my very reality? How do I deal with a liturgy that seems to judge me, when anyone so judged would fail the test? How do I understand a liturgy that implies that my illness is my fault, a punishment for past misdeeds? Most of all, how do I recite a liturgy that suggests that if I am good right now, God will write me in the book of healing and life, but if not, then at this season my doom will be sealed? Is this all my fault?

This question of why we suffer and why people who are clearly innocent suffer has haunted all religions from the beginning of time. The classic rabbinic answer is that suffering is not random. There is a system of reward and punishment even if we cannot understand it (see "After the Words: God," pp. 487–504). One corollary is a belief in life after death in which true justice is meted out. The evil people, who seem to succeed in this world, would be punished then; and vice versa. The liturgy assumes, then, that God intervenes. What happens in life is not random; its operating principle is that of reward and punishment. The High Holiday liturgy, no matter how metaphorical (there doesn't have to be an actual book), is based on this notion of the justice of God's judgment.

There have always been strands within the tradition that questioned this certainty, beginning with Job, continuing with certain rabbis of the Talmud, and so on through the ages. The questioning or even rejection of this simple theology has only increased in modern times—most definitively perhaps in the thinking of Mordecai Kaplan.

The High Holiday liturgy reminds us that there exists something beyond us, larger than we are, over which we have no control, and that something is called God. We are asked to come to terms with something that is fundamentally true but which we most often deny, that we are human, with all the limitations that come from being human rather than divine. The situation of the person in the hospital makes this notion very real. A life-threatening illness strips us of our illusion that death is some far-off experience. We are not in control of our lives, or at least there are real limitations on our control. In this context Yom Kippur is not a Day of Judgment, Yom ha-Din, the way it is traditionally understood. In Kabbalah, *din* (or *gevurah*) is the aspect of God that exists opposite to *hesed*, "loving-kindness," limitless flow. *Din* is the vessel that contains the flow, the boundary set around love, giving the world structure. Yom ha-Din in this understanding is the day that reminds us of our limitations, that brings us face-to-face with our outer limit—with death. We are not all-powerful; we are not masters of our destiny. We are human beings filled with foibles, frailty, and finitude.

Yet even as we see our limitations ever more clearly, we are called to change. I used to think the rabbinic tradition was hopelessly naive about the possibility of change, of *teshuvah*. But I now understand what the rabbis had in mind. Their optimism was based on faith, a belief in the human spirit, a belief in fact in miracles—not miracles like the crossing of the Red Sea, but rather the miracle of reconciliation between two long-estranged relatives or friends, communities, or even nations.

If someone told you that you have only two days to live, you would see to it that each moment of those days you would be fully aware and alive. What if you could obtain such awareness without a decree of death, but rather by being fully aware of the miracle of this moment—of the sunrise, of speech, of movement, of hearing, of smell, of seeing, of relationships, of a friendly hello? The message of Yom Kippur is that the world is re-created anew each day. It is up to you to be fully alive and fully aware.

Unfortunately, there is one truth we all must accept: the most important judgment has already been issued. We, all of us, live under a sentence of death. Everyone dies and, given enough time, even our memory eventually passes away. This decree has never yet been averted. It is expressed in the prayer called *unetaneh tokef*, which begins by reminding us how helpless we are in the face of fate and then lists all the ways we can die: "who by fire, who by water . . ." Yet this otherwise depressing reminder climaxes with the words *uteshuvah utefillah utzedakah ma'arvirin et roa ha-gezera*, "repentance, prayer, and *tzedakah* can avert the severity of the decree." We cannot change the decree, but we can alter its severity through repentance, prayer, and *tzedakah*. To use my congregant in the hospital as an example one last time: she was buoyed by the knowledge that many people were praying for her. On one level, it made a difference to her to know that people cared; on yet another, it actually made a physical difference to her. She came to understand that no matter how many people prayed for her recovery, she could still die, but those prayers made a difference to how she lived.

*Teshuvah, tefillah,* and *tzedakah* are the critical elements of Yom Kippur's process of acceptance and change. *Teshuvah,* "returning," "repentance," and "turning," connects us to the community and to God. *Tefillah,* "prayer," connects us to God and to the possibilities within us. *Tzedakah,* "righteousness/charity," connects us with every living thing in a web of caring and acting. The decree remains the same; it is the severity we can change.

**Teshuvah:** *the path of change*    The theme of *teshuvah,* "change" or "repentance," is central to Yom Kippur and the High Holidays. Earlier we discussed the three paths of Torah, *avodah,* and *gemilut hesed.* *Teshuvah* is actually the fourth path, the one we turn to when we have failed to fulfill the visions of the other three. The High Holidays encourage us to walk the path of *teshuvah.* The first step is to see what we have done wrong. The second step is to regret our mistakes, which is why *teshuvah* is often translated as "repentance." Third, we resolve to change by not repeating our mistakes. Maimonides adds that we really know whether we have truly done *teshuvah* when we are faced with the same situation and find that we can resist the temptation of the past and instead act in a holy manner. This is the traditional view of the path, but it sometimes leads to defeatism, as we seem to engage in an endless war with ourselves—or, at least, with those negative or flawed parts of ourselves.

Another approach to *teshuvah* emphasizes the meaning of "return." Classical Hasidism taught that God is everywhere and in everything. Thus, on some level, whatever happens has an element of God in it. For example, distracting thoughts during prayer, and even lustful desires for inappropriate sex, have some element of Godliness. This, of course, does not imply that God wants you to act on these thoughts; nor are they God's way of testing your saintliness. It does mean that there is no force underlying the universe other than God. You can never say the devil made me do it. There is no devil; there is only God. Thus for Hasidism everything comes from God: lustful thoughts, an overweight body, greediness, or fearfulness. Or, in other words, all of our thoughts, intentions, and deeds are part of who we are. Change does not come by denying or fighting them, but rather by accepting them as intrinsic to our identity.

Sin is not original; nor is it a powerful dark force of the universe. What we call sin, or better yet, what we see as the flaws of our personalities, is part of the structure of the universe. Sins are the fault lines where subterranean aspects of our souls, our personalities, bump up against each other and come into conflict. It is where the needs for dependence and for independence clash, where openness and closedness, generosity and limitations confront one another. All of our parts— those we proudly display and those that, like the dark side of the moon, remain forever hidden—all of these are who we are and all of them partake of the Divine.

Our flaws and faults, all the flotsam of human existence also offer opportunities to come closer to the Holy One. For if they come from God, they have the potential to lead back to God. The *Likutim Yekarim* (an eighteenth-century Hasidic work) asks, if there are sparks of holiness in all things as the mystics teach, then what are the sparks of holiness in sin? It answers that the sparks are *teshuvah*. In the moment we realize that we have done wrong, we gain the opportunity to redeem ourselves by returning to the holy. The High Holidays, then, are an opportunity for self-examination, a chance to greet the worst aspects of ourselves as longtime, if not always welcome, acquaintances. Through this process of facing ourselves in the mirror of the moment, we can begin the process of *teshuvah*, of "turning" or "returning." When we approach our true image as reflected in the mirror of High Holidays, we can see that our flaws are the distorted impulses of the desire that underlies this world for wholeness and holiness. We catch a glimpse of how much happier and whole we could be if we can leave behind that which has made us stuck.

With this attitude, what we ask of God in this season, *selihah*, "forgiveness," is what we will be able to give ourselves. The hardest part is forgiving ourselves for our weaknesses. On the first day of Rosh haShanah, we read the story of Hagar and her son Ishmael. Lost in the desert, Hagar despairs of finding water to save her son's life. God responds to her cries and suddenly Hagar sees a well of water right in front of her that only a minute ago was completely invisible. The High Holidays urge us to see our lives clearly and to find the seemingly invisible wells that could not only sustain us but enable us to grow and change as we stumble through the deserts of experience.

May we be blessed in this New Year to be able to perceive and thus experience all the blessings that surround us and feel embraced by the love underlying the world.

### A TEACHING ON *TESHUVAH*

You have to judge every person generously. Even if you have reason to think that person is completely wicked, it's your job to look hard and seek out some bit of goodness, someplace in that person where he is not evil. When you find that bit of goodness and judge the person *that* way, you really may raise her up to goodness. Treating people this way allows them to be restored, to come to *teshuvah*.

This is why the Psalmist said: "Just a little bit more and there will be no wicked one; you will look at his place and he will not be there" (Psalm 36). He tells us to judge one and all so generously, so much on the good side, even if we think they're as sinful as can be. By looking for that "little bit," the place however small within them where there is no sin (and everyone, after all, has such a place), and by telling them, showing them, that *that's* who they are, we can help them change their lives.

Even the person you think (and he agrees!) is completely rotten—how is it possible that at some time in his life he has not done some good deed, some *mitzvah*? Your job is just to help him look for it, to seek it out, and then to judge him that way. Then indeed you will "look at his place" and find that the wicked one is no longer there—not because she has died or disappeared, but because, with your help, she will no longer be where you first saw her. By seeking out that bit of goodness you allowed *teshuvah* to take its course.

So now, my clever friend, now that you know how to treat the wicked and find some bit of good in them—now go do it for yourself as well! You know what I have taught you: "Take great care: be happy always! Stay far, far away from sadness and depression." [Rabbi Nahman of Bratslav, *Liqqutey MoHaRaN* 282, translated by Arthur Green]

*Customs of Yom Kippur*    The rabbis said that Yom Kippur can only effect atonement for sins between God and human beings. All the prayers we recite in synagogue, however, cannot repair sins and hurts between people. Instead we must approach whomever we have wronged and ask forgiveness. Only the victim can truly forgive our sins. Therefore, some people follow the custom in the weeks leading up to Yom Kippur of asking all their acquaintances, their family, and their friends for forgiveness even if there was nothing specific that they remembered doing wrong.

The day before Yom Kippur, we recite the confessional during the afternoon service, eat a large meal *(seudah ha-mafseket)*, then light *yahrzeit* and festival candles. It is also customary to give *tzedakah* before Yom Kippur. (The usual explanation for the confessional before Yom Kippur is that in case you choke to death during the meal, you will at least have asked for forgiveness before you died!) Some Jews visit the *mikvah,* the ritual bath, before Yom Kippur. A small minority of Jews continue a custom called *kapparot,* "atonements," by twirling a live rooster or hen over their heads, assigning their sins to the bird, in a form of a scapegoat ritual. The bird is then donated to *tzedakah.* Other Jews have substituted money wrapped in a handkerchief. After waving the handkerchief overhead, the money is then donated to *tzedakah.*

On Yom Kippur it is traditional to fast all day. There are other prohibitions, including anointing your body with oil, having sex, and wearing clothing made of leather. These three are seen as giving the body pleasure. Instead of leather, people wear sneakers or shoes of manmade material on Yom Kippur. These prohibitions are meant to help us focus on our striving for repentance on this day.

Nearly all the observance of Yom Kippur takes place in the synagogue. The evening services begin with Kol Nidrei, chanted to its powerful music, and conclude the following evening with Neilah, a service unique to Yom Kippur. It is traditional to wear a *tallit* at the Kol Nidrei service even though in general the *tallit* is not worn at night. Some people wear a *kitel* (a white robe) during services. The *kitel* has been explained in two ways. Its white color is a symbol of purity and thus of forgiveness; and it closely resembles the traditional shroud used for burial and is therefore an appropriate symbol to help us confront our mortality on this day.

The services of Yom Kippur are distinguished by special poetic insertions or *piyyutim* on the themes of the day. Unique to Yom Kippur is the confessional that is repeated throughout the day. There are six *aliyot* for the Torah reading (again unique to Yom Kippur). The *musaf,* the additional service, contains two special elements. The first is the *avodah* section that describes the Temple service of the High Priest, including the ritual of transferring the transgressions of the community to a goat sent to the place of Azazel, the origin of the scapegoat. During the recital of this section, it is traditional to prostrate our bodies at certain moments, as was done in the Temple. The second special element, the martyrology section, describes the deaths of talmudic sages during the Roman persecution. It is most commonly understood that we recite this section to invoke the merit of these martyrs on this day when our fate hangs in the balance. Contemporary liberal prayer books have adapted and reformulated both these sections. Yizkor, the memorial service, is also said on Yom Kippur. The afternoon service is distinguished by the reading of the Book of Jonah. The concluding Neilah service takes its imagery from the closing gates of heaven. It has a sense of urgency (certain prayers are shortened) as well as a sense of accomplishment, as when we come to an end of a marathon or a difficult task. Yom Kippur concludes with the blowing of one long blast on the shofar.

# SUKKOT

The holiday of Sukkot follows Yom Kippur by four days. It is connected to the High Holidays by proximity, but is also the final "pilgrimage" festival. In ancient times, Israelites would travel to the Temple in Jerusalem to offer sacrifices and participate in public rituals during the three pilgrimage festivals of Pesah, Shavuot, and Sukkot. All three festivals were connected to the agricultural cycle, which was itself reflected in the Temple ritual. The three pilgrimage festivals are also connected in a historical sense. We begin with Passover and the Exodus from Egypt, continue on to Shavuot and the Revelation at Sinai, and then come to Sukkot, which recalls the wandering of the Israelites on their way to the Promised Land.

It may seem strange that Sukkot does not mark a specific event like Pesah and Shavuot. If Sukkot had commemorated our entrance into the land of Israel, it would seem to be the perfect ending to our story of the journey from Egypt to the Promised Land by way of Sinai. After all, that is how it "really" happened. Yet there is no festival or commemoration of the entrance to the land. Just as the Torah ends with the death of Moses and the people camped only on the border of the Promised Land, so too in our celebration of our mythic past, we conclude the cycle with the Israelites still wandering in the desert. Should we then look upon Sukkot as marking that dreams do not come true? The answer is a qualified yes.

Of all the holidays, it is only at Sukkot that the Torah commands us to rejoice as part of our celebration. Rejoicing would be easily explained if Sukkot did, in fact, celebrate our entry into the Promised

Land. Yet Sukkot does not represent the fulfillment of the vision, because then the story would be ended. We would be faced with the impossible question of why we are living in an imperfect world if the Jewish myth had already reached its "happily ever after." Instead, Sukkot is the "to be continued" of our story. The story of the Jewish people, the story of each person, goes on. We all wander in the desert on our way to the Promised Land. The only question is how we make the journey. Some travel the landscape warily, always alert to danger. Others are just the opposite, oblivious of all they pass on the way. Many are poised to turn back to the security of some imaginary "good old days." Sukkot suggests that the way to travel is with your "eyes on the prize," with your distant goal always in mind. Yet even as you travel toward that horizon, you are aware of all that occurs to you at the moment. To this present, of course, you bring the past. Most useful in facing the challenges of that journey are the lessons of the Exodus (Pesah) and of Sinai (Shavuot)—that we have the freedom to make choices and an accumulated body of wisdom called Torah that can help guide our choices and give us direction.

Still, Sukkot reminds us that it is not the future goal that sustains us in the face of the hardships of our journeys. Our real goal (and challenge) is to live in the moment. We should do this neither with grim determination nor with an absolute faith in our abilities to overcome any obstacle. Rather we strive to journey in happiness and joy. How? By being aware of each blessing we encounter, especially the greatest blessing—having a Beloved Traveling Companion. For what Sukkot celebrates is not the story of the Israelites complaining for forty years in the desert. The picture evoked by Sukkot is different from the one you get from a simple reading of the biblical account. Rather, it is the picture of Jeremiah, who says, "I accounted to your favor the devotion of your youth, your love as a bride—How you followed Me in the wilderness, in a land not sown" (Jer. 2:2). This is the description of the youthful enthusiasm of a new relationship, of a people who so trust in God that they are willing to leave everything behind and head off into a desert with no real provisions for the way other than a vision of a goal at journey's end. It views the period in the desert not as a story of failure but as a typical life's journey with blessings and tragedies. It suggests that the key to a successful journey is not reaching the promised destination, but rather being aware of every moment of the journey. To be successful you need to rejoice, to travel with *simha*, "joy."

To travel with *simha* makes all the difference to experience. For you can be assured of two things. First, that you will be waylaid by Amalek on the way, will turn aside for Golden Calves, will thirst for sand and hunger for the harmful, and will too often be on the verge of returning to the fleshpots of Egypt. Most of all, you will discover that the fabled Promised Land always lies just over the next hill. Between you and the Land is not the river Jordan but the river Styx. Just as for Moses, death will not let us pass that final barrier. Frustrations, disappointments, suffering, and in the end death are on the itinerary of each of our journeys. It is how we cope that makes the difference.

Sukkot calls us to greet life with joy. It does not expect us to be joyful at the worst moments, but it encourages us to rejoice at the blessings of the everyday—every day that we are not sick, every day that our heart is not broken. It urges us to rejoice in the blessings of life: laughter, tasty food, relationships, or a good book. Sukkot is the explanation of how to live after the Exodus and Sinai—when you are no longer experiencing miracles or hearing God's voice directly. Rejoicing along the path as the way to live life is the message of Sukkot. (For additional development of this theme, see "Numbers/Be-midbar," pp. 396–424.)

## The *Sukkah*

The main ritual of Sukkot is to dwell in a *sukkah*, "booth." We build this temporary structure with a roof made of organic material. The roof should provide some cover and yet be porous enough to enable us to see the stars and thus to let in the elements. The booths can be built from any material in a wide variety of sizes. Most of the traditional rules focus on the roof. It is usually made from branches cut from trees. In warmer climes, Jews eat and sleep in the *sukkah*, making it a kind of temporary home. In the Northern Hemisphere, Jews generally eat in the *sukkah*, but sleep and carry on the rest of their regular activities at home.

You may wish to build your own *sukkah*. Kits for building them are available in local Jewish stores and on the Internet. Or you can plan and build your own. We are supposed to eat in the *sukkah*, but in case of rain, the tradition actually discourages us from doing so. Whenever we do eat in the *sukkah*, we say the blessing for fulfilling this *mitzvah*. We do not say the blessing if we are just visiting the *sukkah*.

It is also customary to decorate the *sukkah*. This can be turned into a joyful project for the whole family. Common decorations include the hanging of fruits or gourds, paper chains, High Holiday cards, pictures of Israel, and children's drawings.

The *sukkah*'s open structure reflects the openness and hospitality of this holiday. Typically, people invite friends for meals in the *sukkah*. In some communities, Jews will go from *sukkah* to *sukkah* on the afternoon of the festival days, stopping to say hello and have a piece of cake. There is also a tradition of inviting *ushpizin,* "symbolic guests," to the *sukkah*. These honorary guests are Abraham, Isaac, Jacob, Joseph, Moses, Aaron, and David. Some include women such as Sarah, Rebecca, Rachel, Leah, Miriam, Abigail, and Esther. Each day one guest or a pair of guests is invited. Perhaps this emphasis on hospitality expresses a desire that in our life's journey we not travel alone.

*The symbolism of the* sukkah    The Talmud records two opinions regarding the symbolism of the *sukkah*. One says that the *sukkah* reminds us of the booths the Israelites lived in while they wandered in the wilderness. Modern scholars suggest that the *sukkah* is actually modeled on the booths in which Israelite farmers sheltered close to their fields during the fall harvest. During the forty years of wandering, the scholars suggest, the Israelites probably lived in tents, especially in the desert.

The second opinion is more intriguing, for it says that the booths are to remind us of the *ananei ha-kavod,* "the clouds of glory," that accompanied the Israelites in their wanderings. According to the Torah, a cloud of glory would lead the Israelites when it was time for them to travel from place to place. When the Israelites encamped, the cloud would rest upon the sanctuary. The cloud was a sign of God's Presence, covering what cannot be seen by humans and showing that God accompanied the people of Israel in all their journeys. But in what sense is the *sukkah* a sign of God's accompanying Presence?

The answer is metaphorical. The *sukkah* is a peculiar structure in that it lacks the basic element of necessary comfort: a protective roof. The *sukkah*'s roof of leaves and branches does not provide real shelter; but allows us to see the sky or the stars—the handiwork of the Creator. It is under God's sheltering Presence that we dwell. Like the cloud, the *sukkah* makes visible that which is invisible—the Holy One. Sukkot reminds us to "see" God in the everyday experience of our lives. The clouds of glory are all around us; they are the presence and pattern of life.

*Lessons on the journey, or why we dwell in a* sukkah    As we journey through life, we construct our homes as places of refuge. We want to feel safe when we close the front door behind us. The *sukkah* is, by definition, a fragile structure. Our homes are supposed to be just the opposite. We try to accumulate enough "provisions" in them to be prepared for any emergency. The truth, of course, is that no provisions are sufficient for life's misfortunes. Yet we all pretend otherwise. We fill our homes with the accumulations of a lifetime, things that reflect our self-image and the image we wish others to see. These reflections of our financial accomplishments are meant to bring us pleasure, both aesthetic and sensory. Yet objects can only provide happiness on a temporary basis. Like good food or wine, life's pleasures should be enjoyed, but they are transitory. Dwelling in the *sukkah* reminds us that our attempts to create permanent castles are illusory. No matter how much enjoyment we get from them, on some level we can only journey through life with as much as our hearts, not our hands, can carry. Our sense of security and our happiness come from what we carry inside. They cannot be purchased; they can only be acquired by understanding what is possible and what is not. Fundamentally, all of us already have everything we need to be happy and secure, that is, the ability to be openhearted.

## The Four Species

The other central ritual of Sukkot employs the Four Species (palm, citron, willow, and myrtle), together known as the *lulav* and *etrog,* from the words for the two most visible of the species, the palm branch and the citron. After the Four Species are gathered in a specified manner, the willow and myrtle are intertwined with the palm to create the *lulav*. Then the *lulav* and the *etrog* are ritually shaken each day of Sukkot.

Particular attention is paid to the aesthetic element on Sukkot. People try to choose the most beautiful *lulav* and *etrog* they can find. While the *lulav* and *etrog* will stay fresh throughout the holiday, it is harder to make sure that the myrtles and especially the willows last. The best method I have found is to keep them refrigerated when not in use.

Some people shake the Four Species in the *sukkah,* others at home. Some will wait to do this until right before Hallel is recited in the synagogue. Specifically, the ritual is to take the *lulav* in your left hand and the *etrog* in your right. Holding the *etrog* next to the *lulav,* you recite the blessing: "Praised are You, Eternal One, our God, the source of the universe, who has made us holy through the commandments and commanded us concerning the waving of the palm branch." On the first day, you also say the *sheheheyanu* blessing: "Praised are You, Eternal One, our God, the source of the universe, for keeping us in life, for sustaining us, and for enabling us to reach this moment."

The *lulav* is shaken a number of times during the Hallel service. The custom is to wave or shake the Four Species in all four cardinal directions as well as up and down; more commonly, the Species are shaken forward, to your right, behind you, to your left, and then up and down. This ancient ritual has no explicit rationale, but it is reasonable to suggest that since Sukkot is a harvest festival, this is a symbolic re-creation of the harvest, a ritualized prayer for future successful harvests, or an expression of gratitude for this year's bountiful harvest.

Rabbi Shlomo Carlebach taught that just as Sukkot marked the agricultural harvest, so do we mark our spiritual harvest "at the end of the year." He thought of Sukkot as the end of the year, since it marked the last of the pilgrimage festivals as well as the end of the High Holidays. In his teaching the order and its meaning go like this: You begin by stretching out the Four Species to the right, shaking them, and then drawing them back toward you and shaking them again. This is done three times. Then the same thing is done to the left, then upward, downward, backward and forward.

As with the counting of the Omer, the mystics have tied the Four Species to the *sefirot,* the emanations of God. We shake to the right, toward the *sefirah* of *hesed* or loving-kindness, becoming aware that just as the world begins in loving-kindness, we should begin with open-heartedness. We continue to the left, toward the *sefirah* of *gevurah* or limitations, becoming aware that just as we need loving-kindness, we also need to set limits and create boundaries for that love. We then point up, calling God's bounty to flow down toward us, and continue by pointing downward to ask that the bounty flow deep into the world. This flow is what gives life to all of creation. We then point behind us to bring forward all of our past, and we end by pointing forward to express our hopes for the future. We thus bring together both openness and structure, both God's bounty and our past, as we continue our journey into the future.

The Four Species are used again during the *hoshanot service.* Each day during Sukkot, we circle the synagogue carrying the Four Species. Someone is honored with holding a Torah scroll inside the circle. As the procession is made, certain poetic prayers are recited that have as their refrain *hosha na,* "save us." Traditionally, neither the circling nor the waving of the Four Species takes place when Sukkot and Shabbat coincide. The book of Kohelet, Ecclesiastes, is read on the intermediate Shabbat of Sukkot.

### Hoshana Rabbah

The seventh day of Sukkot is known as Hoshana Rabbah, "the great or many hosannas." On that day we circle the synagogue seven times instead of just once as we recite all of the *hoshanot* prayers. At the end of the circling, we take a fresh bunch of willows and beat them against a chair. This practice is adapted from Temple times. It is most commonly explained as one last effort of getting rid of our sins. Hoshana Rabbah is seen as the very last day of the High Holiday period.

# SHEMINI ATZERET
# AND SIMHAT TORAH

*Shemini Atzeret* means the "eighth day of assembly." Originally, it was the conclusion to the holiday of Sukkot. In the Torah, God says, Tarry with me one additional day. (This is the traditional interpretation of Num. 29:35.) God is expressing reluctance at seeing the people leave at the end of the pilgrimage festival. Since the destruction of the Temple, Shemini Atzeret is characterized by the prayer for rain that is chanted in services. This prayer for rain still ties the liturgical cycle to the land of Israel. Soon after this time of year, the rainy season begins in Israel. Since almost no rain falls in the summer, a successful agricultural year depends on the winter season's rainfall. Thus this prayer is sung to a solemn melody evocative of the High Holiday liturgy.

Void of the rituals of the *sukkah* and Four Species, Shemini Atzeret seemed characterless until the Middle Ages, when the tradition of reading the whole Torah during the course of one year came to predominate. To celebrate the completion of the cycle, a new holiday developed called Simhat Torah, "rejoicing with the Torah." In communities that observe only one of the two days, Simhat Torah has come to overwhelm the relatively colorless Shemini Atzeret. In those communities that observe two days at the end of Sukkot, Simhat Torah is the second day and Shemini Atzeret is the first.

### Circles of Torah

Both major holiday periods in the year climax with a festival devoted to Torah. Shavuot, which marks the giving of the Torah at Sinai, is linked by the Omer to Passover. Simhat Torah brings to an end the fall holidays of Rosh ha-Shanah, Yom Kippur, and Sukkot. Yet Shavuot is very different from Simhat Torah. On Shavuot, we remember the awesome moment of Sinai, the Revelation of both God and the Torah. There are no rituals for Shavuot other than devoting ourselves to Torah study. Simhat Torah's mood is opposite to the awe and grandeur of Shavuot. We embrace Torah and dance with it. It can be compared to the development of a relationship. At first you are tentative with the other person, unsure of what she or he likes. As time goes on, the relationship seems less fragile and intimacy grows. After receiving the Torah on Shavuot, we have come to know it through study, and so, by Simhat Torah, we are ready to embrace it. As at a wedding feast, we take our partner, the Torah scroll, into our arms and dance the night away.

The month of Tishri is filled with *mitzvot*—the shofar, the *sukkah,* the Four Species. However, when we come to Simhat Torah, there are no *mitzvot,* there is only the Torah itself to be embraced. Instead of an intellectual learning of Torah, we absorb Torah through our dancing, and our feet learn how to walk in *darkhei ha-shem,* "the path of the holy." Throughout the month of Elul and the Tishri holidays, we recite Psalm 27, which includes the verse "One thing I ask of God, only that do I seek: to live in the house of God all the days of my life." We stop saying this Psalm right before Simhat Torah, because on this holiday, as we dance with the Torah, we *are* in the house of God, before the Presence of the Holy One.

As we sing and dance on Simhat Torah, may we experience the Presence of the Holy One in our midst!

### Customs of Simhat Torah and Shemini Atzeret

Simhat Torah and Shemini Atzeret are festival days marked by candle lighting, *kiddush,* and the prohibition on work. On Shemini Atzeret, the memorial prayer, Yizkor, is recited during morning services.

Simhat Torah's celebrations begin after the evening service in the synagogue. All the Torah scrolls are taken out and various people are given the honor of carrying the scrolls. A procession of scrolls circles the synagogue as a few verses are chanted. This is followed by singing and dancing. There are seven *hakkafot*, "circlings." Depending on the enthusiasm of the participants, the length of each one can vary greatly from synagogue to synagogue. There is a custom of giving children paper flags or apples to carry in the procession. After the seventh circling is completed, the scrolls are returned to the ark. One is left out for a reading of a section from the last portion of the Torah. This is the only time the Torah is read at night in a service.

The next morning, in addition to the regular festival services, *hakkafot* are done again, though not as enthusiastically. The highlight of the morning services is the reading of the last verses of Deuteronomy, followed by the first verses of Genesis. We thereby show that the cycle of Torah study never ends. As soon as we finish we begin again. It is considered a special honor to be given one of these *aliyot*. In fact, they are called *hatan/kallat torah*, the "groom/bride of Torah," and *hatan/kallat bereishit*, the "groom/bride of Genesis."

It is also the custom that everyone receives an *aliyah* on the morning of Simhat Torah. This is done either by group *aliyot* or by reading over and over again the verses in Deuteronomy. There is a custom that even children receive an *aliyah*. All children are invited up and a *tallit* is often spread over their heads as a canopy.

In the spirit of rejoicing, some communities include good-natured fooling around during the *musaf* service of Simhat Torah, particularly by children. The person leading services is often the target of the pranks. He or she participates in the spirit of the moment by chanting the service to funny melodies.

# HANUKKAH

Amid the darkness of winter, we light candles to celebrate the story of the Maccabees. The story, as usually told, begins when the Hellenized Syrian rulers of Israel under King Antiochus forbade the practice of Judaism. An uprising led by the priest Mattityahu and his sons ensued. Despite the odds, the Maccabees, as they were called, defeated the Syrians and restored the Temple in Jerusalem to the worship of God. When they went to rekindle the Temple menorah (candelabrum), they could find only one small cruse of oil that had not been defiled. It should only have lasted one day, but miraculously, it burned for eight days. Ever since, we celebrate Hanukkah (which means "dedication") with the lighting of candles for eight days.

The holiday has two connected strands: the victory of the few against the many and the miracle of the oil. At different times in history, one or the other of these strands has been emphasized. In certain periods, the military victory has been the central theme; at other times the miracle of the menorah has been center stage. In the Middle Ages, the stories of martyrdom such as that of Hannah and her seven sons became prominent, reflecting the tragic experience of medieval Jewry. Like the flickering light of the candles, Hanukkah's meaning has continued to shift even in our times.

In modern times, the State of Israel has seen the Maccabees as models for Israel's own struggle for survival against larger foes. In America, Hanukkah has taken on additional significance as a Jewish parallel to Christmas. Since Christmas is so pervasive, Hanukkah became an increasingly important answer to children's question of why we don't celebrate Christmas. This has led to an increased emphasis on the giving of presents at Hanukkah. Though there had been a tradition of giving children small amounts of money, "Hanukkah *gelt*," before the twentieth century, the American Jewish experience made this a major focus of the holiday. For all of these reasons, both its traditional symbolism and new meanings, Hanukkah is widely observed in the Jewish community.

Strikingly, the story we all know exists in none of the early accounts. Each of the ancient versions has only a part of it. Contemporary scholars question even its basic assumptions. They suggest that it was unlikely that King Antiochus, being a Hellenist and a pantheist, would have outlawed the observance of Judaism. Instead, the Maccabean conflict probably began as a civil war between Hellenizing Jews and those who remained loyal to the tradition. At some point, the Hellenizing Jews called for help from their powerful Syrian patrons. This makes the tale less black and white. Is this a fight between liberals and fanatic fundamentalists or between traditionalists and self-hating assimilationists?

Still, the story, with its victory of light against darkness, has inspired hope in many generations. For some, the military victory is itself miraculous, for the small number of Maccabees could hardly have defeated the Syrian armies without God's help. Hanukkah thus remains a story of a struggle for religious liberty. For many others, it is the symbolism of the light that illuminates the deepest dark and that can continue burning beyond all realistic expectation that is the reason to celebrate this holiday.

## The Meaning of Hanukkah

When Adam saw the day getting gradually shorter, he said: "Woe to me, perhaps because I have sinned, the world around me is being darkened and returning to its state of chaos and confusion; this then is the kind of death to which I have been sentenced from Heaven!" So he began observing an eight-day fast. However, as he observed the winter equinox and noted the day getting increasingly longer he said: "This is the world's course," and he set forth to keep an eight-day festivity. [Talmud, *Avodah Zara* 8a]

This ancient proto-Hanukkah festival reflects humanity's deepest fears and hopes. Adam, exiled from the garden and living through the first year in human history, notices the ever-shortening day. He is worried that this trend will continue until there is no daylight left. Perhaps this is the death he has been promised as punishment for eating the fruit of the tree in the garden? Suddenly he notices that the days are getting longer and he understands that this is part of the natural cycle, no different from the daily cycle of night and day.

Afraid of the dark, Adam comes to understand that light will prevail. Like Adam we learn that our lives will be lived amid both light and darkness. Light itself creates shadows. Yet we are not to despair or believe that darkness will overwhelm the light. Instead, we light the Hanukkah candles to remember the miracle that even a small light can illuminate a vast darkness. The light represents the holiness that lies within each of us. Eight is a number that signifies "beyond the normal." Seven is a complete unit, as in the seven days of the week. Eight, then, is one beyond completion.

By lighting the menorah, we ignite the flame in our souls, the sparks that cannot be extinguished, that will burn not for eight days but for eternity. We place the menorah in our windows to be visible to those passing by, just as our inner light must shine against the darkness of evil and indifference and must kindle the spirits of our fellow humans. The menorah reminds us of the miracle that no matter how dark life may be, there remains a source of light deep inside us. The light in our souls reflects and refracts the light from the One who is all brightness. [From *The Jewish Holidays*, p. 177]

### Customs of Hanukkah

The central ritual of Hanukkah is lighting the menorah. It is lit each night after dark. (Some people use oil, especially olive oil, instead of candles.) There is an extra candle on the menorah called the *shammash*, "helper." It is used to light the other candles. To show it does not "count" in the ritual, the holder for the *shammash* is often raised above those of the other candles.

While you have fulfilled the commandment if you light one candle each night, it has become the standard practice to light one additional candle each night. In this manner, someone seeing the number of candles will know which night of Hanukkah it is. Therefore, it is also the custom to have a menorah that keeps each light distinctly in view.

Since there is a desire to proclaim the miracle of Hanukkah, some have the tradition of placing the menorah in a window. Others will place it on a table to proclaim the miracle to the members of the household. Traditionally, you place the candles in the menorah from right to left, but light them from left to right.

After the candle lighting, some people sing Hanukkah songs, such as the hymn "Ma'oz Tzur" ("Rock of Ages") or the children's tune "I Had a Little Dreidl." Presents are given. Latkes (potato pancakes) or doughnuts are eaten. (Food fried in oil reminds us of the miracle of the oil.) It is an old custom to play games of chance during the long nights of Hanukkah. Spinning a top called a dreidl is a popular game. The dreidl has a Hebrew letter on each side—*nun, gimel, heh, shin,* an acronym for *neis gadol hayah sham,* "a great miracle happened there." (In Israel, *sham,* "there," is replaced by *poh,* "here.") The game can be played with nuts or pennies. Each player puts one in the pot and then spins the dreidl and follows the directions associated with the letter that is on top. *Shin* signifies "put in" or add one to the pot. *Nun* signifies "nothing happens." *Heh* signifies "take half the pot." *Gimel* is the big winner, "take the whole pot." You can also try just playing with the dreidl by spinning it upside down or spinning it to knock down other dreidls.

Some have the custom of sitting quietly in a room lit only by the Hanukkah candles. Some recite verses or Psalms related to the theme of light. The candles of the menorah can also be used as a focus for meditation. Or the time can be used to reflect on the meaning of Hanukkah.

Hanukkah is mostly a home observance. There are small changes to the liturgy including adding a special paragraph in the *amidah* and the Grace after Meals. Hallel is recited during morning services.

The mystics taught that the light of Hanukkah partakes of the *or haganuz,* the "hidden light," the primordial light of creation. As we know from the first verses of Genesis, the world was created by setting apart light from darkness. Yet the biblical text tells us that the sun and moon were created only on the third day. According to tradition, there was a primordial light that illuminated those first days of creation. By its light it was possible to see from one end of the world to the other. With the creation of the sun, this light was hidden away until the end of days, hence it is called *or ha-ganuz,* "the light that was hidden." Sitting in the light of the menorah, we can seek to see with the clarity of that primordial light. We can try to see past those things that block our vision or prevent us from having a vision of what could be. Hanukkah, which means "dedication," can be a time for us to rededicate ourselves to that which we "see" as important in our lives. In the midst of the darkness and cold at this time of year (at least in the Northern Hemisphere), months removed from the fervor of the fall holidays, we can reset our bearings by removing our blindness.

> Rabbi Jose said: "I was long perplexed by this verse: 'And you shall grope at noonday as the blind gropes in darkness' (Deut. 28:29). Now what difference does it make to a blind person whether it is dark or light? Once I was walking on a pitch-black night when I saw a blind person—walking torch in hand. I asked: 'Why do you carry the torch?' The blind person replied: 'As long as the torch is in my hand, people can see me and aid me.' " [Talmud, *Megillah* 24b]

The light of the menorah lets us see each other and thereby enables us to help each other on our journeys. Despite the darkness, in its light we can see clearly from one end of world to the other.

---

*KAVANAH*

There is a debate in the Talmud between Hillel and Shammai about how the candles should be lit. Hillel says that we should light one the first night, two the second, and so on. Shammai says that we should start with eight candles the first night and then light seven the second, and so on. I would suggest that Shammai is following his general overriding principle—to tell the truth. The truth is that we live in a world of ever-diminishing expectations. The moment we are born we begin to die. Each day brings us one day closer to our last day. Similarly, as we saw in the section about the Omer, Shammai says that on her wedding day, we should tell the truth about the bride: if she is beautiful, then we say that; if she is not, then we say that. For Shammai, truth is the ultimate value. Hillel says that every bride is beautiful in the eyes of those who love her on her wedding day. Similarly, for Hillel there is a deeper sense of truth at issue here. The deeper truth is that our lives become ever richer and fuller with the passage of time, not increasingly diminished. The light of Hanukkah reminds us of the potential that lies within each moment. The present can be filled with light and that light can increase no matter where we are in the span of our lives. Like life, light can pierce any darkness. It became the custom to follow Hillel's opinion that we light an additional light each night to make known the miracle of Hanukkah; that is, our light can grow exceedingly bright beyond any reasonable expectations.

# TU BISHVAT

The fifteenth (Hebrew: *tu*) day of the month of Shevat (hence *Tu Bishvat*) is a minor holiday known as the New Year for the Trees. In ancient times it affected laws related to tithing. After Temple times, it was marked only by the eating of fruit associated with the land of Israel. In modern times, this minor festival has gained new attention and acquired additional meaning. With the return to the land of Israel, Tu Bishvat's connection to the land has been emphasized. Concerns about the environment have added another layer of meaning to a day associated with caring about nature.

An interesting ritual, developed by the Kabbalists, has also become a common way to observe Tu Bishvat. Loosely modeled on the Pesah Seder, the Tu Bishvat Seder also has four glasses of wine and the ritualized eating of specific foods. These foods are fruits (and nuts) that were seen to symbolize the four worlds of creation. According to Kabbalah, these four worlds move from that which is completely spiritual to the physical world. These worlds are: *azilut,* "emanation"; *beriah,* "creation"; *yetzirah,* "formation"; and *assiyah,* "the physical world." The Tu Bishvat Seder ritual proceeds from the most physical world to the most spiritual while eating fruits associated with each world. The physical world is symbolized by fruits and nuts with inedible skins or shells. The inedible represents the *kelippot,* "shells." In Kabbalah, the world begins with a great shattering that scattered sparks of holiness and encased them in shells of impurity or the mundane. Thus in the world of the physical, the holy is hidden by the shells. In the world of formation, we consume fruits that are edible on the outside but have a pit at their core. In this world, the holy is more accessible, but there remains an element of the inedible/impure. In the world of creation, the fruit is completely edible, and in the world of the spirit or emanation, there is neither fruit nor anything tangible. In the Kabbalistic Seder, there are accompanying texts to be read with each fruit eaten.

The Kabbalistic Seder has served as a model for contemporary Tu Bishvat Seders. Some focus on the environment or on Israel. Others employ a simplified notion of the Kabbalistic Seder and retain the movement from the physical world to the spiritual. Some use all three elements, the environmental, Israel, and the spiritual, in these new Seders. Two such Seders are: *Seder Tu Bishvat: The Festival of Trees,* by Adam Fisher (Central Conference of American Rabbis, 1989); and *A Tu Bishvat Seder: The Feast of Fruits from the Tree of Life,* by Yitzhak Buxbaum (Jewish Spirit, 1998).

One *kavanah* I have used is to see the four worlds as four approaches to the environment. We begin with conflict between humans and nature, move to a concept of stewardship, then to recognizing the "rights" of animals, and finally to a notion of deep ecology with a profound sense that we are one with the universe. (See "Ecology," pp. 475–86, for more on our relationship to the earth.)

A different *kavanah* views the Seder as the evolution of relationships. We begin by keeping a protective shell around ourselves, not willing to let our soft core, our hearts, be vulnerable. As a relationship develops, we open ourselves up, but there is a place deep inside, that which is most vulnerable, that we still keep protected. Finally, a successful relationship moves to where there is nothing held back. Trust is complete and freely given. In such a relationship, there are moments of union when the border between you and the other person blurs or even disappears. This can be true of relationships with human beings or with the Divine.

---

### KAVANAH

In the beginning, we lived in the Garden of Eden, in complete harmony with nature. Then we ate of the tree of knowledge of good and evil. Feeling naked, we experienced a desire for clothing—the first separation between nature and ourselves. With this first manipulation of the natural world for our benefit, we began our exile. "Cursed be the ground because of you; by toil shall you eat of it all the days of your life, thorns and thistles shall it sprout for you" (Gen. 3:17–18). From a symbiotic relationship we were driven into one of bitter struggle with nature.

In that exile from nature, we also became exiled from our bodies, and death came into the world. In the end our bodies will betray us and deliver us to death. Ironically, only in death do we reachieve harmony by returning to the earth. As the verse continues, "by the sweat of your brow shall you get bread to eat, until you return to the ground—for from it you were taken. For dust you are, and to dust you shall return" (Gen. 3:19).

In the modern world, we may think that we have mostly won the struggle with nature. We have been able to harness nature to our own needs. Yet we have discovered that in that harnessing we run the risk of destroying this planet. For it is still true, despite all our accomplishments, that in the end nature will run its course and our bodies will return to dust. Both we and this planet are in need of healing. Let us feel the earth's pain reflected in our pain, for in truth we are part of rather than separate from Mother Earth.

How can we find our way back to the garden guarded by an angel with a fiery sword made up of human hubris and greed?

# PURIM

The festival of Purim (Adar 14) celebrates the story of Esther and Mordecai's triumph over the evil Haman. Its central ritual is the reading of the Book of Esther in the synagogue. Whenever Haman's name is read, we try to drown it out with graggers (rattles or noisemakers).

The story itself is a grand farce, filled with absurdly lucky coincidences where the right person is always in the right place at the right time (or, in the case of Haman, in the wrong place at the wrong time). The story comes to a rather grim end when the empowered Jews kill not only Haman but also hundreds of enemies. There are those who have seen the story as supporting attacks on the enemies of the Jewish people. This seems to me a complete misreading of the tone of the tale. For Jews being persecuted in the Middle Ages, Purim was probably a revenge fantasy and a safe but useful venting of anger against anti-Semites. I think that even the massacres at the end of the book reflect a fantastical yet simpleminded view of good guys and bad guys.

The book's farcical tone is set right at the beginning with the Queen Vashti episode. Called by the dumb King Ahasuerus to dance at his all-male party, she refuses. (The rabbis cleverly suggest that since the text says she was supposed to come with her royal crown, this meant she was to dance wearing *only* her crown. This explains her refusal.) After getting rid of her, the king and his advisers worry that Vashti's disobedience might set a bad example. Therefore, they issue a decree that wives should treat their husbands with respect. There is nothing more ludicrous than a deluded bunch of drunken men issuing a decree ordering respect from their wives. It is left to us to wryly imagine their response.

## Why Celebrate Purim?

We are told to drink on Purim *ad lo yada,* "until we do not know" the difference between Mordecai and Haman. This is a strange tradition if Purim is really about good and evil. But Purim is best understood, like its story, as a time for silliness. As we have noted, various moods are called for in the festival cycle: mourning on Tisha be-Av, joy on Simhat Torah, contrition on Yom Kippur. On Purim, we are to let go and become silly fools. We are to shout out loud to drown out Haman. We are to put on Purim plays or "teach Torah" in ways that make fun of ourselves and even what we usually hold in respect, the Torah. Amid the challenges of the festival cycle, Purim is a day off from seriousness. It is a day devoted to making and having fun. For some people that is harder than repenting on Yom Kippur.

Purim asks us not to become overly serious about Torah or ourselves. In the world of *ad lo yada,* rules and inhibitions are overturned (within reason, of course). Everything is topsy-turvy. Poking fun at ourselves and those things we hold dear gives us a better perspective on life. It helps prevent us from idealizing and even idolizing that which we hold sacred.

On Purim we laugh at our self-righteousness. We make fun of the tradition and text, the Torah that we treat with such respect every other day of the year. In that mockery, we prevent the Torah from becoming an idol frozen in stone. To better value the Torah, we need to laugh at it and ourselves one day a year. Most of all on Purim, we just laugh and laugh.

## Purim Customs

The Book of Esther is read from a scroll similar to the Torah scroll. It is sometimes simply called the *megillah* (scroll), though technically the term applies to any book written on parchment. It is read as part of the evening service. The verses listing Haman's sons are customarily recited in one breath. It is customary to dress in costume for the *megillah* reading as part of the fun and the topsy-turvy nature of the celebration. Some people will wear their costumes during the daytime Purim activities as well (see below). (Traditionally the reading of the *megillah* is repeated during the morning service.) A special paragraph is added to the *amidah* and to Grace after Meals. (Hallel is not recited on Purim.)

A number of customs are observed based on verse 9:22 in the Book of Esther: "They were to observe them as days of feasting and gladness, and as a time for sending gifts one to another and presents to the poor." "Feasting and gladness" became the special meal known as a Purim *seudah* that takes place late on the afternoon of Purim. Some communities will have a communal meal complete with Purim skits that make fun of the story or of the community. This is also an opportunity for Purim Torah, which parodies a regular *d'var torah*, "Torah teaching." "Gifts one to another," *mishloah manot*, became the custom of sending gifts of food to friends. These gift baskets contain cake, fruit, candy, and especially *hamantaschen*—the triangular Purim pastries filled with poppy, prunes, chocolate, etc. They are supposedly reminiscent of Haman's hat. The custom is to include two kinds of food in each *mishloah manot*. Often children are assigned the job of delivering these food gifts and will receive a gift plate back as well as a snack for their effort. "Presents to the poor," *mattanot le-evyonim*, became the custom of giving special Purim gifts to the poor. The tradition is to give to two poor people or charities. A related custom is called *mahatzit ha-shekel*, "a half of a shekel coin." In ancient Israel, each person owed a half of a shekel for the upkeep of the Temple sacrificial system. This tax was collected around the time of Purim. Over time, the custom has evolved into an additional opportunity to give to the poor. Some will use a silver dollar as a way of recalling the half shekel. After "borrowing" the silver dollar, you then donate some of your own money. This donation is often done before the *megillah* reading.

Many communities hold Purim carnivals. In Israel, costumed merrymakers march in large *ad lo yada* parades. Purim is celebrated in Jerusalem on Shushan Purim, the fifteenth of Adar, a day after those outside Jerusalem. This follows the tradition of the Jews of Shushan, Persia (where the Purim story took place), who needed an extra day to defeat their enemies. There is also a minor fast day, *ta'anit Esther,* "the Fast of Esther," that occurs on the day before Purim (Adar 13). This commemorates the Jews fasting in Shushan as Esther, uninvited, approaches the king as part of her plot to save the Jews.

---

### A PIECE OF PURIM TORAH

Rabbah and Rabbi Zera joined together in a Purim feast. They became drunk and Rabbah arose and killed Rabbi Zera. On the next day, he prayed on Rabbi Zera's behalf and brought him back to life. Next year, Rabbah said: "Will your honor come, and we will have the Purim feast together." Rabbi Zera replied: "A miracle does not take place on every occasion." [Talmud, *Megillah* 7b]

---

## Why Does Purim Stand at the End of the Festival Cycle?

The following talmudic text suggests an answer:

"And they stood under [at the foot] of the mountain" (Exod. 19:17). R. Avdimi bar Hama said: This teaches that the Holy One suspended the mountain upon them, like an inverted vat, and said to them: If you accept the Torah, it is well; if not, your burial will be right here. R. Aha bar Jacob said: This story would justify a claim that Israel accepted the Torah under duress [thus nullifying the covenant with God]. Rava said: Nevertheless, the people of Israel freely accepted the Torah in the days of king Ahaseurus, as it is written: "The Jews established and accepted" (Esther 9:27), meaning they established in their time what they had accepted at Sinai. [Talmud, *Shabbat* 88a]

First, this midrash recognizes that there is an element of compulsion at Sinai and at every encounter with the Holy One. The event at Sinai stands near the beginning of the festival cycle. At Pesah, we have just left Egypt and already long to go back. We try to prepare ourselves for Sinai during the weeks of counting the Omer, but at the moment of

Sinai (Shavuot) we feel overwhelmed and flee. We ask Moses to go speak to God and tell us what God says. From Sinai we wander in desert lands through the bleakness of Tisha be-Av and the joy of Sukkot. We celebrate the newness of the New Year and worry about our goodness on Yom Kippur. We come through darkness into light at Hanukkah and strive to gain a glimpse of the garden on Tu Bishvat. In all those ups and downs of the year we struggle to "accept" the Torah by striving to discern its teachings and wisdom. At Purim, we have "grown up" enough to fulfill the challenge of Pesah and Shavuot. God is not only absent but is unmentioned in the Book of Esther. At Pesah, we are told that God redeemed us with an outstretched arm, but at Purim, we need to forge our own redemption, which is what the Jews in the Book of Esther do.

Similarly, after struggling with whether we can really accept the Torah all year, finally at Purim we make the Torah our own. The Jews of that time establish Purim as a holiday, a holiday created by humans, reflecting human endeavors. There are no miracles. The Torah is finally ours.

The irony, of course, is that Purim stands at the end of the festival cycle, for in a month we begin the cycle all over again. We hold the Torah only briefly before we are again immersed in our never-ending cycle of rejecting and accepting the Torah.

Part Four

# LIVING A LIFE
# OF HOLINESS

We live our lives from beginning to end. Each of our stories is similar in summary and yet different in detail. Life-cycle rituals help us mark great moments in a life—birth, marriage, and death. Yet we need not experience every life-cycle moment. Some of us will not have children. Some will remain unmarried. Some will get divorced. Yet all of us will partake of some life-cycle rituals.

One structure that can be laid over our life-cycle rituals is the life cycle of the people Israel as set out in our most sacred text, the Torah. As with any individual's life story, Torah has a beginning, a growing up, a facing of crises, a struggle toward independence, a reaching of middle age, a growing older, and an end in death. To use contemporary parlance, Torah is a story of passages.

Genesis is a book of beginnings. In the beginning, there are Adam and Eve, and a garden where they roam carefree and naked, as innocent as newborn babes. But they disobey God, and when they see themselves for the first time, embarrassment, guilt, and knowledge enter the world. As Adam and Eve leave the garden, real life begins—together with pain and travail, work, and growth. They give birth to children and the future *and* to rivalry, jealousy, and love.

Shemot (Exodus) is a book of leavings—of going out, of Exodus, of fleeing and of breaking loose, of becoming independent, of negotiating and dealing with the parent who knows you need to go but constantly hardens his heart and won't let go, of learning to live in the desert, of longing for the old security, of Golden Calves, of awesome revelations, of intense intimacy. In the end we emerge with a sanctuary, a place for intimate encounters with the Other.

Va-Yikra (Leviticus) is a setting-out of rules, rules relating to the home, relating to the beloved Other. The rules are developed in intricate detail. Movement stops. There is no more wandering in the desert, no more journeying. Leviticus is the season of consolidation, of settling down, of finding God in the details of a microscopic cell, in the tangle of relationships, in the living of everyday life rather than a "wow" moment.

Yet Leviticus is only an interlude. In Be-midbar (Numbers) we soon find ourselves once more wandering in a desert of uncertainty. All the old issues we thought were long ago settled in our Exodus days come back again. Once again we complain about the lack of food and water in the desert. We cry: Nourish me, O Holy One, be supportive, You who took me out of the Egypt that was my parents' home, where they fed me leeks and cucumbers and *my* family's own recipe of *narishkeit* and neuroses.

In the desert, we begin to doubt the vision of our lives. Our spies, our glimpses of the Holy Land, of our inner selves, cause us not to rejoice that the vision is in sight, but rather to doubt our capabilities; we fear we might actually get there. In the words of the spies about the inhabitants of the land of Israel: "They are giants and we looked like grasshoppers to ourselves, and so we must have looked to them." Such doubt and despair and skepticism can lead to rebellion and earthquakes, or just as bad, to zealotry and fanaticism, as we try to anchor ourselves in the shifting sands of the desert surrounded by mirages everywhere.

However, if we remember the past and yet are willing to grow; if we learn from our mistakes and also learn that what was right in the past is not necessarily correct now; if we fulfill the verse *Shiviti YHVH lenegdi tamid,* "I will place God before me" always; then we can avoid the mistakes of even so great a leader and human being as Moses. Moses, faced for a second time with a complaining people and a rock full of water, falls back on old habits, old *halakhah,* and uses a response that was perfectly appropriate the first time, and so he hits the rock. *But to this second rock* he should have spoken. Locked in the past, Moses loses his chance to reach the Promised Land.

To everything there is a season, a time to raise our fist and a time to raise our voice. If we have built our structure of rules and details, but made it a portable sanctuary, and even one ready to change as new challenges arise, then we will reach Devarim (Deuteronomy).

At last, in the wisdom of old age, sight undimmed, we recapitulate in our own version all that has gone before. It is a time of harvesting all that has been. Knowing that we will only see the Promised Land from over the next hill, we look back to the future and forward into the past, and we see the summary of our lives stretched out before us leading off into the distance of tomorrow.

The Midrash says that God looked into the Torah and used it as a blueprint to create the world. I am suggesting that this reading of the text of Torah as a chart of the cycle of our lives can help us echo God's creation by the creating of our world—the story of each of our lives.

# GENESIS/BEREISHIT:
# BEGINNINGS AND BIRTH

In the beginning, there are beginnings. In the beginning, there is life. All things have beginnings. All journeys have first steps, all plays opening lines. All speech begins with the emergence of sound breaking the realm of silence, of the unspoken. Thus we begin with birth. Our births long forgotten, the birth of our children. The birth of our collective future.

For humans, beginnings mean life, consciousness. It is coming awake each morning, opening our eyes, becoming awake to the world, to our being, to our surroundings.

> "Let us make humans in our image after our likeness. . . ." And God created a human in God's image, in the image of God, God created a human; male and female God created them. [Gen. 1:26–27]

Humans were created unique, different from all the creatures, all the creations of the world. We are little lower than angels; we are also creatures like all the other inhabitants of the world. Like angels we can think, walk erect, and speak; like animals we eat and drink, procreate, and die. We have our feet on the ground and our head in the heavens. Our uniqueness lies in part in being so complex, of partaking both of the earth and the heavens, of the material and the spiritual, the tangible and the intangible. Being unique means each of us is different from all other human beings who ever were, are, or will be.

The first human was created alone in order to teach you that if anyone causes a single soul to perish, the Torah imputes to him the destruction of the entire world; and if anyone saves the life of a single soul, the Torah imputes to her the saving of the entire world.

Or, humans were created alone for the sake of peace among them, that one might not say to another: My parents were greater than yours; . . . Therefore people were created unique, in order to proclaim the greatness of the Holy One. For if a person strikes many coins from one mold, they are all exactly alike. But though the King of kings, the Holy One, has fashioned every person in the stamp of the first human, not a single one of them is exactly like another. [Talmud, *Sanhedrin* 37a]

But most important, we are unique because we are created in God's image, in God's likeness. What does it mean that we are in God's likeness? We are unique in the world. We share God's aloneness and yet unlike God we have partners, for God understood it is not good for a human to be alone and so in contrast to all the *ki tov,* "it is good," of the days of creation, a human being all alone is *lo tov,* "not good." Only God remains alone in unfathomable uniqueness.

We taste of God's aloneness. We taste of the heavens. We taste of thought, feeling, and relationships because of the ability to speak—to communicate. Yet most of all we are unique and have a piece of God's image because we have choice. We can choose this path or that, to do this deed or not. To bring holiness into the world or to spread suffering and pain. Choice is the culmination of God's gifts to human beings. Intelligence, speech, and feeling are all means for choosing and ways to express and experience choices.

And one final gift—God. Being in God's image, we can find God reflected in ourselves: a piece of holiness, of the Divine lies within each of us reminding us who we are, for what we were created, and to whom we remain connected no matter what we do, no matter what happens to us: God as the parent who gave birth to us; God whose agents for holiness we are in this world; God whose unity we are to bring about through *tikkun olam*—through the repairing of the world, through transforming the world; God whose unique aloneness reminds us that we are never fully alone—for God is always with us.

> Our masters taught: For two and a half years the school of Shammai and the school of Hillel were divided. The first school said: It would have been better for humans not to have been created than to have been created. The other said: It is better for humans that they were created than it would have been had they not been created. They finally voted and decided: it would have been better for humans not to have been created than to have been created. But now that they have been created, let them search their past deeds. Some say: Let them examine what they are about to do. [Talmud, *Eruvin* 13b]

## Birth

On the sixth day of creation, humans were created. At every birth, the sixth day of creation is re-created. Unlike any other day of God's creation, we are able to re-create this sixth day. We can create human life; we can literally reproduce the sixth day's act of creation.

At that moment of creation of the first humans, God said to us: "Be fertile and increase, *p'ru u'rvu,* and fill the world." The first *mitzvah,* the first commandment, is to create a world, a world of a new human being.

*Sefer ha-Hinukh* says: "Be fertile" is a great *mitzvah* and only because of it do all the other *mitzvot* in the world exist, for the world is given to human beings, not to angels.

### Conception

> A person should leave his parents and cleave unto his partner and be like one flesh. [Gen. 2:24]

In this world of separation and partiality, of *havdalot,* it is in the moment of sexual union that we come close to the wholeness and thus the holiness of the divine. Instead of alienation and loneliness, we join together. We lose our sense of twoness and become as one. And yet it is just at that moment of twoness merged into oneness that we have the potential to create a third, that is, to conceive a child. It is a moment of unity that fosters further separations; a moment in which we are supremely aware of our physical selves and yet we partake of the holiness and the power of the Divine.

The creation of life is a miraculous moment. It is the most godlike act we will ever do and yet it is an act of the everyday world where the moment of miracle is revealed to us only in retrospect, after the passage of time.

**The moment of birth**    There is no traditional ritual or liturgy for the moment of the birth of a child. Perhaps this is because it is not necessary. Often when I ask people when they have experienced God's Presence, they will recount the story of the birth of their child. Amid the pain of delivery, there is an overriding sense of the wonder of creating life. The cry of the newborn is also a release of all the anxiety of the parents hoping for a successful pregnancy. It is a moment beyond words and a moment needing no liturgy to give expression to our feelings.

Yet recently, some people have developed their own rituals for the labor and birth. For example, either as the child emerges or soon after, it may be said, "Blessed and welcome is [he or she] who comes." Appropriate traditional blessings include "Praised are You, Eternal One, our God, the source of the universe, who is good and creates goodness," and "Praised are You, Eternal One, our God, the source of the universe, who has kept us alive and sustained us and enabled us to reach this moment."

A suggested new blessing may be "Praised are you, Eternal One, our God, the source of the universe, who lets the mother rejoice in the fruit of her womb, and the father with his offspring."

Our sages taught: There are three partners in the creation of a human being: God, the father and the mother. [Talmud, *Nedarim* 31a]

## *Brit milah,* Circumcision

The *mitzvah* of *p'ru u'rvu,* "be fertile," is the most universal commandment. In contrast, it is followed by the second commandment, which
established the particularity of the Jewish people, circumcision or *brit
milah.*

> Such shall be the covenant between Me and you and your off-
> spring to follow which you shall keep: every male among you shall
> be circumcised. You shall circumcise the flesh of your foreskin, and
> that shall be the sign of the covenant between Me and you. And
> throughout the generations, every male among you shall be circum-
> cised at the age of eight days. . . . [Gen. 17:10–12]

Beginning with this *mitzvah,* the *brit,* "covenant," between God and
Israel is established. The "natural" process of creation is interrupted. It
is not just the endless cycle of human existence anymore: giving birth,
new life, raising children, marriage, and again giving birth. Now God
creates a *brit,* a covenant, with Abraham and with all of his descendants, the covenant of *brit milah.*

*Brit milah,* as covenant, established a relationship between God
and the people of Israel. It is a relationship in which God asks us to act
in specific ways—*halakhah,* the ways of the Jewish people. It is a relationship that reminds us that we are God's partners in the work of finishing the creation of the world and that God is our partner through
each of our individual life journeys. Because of the *brit,* the covenant,
we walk on this path always accompanied by our covenantal partner, God.

The *brit* begins here at the beginning, at birth. It takes the natural
process and transforms it into a particular process; a process that we as
Jews shape and form. Thus, it is not accidental that the *mitzvah* of *brit
milah* follows the *mitzvah* of "be fertile," nor that the covenant between God and Israel is established by a circumcision of the foreskin of
the male reproductive organ.

Circumcision is an *ot,* a "sign" of this covenant. The covenant says that even the most universal impulse, to reproduce, is shaped by the relationship between God and Israel. What can be seen as natural, almost accidental, now has become purposeful. The reproduction of human beings, the continuity of generations, is now set in the context of the history and the role of the Jewish people.

For creation itself is given to us to transform. We take the male body as it is born, "the way God intended it to be," and we cut off the foreskin. Even the most natural is to be transformed by the act of circumcision; even the most natural is to be given specific meaning by the act of reproduction. That is why males are not born circumcised, as we learn from the following story:

> The tyrant Rufus asked R. Akiva: "Whose works are more comely—those of the Holy One or those of flesh and blood?" R. Akiva: "Those of flesh and blood are more comely." The tyrant Rufus: "But think of heaven and earth—can humans make anything like them?" R. Akiva: "Do not speak to me of matters that are above mortals and over which they have no power, but only of matters that are to be found among human beings." The tyrant Rufus: "Why do you have yourselves circumcised?" R. Akiva: "I knew that you were going to ask me this question. That is why I anticipated you by saying, 'The works of flesh and blood are more comely than those of the Holy One.'" [To prove his point] R. Akiva brought Rufus ears of grain and delicate breads, saying, "The ears of grain are the work of the Holy One, the breads the work of flesh and blood—are not the loaves more comely?" . . . Then the tyrant Rufus asked, "Assuming that God desires circumcision, why does the infant not emerge from his mother's womb circumcised?" R. Akiva replied, "Why does the umbilical cord emerge with the infant? Should not the mother have had the infant's umbilical cord cut off [in the womb]? As to your question of why an infant does not emerge circumcised, it is because the Holy One gave the *mitzvot* to Israel to purify them!" [*Midrash Tanhuma, Tazria* 5]

The ritual of circumcision is seen as an essential ritual of Jewish life. The *gematria* (numerical value) of the Hebrew word *brit* is 612.

This teaches that the *brit* is the equivalent of all the other *mitzvot* combined, for *brit* itself and its value total 613, the traditional number of commandments.

The main reason most Jews continue to observe circumcision is to place themselves within the Jewish people, within its long chain of tradition stretching back to our beginnings. It is not an easy ritual and many parents have qualms about it. In recent years there has been much discussion in the medical community about the effects of circumcision. While some say circumcision can have a number of medical benefits, others argue it has no medical benefit and therefore is an unnecessary procedure. However, the *mitzvah* of *brit milah* is not based on its medical benefits, just as *kashrut* is not based on health issues. It is a *mitzvah*. However, it is also clear that circumcision is a very safe procedure, particularly when performed by a *mohel* (plural: *mohelim*), a specialist in circumcision.

Parents are faced with a choice these days of having a circumcision done by a doctor in the hospital (as is done with most American non-Jews) or having a *brit milah* done by a *mohel*, either at home or in the synagogue, on the eighth day. The most cogent reason to have a *mohel* perform the *brit milah* is that a medical circumcision is not considered a valid fulfillment of the *mitzvah* of *brit milah*. Even more important, given the current medical uncertainty about the benefits of circumcisions, the only compelling reason to circumcise a child is to bring a son into the chain of tradition of the Jewish people. In other words, a circumcision for Jews should have the significance of a *brit milah*, not of a minor hospital procedure. A circumcision performed by a *mohel* is done to fulfill the *mitzvah* and therefore is accompanied by blessings, prayers, and the giving of a Hebrew name to the child. There are more pragmatic advantages to a *brit milah* as well. A *brit milah* is always performed in a loving environment rather than an impersonal hospital room. At a *brit milah* the child is not strapped down, as in a hospital "circ" room. *Mohelim* are skilled, experienced professionals who do nothing but circumcisions. There also seems to be some evidence that blood coagulates faster by the eighth day of a baby's life (making healing faster) than it does in the first few days (when hospital circumcisions are often performed).

The more difficult question for some parents is whether to have a *brit milah* or not. For many parents the notion of causing pain to their newborn child is troubling. There are those who wonder about the psychological impact, or see the whole procedure as a symbolic castration. To alleviate parental anxiety, some used to maintain that the infant cried at the *brit* only because he was cold and felt uncomfortable being held firmly during the procedure. Unfortunately, the truth seems to be that the baby does feel pain during the actual cutting of the foreskin. However, all evidence suggests that there are no deep psychological wounds and that the procedure is almost certainly more difficult psychologically for the parents than for the child. The child's physical pain seems to ease quickly following the procedure, which in itself takes less than a minute. Most infants are easily comforted, often with the help of a drop of wine or by being fed.

Thus the difficulty seems to come back to the natural reluctance of parents to cause their child pain. The tradition is not unaware of this. The Ramah (a traditional commentator) says that the *sheheheyanu* blessing usually recited at joyous occasions is not said at a *brit* because we are causing pain to the child. The reason that *brit milah* is still so widespread among Jews is that, like giving your child an inoculation shot, *brit milah* is done for a longer-term good: the formal entrance of the child into the covenant, the special relationship between God and Israel, a joining of a chain of tradition that links us back all the way to the first male Jew, Abraham. To withhold a *brit milah* is to break that chain.

> The tension, release, and celebration that attend every *bris* reenact the drama of birth: the tension and worry of pregnancy, the life-and-death, bloodstained release of delivery, the wail and acclaim that announce a new life. At the heart of the ritual, *brit milah* is not about the circumcision; it is about the flesh and blood miracle of our lives as human beings. [Anita Diamant, *New Jewish Baby Book*]

*The ritual*    Brit milah always takes place on the eighth day after birth. Traditionally, eight is seen as the number beyond completion. Thus we wait for a full week of the child's life (seven days) and only then circum-

cise him. Originally, this was probably linked to a concern for the via-
bility of the newborn, but by waiting until the symbolic completion of
seven, it is also an expression of a wish for a long life for the child. As
the number beyond completion, eight also implies perfection. The *brit
milah* completes the birth process, since every birth brings an element
of completion and hints of perfection to a family.

The tradition of having the *brit milah* on the eighth day is so important that if the eighth day falls on Shabbat or Yom Kippur, the *brit*
still takes place. The only exception to this is if the child is ill or jaun-
diced, and the pediatrician and the *mohel* are the ones who make this
judgment. The *brit milah* is postponed in such a case and no longer
takes precedence over Shabbat or Yom Kippur. While the *brit milah*
can take place at any time during the day, the custom is for it to take
place in the morning (often right after morning services). In general, we
demonstrate our eagerness to perform a *mitzvah* by doing it as soon as
possible.

The *brit milah* can take place at home or in the synagogue, depending on the family's preference, the number of guests, etc. A *mohel* can
be found through a rabbi or the local board of rabbis. Each of the
major religious denominations now has trained *mohelim*. The ritual is
basically the same; it is the attitude toward participation of the mother
and to *metzitzah* (see below) that might distinguish liberal *mohelim*
from their Orthodox counterparts. Some of the Reform *mohelim* are
physicians (male and female) who have undergone special training.
(There is no halakhic reason preventing a woman from being a *mohel*.)

It is important to call the *mohel* very soon after birth, since everyone
else who gave birth that day will be making the same phone call. A
*mohel* does not take advance reservations (except for scheduled births)
for obvious reasons. Some traditional *mohelim* are coy when asked
about their fee. This is because performing a circumcision is viewed as a
*mitzvah,* and the performance of a *mitzvah* should be "its own reward." If a *mohel* is being coy, you can elicit the information by indi-
rection, as by asking, "What do people generally pay a *mohel*?"

The *mohel* will tell you if he wants you to buy anything in preparation for the *brit*. A *mohel* needs good light to work under and a sturdy

surface for the baby to rest upon (though sometimes a person's lap will be sufficient). The *mohel* will give you instructions for caring for the infant after the circumcision. The penis will be red and swollen for a number of days or even a week or more after the *brit*. The *mohel* can be phoned if you have any concern after the *brit* and will come back to see the infant if necessary.

The typical *brit milah* is an occasion for family and friends to mark the ceremony itself and also in a formal way to celebrate with the parents the birth of their child. There are a number of roles that can be given to people to include them and honor them in the ceremony, including the *kvatter* and *kvatterine* (godparents) who carry the infant into the room, and the *sandek* who holds the baby's legs down during circumcision (this is a great honor, not to be given to the fainthearted).

These traditional roles can be expanded, for example, by having the baby brought into the room by one set of people, then passed to a second set to bring the baby all the way forward, and so on. There are some people who feel uncomfortable with a "public" *brit milah*. It can also be a strain for a mother who has not fully recovered from a cesarean birth. Yet *brit milah* is a *mitzvah* and a statement of joining the chain of the Jewish people. Also, this birth is an occasion that relatives and friends want to share with you, and therefore the tradition of its not being "private" is a sound one. There is, in fact, as with all important life-cycle events, a tradition to have a *minyan* (a quorum of ten) present. However, if desired, there is no reason why a *brit* cannot be attended by just the parents and the *mohel*, or be restricted to the immediate family. Some people have had a small *brit milah* and then held a party later for a larger group of relatives and friends.

The ritual centers on the act of circumcision. The parents (traditionally the father) authorize the *mohel* to act on their behalf. After the foreskin is cut, prayers of blessing are said. In that context the baby is named. (On the significance of naming, see below.)

*Customs*    One chair is designated as "Elijah's chair." If an ornate chair is available, it is used for this purpose. In some communities, they had a special chair or a decorative cushion in the synagogue that was used for Elijah's chair at every *brit milah*. The prophet Elijah, who went up to heaven in a fiery chariot and thus never "died," has been seen through the ages as an advocate and a protector of the Jewish people.

Many people have incorporated a new custom in the *brit milah*, which is to speak about the person for whom the child is named. If the child is named after a relative, something is told about the relative and wishes are expressed that the child might "inherit" some of the special qualities of that relative. If the child is named after a biblical or historical character, an explanation of why that person's name was chosen is shared.

Since light is a general symbol of joy and good wishes, some people have adopted the custom of lighting candles before the *brit milah* begins. (No blessing is recited.)

*Metzitzah* is the traditional practice of drawing blood from the circumcision wound. The traditional sources discuss whether this is part of the circumcision itself or is just a health measure to prevent infection. The traditional method for doing this is via the *mohel*'s mouth. Another common method is to use a glass tube to draw off the blood by mouth or by a suction device. A third method is to use a swab or cotton wool to absorb the blood. With the advent of AIDS, even in traditional communities there are those who advocate against *metzitzah* directly by mouth. Both the indirect method and swabs are hygienic and medically safe. If this issue is of concern to you, discuss it with your *mohel* ahead of time.

Since attending a *brit milah* is participating in a *mitzvah*, among traditional communities people are not literally invited to one. If you are invited to do a *mitzvah*, it is considered "impossible" to refuse. Therefore, the custom arose of inviting people indirectly, that is, by simply telling them when the *brit* is happening without officially inviting them and thereby forcing them to attend.

Since a *brit milah* is a *mitzvah*, the food served afterward is not just refreshments or part of a party but rather is a *seudat mitzvah*, a "festive meal." A *seudat mitzvah* means that we are joining with the parents to celebrate this occasion. Part of that celebration is eating good food, literally "breaking bread together." It is traditional to add special lines to *birkat ha-mazon,* the Grace after Meals, on the occasion of a *brit milah.*

***And what about girls?***   Until recently there was no equivalent to *brit milah* for girls. The most widely observed custom was the naming of the girl while her father was called to the Torah on the Shabbat after her birth. This is reflective of the differing status of men and women in traditional Judaism. Some contemporary critics therefore make the argument that Jewish women are not really part of the covenant with God. Yet the fact that women do not have a *brit milah* or its equivalent is not grounds for an argument for total exclusion. For the truth is that a Jewish male who is not circumcised is still a Jew. Your status as a Jew derives from being born of Jewish parents, not from any ritual. As we saw in the section on festivals, the larger notion of the covenant between God and Israel derives from the Exodus from Egypt and the giving of the Torah at Sinai, not from the covenant of circumcision.

While women are certainly Jews, for many contemporary Jews, the inequality between men and women in traditional Judaism begins at birth. For some, the absence of an equivalent ritual for girls implies that male children are more welcome than female children. (It is not uncommon to hear a traditional relative living at a distance say: "If there's a *brit,* I'll come; if it's a girl, I won't make it.") Therefore, people have created elaborate naming rituals that acknowledge the birth of a girl with as much pomp and circumstance as the birth of a boy. For others, without some notion of *brit,* of covenant, their egalitarian notion of Judaism would be violated. Thus a number of suggestions have been made for a *brit* for girls that while not the same ritual as for boys would be egalitarian in its notion of equal importance.

These suggestions include the use of candles, wrapping the baby in a *tallit* or prayer shawl, awakening the five senses of the baby, washing the baby's feet, and a ritual immersion. These new ceremonies share a common structure that roughly parallels the *brit milah:* an introduction, a ritual or central theme, and blessings and naming. There are many ceremonies conducted nowadays, all of them borrowing from one another. To construct your own, look over a number of these ceremonies and choose the blessings, readings, and wordings that seem most appropriate to you. Two good sources for such ceremonies are the Jewish Women's Resource Center (9 East 69th St., New York, NY 10021) and Ma'yan: The Jewish Women's Project of the Jewish Community Center in Manhattan (15 West 65th St., New York, NY 10023). Ma'yan, with others, also has a Web site devoted to such material: *ritualwell.org*. There are also a number of ceremonies printed in *The New Jewish Baby Book,* by Anita Diamant (Jewish Lights Publishing, Woodstock, VT, 1993).

New rituals have the advantage of being personal and therefore meaningful to you. But they have the disadvantage of feeling untraditional and therefore arbitrary or phony. The latter is a particular problem with the creation of the ritual part of the *brit* for girls. The goal is to create a ritual that feels appropriate, of equal weight as the circumcision, and somehow also traditional in feeling. No one ritual has yet gained wide acceptance.

### SUGGESTED READINGS

A blessing—
May your eyes sparkle with the light of Torah,
    and your ears hear the music of its words.
May the space between each letter of the scrolls
    bring warmth and comfort to your soul.
May the syllables draw holiness from your heart,
    and may this holiness be gentle and soothing
    to you and to all God's creatures.
May your study be passionate,
    and meanings bear more meanings
    until Life itself arrays itself before you
    as a dazzling wedding feast.
And may your conversation,
    even of the commonplace,
    be a blessing to all who listen to your words
    and see the Torah glowing on your face.
[Danny Siegel, based on Talmud, *Berakhot* 17a and *Eruvin* 54a]

---

When Israel stood to receive the Torah, the Holy One said to
   them: I am giving you My Torah. Present to Me good
   guarantors that you will guard it, and I will give it to you.
They said: Our ancestors are our guarantors.
The Holy One said: Your ancestors are not sufficient guarantors.
   Yet bring Me good guarantors, and I shall give you the Torah.
They said: Master of the universe, our prophets are our
   guarantors.
God said to them: The prophets are not sufficient guarantors. Yet
   bring me good guarantors and I shall give you the Torah.
They said: Here, our children are our guarantors.
The Holy One said: They are certainly good guarantors. For
   their sake I give the Torah to you. [Midrash, *Song of Songs
   Rabbah* 4:1]

---

***Some musings on creating a new ritual***    A *brit milah* marks the entrance of a male into the covenant of Israel. It is not just the celebration
of the birth of a child. Thus those rituals whose image is of welcoming a
girl child seem closer to the notion of *brit milah*. However, wrapping
the baby in a *tallit,* having her touch a Torah (isn't that the *brit* of
Sinai?), using *sheva berakhot,* "seven blessings," as in a wedding, seem
a confusing use of Jewish symbols. The washing of a baby's feet does
suggest the notion of welcoming, though it lacks a ritual resonance or
any particular connection to girls in distinction to boys. I still like the
ritual we created for our daughter, a ritual immersion, though it has not
gained a wide following. I think it has not become popular for two reasons: for too many people it resonates with baptism, and it is a little
scary. Yet baptism, that is, ritual immersion, existed in Judaism long before Christianity. If this custom became widespread among Jews, it
would take only a short time for it to feel "Jewish." As for its scariness,
while there is no danger to the infant, the trepidation it evokes parallels
those same feelings in regard to circumcision. Most important, a ritual
immersion is like circumcision in that it is used for those converting to
Judaism, who are becoming part of the Jewish people (see pp. 326–29).

Thus it seems an appropriate ritual to welcome a newborn into the Jewish people. Since women traditionally immersed themselves monthly, it is also a ritual that evokes women's sexuality, just as circumcision evokes male sexuality (see pp. 308–9). It is not surprising then that the Meiri (a medieval commentator) quotes an opinion that when Abraham was circumcised and thus entered the covenant (and began the tradition of *brit milah*), Sarah was ritually immersed to enter the covenant.

### Other Birth Customs

*Amulets*    In the past, birth and death were closely linked, as often the mother or the baby would die in childbirth. To protect them from the "evil eye" and from demons, a number of customs arose.

The most widespread was the use of amulets to protect mother and child. Lilith, the queen of the demons in traditional Jewish folklore, is described as particularly set on killing newborn human babies. One traditional amulet text reads as follows: "Sinoi, Sinsinoi, Semanglaf, Adam and Eve barring Lilith." (This is the text of the amulet revealed to Elijah by Lilith in a legend. The irony is that some scholars suggest that Sinsinoi is actually a Christian saint, Saint Sisinnius, about whom a similar legend is told. We have here then a borrowing of folk customs across religious lines. This was possible because the original meaning of the words was lost. In effect, Saint Sisinnius's role was taken over by a Jewish "saint," Elijah.)

Today, some people still hang amulets both as a folk tradition and, despite our rational selves, "just in case." (Some feminists have reclaimed the figure of Lilith, who as Adam's first wife insisted on being equal to him. They see Lilith as a model of an independent woman transformed into a demon by men threatened with her demand for equality.)

Other amulets are in the shape of a *hamsa*, an open palm, or use as their text Psalm 121, which is reputed to be effective against demons. A related custom is not to buy baby furniture before the birth. Today this is explained as a sensible idea in case something goes wrong with the pregnancy or birth. While that notion has validity, this custom also reflects a concern for the "evil eye."

**Shalom Zakhor** *and* **Shalom Nekavah,** *wishing peace to the newborn*
There is a traditional custom for people to gather in the parents' home
the first Friday night after the birth. This was both a way for the community to celebrate the birth and a way to help guard the baby from
demons. Similarly, there is a custom to stay awake all night before the
*brit* ceremony. This is a vigil of protection for the baby. It is called *leil
shimurim,* "night of watching" (or *Vach Nacht,* "watch night," or by
Sephardim *brit Yitzhak,* "the covenant of Isaac"). In some traditions,
this was a celebration for the community, not just the family. In some
communities, these celebrations were held at the home of the *sandek.*
Neither of these customs is widely observed today.

An old birth custom, no longer widely observed, was to plant a tree
at the birth of a child—a cypress for a girl and a cedar for a boy—and
later to use its limbs for the *huppah,* the wedding canopy, at that child's
marriage. Today some people plant a tree in Israel through the Jewish
National Fund at each birth.

*The* **wimpel**    A *wimpel* is a long piece of material used in the synagogue to bind up a Torah scroll (it is traditionally used in German Jewish communities). An old tradition was to use a piece of material at the
*brit,* either to decorate Elijah's chair or to put around the baby as the
baby is carried into the room. Later the material can be cut and sewn
into a long strip (usually at least six inches wide by eight feet long). It
can be decorated and have painted or embroidered upon it the child's
name, date of birth, a *mazal tov,* etc. The *wimpel* is then donated by the
family to their synagogue for use in binding the Torah. An alternative
suggestion is to use the material as part of the *huppah* or for the *atarah,*
the "neckpiece" of the *tallit* (prayer shawl), or for the *tallit* itself.

**Pidyon ha-ben,** *the redemption of the son*    There is an ancient
custom of redeeming a firstborn child. In biblical society, the firstborn
had a special status. Whether first fruits or the firstborn of animals, the
first of things were seen as holy and as belonging to God. As we know
from the story of Jacob and Esau, the status of firstborn was worth
fighting for. According to law, the firstborn inherited a double portion
of his parents' estate. Originally, the firstborn were designated in the

Torah to be the servitors of the Temple. "For every firstborn among the Israelites . . . is Mine; I consecrated them to Myself at the time that I smote every firstborn in the land of Egypt" (Num. 8:17). Subsequently, because the Levites did not participate in the sin of the Golden Calf, they were rewarded by letting them replace the firstborn as the servitors of the Temple.

Because of their onetime special status, the firstborn was still redeemed from Temple service by giving a *kohen,* a priest, five shekels (an ancient Israeli coin). This has continued as a traditional custom even since the destruction of the Temple.

The traditions related to *pidyon ha-ben,* "the redemption of the son," are as follows:

The ritual takes place on the thirty-first day after the birth of a child. (Thirty is a complete unit.) If the thirty-first day falls on Shabbat or a festival, the ritual is postponed to the next day. *Pidyon ha-ben* applies only to the firstborn son of the mother, not the father. If a woman had a miscarriage after forty days of pregnancy or she gives birth by cesarean section, then the custom of *pidyon ha-ben* is no longer applicable. This is because, based on the biblical verse, the tradition emphasizes that the child must be the first issue from the womb. The firstborn of a *kohen,* a Levi, the daughter of a *kohen,* or the daughter of a Levi is exempt from *pidyon ha-ben.*

During the ceremony, five shekels or five silver dollars are given to a *kohen* to "redeem" the child.

Today, *pidyon ha-ben* is mainly observed in traditional circles, but some nontraditional Jews have revived the custom and include any firstborn child, male or female, delivered in any fashion. It is an opportunity for parents to reflect upon and celebrate the experience of becoming parents for the first time. Newer rituals tend to adapt the traditional ritual of *pidyon ha-ben.*

*And more*  Any Jew who has successfully passed through a dangerous situation can recite *birkat ha-gomeil* during the Torah service. (It is the one time in traditional communities when a woman can publicly recite a blessing.)

"Praised are you, Eternal One, our God, source of the universe, who bestows good things on one in debt to you, and who has granted me all good."

To which the congregation responds: "And may the One who bestowed upon you good, continue to bestow upon you good. Let it be so!"

Some people have included this blessing and its communal response as part of the birth rituals. Similarly, some have included the blessing *ha-tov ve-ha-meitiv,* normally recited upon hearing good news.

## Childbearing Issues

*Contraception*    Many authorities in Judaism have no problem with the use of contraceptive methods by women. For many traditional authorities the use of a condom could be problematic. If you understand the story of Onan in the Bible as teaching us that "spilling seed" is wrong, then masturbation or using a condom can be considered onanism. Liberal authorities understand the story as being about a self-centeredness and an unwillingness to fulfill a responsibility. In that case, coitus interruptus and even masturbation are not wrong and the use of condoms is permissible.

*Abortion*    Judaism is not categorically opposed to abortion. Even the most traditional authorities permit an abortion when it endangers the mother's welfare, which is understood to mean not just her physical health. Most authorities have a position similar to that of the U.S. Supreme Court—that is, before a certain time the fetus is not viable and therefore abortion is allowed. Since the fetus is a potential life, Judaism would maintain that abortion should never be treated as a casual decision.

*Adoption*    There is no legal mechanism in Judaism to adopt a child as there is in American law. On the other hand, Judaism does consider people who raise a child as being like parents. Hence the *mitzvah* of honoring parents applies to them. Some traditional authorities discourage the adoption of Jewish children out of a concern for possible incest when the child grows up and marries. Adopting a non-Jew eliminates that problem. An adopted non-Jewish child needs to be converted (see pp. 329–30).

*Miscarriage*   While traditionally there are no mourning rituals for a miscarriage or even a stillbirth, contemporary practice increasingly marks these losses. If the miscarriage takes place early in the pregnancy, the loss is observed more privately. Depending on the wishes of the couple, a rabbi can create a ritualized expression of grief and loss.

### A READING FOR A MISCARRIAGE

You know when the wild goats of the rock give birth. You mark when the hinds calve. You created the miracle of birth and the wonder of the body that cares for mother and child. *Dayan Ha'emet,* Judge of Truth, You care for Your creatures even when such care tastes bitter. Who are we to understand Your ways, to know what future would have lain ahead for myself and my child had it come to term? *Harahaman,* Merciful One, heal my body and my soul; heal my womb so that I may carry to term a healthy soul, that I may come to sing Your praises as a happy mother surrounded by her children in the courtyards of a Jerusalem at peace. [From the Rabbinical Assembly *Moreh Derekh*]

For miscarriages after five months and for stillborn babies, burial should take place. Discuss with your rabbi the forms of mourning in such circumstances.

### KAVANAH

At first God created many worlds, but destroyed them when God saw their imperfections. Finally God created a world with human beings, but though they tried they constantly failed in their attempts to get closer to heaven. After a while they grew tired and ceased struggling. So God created Death and killed every living thing and created everything anew. But God grew tired always starting at the beginning again, seeing humankind do exactly the same thing, struggling with no memory, no inherited wisdom—a Tower of Babel of generations, for none spoke to one another. God looked and saw the world was too imperfect and God decided to create birth, the womb, generations, parents and children, progress, and history. But first God created a flood to come upon the earth to make a new beginning, and God caused life to enter the ark/womb by twos, X and Y, male and female. And the ark was surrounded by water and darkness. And behold after nine months, the waters dropped and the ark sent forth life into the world and it did not return and the umbilical cord between life and the ark was broken. Life left a state of rest and became alive. And God made a promise that though Death should remain, Life would never cease, and so God took part of the line called Horizon, which marks the sacred place where the earth meets heaven. And God bent it and placed it in the sky and called it Rainbow. And God said: "This rainbow shall be a sign of the *noah* renewal of life and whenever one sees a straight line swelling, like a pregnant woman, like a dough filled with yeast or like this rainbow, you shall know that I will keep My covenant." And thus, when people will see these things, they will know that life is ever renewing and they will feel enclosed and secure once more in the womb of God, the Mother of all creation, and they will say: "Holy Holy Holy is the Creator of Hosts; The whole earth is *maleh*, 'pregnant'/'full,' of God's glory."

# GENESIS/BEREISHIT: CONVERSION

To choose to become a Jew is a new beginning marked by taking a new name, a Hebrew name. The process of conversion is inherently a spiritual one as the convert explores the meaning of being Jewish. The ritual of conversion, especially the immersion in the ritual bath, while simple, is nevertheless a powerful expression of the new beginning that conversion represents.

*Ger* is the Hebrew word for "convert." Yet Bible scholars maintain that in the Bible *ger* refers to a non-Jew living among Jews. Apparently, in biblical times people became Jewish simply by marrying into the Jewish people. Beginning with the rabbis of the Talmud, *ger* comes to mean a formal conversion with its associated ritual.

It is often said that unlike other monotheistic religions, Judaism never sought converts and certainly did not convert people at the point of the sword. Both those commonly held views are incorrect. Jews living in Hellenistic times did actively seek converts, and under some of the Hasmonean kings certain groups were forcibly converted. With this exception, proselytizing and forced conversion are absent from most of Jewish history. However, it could be that Judaism gave up seeking converts because it had no choice. As a religious minority living under the control of governments influenced by the religious doctrines of Christianity and Islam, Jews were forbidden to seek converts. Both of those religions believed that all people should be followers of the one true religion (theirs) and that salvation could only come to those who believed in Christ or Allah. At times, the punishment for trying to convert a non-Jew was death. During most of the Middle Ages, there was a wide religious chasm between Jews and their neighbors. Persecutions and efforts to convert Jews served only to widen that chasm.

That history and the infrequency of conversion (there were a few cases even in the Middle Ages) influenced Jewish attitudes toward conversion even in the modern period. Though no longer forbidden from actively seeking converts, Jews still did not actively proselytize. Even centuries after the fall of the ghetto walls, the chasm between Jew and Gentile left some Jews suspicious of the motives of those seeking to become Jewish. There was even some feeling that "once a *goi* always a *goi*" (*goi* means "nation" but can be a disparaging term for non-Jews).

I wanted to share this history not only to put some myths to rest but because we are now living in a very different period in Jewish history. Jews today are very much accepted as part of America's open society. The walls between Jew and Gentile are gone. If this means that some Jews will convert to other religions and others will marry non-Jews, it also means that some non-Jews will want to convert to Judaism and marry Jews. The "once a *goi* always a *goi*" attitude (held in any case by only a portion of the Jewish community) is disappearing with the older generation. Baby boomers and younger Jews who have grown up in this "wall-less" society have little or no discomfort around people of diverse background. As more and more people convert to Judaism, more and more Jews know someone who is a convert. It is no longer a rare phenomenon. In fact, there are a number of rabbis who are converts. A few religious leaders, primarily in the Reform movement, have even advocated that Jews make a concerted effort to attract non-Jews. Whether that will happen remains to be seen, but we live in a world where conversion and converts are a part of the fabric of the Jewish community.

Traditionally, Jews were cautioned not to "remind" converts that they had converted, that is, that they come from a less-than-noble past. Nowadays, many converts term themselves "Jews by choice" and are very open about their conversions. For a number of years my synagogue had an annual Shavuot breakfast for converts. Those who are contemplating conversion should feel reassured that they will be not just accepted but welcomed in the Jewish community.

As a congregational rabbi who has worked with a sizable number of people considering conversion, I have found that the most frequently raised concern is whether the conversion will really take. Accepting religious tenets often seems far easier than feeling part of the Jewish people. Converts worry, Will they ever be able to learn enough? Will they ever feel intrinsically Jewish? These are not easy questions, but many people with whom I have worked have found positive answers. With time Judaism does become woven into your identity rather than a garment that you are conscious of wearing.

## The Process of Conversion

Conversion involves a course of study followed by the actual ritual of conversion. A sponsoring rabbi oversees this process. Any rabbi can do it, though not all rabbis in fact do conversions. The first step is to speak with a rabbi. The rabbi will want to know why you are considering conversion. The rabbi will set out what she or he requires for someone to be ready to convert. This first conversation can be exploratory on your part. You do not need to make a commitment to convert to begin the process or at any time in the process. No rabbi wants to convert someone who is uncertain.

If neither you nor any of your friends knows a rabbi, you can call the local Jewish federation, Jewish community center, or Hillel (the Jewish student organization established on many college campuses). All three of these types of organizations are transdenominational, which means they will provide the names of rabbis from any or all of the Jewish movements. (The denominations are discussed below.) Obviously, you can also call the nearest synagogue. You may have an idea of which kind of rabbi you are looking for. A number of potential converts told me they attended my synagogue first, to check it and me out. If after your first meeting the "chemistry" between you and a rabbi does not seem right, then consider finding another rabbi.

The rabbi will tell you what you need to learn in preparation for the conversion. While no one expects you to learn everything, a basic knowledge of Jewish practices, beliefs, and history is standard. Some rabbis themselves teach an introduction-to-Judaism class. Others will tell you where you can take such a class or recommend a tutor. The Conservative and Reform movements in large cities often offer such a class for the area. A number of Jewish community centers offer the Derekh Torah program, an intensive introduction to Judaism pioneered by Rabbi Rachel Cowan (herself a convert). During your course of study, your sponsoring rabbi will occasionally meet with you to answer any questions and to help guide you through the process.

Once the required study is completed, if you are certain you want to convert and the rabbi feels you are ready, then the ritual of conversion can be scheduled. This involves convening a Jewish court called a *beit din* (literally, "house of judgment") to confirm the legality of the conversion according to Jewish law. Though in theory any Jew is eligible to serve on the *beit din,* the panel is usually composed of three rabbis. Your rabbi is one of the three. For a woman, conversion involves immersion in a *mikvah,* "ritual bath." (Where there is no *mikvah,* a lake can be used.) For a man, conversion involves *milah,* "circumcision," in addition to immersion in the *mikvah.*

The *beit din* meets you at the appointed time at the *mikvah.* Check with your rabbi, but it is usually appropriate to bring a close friend or two with you to "hold your hand" through the experience. Most converts are nervous. For some it feels like a momentous permanent decision. For others it feels like entering into an unknown and still-alien land.

The members of the *beit din* ask you a few questions. There are variations in how much and what kinds of things a *beit din* asks. Some ask specific questions such as, What is the meaning of the Sukkot holiday? Some have an extensive conversation with the prospective convert. In the ones in which I have been involved, the questioning is pro forma. The other rabbis rely on the assumption that the sponsoring rabbi would not have brought this person to the *beit din* if the person was not ready. The questions themselves generally explore your motivation rather than your knowledge of Jewish tradition. Ask your rabbi what to expect from your *beit din.* Once the *beit din* is satisfied, you move to the next step: immersion for a woman, circumcision and immersion for a man.

Circumcision is a sign of the covenant between God and Jewish males (see pp. 308–11). It is performed by a *mohel,* a person trained to perform a *religious* circumcision. Though males may have been circum-

cised by a doctor at birth (as are most American males), for most traditionally oriented rabbis medical circumcision does not fulfill the ritual.
A symbolic ritual circumcision, *hatafat dam brit,* "the drawing of a
drop of blood," is still necessary. A *mohel* pricks the penis and draws
a drop of blood. Male converts tell me that despite the sensitive location, the procedure was no more painful than a pinprick. (If a male has
never been medically circumcised, a circumcision is usually required.
This should be discussed with your rabbi.) The ritual circumcision is
followed by the immersion.

*Immersion*   Jewish law requires that the water of the *mikvah* touch
your whole body. To do this you basically float underwater, making
sure to lift your feet off the bottom of the pool while ducking your head
underwater. It is simpler than it sounds. The ritual immersion is instan-
taneous. You do not have to be submerged until the count of ten. To get
ready for the immersion, you take off all your clothes, jewelry, contact
lenses, etc. This is to ensure that the water touches all of you. The symbolism of the *mikvah* is of cleansing and rebirth.

The actual procedure is as follows: You enter the *mikvah* and immerse. Then you recite two *berakhot* (blessings), one for the immersion
and one (the *sheheheyanu*) that is said for new occasions. (If you are
male, you may wear a skullcap while reciting the blessings.) You then
immerse twice more before leaving the *mikvah* and getting dressed.

Of course, members of the *beit din* who may be of the opposite sex
are not inside the *mikvah* with you. They stand outside the room with
the door ajar so that they can hear but not see you. A person of your
sex is inside to make sure that you perform the immersion correctly.

After you are dressed, you come before the *beit din* and are presented with a document confirming your conversion. The members of
the *beit din* sign it. At this time you can choose a Hebrew name. If your
English name is a biblical one, the choice may be obvious. Otherwise,
you can choose a name that means the same thing as your English name
or one that sounds like it. Alternatively, you can choose the name of a
biblical character you admire, or just a Hebrew name you like. It is an
unusual and fun experience to choose your name as an adult. The He-

brew name becomes part of the official conversion document. This completes the conversion ritual.

The above describes a usual conversion. There are some Reform rabbis who do not require *mikvah* or *hatafat dam brit*. Some rabbis will go with the convert to a synagogue for an additional ceremony. This is a new custom and practices differ. Often it involves the convert's standing before the ark in the synagogue. The ark is opened and then the convert recites the Shema or other prayers.

Some converts will be called up for an *aliyah* to the Torah on the Shabbat following their conversion. This is an honor that, as Jews, they may now receive, as well as a way to announce to the community that the conversion has taken place.

## The Conversion of Children

The procedure for converting a child is basically the same as that for an adult. If it is a newborn baby boy, then a *brit milah*, "ritual circumcision," should be performed by a *mohel*, as is done for a Jewish child. In this case the circumcision is considered the first step of the conversion process. Only when the baby is immersed in the *mikvah* is the process complete.

Of course, there is no course of study for an infant. The assumption is that in time the child will be given an appropriate Jewish education. There is no interview by the *beit din* either. While the immersion can happen at any time, people will often wait three to six months until they feel comfortable about immersing their baby in the *mikvah*.

The major difference in a conversion of a child is that it is conditional. Conversion is predicated on the convert's making a conscious decision of his or her own free will. Clearly, this is not true for a child, never mind for an infant. Therefore, when a child is converted, the *beit din* acts on behalf of the child. The conversion is conditional in the sense that the child can renounce it upon becoming an adult at age twelve or thirteen. There is no required reappearance before a *beit din* to affirm the conversion. If, when the child reaches Jewish adulthood, she or he publicly identifies as a Jew, then that is a clear enough sign that they have agreed to the conversion. Celebrating a bar or bat mitzvah is such a sign.

## The Politics of Conversion

Anyone considering conversion should understand the "politics of conversion." Basically, most Orthodox rabbis do not accept conversions done by non-Orthodox rabbis as legitimate. This means that the convert is not Jewish in the eyes of Orthodox rabbis. All other rabbis accept each other's conversions. There are two reasons that Orthodox rabbis have such a policy. One could be described as political, that is, it is simply because the sponsoring rabbi is not Orthodox. In other words, a sponsoring rabbi could require the same course of study as an Orthodox rabbi, use the same *mikvah,* and so on, and the Orthodox rabbis still would not consider the conversion legitimate. This is because Orthodoxy considers itself the only legitimate form of Judaism. The second reason has to do with an actual difference. An Orthodox rabbi will ask for a commitment by the person undergoing conversion to observe the major practices of Judaism. This may vary somewhat from one Orthodox rabbi to another, but generally can be assumed to include observing the Sabbath and keeping the dietary laws *(kashrut).* The Orthodox rabbi would say that someone who is not willing to commit to observing these rituals should not convert, because that is what it means to be Jewish. Of course, Orthodox rabbis are fully aware that there are many people born as Jews who do not observe at all. Yet for Orthodox rabbis to convert someone to Judaism means that person must commit to live a Jewish life, defined as observing the *mitzvot.*

Non-Orthodox rabbis will take a different approach to the issue of a commitment to practice. While they certainly want the convert to express a commitment to some form of Jewish practice, they will be more flexible about what that means. Thus, a rabbi might expect a commitment by the convert to some Shabbat observance, such as lighting candles, but not specify a commitment to a complete traditional Shabbat observance. Non-Orthodox rabbis take this approach because they believe that there is more than one legitimate way to be Jewish. They thus validate the spectrum of the ways that the vast majority of Jews actually practice. Some rabbis also believe that becoming Jewish is a process that continues after conversion. The practice of a person who has been Jewish for several years may be very different from the practice of someone who has just become Jewish. Thus, many rabbis feel it is not critical at the moment of conversion to commit to what your practice will ultimately be. Obviously, conversions performed by non-Orthodox rabbis are accepted as legitimate by the vast majority of the Jewish people.

This dispute between the Orthodox and non-Orthodox world is deeply disturbing, but at the moment seems only likely to get worse rather than better. While someone can always reconvert under Orthodox auspices (a non-Orthodox conversion does not prevent that from happening), it can be very disturbing to be told by some Orthodox authority that you are "not Jewish" after many years of thinking otherwise. Some converts I have worked with considered having an Orthodox conversion only to forestall any future problem. In the end, they did not, since to do so they would have had to lie about being committed to practice in an Orthodox way. For them, lying would have undermined the whole meaning of the conversion. Though there is no simple solution, in truth, for most converts the issue of who did their conversion will not arise. However, here are the possible scenarios that it could arise. (1) Some time after you convert, you decide to join an Orthodox synagogue and are asked about your background and told you are not really Jewish. (2) You decide to move to Israel. Unlike in the United States, where every rabbi and synagogue is basically religiously autonomous, in Israel matters of religion are under the Chief Rabbinate, which is Orthodox. While the State of Israel will treat anyone converted by a rabbi as a Jew in terms of Israeli citizenship, on issues of personal status, such as marriage, the Chief Rabbinate could decide you are not Jewish. Since there is no secular marriage in Israel, you would not be able to be married to a Jew in Israel. If you are a woman, your children would also not be considered Jewish. (3) You are a woman and your child grows up and falls in love with an Orthodox person and wants to be married by an Orthodox rabbi. The rabbi informs your child that she or he is not Jewish, saying that only children of a Jewish mother are actually Jewish by birth.

## A Related Issue: Patrilineal Descent

It is clear that in biblical times, the status of a Jewish child was determined by the father. The term for this is *patrilineal descent,* meaning that if the father was Jewish, then the child was Jewish, too. It is equally clear that in rabbinic times, the definition was changed from patrilineal descent to matrilineal descent. It is not clear why. One common rationale is that it is easier to determine who is the actual mother of a child than who is the father. (Of course, today with genetic testing that is no longer as true.)

For centuries, then, Jewish identity has been determined by the Jewishness of one's mother. Having a non-Jewish father did not affect your status as a Jew. A number of years ago, the Reform movement decided to regard anyone with one Jewish parent as Jewish, provided that person is raised as a Jew. This means that someone can be patrilineally Jewish (through the father) or matrilineally Jewish (through the mother). This controversial decision meant that there was no longer one agreed-upon definition of who is a Jew. The Reform movement felt the new definition more accurately reflected the reality of the modern world. They argued that matrilineal descent was an arbitrary standard, particularly since in the Bible, the father was the determining factor in a child's Jewish status.

Both the Conservative and Orthodox movements have rejected the Reform position. This means that potentially there will be people considered Jewish by the Reform (and also the Reconstructionist) movements who will not be considered so by the other movements. It also means that in the Reform movement someone whose father is Jewish (and mother is not) does not need to undergo conversion, assuming he or she was raised as a Jew.

## A Guide to the Denominations

It might be helpful for someone considering conversion (and, possibly, for the rest of us) to understand the various major denominations in contemporary Jewish life in order to choose what kind of rabbi to work with.

The rise of the present denominations in Jewish life is an outgrowth of historical developments of the modern period. The Enlightenment and then secularism raised challenges to all traditional religions. For the Jews, the modern world also offered the possibility of leaving the ghetto behind. In response, the Reform movement began as an attempt to reform traditional Judaism in light of modernity. Reform Judaism wanted to create a Judaism that allowed the Jew to fully participate in the world while remaining Jewish. It also sought to eliminate practices that it felt were no longer relevant to modern life. In response to the Reform movement, Orthodoxy emerged as a movement to defend and uphold the tradition. Conservative Judaism became another option at the turn of the twentieth century in America, in response to the widespread practice of Reform Judaism in America. It wanted to "conserve" more of the tradition. It thus took a middle ground between Orthodox and Reform Judaism. In the middle of the twentieth century, Reconstructionism became a movement inspired by the teachings of Rabbi Mordecai Kaplan. It began as a response to the rejection of supernatural theology by many Jews.

What follows is a capsule description of each of these denominations. Though each is internally diverse, they are quite different in their ideological and theological view.

*Orthodox Judaism*    Orthodox Judaism starts with the belief that the Torah was given by God to Moses at Sinai. The written Torah was accompanied by the oral Torah, which expanded upon the laws in the written text. Thus *halakhah*, Jewish law, is based on a written and oral tradition that is the word of God and is therefore unchanging. As new questions arise, the leading rabbis of each generation make decisions based on their understanding of the tradition. Orthodox Judaism believes that God rewards the righteous and punishes the sinner. It also believes in life after death and a future resurrection of the dead.

Orthodox Judaism has had an ambivalent relationship with modernity. There is a spectrum within Orthodoxy ranging from the modern Orthodox to the ultra-Orthodox. Modern Orthodoxy, while rejecting some of the values of modernity, believes others are compatible or even enhance Judaism. The current trend in Orthodox Judaism is away from the modern toward more right-wing elements, which perceive modernity as a threat because of its corrupt moral values. Thus, while under pressure from feminism, the religious authorities have maintained the nonegalitarian nature of premodern Orthodox *halakhah*.

*Conservative Judaism*    Conservative Judaism's slogan is "Tradition and Change." It advocates adhering to the tradition and yet sees change as necessary. In fact, it believes that *halakhah*, Jewish law, has constantly been changed to meet new historical realities. Thus, for example, the Conservative movement has become egalitarian with respect to the participation of women in religious life. Conservative Judaism has understood that the study of Torah also includes the scientific approach to Jewish texts. Thus biblical and talmudic scholarship have been hallmarks of the Conservative movement.

The Conservative movement considers *halakhah* as binding upon Jews. Conservative *halakhah* is similar in many respects to Orthodox *halakhah*, except in certain major areas such as the role of women and a variety of leniences related to modern life, for instance, permission to drive a car to synagogue on Shabbat. Yet in practice there is a wide spectrum of observance even within Conservative Judaism. There is also a wider gap between theory and practice among Conservative laypeople than there is in Orthodox Judaism. Theologically, Conservative Jewish belief is diverse, ranging from believing in a supernatural God who acts in the world to seeing God not as a being but as a force that works through the world (a natural God). In the latter view, God does not reward or punish individuals. In this way Conservative Judaism reflects the diversity of theological views that for centuries has existed among Jews.

*Reform Judaism*    Reform Judaism does not see *halakhah* as a binding system of law. The decision to practice is left to the individual. Individual autonomy is one of the hallmarks of Reform Judaism. The other is a stress on ethics and social justice. For Reform Judaism, the purpose of religion is to help us live moral lives. While Orthodox and Conservative Judaism also believe in the importance of the ethical, Reform Judaism has emphasized it. In the days of the early Reform movement, this emphasis was accompanied with a de-emphasis on ritual. In the last few years, Reform Judaism has encouraged its adherents to observe more rituals along with living an ethical life.

Reform Judaism is more willing to change the tradition than Conservative Judaism and thus moved to be egalitarian before Conservative Judaism. It has also welcomed gay and lesbian Jews as rabbis and laypeople in contrast to an ambivalent attitude in Conservative Judaism (see facing page for more details). Currently, it is the largest denomination in North America, followed by Conservative Judaism and Orthodox Judaism as a growing but distant third.

*Reconstructionist Judaism*    Reconstructionist Judaism is the fourth and by far the smallest denomination. Some, however, claim that most Reform and Conservative American Jews adhere to a Reconstructionist understanding of Judaism. The movement was founded by Mordecai Kaplan and became its own denomination in the 1960s with the creation of its own seminary. Before the movement began, Kaplan himself taught for many years at the Jewish Theological Seminary of the Conservative movement, influencing many Conservative rabbis, some of whom helped to found Reconstructionism.

Kaplan spoke of Judaism as an evolving religious civilization. He taught that Judaism had continually changed and, moreover, needed to continually change in order to be vibrant. Each generation needed to "reconstruct" Judaism for itself. Though his teaching sounded radical, in fact, he encouraged Jews to reinterpret the practices of the past rather than discarding them as obsolete. The forms might remain much the same, but the reasons behind practices might change. However, there were some practices and beliefs that he thought could not be reconstructed. Kaplan rejected the notion of the Jews' being a "chosen people" as a concept that inherently encouraged negative feelings toward others; and he removed all mention of the chosen people from his Reconstructionist prayer book.

Kaplan also did not believe in a supernatural God, but rather saw God as the "force that makes for salvation." Reconstructionism has continued to evolve and has become more theologically diverse. It considers the tradition as having a "vote not a veto." It believes that communities should make decisions about practice (unlike Reform Judaism's stress on the individual). It has taken positions similar to many of the liberal positions of Reform Judaism, such as encouraging inclusiveness for gays and lesbians, and yet has had a somewhat more traditional religious style than its Reform counterpart.

# GENESIS/BEREISHIT:
# PARENTS AND CHILDREN

The book of Genesis is full of stories of families, of parents and children, of siblings. They are all dysfunctional families, in other words, families just like ours. Instead of *Father Knows Best,* we have Abraham, Sarah, Hagar, Ishmael, and Isaac. Instead of Wally and Beaver, we have Jacob and Esau. Running through Genesis is a variation on these human stories, the story of God as parent learning what it is like to have children.

We begin with the first story that includes all the rest. God creates the first humans, Adam and Eve. They live in a sheltered environment where all their needs are met. They are naked and innocent. Apparently, they spend most of their time in the garden giving names to all the creatures and plants. God the Parent tells them not to eat of the tree in the center of the garden. Eve breaks the rule and then involves Adam in her rule-breaking. Adam and Eve hide and deny. God gets angry and punishing. Innocence is lost. Clothing, self-protection, defenses come into the picture.

Rules are necessary. Rules will be broken. Sometimes rules need to be broken in order for growth to take place. Relationships create distance as well as intimacy, support as well as disappointment. Life is complex. Life in any garden lasts only for a short period. (Corollary paradoxical lesson: Maybe God gets to rest every seventh day, but parents of newborns *never* do.)

Story two: There are two brothers who bring food to their Parent. The Parent can eat only one offering, so the Parent chooses to have a meat meal tonight over the vegetable offering. Cain, feeling rejected, kills his brother Abel. The Parent now understands that choices have consequences. In a limited world, choosing one means another is left unchosen. Someone falls in love with you but you love another, etc. Even unintentional, hurt is inevitable.

Having made mistakes, you might think the best thing to do is to start all over again. You could bring a flood and begin again. However, as soon as the kids are out of the ark, they get into trouble again. At this point, God turns the story over to human families, with no better results.

What then are we to learn from Genesis? Family life is not easy. God had less trouble creating the world. Parenting is about recognizing both the possibilities and limitations of the role.

The possibilities: To our children, we are all-powerful, Godlike. We can do anything and know everything. We can make everything okay. Even knowing that this is not really true, as parents we want to make it as true as possible. We feel responsible and protective of our children. With the birth of a child, we enter into a relationship of complete trust. There is no weighing, as there is in romantic love, whether this is the right person. No one is worried about whether they are just settling by being in relationship with this child instead of another. The baby is born and embraced. The relationship is assumed. We do try to create a garden where children are safe and where we can provide for all their needs.

It is a world of *hesed*, "loving-kindness," of giving. We like being needed and we want to give. We do not measure it out or check to see if it is being reciprocated in equal measure. We just give. Our love flows forth.

Having a baby brings us back to innocence by reminding us not to take the world for granted. Everything is new and first in the baby's eyes. Turning a light on and off fascinates an infant even as it reminds us of the distinction between light and darkness. As the baby grows, we eagerly anticipate the first appearances of all those activities we have so long taken for granted—rolling over, crawling, standing, walking, speaking, feeding yourself, using the bathroom. (Well, maybe we don't *eagerly* anticipate the baby's first missteps, when they are prone to come crashing down.) It is a world of firsts, not just in the baby's eyes but in our experience of our baby's growth.

## Limitations

Yet, as all-powerful as we feel, we also feel constrained. Constrained by the truth that we are not all-powerful. Instead, we worry about all the things that could go wrong with this vulnerable little being. One of the worst experiences of my life was when our daughter was too young to speak and woke up in the middle of the night crying in pain. She was in so much pain that she kept on pushing herself out of our embracing arms. We rushed to the emergency room as she kept on crying nonstop. We sat there for thirty long minutes waiting for the one pediatrician on duty to come. (It was the middle of the night on a holiday weekend.) Of course, she quieted down a few minutes before the doctor arrived. It turned out she had an ear infection, a very painful condition. The worst part, of course, was not knowing what was wrong, since she could not tell us. More broadly, there is the worry about everything that could go wrong. How many parents have checked on their baby in the crib to make sure the baby is breathing? Babies bring us an awareness of the fragility of life.

More important, babies mean we have lost control over our lives. We cannot negotiate with a baby. "Just wait five minutes to eat, I'm on the last pages of my murder mystery!" Time, the basic currency of control, is no longer our own. Someone else is establishing our schedule.

There is another way that your "all-powerfulness" has been limited. We have made a lifelong commitment to this child. We cannot change our mind and give the child back. It is as permanent as anything can be in this world.

Thus, like the Parent in the first stories of Genesis, we learn that we are extremely powerful and yet without control of time or of the relationship.

How then should we parent? The same way we do everything else. Trying to be fair and just. Trying to listen. Trying to balance letting go and holding on. Trying not to be confused by our frustrations. Striving to punish appropriately and purposefully, that is, being clear about what we want to accomplish. Striving for consistency.

What is the most important thing we should remember as parents? Forgiveness. God forgives Adam and Eve and even Cain, for God understands that we are only human. We need to forgive our children and also need to forgive ourselves for the mistakes we make as parents.

> R. Simeon ben Eleazar said: . . . a child should be thrust off with a left hand only so long as one brings them near with the right hand. [Talmud, *Sotah* 47a]

The other most important thing is to benefit from the opportunity of having a child.

> There is a story about a man who made out his will with this provision: my son shall not inherit anything of mine until he acts the fool. R. Yose bar Judah and Rabbi went to R. Joshua ben Korhah to get an opinion about this [strange] provision. When they peeked in from outside [R. Joshua's house], they saw him crawling on his hands and knees, with a reed sticking out of his mouth, and being pulled along by his child. Seeing him thus, they discreetly withdrew, but they came back later and asked him about the provision in the will. He began to laugh and said, "As you live, this business you ask about—acting the fool—happened to me a little while ago." [*Midrash Tehillim* 92:13; *Yalkut*, Ps. #846]

## A Parent's Obligation

Our masters taught: With regard to his son, a father is obligated to circumcise him, to redeem him [if he is the firstborn], to teach him Torah, to teach him a craft, and to get him married. Some say: Also to teach him how to swim. R. Judah said: When a person does not teach his son a craft, it is as though he taught him brigandage. . . . Rabbi [Judah I, the Patriarch] said: A father is also required to teach his son civic obligations. [Talmud, *Kiddushin* 29a–30b; *Mekilta de-Rabbi Ishmael, Bo, Pis'ha,* 18]

Rabbinic values are much in evidence in this text. First, it should be remarked that this is a text only about fathers and sons. The only similar text about daughters debates whether it is a bad idea or an obligation to teach Torah to daughters. It is also a traditional text in that the father arranges for the marriage of the son. Yet, the broader teachings of the text apply to all parents and children in any age. We should teach our children our value system (Torah). They need to learn how to make a living, otherwise we may be setting them up for failure, if not brigandage. We need to teach them the basic skills for making it through life (represented by swimming). Finally, we need to teach them that engaging in civic life is also part of what it means to live a life of holiness.

How do we teach our children the values we want them to acquire? It is not the Torah that you say that is most heeded; it is the Torah that you do. Just as we are to imitate God by being merciful as God is merciful, so too our children will learn how to act from the way we act. If we engage in civic life, if we study Torah, if we speak with caring to other people, if we take care of our physical well-being, then they will learn "our parenting Torah."

## Children's Obligations to Parents

*Kabeid* [honor] your father and mother that you may long endure on the land. [Exod. 20:12]

The obligation to honor parents is one of the Ten Commandments.

How far should honoring one's father and mother extend? Go and see what a certain heathen named Dama ben Netinah did for his father in Ashkelon. Once, the sages sought some merchandise from him involving a profit of sixty myriads [of gold dinars]. But the key to where the merchandise was kept was under his [sleeping] father's pillow, and he would not disturb him. [Talmud, *Kiddushin* 31a]

When R. Joseph heard the sound of his mother's footsteps, he would say, "I must rise before the Presence, which is approaching." [Talmud, *Kiddushin* 31b]

These two stories suggest the importance of honoring one's parents. This respectfulness derives from who they are. Thus, in the second story, Rabbi Joseph's mother is a form of God's Presence. The link between parent and Parent is made explicit here. We want God to act as a caring parent. We want our parents to be as forgiving and as able to protect us as the Almighty. Certainly, this idea is rooted in a notion of a traditional society with a hierarchical structure. Yet honoring parents ultimately derives from an appreciation of all that parents give to a child. All of us have been given huge amounts by our parents, both in our genes and in our upbringing. Parents may never feel appreciated enough, but we are to strive to appreciate their efforts and honor those who gave us life. Honoring them also means at some point in our lives being willing to forgive them for their human flaws. Most parents try to do their best at parenting. Most children feel not loved enough, criticized too much, etc. Part of growing up and ultimately offering respect to our parents is to come to an acceptance of their flaws.

What about parents who betray their trust?—for example, those who sexually abuse their children. There is of course no easy answer, but the tradition recognizes that a parent can behave in such a manner that they no longer deserve to be treated with honor. While ideally *teshuvah* and forgiveness should happen for both parent and child, this is not always possible. Thus, there are traditional opinions that a child does not have to say *kaddish* (i.e., to mourn) for a parent who has acted in ways that make it impossible to honor them even in death.

## Siblings

Cain and Abel, Isaac and Ishmael, Jacob and Esau, Rachel and Leah, Joseph and his brothers. There seem to be no models of siblings that get along in Genesis. Is it really that bad?

One way to understand Genesis is that it is not so much about siblings as about people. What Genesis represents, then, is how difficult it is for people to get along with one another. Many of the characters in Genesis are the founders of a nation, or at least larger than life. It is not just two brothers who fight over the birthright but all of us and all nations.

Seemingly Genesis begins and ends with stories of fratricide: Cain slaying Abel and the near-fratricide of Joseph by his brothers. Yet the picture is more hopeful than that. It is not only that a near-fratricide is significantly different from actual killing, it is how Joseph reacts. He forgives his brothers. He is the first person in the Bible to clearly forgive others who have deeply wronged him (though a case could be made for Esau's forgiving Jacob at their reunion). Even after his father's death, Joseph reaffirms that he bears no ill will toward his brothers. Joseph has come to understand that this was all God's plan. He describes it as the means for bringing the Israelites down to Egypt. They are thus saved from the famine and their future destiny is set in motion. Perhaps all this was necessary if Joseph was to grow from an obnoxious, arrogant youth into a sage. Joseph's wisdom aids him in planning to avert the worst effects of the famine as well as in coming to understand his own role in provoking his brothers' anger. Joseph has really grown in this story, and not just to a position of power. Joseph outgrows the rivalries of Genesis and thus points beyond to the Book of Exodus, where siblings like Miriam, Moses, and Aaron collaborate instead of compete.

> Rav said: A person should not single out one of his children for special treatment, for on account of two *sela* of silk [the coat of many colors]—the one thing Jacob gave to Joseph and not to his other sons—Joseph's brothers grew jealous of him, and the consequences grew until our forebears had to go down into Egypt. [Talmud, *Shabbat* 10b]

A traditional folktale of two brothers:
Once there lived two brothers. One had a wife and children and wealth; the other was unmarried and poor. Their fields were side by side. It was the time of the harvest. The bachelor brother said to himself: While I do not have much, I do not need much, since I am alone. On the other hand, my brother has a large family. At night, this brother would throw sheaves over onto his brother's land. At the same time, the other brother said to his wife: I have the riches of a family. My brother is poor and alone. I will give him extra grain from my land. This went

on during the harvest until one night the brothers met as each was sur-reptitiously throwing sheaves onto the other's land. They laughed and embraced.

It is because of their brotherly love that their fields were chosen by God to be the land upon which the Holy Temple in Jerusalem would be built in King Solomon's time.

# EXODUS/SHEMOT:
# BAR/BAT MITZVAH

After those first dramatic years of infancy, when there are so many skills to acquire, the pace of growth seems to slow. There is a period when children just seem to be kids. Then, of course, comes adolescence. In like form, the book of Exodus tells the story of the adolescence of the Jewish people. The Israelites leave behind everything they know and embark on an uncharted future. God, as parent, constantly reminds the Israelites of everything that God has done on their behalf. The Israelites are constantly unappreciative and rebellious. At times they want to go back to the undemanding simplicity of childhood. At other moments, they refuse to be patient in waiting to get to the Promised Land and decide to rush foolishly and dangerously ahead. The Exodus story of the Israelites and God is reflected in the story of every parent and child.

The rocky period of transition from child to adult is mirrored in our parental confusion about when to let go and when to continue setting limits. It is never clear to us as parents whether we are speaking to a child who, despite demands for independence, really wants us to say no, or to a young adult who needs additional responsibility. Both forms inhabit our offspring. Each appears and disappears; though at times both appear simultaneously. It is not only the adolescent who is confused and confusing. We are ambivalent about letting go. We can see how this chapter of the story will end: our child will leave home for good. After some years of little change, we enter not only a period of turbulent change, but also a period that will end with leave-taking. We cannot believe our baby has grown up. We cannot believe we are old enough to have a teenager. The passage of time in our own lives is troubling.

## Bnai Mitzvah

It is this getting ready to leave (though the adolescent may be only dimly aware of how this story inevitably ends) that creates the context of *bnai mitzvah* (singular: bar or bat mitzvah). I used to think that *bnai mitzvah* should be postponed until age sixteen or eighteen, when teenagers could engage meaningfully in this ritual. I have subsequently come to understand the wisdom of the tradition, that twelve or thirteen marks the beginning point of change and therefore is the better age for this rite of passage.

While every child has her or his own biological and psychological clock, adolescence sets in around the time of the bar/bat mitzvah. Children's bodies begin to change in significant ways. Some of these changes are particularly important as they point to adulthood and sexuality. An adolescent begins to shift the primary focus of relationship from parents to friends. Parents are no longer the all-powerful beings of childhood. Instead, they are seen more realistically as human beings with flaws. They are also seen as outdated relics of another age whose favorite activity is to be embarrassing in front of friends. Instead of the closeness of childhood, a divide, at some moments a chasm, appears between adolescent and parent. The adolescent's sense of self is in flux. The desire to be like everybody else, that is, like the "in" group, often becomes a major goal of adolescents. The growing awareness of sexuality and the desire for romance becomes a major preoccupation.

Into this explosive stew comes the life-cycle moment of the bat/bar mitzvah. The ritual comes out of obscure origins. It is clear that there existed a notion that boys at the age of thirteen and girls at the age of twelve are considered adults. This reflects the emergence of sexuality and thus the possibility of marriage. In the past, it also reflected the reality of a society with much shorter life spans and where adolescents were necessary participants in the economic life of the family. In the rabbinic tradition, becoming thirteen (or twelve for girls) meant that you were now obligated to fulfill the *mitzvot,* commandments. Hence the term *bar* or *bat mitzvah,* meaning "son" or "daughter of the commandments." Over time, the notion of the bar/bat mitzvah as a rite of passage and a celebration developed. In modern times, it has become a central life-cycle event.

An important secret: I often meet people who say to me that they were not bar/bat mitzvahed (the word has been turned into a verb in English). I explain to them that by turning twelve or thirteen they became a bat/bar mitzvah even if they never walked into a synagogue. It is the coming of age, not the learning of a Torah portion, that makes you a Jewish adult. The ceremony is not necessary, however much it provides an opportunity to mark this important period in the life of an adolescent, his or her family, and the community.

### What Is a Bar/Bat Mitzvah?

On one level, the bar/bat mitzvah is a public recognition of the new adult status of this adolescent. Since only Jewish adults can have the honor of being called up for an *aliyah* to the Torah, the *aliyah* serves as an announcement to one and all that Joey or Jane has become a Jewish adult. It has become customary that a bar/bat mitzvah not just be called to the Torah but also read from the Torah and/or *haftarah* (the prophetic reading). This demonstrates that the child has had a Jewish education. It can also reflect a commitment to Judaism. Having an *aliyah* and reading from the Torah/*haftarah* together show a connection to Torah, the central expression of Judaism. Finally, it also reflects a certain mastery of a challenge. In many cultures, entry into adulthood is marked by a rite of passage that requires overcoming a challenge. In this case the challenge may not be terribly difficult—learning to chant the Torah/*haftarah* selection. Yet for the bar/bat mitzvah it takes work and some commitment. For many children it is no small feat to stand before a large group of people and perform. Thus this act involves forming a link to Judaism and the Jewish people, becoming an adult, and mastering a challenge while being center stage. Everything else that the bar/bat mitzvah may do during the service, such as delivering a speech or leading parts of the service, are further reflections of the meaning of this ritual.

The hope then is that the bar/bat mitzvah will feel welcomed into the chain of the Jewish people. This is a rite of passage that takes place not just before family and friends, as does a *brit milah* (naming) or a wedding. It occurs (in most cases) during a Shabbat morning service that includes the regular worshipers. The ritual is placed within the context of a Jewish community to express the hope that children will take their place in the Jewish community. It recognizes that as they begin the transition to adulthood, they will be making their own decisions about what is important in their lives. It underlines that just as they will need to be responsible for their actions as adults, the *bnai mitzvah* now need to be responsible for their actions as Jewish adults. The bar/bat mitzvah is a challenge to remind Joey and Jane that much of what is worthwhile is accompanied by hard work; it can no longer be a gift from a parent.

For parents, the bar/bat mitzvah is a rite of passage that marks this transition in the life of their child. They can take pride in the accomplishment of their child learning what they needed for the ritual. They can feel bittersweet about reaching this stage in their child's life. And they can realize that their child is a marker of their own life. Thus the bar/bat mitzvah serves as a reminder of their own passing years. As on all such family occasions, there is a connection to the past and to the future. There is often the remembrance of past bar/bat mitzvahs. There is a recollection of family members who have died, but whose presence is felt at the occasion. There is recognition of the new generation as the future of the family, with all the hopes and concerns that that raises. Since people are getting married later and having children later, it may be at the bar/bat mitzvah rather than the wedding when grandparents are still alive and all three generations are able to be present. Thus the moment of the bar/bat mitzvah can be laden with a great deal of emotion, even if it is not always expressed.

## What Happens at a Bar/Bat Mitzvah?

Most bar/bat mitzvahs take place on Shabbat morning, though they may occur at any time the Torah is read. A small but increasing number take place at Shabbat *minhah*—(afternoon) service. At the center of a bar/bat mitzvah and of Shabbat morning services is the Torah service. It is traditional for the bar/bat mitzvah to read the *maftir*, the final verses of the weekly portion, and the *haftarah*, the prophetic reading. In most synagogues, the young person also gives the *d'var torah*, the sermon. This focuses on the weekly reading more than the experience of becoming a bar/bat mitzvah. (The latter used to be the focus of the bar mitzvah speeches of my childhood.) In some synagogues they lead part of the service and/or read additional sections of the Torah portion. The family is given a number of honors to give out to their guests. These can include a number of *aliyot*, opening the ark, etc.

## Creating a Spiritually Meaningful Occasion

The first step in making the ritual meaningful is to be thoughtful about what you are trying to accomplish. This process should involve both you and your child. Begin with a discussion of what this event means to each of you. Share your experience of your bar/bat mitzvah, if you had one. Discuss expectations and concerns. Try to explain why this might be important, besides being a task to be accomplished and an opportunity to get lots of presents. Hopefully, this discussion might lead to making this a celebration of an important moment rather than a hurdle to be overcome.

While only the bar/bat mitzvah has a specific role in the day, you can participate in a number of ways. Depending on your synagogue's practice, there may be a customary role for the parents beyond being called up for your own *aliyah* (see below). It may be the custom for parents to speak or share a reading as part of the service. Find out what is expected, as well as what you can do beyond the expected, and figure out how that fits with your own notion of the occasion. If you are doing something that requires practice or forethought, give yourself enough time to do it well. If you are having an *aliyah* and are unfamiliar with how the blessings are chanted, have your child teach you. If that is not a good idea, then her or his tutor or the rabbi can make you a tape.

Some families will have a number of family members and relatives read from the Torah. There is nothing that more validates a child's experience than to see one's parents doing the same thing. Even if this is much more than you are able to take on, there are lots of ways to show an interest in and thus support for the effort of your child. The larger discussions about the occasion signify that this is not just an event in the child's life. As with anything else, demonstrating involvement beyond checking to see if your child has done the assigned practicing for the week conveys more than casual concern. One way for you (and even siblings) to participate is by studying together your child's Torah portion. This not only shows your interest, and may be helpful in your child's preparation, but it also can help you feel a participant rather than an outsider at the bar/bat mitzvah service. There are a number of useful commentaries (some are available on a CD-ROM or online). Ask your rabbi for advice. If your child is giving a speech about the Torah portion, be careful not to select the focus. It is important that it should be a topic that the child is interested in. Of course, you can be helpful in the process. A few synagogues have a practice of a family *d'var torah*—that is, the speech is presented as a discussion among the family rather than just a monologue by the child. Finally, studying the Torah portion together creates an opportunity for the family to spend some time together beforehand focusing on the event but in an indirect fashion.

### Framing the Experience

Beyond focusing on the service and the Torah portion, some families see this as an opportunity to express important family values. The bar/bat mitzvah as a coming of age can also be seen as the beginning of taking on the responsibilities heretofore assumed only or mostly by adults. For others, they want to make clear that *mitzvah* is not confined narrowly to ritual and synagogue. Some people have explored doing a variety of *mitzvot* and deeds of social justice. One child spent the year before his bar mitzvah volunteering weekly at a soup kitchen serving meals.

Another way values can be expressed is in planning for the occasion and for what to do with the gifts of money that are given to the child. Each family will decide how much money it wants to spend on the dinner or party. Some families also donate money to a charity at such an occasion. The concept of sharing your wealth with those less fortunate at moments of great joy is an old tradition in Judaism. Two modern versions: (1) Mazon is a project that encourages people to donate three percent of the cost of their *simha* (celebration). Mazon, in turn, allocates all the money it collects to hunger projects here and abroad. (Mazon: A Jewish Response to Hunger, 1990 S. Bundy Dr., Suite 260, Los Angeles, CA 90025-5232.) (2) One bat mitzvah asked each of her friends to bring new or slightly used books to her party. She then took the books and donated them to public school libraries.

While most often the bulk of bar/bat mitzvah money is put away in a future college fund, some decisions about money are necessary. This is usually the first time your child will have large sums of money at her or his disposal. What percentage of the gift money should they keep? Should there be any limitations on how it is spent? It would seem that letting them keep some is both fair and a useful introduction to managing money. Leaving it to the child to decide whether to spend it on one gift (that you will inevitably think extravagant) or on many smaller ones is the most common practice. Is some of that money donated to a *tzedakah,* a "charity"? Is there a process for deciding which worthy causes should be given to? Each of these provide opportunities for discussing values related to money and social justice. They all convey the message that with adulthood there comes a responsibility for others besides yourself. This responsibility goes beyond family and friends and beyond what is "owed" to other people. This too is what it means to be a bar/bat mitzvah.

Jewish federations have encouraged bar/bat mitzvahs to sign up for a summer program in Israel. By offering a small grant redeemable when the teenager is sixteen or seventeen, they hope more teenagers will have the experience of visiting Israel. Ask your rabbi or local federation for more information.

Finally, it is key to the spiritual component of the occasion to make sure to create moments to appreciate this life-cycle event. Amid all the details and planning, the peer pressure for the best party, etc., it is easy to lose track of the meaning of this moment in our lives and that of our child. Almost invariably, we will end up spending more money than we had planned and more time on details that do not ultimately matter. Strive to balance that time and energy with creating moments for the child and yourself that acknowledge the significance of the moment. Those moments and that recognition should be our bar/bat mitzvah gift to ourselves.

# EXODUS/SHEMOT:
# ON BEING A *MENTSCH*

In the old days, proverbially, a boy would begin his bar mitzvah speech with the words "Today I am a man." What does Judaism have to say about being an adult? The answer can be summed up by the Yiddish word *mentsch,* "a decent human being."

Who are we as human beings? We exist because of a choice—a choice by God to create the world. The world was created unfinished, incomplete, and flawed. God created humans to be partners in the completion of the world. Who better than humans, who are of this world and yet are created in God's likeness, to finish the work of creation?

What are we to do? What is asked of us?

Something both simple and immensely complex—to be a *mentsch,* a caring, ethical human being.

Maimonides (the great medieval Jewish thinker), near the beginning of his code, the *Mishneh Torah,* sets out the prime directive: *ve-halakhta be-drakhav,* "you should walk in God's ways." This is how we are to journey through the world.

We are always to remember that we are created in God's image. As the rabbis said: "Just as God is kind so should you be kind; just as God is merciful so should you be merciful; just as God is holy so should you be holy" (Talmud, *Shabbat* 133b).

Maimonides says: "There are many different attributes. One person is temperamental and always angry, another is very even tempered and is never angry, one is arrogant, another humble, lustful or pure, etc." (1:1—all references are to the *Mishneh Torah, Hilkhot Da'ot,* chapter and section, unless otherwise noted).

We thus have characteristics that are both hereditary and acquired. For Maimonides the right path, God's way, is that of the middle ground. We should "neither be easily angered nor be like one dead that does not feel" (1:4).

We should try to live a simple life. "Don't desire except those things your body needs, that without them you could not live. Do not become obsessed with your work. Remember its basic purpose is to secure the necessities of life" (1:4). How do we achieve this middle path, the way of balance? We are to repeat a measured response over and over until it becomes a part of us.

Maimonides uses the image of a sick person to explain why we do not all follow his measured way. When we are sick, our senses are distorted. We perceive the bitter as sweet and the sweet as bitter. We want to eat things that are not good for us. So too when souls are sick. They desire and love bad ideas, and reject that which is healthy, the good path. It is easy for them to continue on as they have, even though this has been bad for them.

Maimonides sets out a method of change through behavior modification. He believes that if a person has an extreme quality, such as stinginess, that person should behave in a way that is the opposite extreme—that is, be very generous. One extreme will uproot the other and the person will then be able to follow the middle path.

Maimonides understood that motivation is the key to all our actions. We can be long-suffering not because we strive not to be angry but because we are passive. While a rabbinic maxim states: "Who is rich? A person who is satisfied with his lot," Maimonides knew self-satisfaction could be an excuse for laziness.

Maimonides adds: "In your quest for the middle ground, to avoid lust or envy, do not say I won't eat good food, or marry. This is an evil way. . . . One who follows that path is a sinner" (3:1). The Talmud teaches: "Isn't it enough for you what the Torah has forbidden, that you should want to forbid additional things to yourself?" (Jerusalem Talmud, *Nedarim* 9:1). Or as Kohelet/Ecclesiastes (7:16) said: "Don't be too big a *tzaddik*, a righteous person, and don't be too wise."

Maimonides' vision is just one vision of the *darkhei hashem*, "the path of God," on which we are called to travel. Even within Jewish tradition, there are other models.

In Hasidism, for example, humans are perceived as more dynamic in character. Therefore, a golden mean is not only an impossible goal to achieve, but also perhaps not even the correct goal. Rather than searching for the perfect balance between opposite qualities, the Hasidic model elevates our ability to make the appropriate choice in a particular circumstance. This is more in line with the words of Kohelet (3:1ff): "There is a time and place for every thing under heaven. A time to be born and a time to die . . . a time to love and a time to hate. . . ."

In this model, there is a time to be angry and a time to be placating, a time to be generous and a time to hold back. In the ebb and flow of life, we are often stuck in one place—too often angry; too often generous; too often scared.

We tend to abrogate choice, acting instead in a routine created from our past. The task then is to try to see clearly, to be aware, to avoid the kind of confusion described by Isaiah: "Ah, those who call evil good and good evil; Who present darkness as light and light as darkness" (Isa. 5:20).

In the world of creation, God's first act is to separate light from darkness. And yet we can only see light because of the contrasting darkness. We live our mortal lives knowing that darkness inevitably follows light. Both light and darkness are necessary, and together they help us see.

We strive to gain clarity, sight, and insight even as we know it will pass, knowing we will achieve clarity only for a brief moment.

We live in a world of differentiation, a world of *havdalot*, "separations," that give us perspective. We need to see that this is the nature of our world; perhaps we need even to celebrate these separations. Even as we try to repair the world, to restore it to its unity, the world continues to exist with its unbelievable diversity. God, as the underlying unity, gives affirmation and value to all people and all things, even to anger and pride.

God then calls upon us as our first act of creation to become aware, to see clearly, to separate the light from the darkness, and to accept the knowledge that darkness will always be present until the end of time.

And in that awareness, we must remember that we are to be merciful as God is merciful, for all humans are created in God's image. We are taught *kavod ha-beriot,* "respect and honor for all human beings." For we are truly all equal, all created in the image of the One, all descendants of one set of parents. As different and as unique (and as problematic) as each of us is, we all share the bonds of our humanity, because we are all God's creatures.

What is the most important verse in the Torah?

> Rabbi Akiva said: "You shall love your neighbor as yourself." This is a great principle of the Torah. Ben Azzai disagreed: The verse "This is the book of the descendants of Adam . . . the human whom God made in God's likeness" (Gen. 5:1) utters a principle even greater. [Jerusalem Talmud, *Nedarim* 9:4, 41c]

Why does Ben Azzai find such an obvious choice as "love your neighbor as yourself" inadequate? Perhaps, quite simply, because some people don't know how to love themselves. Perhaps because it demands too much of us—to love *everybody*! Or perhaps Ben Azzai thinks that the simple statement of human existence is enough: "This is the record of Adam's descendants." For as we look in the face of another human being, we see the image of God, the image of all God's creatures who have ever existed. Ultimately, we are looking in a mirror and seeing our own face. Through the realization that we are all equal, both in our humanity and in our having been created in the image of God, we learn to treat the other with respect and with kindness.

# LEVITICUS/VA-YIKRA:
# RELATIONSHIPS
# AND SEXUALITY

As the exhilaration of leaving Egypt behind wears off, we struggle with the day-to-day challenges of our journey to the Promised Land. We are excited by being on our own and at the same time worried about being all alone. The challenge of Leviticus is how to create the structures that will aid us on our travels. One of those "structures" is having a clear goal that is kept always before you. For Leviticus that goal is to live a life of holiness. "You shall be to me a kingdom of priests and a holy nation" (Lev. 19:6).

In the Bible, holiness is a quality ascribed to God. Nothing else is intrinsically holy—not a mountain or a sacred grove (see "Eating and Food," pp. 66–93). In the teaching quoted in the previous chapter that we should be merciful as God is merciful, we are also told to be holy as God is holy. While it is clear what being merciful means, it is not very clear what it means to be holy. It is not even clear what it means for God to be holy. This teaching in fact suggests that holiness is not a quality but a way of acting, like being merciful. Holiness is what brings all those qualities together: merciful, forgiving, forbearing, acting justly. Holiness is acting with a consciousness that there is a right way to behave and to respond.

The Book of Leviticus sets out in great detail the striving for holiness. It includes laws of impurity related to bodily emissions, the dietary laws of keeping kosher, and ethical laws such as loving your neighbor. In Leviticus, these laws help us to achieve holiness and reject impurity. What is their context in the Book of Leviticus? What is the context of Leviticus itself? In the Book of Exodus, we have left home and have begun our independent journey. At the end of the Book of Exodus, the Israelites are commanded to build the sanctuary as a place for God's Presence to dwell. Like the Israelites in the desert, we too are faced with the challenge of building our own home when we have left our parents' home behind. That home is constructed not only of straw or sticks or even bricks; in the vision of Leviticus it is constructed of holiness.

In the Torah's picture of a holy nation, we are to live as the Israelites did when they camped in the desert. In the middle of the camp is God's Presence hovering over the sanctuary, with the Israelites encamped all around. In Leviticus, we are told to be careful to keep the sanctuary free from impurity and to cleanse it periodically. For if the sanctuary becomes too tainted with impurity, then the Presence of God will be forced to abandon it and in so doing abandon the camp of Israel. Thus Leviticus is concerned with the question, How do you live with God as your next-door neighbor?

How then do we create our homes/lives as a reflection of the ideals of holiness?

The construction of that home takes place in career and in relationships much more than in some spatial sense. I discussed the subject of work earlier in this book and so would like to focus on relationships.

### A MIDRASH

Therefore the Lord has sent *him* forth from the Garden of Eden to till ground whence he was taken. So he drove out the *man*. [Gen. 3:23–24]

He looked around him. Everything seemed different. Everything. Then he heard a noise. Startled and afraid, he turned. "Oh, it's you."

"Yes, it's me," Eve answered quietly.

They stood quietly, looking at each other, then looking away when their eyes met. They felt naked again, though in a different way.

"Why are you here?" asked Adam in a voice thick with hope, anger, and confusion.

"Here—why here?—isn't it obvious?"

"You weren't expelled by God from the garden, only me. Only *me*," Adam said emphatically. He looked past Eve toward where he thought the garden should be. "You don't have to leave. You could stay in the garden with all it contains."

She looked at him and said slowly, "I want to be here."

"Here!? I have no idea where 'here' is."

"I want to be here with you. 'Here' is with you." Hesitantly, Eve said, "I'm sorry about what happened. I'm sorry that you were hurt. I'm sorry that so much lies between us."

"Sorry?"

"Yes, sorry."

"But you gave me the apple."

"And you turned on me and told God it was my fault."

"Yeah, that's because—"

"Adam, we don't need to go over again what happened, who did what to whom, and why. I'm sorry for what I did. I'm sorry for what you did to me, but most of all I'm sorry about what has happened to us."

"I'm sorry too, but I don't know if I can trust you." Adam looked around and looked at her and said, "Everything seems different."

"Everything doesn't have to be different. This place is different but we don't have to be different. I care about you. I want to be with you."

"You want to be with me? You are willing to leave the garden for this? For me?"

She nodded.

They looked at each other. He stretched out his hand to her. She took it. Then they both said, "I love you."

They felt naked to each other and they knew the wonder of love. Hand in hand they walked off.

God watching all this smiled pleasantly.

Satan said to God, "I don't understand. What was all that about and why do you seem so pleased with yourself?"

"Don't you see, they have found each other again. They forgave each other. They reestablished trust. They discovered love."

"Love," said Satan, "how does love come out of such a mess?"

God said: "Love only comes out of a mess. Only from brokenness can real wholeness come. Trust can only follow distrust."

"But why so complicated, why not tell them all this?"

God said, "They had to find out for themselves, they had to eat of the fruit of the tree."

"What were those fruits? They looked sort of like apples."

"Not apples, the tree's fruit were argument, discord, betrayal, anger, hurt feelings, and alienation."

Satan asked, "And from eating such fruit you create love?"

"No, you don't create love, but you can find your way *to* love. *If* you can remember what was before, what is really important, and can see the other's nakedness in all its fragility and beauty. And you have to remember that all other humans are equal in their nakedness, and all humans are equal in containing a piece of Me, of holiness."

"But why did you expel only Adam and not Eve?"

God chuckled. "It was the only way they could rebuild their love. Otherwise Adam would never be really sure that Eve was sorry. But because she was willing to give up Eden for him, he knew her love. And she too wouldn't have been able to trust his forgiveness if both were expelled and she just simply asked him for forgiveness. In fact both would probably still be waiting for the other to make the first gesture. Nothing would have happened. Creating the inequality created a choice for Eve. It was the only way."

Satan frowned. "I still think you just could have told them straight out, none of this forked-tongue stuff."

"Satan, you don't have children, do you? Someday maybe you'll understand how My children learn."

And God placed an angel with an ever-changing sword made

of the flames of love to prevent humans from going backward into the garden.

It would be correct but still too simple to say that the tradition sees the goal of relationships to be marriage. Coming out of a traditional culture, it regarded sex as restricted to married couples.

Unlike some other religions and cultures, Judaism does not see the body as the enemy of the spirit, or sex as "dirty" or grossly physical. The picture of sexuality in Judaism is more complicated. The tradition contains strands that are very ascetic and puritanical, as well as those that see sex as something to be enjoyed for its pleasure.

Yet I would suggest that attaining holiness through relationships is central to Judaism as a spiritual practice. Let us develop a notion of holiness in relationships by returning once again to the beginning of creation.

"Be fertile and increase, *p'ru u'rvu,* and fill the world" (Gen. 1:28) are the first words addressed by God to human beings. Not "keep the Sabbath"; not "don't steal" or even "you should have two dish drainers, one for dairy and one for meat."

"Be fertile and increase, *p'ru u'rvu,* and fill the earth." At this moment of the creation of the first humans, God calls upon us to be like God and create a world—a world of new human beings. According to the rabbis, *p'ru u'rvu,* "be fertile and increase," is the first *mitzvah,* the first commandment of the Torah. There is a paradox here. The *mitzvot,* all 613 commandments, are meant for the Jews. And yet we begin with one which is universal—all human beings should be fruitful and fill the world (not just the Jews).

Sex then begins right at the beginning. It doesn't even wait for the Garden of Eden story. What then is the primary purpose of sexual relations: procreation, enjoyment, *kedushah* (holiness)?

With just this verse one could argue that procreation is the prime directive for humans and thus sex is primarily for procreation. Or one could argue that since God says *ki tov,* "it is good," that sex like the world at large is given to humans to enjoy, and so sex, like food, like life itself, is to be savored for its rich pleasures. Certainly Judaism sees sex as involving procreation, and also enjoyment. Both are of importance to Judaism. Yet it is the third possibility, *kedushah*, "holiness," that is the primary purpose of sexuality.

Judaism looks at the human condition and invites us to take those things that we have in common with the animals and make them holy. We regulate what we eat and recite a *berakhah* before we eat to make the act of eating holy. We are called to do this in the area of sex as well. We are not just animals reproducing our species. Or just seekers of sensuous pleasure. The act of sex primarily involves another person. We are in relationship with that person—and in that relationship holiness can be created. Relationships of caring, intimacy, affection, mutuality, are relationships of holiness, and sexuality is one way to create such relationships.

For Genesis goes on from "Be fertile and multiply" to say, "A person should leave their parents and cleave unto their partner and be like one flesh" (Gen. 2:24). This one verse captures the basic underlying rhythms of the universe. Separation and striving for union. The world of Genesis is one of separation: light from darkness, sea from land, etc. We each of us know the utter aloneness of human existence. Our world is one of partiality, of brokenness, of loneliness, a world of light but of darkness as well.

Yet as God said to the first human, *lo tov heyot ha'adam l'vado*, "it is not good for a human to be alone." All the rest of creation from the first day on is described as *ki tov*, "it is good." The one thing *lo tov*, "not good," is a human alone. The rhythm of the universe is set. We begin in separation and strive for wholeness. A person should leave their parents and cleave unto their partner and be like one flesh. We leave our parents (separation) to find another (unity). It is in the moment of sexual union that we come closest to wholeness. Instead of alienation and apartness, we become as one flesh. We lose our sense of twoness and become as one. In sexual union and in love there is the holiness of being in relationship to rather than in alienation from the other.

In fact, the mystery and power of sex is a gateway not just to the holiness of relationships but the holiness of God. For Genesis tells us we are all created in the image of God. Interacting with other people is interacting with other divine images, thus reminding us of who we are and reminding us who created us and who calls us to restore holiness and wholeness to the world: God.

By now, you're probably thinking that this is all very nice. For surely love, deep love, expressed romantically and erotically, is holy and wonderful. But there is a kind of sexual love that feels more like partiality than wholeness, more like lust than love, or more like simply sex. So where is holiness in those moments? Despite the fact that more people say the words "Oh God" with fervor in a moment of passion in the bedroom than in any synagogue, I'm not sure that it is an expression of supreme religious faith.

Judaism calls us to strive for an ideal. That ideal is not platonic love but rather a love that is deep, mutual, caring, and expressed in every way, including and especially through the physical. The tradition understands that we will live far from that ideal but nevertheless believes the closer to the ideal the better, and recognizes that we deeply long "not to be alone" but to cleave together as one flesh.

Hasidism believed not just that the underlying impulse in the universe is human beings striving for wholeness, but that the whole universe is striving for wholeness. Our task is *tikkun olam,* "repairing the world," and restoring even God to wholeness. The Hasidic writers therefore taught that when you are trying to pray and instead find yourself distracted by thoughts of attraction to another human being, instead of saying "*Feh!* I'm such a lowlife," you should realize that all attraction, all love is just a reflection of this impulse underlying everything to love God, to come close and cleave to God, to experience the unity of the world.

Even pure lust is only a distorted reflection of the impulse buried deep inside us to love God. Hasidism calls us to follow that lust back to its sources as the love of God. But even if we are less ambitious, we should understand that sex and love are doorways to Judaism's deepest value: holiness. To love God, one must first love another human being; one must first love oneself; and then together with the other loved ones we can restore the world to peace, wholeness, and harmony. Judaism then is not setting boundaries or trying to keep in check the powerful sexual urge. Rather it sees sexuality and its highest form, love, as among the most critical gifts of holiness given by God to us to live in and beyond this world. Love of humans and love of God are inextricably linked, and are Judaism's answer to the human condition.

Bernard of Clairvaux, founder of the Cistercian order of monks in the Middle Ages, wrote in his commentary on the Song of Songs:

> Love is alone sufficient by itself; it pleases by itself, and for its own sake. It is itself a merit, and itself its own recompense. It seeks neither cause, nor consequences beyond itself. It is its own fruit, its own object and usefulness. I love, because I love; I love, that I may love.

There are a number of specific values that are part of this notion of the holiness of sexuality.

First, we are created by God. This means that the penis and vagina are also created by God. The sex drive is also God's rather than Satan's creation. Our bodies are a gift to us from God. There is nothing disgusting about any part of them.

Even more important is to remember that what makes humans special is that we are created in the image of God. We are all equal and should be treated as such. To treat another person as an object is to deny at that moment this basic teaching of Judaism. In that way, sex is different from other pleasures, such as food. Even if we eat food without appreciation of it as a gift or without any awareness of the holiness of the act, at worse we hurt ourselves by self-destructive eating habits. Sex (except for masturbation) involves another person.

This concept of treating another person with respect is called *kavod ha-beriot*, "respect and honor for all human beings." The potential to hurt someone else is particularly present in sex because the act, no matter how "casual," involves vulnerability. You are naked before another person. If the Torah urges us to take special care of the widow, orphan, and stranger because they were particularly vulnerable in ancient Israelite society, how much more so, when we lie naked physically and emotionally with a lover. Knowing our common vulnerability, we need to be especially protective of the other person in their nakedness. Needless to say, rape and sexual abuse are terrible personal violations, made even worse if done by someone who is supposed to be a protector, such as a parent. There are many forms of coercion that do not have the violence of rape, but still do violence to the integrity of a person's soul. Sex needs to be fully consensual. Taking advantage of another's emotional neediness or when a person is not in full control of his or her faculties is not consensual. Sex is not about power; it is about pleasure and love.

These attitudes translate into the following traditional teachings about sex:

- In an appropriate context (for the tradition that means a married couple), all varieties of sex are permissible. There are no restrictions about what can happen in bed as long as both people want it to happen.
- The tradition recognizes women as sexual beings with equal needs and rights equal to men's to have those needs met.
- Sex is not just for the purpose of procreation. The tradition stresses the importance of having children. Yet it also sees nothing wrong with sex as pleasure. Even if conception is not a possibility, sex should be part of a couple's relationship.

## *Taharat ha-Mishpaha,* Laws of Family Purity

Traditionally, sex was prohibited while a woman had her period. Menstrual blood was considered *tameh,* "impure," and physical contact with someone in a state of impurity was discouraged (see Lev. 15:19ff). This was part of a larger system of purity and impurity including other bodily discharges, biblical leprosy, and corpses. As developed by the rabbinic tradition, this meant a woman counted a minimum of five days from the onset of her period followed by seven days without any bleeding. At the conclusion of this time, she would then go to the *mikvah,* the ritual bath. Immersion in the *mikvah* would restore her to a state of purity and allow for sex.

With the destruction of the Temple in Jerusalem, the laws of purity and impurity basically fell into disuse except for the law concerning menstruation. In traditional circles, this is still widely observed. It is praised as regulating sex between a couple, just as Judaism regulates what we can eat, etc. Thus it is seen as taking the natural act of sex and putting it into a religious context. For some, observing a time of enforced abstinence prevents the pleasure and blessing of sex from being taken for granted. Some argue that the blood of menstruation is impure because blood is a powerful symbol of life and death. Underlying the whole structure of purity and impurity in the Bible, according to one understanding, is the separation of life from death.

Nevertheless, many in the Jewish community reject these laws. Since the laws of impurity nowadays only apply to menstruating women, it is argued that this fosters a negative attitude toward women and menstruation. Women and women's things are unclean. A woman's period, which is a part of her body's natural monthly cycle, thus has a negative connotation. Only the woman is impure and only she goes to the *mikvah*. If this was to renew a couple's sexuality after a period of abstinence, why shouldn't both immerse in the *mikvah*? These laws feel too much part of the strand in the tradition that perceives women as the mysterious or even dangerous "other." Without a larger context of laws of purity and impurity, one cannot escape the question, why are these laws the only ones still in effect today? Thus for many people the negative connotations of the law of family purity are overwhelming. In contemporary practice, they are not observed outside the traditional community.

There are other traditional attitudes that are also problematic. Some are just strands within the tradition, such as the Kabbalah's view of male masturbation as a terrible sin. Or the more puritanical traditions that say intercourse should be done only in the dark or as quickly as possible. These strands can be ignored, since there are strands of equal authority that are more celebratory of sex. There are, however, two areas where the tradition stands in contrast to trends in modern society: premarital or nonmarital sex and homosexuality.

### Sex Between Unmarried Adults

The norm in our society is not to limit sex to people who are married. The sexual revolution of the late twentieth century came about for a variety of reasons. The availability of effective female contraception removed the concern about unwanted pregnancies. Women's liberation and the rebellion against old norms in the 1960s all played a role in fostering the new sexual freedom. For a while, sex seemed relatively risk-free; then AIDS made sex not just risky but possibly deadly.

While the tradition has seen married sex as the only permissible form, what should our response be to the current societal norm? The more traditional elements continue to argue for abstinence before marriage. In fact, in the Orthodox community, any physical contact between the sexes, even holding hands and kissing, is forbidden. I think a more nuanced response is needed. Sex, as we have seen, is a response to a number of urges. The tradition is clear that having babies is not the only valid reason for sex. Experiencing pleasure, expressing intimacy, and manifesting one's love can all be purposes of sex. These can be experienced outside the state of marriage.

We live in a world of certain realities. People are getting married at a later age. Therefore there is more time between puberty and marriage. Not everyone is going to get married. Some will choose not to marry; others will not find the "right" partner. Many get divorced, which means that in a traditional model people who have been sexually active while married must now forgo sex until remarriage. Is the correct position to say that all such people should practice abstinence?

There is something attractive about being sexually intimate only with your marriage partner. Yet that would mean the exploration of that part of your identity and your partner's identity would only begin on your wedding night. Sexual compatibility has become, along with all other forms of compatibility, part of the mix that we use in deciding upon a marriage partner. We live in a world of romantic love, not arranged marriages. Our expectations are different. Perhaps they are too idealized, but we want to know whom we are marrying so as to be sure we are making the correct choice. That knowing includes the biblical meaning of *knowing*, that is, sexually.

Why is it that the word *yada*, "know," in the Torah can refer to sex? Because to have sex with someone is an opportunity to know that other person. There is a revealing not just of our bodies but that which we keep most private—our sexual selves. There is an intimacy in the sexual act, and thus a knowing of the other person.

Let us for a moment turn the question on its head. Why not have sex before marriage? Well, one answer focuses on virginity. Yet virginity has almost always applied only to women. It thus seems part of a larger view of women as different and thus not equal to men. Their virginity is to be protected. Women who were not virgins were less desirable as brides in ancient times.

Let me suggest, then, two complementary ways to look upon sex before marriage. The first is that sex as a source of pleasure is not denied us by the Torah. We are to enjoy this world and see it as God's gift to us. As we learned in the chapter on "Eating and Food," there is one talmudic teaching that says we will be called to account in heaven for those good foods that we abstained from eating during our life on earth. Sex, too, is one of the great pleasures of life. Like food, it needs to be enjoyed not in excess and with the right intention. It cannot replace real relationships and intimacy; it can help create them. There is, then, "junk sex" just as there is "junk food"—that which seems fine, but actually is not good for us. What then is "good" sex?

That takes us to the second way of viewing sex. Sex is a means to *kedushah*, "holiness." Marriage is called *kiddushin*, from the same word. There is a sanctity to the act of sexual intercourse, for all the reasons we have talked about. It is a holy connection between two people that brings a sense of wholeness and unity, even if only for a brief period. That is no small thing in a world of brokenness. This is a world where we experience existential aloneness. This is an act of togetherness, not aloneness. For most people it is the closest they will come to experiencing a union with someone beyond themselves. The possibility that the masks that we wear and the walls that we have erected should be removed to allow for the joining of two people in warm embrace is an opportunity that should not be restricted only to those who are married.

On the other hand, it is important to recognize not only the powerful urge toward sexuality, but its power to hurt as well. We begin our exploration of this powerful force as adolescents. It is a great challenge to teenagers to both explore this (for them) unknown territory and to do so wisely. If with experience this territory becomes familiar, it still can be very wonderful or very hurting. Therefore, all the principles we discussed earlier should provide guidance to our sexual behavior. We need to treat this other divine image respectfully and be protective of his or her vulnerability. It should be an act of mutual consent.

Of course, honesty must be the common language of sexual partners. Whether being misleading in order to get someone into bed or being untruthful about your commitment, these are forms of lying. Lies can also be what is hidden, such as secretly being involved with someone else. You need not be in a marriage for an affair to be a betrayal of an understanding of commitment and trust between two people.

Finally, even when not secretive, promiscuity or one-night stands challenge anyone's ability to treat sexuality as a form of holiness. Is it possible for sex to be just sex, a physical act of release and pleasure? Possibly, but most of the time there is an emotional element involved, at least for one of the partners. It is rarely just the equivalent of eating a good meal, much as we might try to pretend otherwise. Once there is more at stake, all the ethical principles then come into play. Ultimately we need to acknowledge sexuality as a powerful force that also provides the opportunity for two people to touch the deepest parts of each other's being.

## Homosexuality

Within the Jewish community (and the greater society) homosexuality is a matter of much debate. Traditional elements in the community see the biblical text as clear and unequivocal about homosexuality: "Do not lie with a male as one lies with a woman; it is an abhorrence" (Lev. 18:22). There are some in the traditional camp who have ceased stressing that it is an abomination. Instead, they urge having compassion for someone who engages in homosexual sex, just as for someone who engages in any other violation of the *mitzvot* (commandments). Yet it still remains a violation and behavior that should be discouraged. There are of course many other people who think homosexuality is wrong for "nonreligious" reasons. These range from thinking that heterosexuality is the natural way of the world as it leads to propagation, to homophobia, an irrational fear that homosexuality sometimes evokes. There are those in the Jewish community who have tried to take a seemingly middle ground. The Conservative movement has come out in favor of the civil rights of homosexuals and against discrimination toward them. Yet at the same time, in the religious sphere, it will not ordain openly gay and lesbian rabbis and more broadly upholds the Bible's prohibition of homosexuality. The Reconstructionist and then the Reform movement have taken a position that affirms homosexuality. They have ordained gay and lesbian rabbis and some rabbis in both movements will perform same-sex commitment ceremonies (the equivalents of marriages). These policies reflect a larger attitude that no longer sees homosexuality as wrong, but rather as another form of human sexuality. They suggest that our attitude has changed from that of the Bible, just as it has on other issues such as slavery and the status of woman. For some this change in attitude has to do with evidence that suggests homosexuality is not a choice but part of the genetic makeup of some people. For others, it reflects an understanding that relations between homosexuals are no different from those between heterosexuals. At their best, they are relations of deep love and commitment. This is also part of an expanded definition of what constitutes families. For me, an affirmation of homosexuality follows from all that I have already said about sexuality. There is an opportunity to experience holiness through the intimacy between two people. Since sex for Judaism is not just about having children, I would suggest that the Talmud's statements that permit any act that both people want be expanded to include two adults of the same sex. Ultimately homosexuality and heterosexuality should be seen as aspects of the same Divine desire: "it is not good for a human to be alone."

## Getting Married and Having Children or Not

The tradition has many statements that suggest that a person is incomplete unless married. It also stresses the importance of having children. As mentioned above, it is the first commandment. Yet we live in a world that provides more options than in premodern times. Before effective birth control and while the family was still an economic unit, traditional family structures were almost a necessity. When the rabbis talked about needing to settle the uninhabited areas of the earth as part of the mission to be fruitful and multiply, they were living on a largely uninhabited earth. We, on the other hand, are pushing the limits of human growth. Zero population growth, while only a passing phase as a movement, is a notion that would have seemed ludicrous in premodern times.

The tradition has always realized that the world was far less than the ideal. Certainly we live in a world where some of the people who do not get married are in fact eager to be married. With an expectation of romantic love, it may not always be possible to find the right someone, even if you are "really" looking. Just as couples who cannot have children are no longer obligated to observe the commandment to be fruitful, so one could argue that someone who cannot find the right partner should not be criticized for not being married. Yet the challenge to traditional attitudes is greater than that. For there are people who have decided not to get married. There are also couples who have decided not to have children. (If having children is the ultimate primary reason for marriage, then single parents would not be an issue in this discussion.) What should the tradition's response be?

> We have been taught that R. Eliezer said: A person who does not engage in fruition and increase is as though he shed blood. . . . R. Akiva said: Such a one is as though he diminished God's image. . . . Ben Azzai said: He is as one who both sheds blood and diminishes God's image.
>
> R. Eliezer said to Ben Azzai (a bachelor without children): "Such words sound well when they issue from the mouths of those who practice them. There are some that preach well and practice well; others practice well but do not preach well. You preach well but do not practice well." Ben Azzai replied, "But what shall I do, seeing that my soul yearns for Torah? The world can continue through others." [Talmud, *Yevamot* 63b; *Tosefta Yevamot* 8:7]

This text is one of the most quoted on the importance of having children. Often only the first half is quoted, yet the text is more nuanced than that. Ben Azzai, a bachelor, who has the strongest statement advocating having children, is called to account by his colleague. Ben Azzai can only say that his soul yearns in a different direction from marriage and children. He both concedes and suggests that the world will have to be continued by other people having children. It would have been simple to edit Ben Azzai out of this text. Having the whole text suggests that the tradition is saying here that having children is important and not everyone will do it. There will be people like Ben Azzai whose priorities lie elsewhere. As much as the tradition advocates marriage and having children, this text gives Ben Azzai the last word. To the criticism of him, he answers that is the way it is. I would suggest that the Jewish community follow in the path of this text. We should continue to talk about the holiness of marriage and the unbelievable gift that children are, and allow people the room to make personal decisions. The truth is none of these choices is simple. Whether to get married or not, have children or not, are never casual decisions. Ultimately we are living in a much more diverse world than our ancestors. There are all kinds of families and people single at various stages of their lives. Rather than lamenting the loss of some idealized, never-really-existed past, let us celebrate that diversity. It has allowed greater freedom to people to create the life that might bring to them the most happiness, wholeness, and holiness.

# LEVITICUS/VA-YIKRA:
# MARRIAGE

From every human being there rises a light that reaches straight to heaven. And when two souls that are destined to be together find each other, their streams of light flow together, and a single brighter light goes forth from their united being. [Baal Shem Tov, as told by Meyer Levin in *Classic Hassidic Tales*]

A marriage is a work of holiness. It is not just an expression of love for another. Marriage also involves a willingness to make a commitment to another human being, thereby linking lives. For the first time really since an infant discovers that she or he and the world are separate, the "I" is willing to join with another in a profound and lasting way to become a "we." This commitment excludes comparable relationships with other people. In its positive formulation, it is expressed in devotion and caring for another person. Facing the future together as a married couple means decisions will now involve what is good for *us*, not just for *me*. Part of the holiness comes just from this we-ness. We diminish the boundaries between two people through an intimacy that involves many dimensions. Marriage does return us to the garden, not in our innocence but in our willingness to be naked before each other. In that nakedness, innocence is reestablished, the innocence of a trust built in an ever-deepening love for the other person. In marriage, that love comes not from new revelations as much as from the familiar becoming dearer. The wrinkle above her eye, his oft-repeated expression, the way she arranges the pillows, etc., become

373

part of the fabric of this love. Marriage understands that deep love comes from the everyday, not from the extraordinary moment. This too is why marriage is a path to the holy, since it takes the everyday of a relationship between two people and challenges us to work to make it a source of holiness. After all, for married couples the marriage is the primary relationship in their life. Potentially, your partner is the person you will spend more of your life with than anyone else. You left home and so will your children. You and your partner will be together for the rest of your life.

As a lifelong partnership, marriage is a commitment to grow together. This is one of its greatest challenges, made even more so by longer life expectancies. We may feel we know our partner deeply at the time of our wedding, but what will he or she be like ten and twenty years from now? Marriage is a contract that must allow for growth if people are not going to be stifled. Yet that presents the all-too-real danger that people will grow apart rather than together. As much as the couple is a "we," they are also "I"s. The challenge is to grow with an expansiveness that allows both persons to move in the directions that they find necessary, yet at the same time feel that theirs is a joint enterprise. The hope is that ultimately the growth of each will be part of the growth of the marriage.

Marriages also point toward holiness because they require a leap of faith. As much as we may know the beloved other, she or he is still an other. As much time as we may have spent together as a couple, there are still things that I do not know about you. Nor can anyone predict the future—as we all have seen, marriages that seemed strong sometimes come apart. Thus as we approach a decision to marry, we can use our rational minds only so far. In the end marriage does require a leap of faith—a belief in the other person, in yourself, and in the potential of this relationship. Particularly in our time, with the high divorce rate, marriage can seem an act of courage. Ultimately a loving relationship ensconced in a marriage reminds us that we can have a form of such a relationship with the Holy One. Both relationships depend on a faith in the other beyond reason. What makes marriage holy is not the taking of sacred mutual vows, but the knowledge that marriage emanates from the impulse to love and cherish another person. There is nothing holier than that, or more reflective of God's love and caring for all God's creatures.

A [Roman] noblewoman asked R. Yose ben Halafta: "In how many days did the Holy One create the world?" R. Yose replied, "In six days." She asked, "And what has God been doing since?" R. Yose replied, "The Holy One has been busy making matches: the daughter of So-and-so to So-and-so." The noblewoman said, "If that is all God does, I can do the same thing. How many menservants and how many maidservants do I have! In no time at all, I can match them up." R. Yose: "Matchmaking may be a trivial thing in your eyes; but for the Holy One, it is as awesome an act as splitting the Red Sea."

R. Yose ben Halafta left the noblewoman and went away. What did she do? She took a thousand menservants and a thousand maidservants, lined them up in row upon row facing one another, and said, "This man shall marry that woman, and this woman shall be married to that man," and so she matched them all up in a single night. In the morning, the ones thus matched came to the lady, one with his head bloodied, one with his eye knocked out, one with his shoulder dislocated, and another with his leg broken. She asked, "What happened to you?" One replied, "I don't want that woman," and another replied, "I don't want that man."

The noblewoman promptly sent to have R. Yose ben Halafta brought to her. She said to him, "Master, your Torah is completely right, excellent, and worthy of praise. All you said is exactly so." [Midrash, *Genesis Rabbah* 68:4; *Leviticus Rabbah* 8:1; *Numbers Rabbah* 3:6]

### Remembering What Is Important

Once a decision to get married is made, the couple begins the intensive process of wedding plans. Weddings may be the most complex of the standard life-cycle events in terms of the organizing necessary to make it happen. Most of that work will fall to the couple, though if they are young, parents may be more involved. The spiritual challenge is to hold on to what marriage is all about in the midst of the flurry of preparations. Too often arguments arise between the bride and groom or between the couple and their parents about some detail of the wedding. These arguments can reflect the nervousness of all the involved parties. It can also reflect a tension between parents and the couple over who makes final decisions. Despite all that needs to be accomplished, the couple should not lose sight of one truth: you do not need to have a perfect wedding to have a great marriage. It is natural to want to have a wonderful wedding to celebrate your love for each other. But that love does not depend on the color of the tablecloths or who is asked to walk down the aisle. The challenge is to be clear about what is important for your wedding and what is just a nice extra.

The good thing about making wedding plans is that it helps keep in your consciousness that you will be taking this big step soon. An engagement is a preliminary announcement of the upcoming wedding. Instead of a "save-the-date notice," its purpose is to hang a "sold" sign on both bride and groom. They are removed from the social marketplace. An old Jewish tradition, no longer observed, was to treat an engagement as a legally binding contract called *tena'im* (conditions). (Today, in traditional circles the signing of *tena'im* is done right before the wedding ceremony.) There are no Jewish customs concerning showers or bachelor parties. Throughout the period leading up to the wedding, as you make decisions, buy the rings, etc., try to take a moment at each step to focus on your marriage (for example, "I am buying this ring which will be placed on the finger of my loved one as a sign of our love and of our marriage"). Mostly, that *kavanah*, "intention," is present as we prepare for our weddings, but occasionally it gets lost under the press of getting everything done.

## Basic Preparations

The Jewish wedding ceremony is simple and yet rich with meaning and tradition. There are many decisions to be made about the wedding, some trivial, some important. Most of the trivial ones seem extraordinarily important at the time. There are, however, some basic decisions that determine the general character of your wedding.

How formal or informal do you want the overall style to be? How many guests will you be having? How traditional do you want to be? Do you want to involve many people in the ritual or keep that number small? As these basic questions are clarified, the general style of your wedding will emerge.

There are a number of elements needed for the wedding that require advanced planning.

*Finding a rabbi* If you know a rabbi, you should call and discuss her or his availability. If you don't know a rabbi, ask people in the community, especially friends who have recently married. Call a rabbi and discuss your plans. Besides general availability, if you have specific concerns you should not hesitate to ask. Some congregational rabbis are too busy to perform weddings for nonmembers. If this is a problem, ask the rabbi for a referral to a colleague who might be available. The next step is to make an appointment to talk more in depth, so as to find out whether this rabbi is the right person to officiate at your wedding. Unlike therapists, rabbis do not charge people for an initial session, even if they are shopping around. Therefore, you should both feel free to ask to speak to a rabbi and yet be careful not to waste his or her time. You mostly want to gauge whether the right chemistry is present. How does this rabbi relate to tradition, flexibility, feminism, making non-Hebrew-speaking guests, whether Jew or Gentile, welcome? How would they describe their religious approach? How would they broadly describe how they perform a wedding? How often do they meet with the couple before the wedding and for what purposes?

Some rabbis are uncomfortable talking about their fee, so you should ask. Also find out how and when the rabbi wants to be paid. A rabbi should never have to bill for a fee. In many synagogues, members of the congregation do not pay a fee to the rabbi for officiating at their life-cycle events. It is, however, customary to make a donation to the rabbi's discretionary account in such circumstances. You can ask the rabbi's secretary or the synagogue's administrator for some guidance on what would be an appropriate donation. If out-of-town travel is involved, the rabbi should be reimbursed.

By the way, it is customary to invite the rabbi and her or his spouse to the wedding reception, though many rabbis have a general rule not to stay for receptions. Some couples and some rabbis like to have a cantor also participate in the ceremony to chant certain parts of the ceremony. This should be discussed with the rabbi.

*Some possible hitches to getting hitched*    Rabbis with a traditional bent will ask questions regarding you and your fiancé's personal status. The rabbi raises such questions to find out if there is any reason that he or she would be unable to officiate at your wedding because of issues of Jewish law. It certainly makes sense for you to raise an issue that you think might be problematic in your initial conversation to avoid wasting everyone's time. If you are marrying a non-Jew, that should be mentioned. (See section below on intermarriage.) Potential issues are reflected in the following questions: Are you both Jewish? Are all your parents Jewish? Were either of you married before? If you were married to a Jew, did you receive a *get,* a Jewish divorce? Are you a *kohen,* of priestly lineage? If you or your parents (especially your mothers) were converted, by what kind (that is, by what denomination) of rabbi were you converted?

There are three types of issues the rabbi is trying to ascertain: (1) Is the couple Jewish according to the rabbi's definition of Jewish law? If not, then this is an intermarriage at which many rabbis will not officiate. (2) Traditionally oriented rabbis want someone who has been previously married to a Jew to have a Jewish divorce. This is because they believe that just as there was a religious ceremony to begin the marriage, so should there be one to end the marriage. There are also serious Jewish legal consequences involved. According to Jewish law, even if you had a civil divorce you are still considered married. For more details about Jewish divorce see pp. 403–10. Reform rabbis consider a civil divorce the equivalent of a Jewish divorce and for them this is not an issue. (3) There are certain marriages that were traditionally forbidden according to Jewish law, including some special restrictions on someone who is of priestly descent. Orthodox and some Conservative rabbis will be concerned about this.

Another set of concerns for a rabbi might be the time of a wedding ceremony. If you have fixed on a time and date or are considering a time and date, see if the rabbi has any problem with it beyond just her or his scheduling.

Similarly, there are some traditional rabbis who care if the reception following the ceremony is kosher, whether or not they are staying for it. I had one couple approach me a month before their wedding because they had just told their Orthodox rabbi that the planned meal was not kosher. Having assumed that it was kosher, he had never asked and now refused to officiate. The couple never thought of it as an issue and so had never mentioned it to him. Even if the rabbi is not staying for the reception and does not care that it is not kosher, if you are having hors d'oeuvres before the ceremony, they may be uncomfortable with non-kosher foods like shrimp.

### Ketubah: The Jewish Wedding Contract

The *ketubah* ("wedding contract") is an essential part of the wedding. There are a number of choices here. In the last couple of decades, there has been a revival of the art of illuminating *ketubot*. Contemporary artists will create a unique *ketubah* for you that has a calligraphed text and decorative border design. Such *ketubot* are beautiful reflections of the joy and specialness of the occasion. These are works of art and cost accordingly. After the wedding, the *ketubah* can be framed and hung in the couple's home. Calligraphers may need six months or more to create a *ketubah* for you. Most calligraphers will incorporate into the design a personal element—for example, the official flower of your birth state, something that reflects your occupation or hobbies, a symbol of the place you met, and so on.

If you don't want an individualized *ketubah*, you have two choices. A number of these calligraphers have created limited editions of one of their *ketubot* as lithographs. These cost substantially less than an original *ketubah*. There are blank spaces left for the date of the wedding and the couple's names. Jewish bookstores carry a wide selection of these *ketubot*. For an additional fee, some calligraphers will fill out the specific information for your wedding. In this way all the writing on the *ketubah* is in the same calligraphed hand. (Additional time is required to send it to the calligrapher.) These too can be framed and hung after the wedding.

Finally, there are inexpensively mass-produced *ketubot* that the rabbi can provide upon request. The various denominations publish a number of these as well as egalitarian versions (see below). They present the text with a simple design.

All three choices of *ketubot* are equally valid according to Jewish law; it is an aesthetic and financial decision.

*The text*　Another factor in deciding on a *ketubah* is the text. There is a fairly standard traditional text, in Aramaic, which was the language that Jews spoke in talmudic times. The traditional text has been found unsatisfactory by some on two grounds. The first is that it is not egalitarian. The traditional *ketubah* is a document that sets out what the groom is obligated to do for the bride. Some have even characterized it as the acquiring of the bride by the groom. It is certainly one-sided. Clearly the groom is the actor and the bride is the acted upon. Some claim the *ketubah* was in fact a step forward in that it provided rights and financial support for the woman. Yet it remains a document without mutuality. The other criticism is that it is only a legal document. It never expresses the romantic commitment of the couple to each other. (Often rabbis using the traditional text will not read an English translation but rather a rendering that captures the "spirit" of the *ketubah*.) Therefore in the last couple of years new texts have been written that are both egalitarian and romantic. While affirming the legal nature of the wedding, these *ketubot* express both a romantic and a legal commitment of the couple to each other. For the most part these new texts are written in Hebrew rather than Aramaic. No single new text has become the standard yet. Many calligraphers have at least one egalitarian text that they can show you. Similarly, they will often do two versions of the same lithograph, one traditional and one egalitarian. If you are trying to choose in a bookstore and can't read the original, ask the people who work there for help. Remember the English is not always a translation. If you are thinking of using a new text, you should make sure your rabbi feels comfortable with it.

## The Marriage License

To be legally married in the United States and Canada you need to register your marriage with your state or province. Contact the appropriate office in city hall. States have different regulations, so call ahead. The license is valid for a certain period, so you can pick it up more than a few days before. Make sure the rabbi is registered as an officiant in that state, though it is possible for an out-of-state rabbi to arrange "visiting privileges."

## The Pre-ceremony Details

*Rings*   These days the custom in traditional circles is to use a gold band for the wedding ring. The giving of the ring is part of the legal proceedings of the ceremony. Traditionally, a marriage is consummated in three ways: through a contract *(ketubah)*, through the giving of something of value to the bride (a ring), and through sexual intercourse. (As will be explained, all three elements are part of the wedding ceremony.) There is concern that the value of the object can be misleading if it is a precious stone, for example he says it is a diamond but it is really zirconium or glass. Since a wedding is a legal transaction, for one party to be misleading might jeopardize the marriage's legality. Therefore a plain gold band or one with letters engraved on it is traditionally used, since its value is clearer. Despite this tradition, we have elaborate wedding rings from the late Middle Ages. In some communities these were communal rings, used by successive couples of the community for their weddings.

In a traditional wedding, the groom gives the bride a ring. As with the traditional *ketubah,* the groom is the actor and the bride the recipient. Most couples today have a double ring ceremony where both the bride and groom give each other rings. However, most Orthodox rabbis will not officiate at a double ring ceremony out of concern that the fulfillment of the legal requirement of the giving of the ring might be compromised by an exchange of rings.

*The* huppah   The *huppah,* "wedding canopy," is usually a fabric suspended at its four corners from poles. The rabbi (or the wedding site or your florist) can provide you with a *huppah*. Some people or their guests make their own *huppah* or commission one to be made.

The *huppah* symbolizes the home that the couple will create together as an essential part of their married life. For some, it evokes the tent of Abraham and Sarah, which had doors on every side to offer hospitality to travelers. The *huppah* as roof symbolizes the home, and yet it is open on all four sides to welcome family and friends, who support and help to provide a foundation for a marriage. A home should then be like the *huppah* and the moment of marriage—a moment when the couple are joined intimately together and the various strands of their lives are gathered to mark and celebrate this occasion with them.

The other things you need for the ceremony are fairly simple to obtain. Sometimes the caterer or catering hall will provide them. They include wine, the wine cup(s), and the glass to break. Traditionally, kosher wine is used. The wine cup can be any glass, yet many people use a special cup, whether a new *kiddush* cup or a family heirloom.

*When*    According to Jewish law, there are no limits to the time of day when a wedding can take place. However, there are limits to the specific dates upon which weddings can occur. Traditionally, weddings are not held (1) on Shabbat or on festivals—Rosh ha-Shanah, Yom Kippur, first day(s) of Sukkot, Shemini Atzeret/Simhat Torah, first and last day(s) of Passover, or Shavuot; (2) during periods of mourning, such as the Omer period between Passover and Shavuot, the Three Weeks (between the Seventeenth of Tammuz and Tisha be-Av, which falls during the summer), or any public fast day; or (3) during *hol ha-moed*, the intermediate days of Passover and Sukkot. The tradition is not to mix two kinds of rejoicing, for example, the holiday and a wedding, or to interrupt somber periods with rejoicing.

Where your rabbi or synagogue falls on the liberal/traditional spectrum will affect how many of these days will be considered "out of bounds" for marriages. Recently, the Conservative movement has accepted as a valid opinion a liberal policy concerning the two long mourning periods of the Jewish calendar.

*The place*   A wedding can take place anywhere. Many Jewish weddings take place in synagogues. In some cities there are *simha* (literally, "rejoicing") halls that specialize in weddings. Some couples look for a beautiful or unusual place for their wedding. There is an old tradition for weddings to take place outdoors under the heavens. If you choose a space not regularly used for weddings, try to anticipate all your needs. Is the space accessible to all your guests? Is it air-conditioned? Is there a little table to hold the wine, etc., for the ceremony? Is there a place to get dressed? To leave your things? A table and a place to sign the marriage documents? And so on. If you are going to be outdoors, you need to take Mother Nature into account. What if it rains? Is there any shade if it is boiling hot? Nearest bathrooms and phones? Will there be seating for some or all? (There are agencies that rent everything from chairs to large party tents.)

Three helpful hints for outdoor weddings: (1) Make sure the ceremony isn't any longer than necessary and that it starts promptly after your guests sit down. I've watched guests wilt while waiting twenty minutes for the wedding party to line up. (2) Have the wine bottle open but don't pour the wine ahead of time, so that you are not unduly visited by bees. (3) If you are going to be outdoors, make sure the site doesn't have problems that weren't apparent when you first visited, such as being under the flight path to an airport or next to a Little League baseball field used only on weekends.

*Photography*   These days you have a choice of commissioning photos or video, and many people choose both. Photographers usually have a variety of packages that you can purchase. Typically, they will take many photos from which you choose a certain number for your album(s). You should tell the photographer what kinds of pictures you want, that is, a photo of everyone at each table, informal shots, lots of dancing pictures, many pictures of relatives (or not!), and so forth. Photographers constantly balance getting all the important shots and not being overly intrusive. Since their job is getting the pictures, they often tend to be too intrusive, assuming people will be more angry at them later for not getting that picture than for being a little pushy at the wedding. Rabbis often have rules about photography during the ceremony.

Some will not allow it or will not allow flash photography. My own feelings have to do more with the distracting nature of the photographer rather than the sacredness of the occasion. A photographer who keeps moving about during the ceremony distracts the guests from the rightful center of their attention: the couple. In any case, make sure to convey the rabbi's feelings or rules to the photographer. Most rabbis have no rules for photography either before or after the ceremony (including the processional and the recessional). Finally, as we will see below, there is an old custom for the bride and groom not to see each other before the wedding. Photographers will often want to take pictures of the couple and of the immediate family and wedding party before the ceremony. If you don't want to see each other, the other time to take such pictures is after the ceremony, before the bride and groom have gone into the reception. Since the pictures could take a while, you might want to have your guests start the meal without you, serve hors d'oeuvres, or ask the band to start playing dance music.

*Wedding booklets, bentschers, and* **kippot**    Some couples prepare a booklet for their wedding that describes the various parts of the ceremony with short explanations of their meanings. These booklets are also in the nature of a program for the day. They are mostly done to help those unfamiliar with the Jewish wedding ritual to feel included. They also serve as mementos of the day for the guests. Your rabbi can help you prepare the material and may have samples from other weddings. The booklets are usually simply done, often using a computer and photocopy machine.

Some couples give out a bentscher, which is a booklet that includes the Grace after Meals and the special additions for a wedding feast. These can be obtained at Jewish bookstores and can be imprinted with the couple's name, wedding date, etc.

Similarly, some couples have *kippot,* "skullcaps," imprinted with their names to provide both head coverings for the ceremony and mementos of the occasion. It is traditional for men to cover their heads during Jewish services, including a wedding ceremony. (Some women prefer to cover their heads as well.) Whether imprinted or not, if you want men to cover their heads during the ceremony you must make sure *kippot* are available for those who don't bring their own. If the wedding is taking place at a synagogue, check to see whether the synagogue provides *kippot* or you need to. Plain black or white *kippot* can be obtained inexpensively at a Jewish bookstore, which will also carry additional more expensive *kippah* choices.

*Dress*    It is customary for the bride to wear white at a wedding. Actually, there is a tradition for the groom to wear white as well, that is, to wear a *kitel,* a white robe, over his clothes. The *kitel,* like the color white, symbolizes purity. It is traditionally worn on Yom Kippur in the synagogue. (It is also similar to what a corpse is dressed in.) Wearing a *kitel* is not common outside of traditional circles. Usually it is put on after the groom walks down the aisle to the *huppah.* Traditionally, the bride wears a veil.

*Preparing for the day*    The time just before the wedding is focused on the transition from not being married to being married. Today, as many couples are living together before marriage, this distinction may be more important than ever. Traditionally, this distinction was created by the bride and groom's not seeing each other for up to a week before the wedding. I encourage couples who are living together not to spend the night before the wedding together. Partially, this is to prevent the natural anxiety of the moment from leading to a huge fight, but the basic idea is to create a symbolic separation between the unmarried state and marriage. It is your last night "alone." It can be used by you for reflection on the meaning of your marriage.

*The* mikvah    It is also traditional for a bride to immerse herself in the *mikvah,* the ritual bath, before the wedding. This is connected to the laws of female purity (see pp. 365–66) that begin with marriage. While most women no longer observe these traditional laws, many brides go to the *mikvah* before their wedding, sometimes accompanied by close friends (or by a woman rabbi). The symbolism of cleansing and rebirth by immersion in the waters of the *mikvah* fits well with the notion that marriage represents a new stage in life. Some grooms go to the *mikvah* for the same reason.

This notion that marriage is a new stage in life is also reflected in the traditional custom of the bride and groom fasting on their wedding day. There is a tradition for them to recite the confessional (as on Yom Kippur) as a way to express a desire to enter their marriage "sinless." (Hence also the custom of wearing white at a wedding.) All these practices reflect a desire to start afresh and take on added meaning for those who have been previously involved sexually with other people. It does not pretend the past has not happened, rather it expresses a notion that this relationship of love leading to marriage is different from all that preceded it. This, indeed, is a new stage both for each of the individuals and for the couple.

The other tradition before the wedding is the *aufruf*. This takes place on the Shabbat before the wedding (or the Shabbat before that). Traditionally, the groom is "called up" (the Yiddish meaning of *aufruf*) to the Torah for an *aliyah*. Some will chant the *haftarah*. In egalitarian communities both the bride and the groom are called up for an *aliyah*. The *aufruf* is a way to share with the community your upcoming *simha,* particularly with those people who are not invited to the wedding.

Finally, the long-awaited day of the wedding arrives. Before the ceremony begins there are a number of important preliminaries.

*The signings*　Both the *ketubah* and the marriage license need to be witnessed to make this marriage legal from a Jewish and secular perspective respectively. If the *ketubah* has not been filled out beforehand, the rabbi fills it out now with the Hebrew and secular date, the place, and the bride's and groom's Hebrew names. Your Hebrew name is "So-and-so, the son (or daughter) of Such-and-such." Traditionally the "Such-and-such" would be your father's name. Egalitarian Jews use both the father's and the mother's names—for example, David ben ("son of ") Abraham v' ("and") Ruth, or Sarah bat ("daughter of ") Moshe v' Naomi. Make sure you know what your Hebrew name is (and the Hebrew names of your parents) before your wedding day. After this information is written into the *ketubah,* it is witnessed by two witnesses. It is an honor to be a witness at a wedding. The *ketubah* witnesses must be Jewish and not related to the couple even by marriage.

(The witnesses cannot be related to each other either.) While egalitarian Jews will use both men and women as witnesses, traditionally only men could serve as witnesses in Judaism. (Some compromise by having four witnesses, two female and two male, assuming that from a traditional point of view the two male witnesses make it legally valid.) The witnesses sign their names in Hebrew. Therefore, they too should know their Hebrew names and at least be able to copy their names in Hebrew if written out by someone else. Traditionally, only the witnesses sign the *ketubah*. Today, since *ketubot* are often framed and hung, many *ketubot* have places for the couple and the rabbi to sign.

The marriage license needs to be filled out and witnessed. These witnesses can be any adults. The state does not care as long as they are alive. (Actually you might want to check if you plan to use witnesses who are not citizens.) You can choose the same two people to sign both the *ketubah* and the marriage license or involve and honor more people by choosing different ones.

These signings can be done privately with just the couple, the witnesses, and the rabbi (and the photographer), or more publicly. It depends in part on what you want to be happening before the ceremony actually starts.

*The* tena'im *and the* bedeken    Long ago, marriage was a two-stage process consisting of betrothal and wedding. Like our modern engagements, the betrothal often took place up to a year before the wedding date. Beginning in the Middle Ages, the betrothal and the wedding ceremony happened together. The first half of our wedding ceremony is actually the betrothal. Traditionally, a legal document of betrothal (called *tena'im*, or "conditions") was drawn up and witnessed right before the *ketubah* is witnessed. Today this is done only in very traditional communities.

Usually this witnessing is followed by the custom of the two mothers taking a plate wrapped in a napkin and smashing it. The meaning of the custom is unclear, though it clearly resonates with the breaking of the glass at the end of the wedding ceremony (see below).

There is a traditional custom called the *bedeken,* "the veiling," during which the groom, accompanied by friends, is brought before the bride and veils her. By tradition this custom originated after Jacob was tricked into marrying the wrong sister. Some have used this moment as a prelude to the wedding. Rabbi Neal Borovitz encourages each set of parents to bless their child with the priestly blessing or with words of their own. This acknowledges the change in status as the child enacts the words of Genesis—of leaving parents and cleaving to a spouse. I encourage the couple to hold hands and face each other. I acknowledge that these are the last moments before they become married. I ask them to remember when they first met, when they first knew they loved each other; and ask them to remember how they feel at this moment so they can recall those feelings in the years to come.

The moment of the *bedeken* is often the first time the bride and groom see each other on the wedding day. At traditional weddings, the bride and groom are in separate rooms. In the groom's room, the *tena'im* and the *ketubah* are signed. There is also a tradition for the groom to try to speak—only to be interrupted with singing. The *bedeken* is immediately followed by the ceremony.

## The Ceremony

*The processional*   The ceremony is ready to begin. Either the *huppah* holders and the rabbi walk down first in the processional or they set up the *huppah* and the rabbi stands under it and only then does the processional begin. There are no Jewish traditions of who, how many, or in what order people should march in the processional. It is really the couple's decision. The *huppah* holders and the wedding party are opportunities to honor people by having them participate in your wedding. It is customary for the bride to walk down last. The Jewish custom is for the groom's parents to accompany him and the bride's parents to accompany her. Sometimes the bride stops halfway and her parents continue. She either then walks alone or the groom goes back to escort her to the *huppah*. It is an aesthetic decision whether members of the wedding party stand around the *huppah* or only the parents or only the rabbi and the couple (and the *huppah* holders).

Even if the *huppah* is freestanding, some people still have symbolic *huppah* holders. If the *huppah* is being held, you might want to check whether the poles reach the ground or need to be held aloft. While a *huppah* is not heavy, not everyone can hold a pole that is not resting on the ground for the twenty to thirty minutes that a ceremony can take.

*The ritual*    The wedding ceremony begins with words of welcome that are chanted or read. Besides welcome, these words also invoke God's blessing on the groom and bride. The Jewish wedding ceremony is framed by blessings recited over wine, giving it a symmetrical structure. It also reflects that the two stages of marriage have been combined into one in ceremonies performed today (and for many centuries). Since the Middle Ages, betrothal *(kiddushin)* and marriage *(nisuin)* are both done as part of the wedding ceremony.

Wine is an ancient symbol of rejoicing used in many Jewish rituals. The blessings are recited over the wine, which is then sipped by the groom and the bride. (Some have the custom for the mother of the bride to lift the bride's veil so the bride can drink and then lower it again.) Whenever wine is traditionally used, grape juice can be substituted. Sometimes parents share the first cup as well.

The next part of the wedding is the ring ceremony. Most couples today prefer a double ring ceremony. The giving of the ring is part of the legal component of the wedding. The groom recites the ancient formula *harei at mekudeshet li be-taba'at zo ke-dat mosheh ve-yisrael,* "By this ring are you consecrated to me according to the laws of Moses and Israel." Then he places the ring on the bride's finger. If it is a double ring ceremony, the bride then says, *harei attah mekudash li be-taba'at zo ke-dat mosheh ve-yisrael* (the same phrase as the groom, just changed for gender). Traditionally, the ring is placed on the right index finger. This is done because it used to be the ring finger or because it is easier for the witnesses to see the ring better. It can later be moved to the ring finger. Some people just place it on the ring finger right off.

Next, the *ketubah* is read. Traditionally, the complete text is read in its original Aramaic. Many rabbis will read part of it and read an English rendering (rarely is a translation read). Those using an egalitarian version will usually read it in Hebrew and in its translation. The giving of the wedding contract is another method for making the marriage legal. In a traditional wedding, the *ketubah* is given to the bride to keep after it is read. In an egalitarian ceremony, the *ketubah* is given to the couple. Some rabbis will speak here, while others speak after the *sheva berakhot* (see below).

The final part of the wedding ceremony begins with the *sheva berakhot,* "the seven blessings," recited over a cup of wine. (Some use a second cup of wine; others use the first, though they may refill it.) These are blessings recited for the groom and bride. At some weddings, each of the blessings is given to a different person to recite. More commonly, the rabbi recites them all. The groom and bride then sip the wine.

The wedding ceremony concludes with the breaking of the glass. This ancient custom has been explained in a number of ways, most commonly as a way of acknowledging the imperfection of the world. All joy contains a realization of the world's suffering and sadness. The breaking of the glass at this moment of great joy is then a call to work toward the perfection of the world, as just described in the final blessing of the *sheva berakhot.*

The glass is wrapped in a napkin to prevent shards from getting into a carpet and to make cleanup easier. Most commonly, the groom breaks the glass by stamping on it with his foot. A few couples choose to break separate glasses or break one glass together.

The breaking of the glass also marks the end of the wedding ritual, and the signal to wish *mazal tov,* "congratulations," to bride and groom by the witnesses to the event, family, and friends.

*The recessional and time alone*    If you have musicians they will now play *simha,* "joyous" music, for the recessional. The recessional is in reverse order, led by the bride and groom. Traditionally, the bride and groom spend some time alone in a room. This was the third part of the legal enactment of the marriage, since in traditional society this would be the first time the couple would be alone, unchaperoned, and thus is symbolic of their now-permitted sexual intimacy.

For couples who are fasting on their wedding day, or were too nervous to eat, it is also an opportunity to get something to eat before the reception, when you are often too busy and distracted to eat. Ask the caterer to leave some food in the room for you.

I encourage couples to take this time in *yihud* ("privacy") not for its traditional symbolism, which is no longer relevant for most couples, but for the opportunity it provides for the couple to spend a few moments alone with each other celebrating their newly married status before the reception. While the reception is a wonderful part of the event, the bride and groom are very public figures and are in demand by all the guests. *Yihud* then is an opportunity for some private time.

## The Reception and Festive Meal

It is a *mitzvah,* a commandment, to rejoice with the bride and groom. The reception and meal then are important parts of the wedding. The meal is in the category of a *seudat mitzvah,* "a sacred meal," a meal in celebration of the fulfillment of a commandment. Singing and dancing with the couple is an old tradition. Telling stories and making up songs about the couple and their families can all be part of the traditional merrymaking.

While the rejoicing at the wedding is the main religious requirement, the meal traditionally has its customary rituals. The meal begins with a *motzi,* the blessing said over bread (see "Shabbat," pp. 103–34). Usually there is a large braided bread known as a *simha hallah* ("hallah of rejoicing"). Because of its use on Shabbat, *hallah* has a Jewish "flavor." However, any bread can be used and two *hallot* are not required, that custom being reserved for Shabbat. Similarly, there is no reason to begin the meal with a blessing over wine (*kiddush* is related to the sanctification of Shabbat and festivals). Traditional Jews will wash their hands before the *motzi.* There is no standard wedding food.

At the end, the recital of *birkat ha-mazon,* the Grace after Meals, is traditional (see p. 80). The text can be found in bentschers (see above). There is a special version of *birkat ha-mazon* for a wedding meal. The opening responsive lines are changed for the occasion. At the end of *birkat ha-mazon,* the *sheva berakhot* are recited again over a cup of wine. The order is changed so that the first blessing over wine is recited last. Since there is a general custom to recite *birkat ha-mazon* over a glass of wine at special occasions, some use two cups of wine, one for *birkat ha-mazon* and the other for the *sheva berakhot.* At the conclusion, some of the wine from each of these two cups is mixed into a third cup, which is then given to the bride and groom to share.

This brings the meal and reception to a close. At nontraditional weddings, the blessings are usually omitted and guests leave as they're ready following dessert.

## Intermarriage

The widespread phenomenon of intermarriage is the focal point of concerns for the future of Judaism and the Jewish people. This is an issue for all Jews living in the modern world, but it is in America that this has become the prime issue on the communal agenda. There is much debate about what should be done. Should there be more energy devoted to outreach or should that energy be used to strengthen the existing core of the Jewish community? Is this the end of the Jewish people? Should the Jewish people be placed on the endangered species list?

I would like to suggest that the phenomenon of intermarriage is more complex than the doomsayers suggest. It is clearly a by-product of an extraordinary level of social acceptance of Jews. Since coming to America, Jews have experienced an unimagined freedom. They could become full participants in American society. A committed Jew was chosen as the vice-presidential candidate of the Democratic Party in 2000. Jews also discovered that they could observe Judaism and still be part of America. It was not an either/or choice. Again, Senator Joseph Lieberman was striking proof of this. Intermarriage is part of the package that comes with all this freedom. It is in fact the best proof of Jews' being accepted in America. Non-Jews actually want to marry us!

Yet intermarriage has not always been the same phenomenon since Jews arrived on these shining shores. In the first half of the twentieth century, a goodly number of the Jews intermarrying were making a conscious decision to assimilate or perhaps even to reject Judaism. In the second half of the century, many intermarrying Jews were uninterested in Judaism. Judaism was not being rejected; it was simply relatively irrelevant in the life of these people. This is still true for a number of Jews intermarrying in the last decade or so. Yet there are also Jews who are intermarrying today and who neither reject nor are indifferent to their Judaism. Their intermarriage reflects the "simple" fact that they met a non-Jewish person whom they came to love. Being Jewish is still an important part of their identity. They may plan to instill in their children a Jewish identity. Often their spouse is not an active believer in another religion. However, they both feel a conversion to Judaism would be inauthentic unless the non-Jew could do it sincerely.

It is no longer so black and white. Intermarriage is not so clearly an indicator of the failure of Judaism in America. The Jewish community will have more and more people sitting in our synagogues with non-Jewish relatives or non-Jewish spouses, some joined by these non-Jews themselves.

All this is not to say that intermarriage and a Jewish-Jewish marriage are of equal validity from the standpoint of the Jewish people. Clearly, having a parent who is not Jewish has a potentially significant impact on the Jewishness of the home and the strength of the Jewish identity that is conveyed to children. Yet conveying a Jewish identity in the land of the free is an often unsuccessful task, even with two fully committed Jewish partners. Still, intermarriage can make that task even more difficult.

Being Jewish in America has taken on new varieties of possibilities. We need to welcome those possibilities, in part because we have no choice. The price of freedom in America is also the freedom not to be Jewish anymore. We Jews are firm supporters of the notion that in America all people are equal. We live in two civilizations, the American and the Jewish, and validate both as worthy of respect and support. It is a hard distinction to uphold the freedom and equality of America and at the same time draw the line at marriage, saying here we are not all equal.

Yet we, the Jewish people, have a right to survive. As Jews, we need to find ways to affirm that right even as we welcome into our community Jews and their non-Jewish partners. We welcome them as an acknowledgment that they and their partners are part of the complex Jewish experience in America. This is no easy challenge.

In trying to balance these competing notions, each of us will draw those lines in different places. This is most evident within the rabbinic community. There are those rabbis (especially Orthodox and Conservative rabbis) who will not officiate at an intermarriage. A generalization of their position is that as rabbis, they are religious officiants at Jewish weddings. For them, a Jewish wedding marks a marriage between two Jews. An intermarriage does not meet that criterion. Other rabbis (some but not all Reform and Reconstructionist rabbis) will officiate at intermarriages. These rabbis have varying criteria for when they will officiate at such a marriage. Many will not co-officiate with a clergyperson of another faith. Some will want a commitment that the children of the marriage will be raised as Jews and be given a Jewish education. A generalization of their position is related to two notions. First, the purpose of a marriage is the creation of a Jewish home. Such a home can be created even if one parent is not Jewish. Second, rabbis serve Jews. A Jew is requesting a rabbi's assistance at a critical life-cycle event. To refuse could potentially drive this Jew away from the community.

These are difficult questions for every rabbi. No rabbi anymore believes that if enough rabbis say no to intermarriages they will cease. Is it better to accommodate the intermarrying couple to keep them within the Jewish community or are these families unlikely to produce committed Jews in the long run? These are hotly debated questions. The truth of course is that each family is different. There are intermarried families that are much more committed to Judaism than families with two Jewish partners. There are many intermarried families with attenuated connections to the Jewish community. Whatever their policy, many rabbis are sensitive to the pain that these questions raise for Jews who are marrying non-Jews. It is an increasingly difficult question as intermarriage remains so prevalent in the Jewish community.

Beyond the question of the marriage itself, the Jewish community wrestles with how to welcome such Jewish families into the community. There is again a wide spectrum of responses. Is an intermarriage announced under the *mazal tov* column in the synagogue bulletin, like all other congregants' marriages? Can the Jewish partner receive an *aliyah* marking his or her wedding, as they would if they were marrying someone Jewish? These and similar questions will be points of debate and evoke diverse answers within the Jewish community in the years to come.

For those who seem sure of the answers and how to ensure the survival of the Jewish community, I would urge a modest humility. I think no one knows *the* answer. I think all we can do as a community is live vibrant Jewish lives infused with meaning and awareness. If we do that, then Jews will want to be Jewish and non-Jews will want to become Jews. For the flip side of assimilation and intermarriage in open-society America is that people are also converting to Judaism.

The story of Ruth is the paradigmatic story of conversion in the Jewish tradition. Ruth, having married a Jew, is widowed. Her mother-in-law Naomi wants to move back from Moab to Israel. Ruth insists on accompanying her, saying, "For wherever you go, I will go, wherever you lodge, I will lodge; your people shall be my people; and your God my God" (Ruth 1:16). We do not know what brought Ruth to that decision. One could surmise that there was something about her mother-in-law and her Jewish life that Ruth found important enough to leave all she knew behind. She did not do this for the sake of marriage (her Jewish husband was dead). She did it for herself. We, the Jewish community, need to be Jewish for our own sake and have faith that others will find our Judaism worth emulating.

The larger lesson we learn from the Book of Ruth is that you just never know. The book ends with the genealogy of Ruth leading to the birth of David, the future king of Israel and the ancestor of the future messiah. David, one of the most important figures in Jewish history, comes not from some pure-blood Jewish genealogy. Rather his ancestry comes through incest (see Genesis 19 for the birth of Moab) and non-Jews. We should be modest in our predictions of who shall be committed to Judaism and who not a hundred years from now. In our own lives, we have seen the rebirth of the Jewish community of Russia after it was cut off from Judaism for decades. You just never know. We can only plant the seeds and wait for them to bear fruit.

# NUMBERS/BE-MIDBAR:
# LIVING IN THE DESERT

The Book of Be-midbar (Numbers) is the book that describes the time between the Revelation at Sinai and the arrival at the Promised Land. It tells of thirty-eight of the forty years wandering in the desert. There are no great moments in Be-midbar: no Exodus, no Sinai, just the complaints of daily life.

For some of us, then, Be-midbar is that whole stretch of life between major life-cycle events. Or, perhaps, it is those years between youth and old age, the years when there is little external reminder of time's passage. It is those years when our bodies become familiar, the changes of adolescence a distant memory. In the middle of this time, our trusty companion does begin to give us signs of aging. Gray hair and failing eyesight are the most common and least physically problematic. Be-midbar symbolizes the whole middle of our lives, which is much longer than what we commonly refer to as middle age. We are no longer just past youth. All of the firsts of our lives are past us—first love, first job, first car. It is a time of building—our careers, our relationships, and most of all who we are and hope to be.

However, like the desert, it may lack any milestone moments that serve as directional markers. There certainly are no signs telling us how many more miles to the Promised Land. At times, we weary of the responsibility of the journey and want to turn back to live in our past. Then too the desert is filled with mirages. Many spend their time chasing will-o'-the-wisps and too late awaken with mouths filled not with the bounteous fruit of the Promised Land but instead with sand. Others discover that the castles they had spent so much time building have no real substance and shimmer in the blazing sun only to disappear. Some of the complaints are real; there are dangers in the desert beyond those we imagine. Disappointments, heartaches, and failures, not just manna, rain down from heaven in this desert and lie in wait for even the most careful traveler.

While each of us has our own unique journey to make, there are some common challenges and goals. The challenges include illness, divorce, and overall disappointments. To meet those challenges, we will need to build a caring community that can accompany us on our journey. Most of all, our task is to find happiness and peace in order to pass successfully through this desert of discontent and distractions.

## Illness

At a certain point in life, our body begins to send us reminder messages that we will not live forever. Slowly at first, we notice that things don't work as well as they once did. We do not seem to have the same energy as twenty years ago. At some point, we are shocked to discover we are the oldest person in the room or in the office, for we still think of ourselves as young. Or the biological clock's ticking sounds louder and louder. Or we may realize that most professional athletes have long since retired by the time they reach our age. More than reminders of our ultimate mortality, aging can bring an increased onset of illness.

Whether life-threatening or just painful, a serious illness can shake our sense of well-being. Our world seems to have spun out of our control. We feel as if we have entered another land. In the war between our doctors and our illness, our only role is to present our body for use as a battlefield. If we are in the hospital, we find ourselves in unfamiliar surroundings, most often not wearing our normal clothes. We feel completely isolated from our regular world. People who are not ill seem to be totally different from us. We feel they have no real understanding of our situation. Despite our speaking the same language, it is as though there is an invisible wall that separates us from them. We lie in our sickbeds worried about our future, wondering what we did to make this happen, or why we deserve this. Feeling betrayed by our bodies, abandoned by our assumption of normality, feeling distant from family and friends and God, we feel a profound sense of aloneness. That is why visiting the sick is such an important act of *gemilut hesed,* "loving-kindness."

**Bikkur holim—***visiting the sick*   There are two purposes for visiting the sick. The first is to combat all these feelings of isolation. A visit from another person reconnects those who are sick to the network of love and caring that surrounds them. They are reminded that they are not alone. Often people ask me what they should say when visiting someone in the hospital. There is, of course, no right answer to this question. There are obvious things to avoid such as stories about other people who died from the same disease. Neither is it helpful to tell the patient about other people who are even "sicker." This does not cheer people up; it only makes them feel that their own experience is being belittled. For them, their pain is the only pain that is real, their prognosis the only important one. Hearing about other people does nothing to lessen the actual experience of pain or change their prognosis. Our role is not to "jolly" people up who are in hospital beds, or in any way to minimize their experience.

Once a patient complained to me about how he was failing in his attempt to meditate to help him during his illness. Someone had suggested that he imagine himself on a beach of a Pacific island. The patient, who had been meditating for years, felt like a miserable failure because he could not successfully meditate himself to the beach. I looked at him puzzled and said, "But you're not on a beach, you're in a hospital bed with a serious illness!" We cannot deny reality. Both patient and visitor need to be present to that reality. For the visitor, not being challenged by pain and the anxiety of an iffy prognosis, that is much easier to do. As a visitor what we can do is offer our caring presence, to listen empathetically to their experience, to offer to help if we can.

Sometimes there are ways to offer concrete help, perhaps by bringing a book or by helping the family manage without the patient. Knowing the children are being chauffeured around helps relieve the concern of the patient for his or her children and for the burden that has fallen on his or her partner. Yet most of all it is the visit itself and the words "I can only imagine how hard this is for you" that is the essence of *bikkur holim,* "visiting the sick."

The other component is prayer. Traditionally this was the central purpose of the visit: to pray to God for the recovery of the sick person. The notion that God can answer such a prayer and heal an individual has been rejected by many Jews in the modern world. Yet recently the notion that prayer can be effective in healing has gained new adherents. Some studies have been done that support the idea that patients who have people praying for them do better than patients without a supporting network of prayer. Clearly, it is difficult to make a claim that prayer alone can cure disease. Nor does this mean that someone who in the end succumbs to cancer had an insufficient number of people praying on her or his behalf. This insight is found in the following Talmudic teaching:

> R. Huna said: When a person visits the sick, the sick person's illness is diminished by one-sixtieth. At this, R. Huna was challenged: If so, let sixty people visit the sick person, and she immediately will be able to go down with them to the marketplace. R. Huna replied: [It would work] only if each of the sixty loved her as a person loves themselves. In any event, they will afford her some relief. [Midrash, *Leviticus Rabbah* 34:1]

This teaching tells us that visiting helps a little bit (one sixtieth) and the more empathetic the visitor is (love the sick person as you love yourself) the more beneficial the visit will be to the sick person. However, this process is not a mathematical formula. Rather, it suggests that even though we do not know how the universe works, things we do have an impact on the cosmos. These are not laws of physics. How this happens and how much of an impact are not questions that can be answered. Yet there is emerging evidence that prayer and good wishes have a beneficial effect on those who are ill.

This resurgence of a connection between healing and religion is reflected in a number of new phenomena in the Jewish community such as healing services, a greater emphasis in regular services on the *mi-sheberakh,* the traditional prayer for healing, the widespread use of songwriter Debbie Friedman's *mi-sheberakh* composition, and a growing number of organized Psalm-reciting groups in traditional communities.

All this reflects a desire to give space within Judaism to the experience of those who are ill. At its best, "visiting the sick," or more simply acknowledging their situation, allows them to feel connected rather than isolated, cared for rather than alone, and gives them some measure of hope in the midst of their pain and suffering.

*A theology of illness*    What should the sick person do in the face of illness? While much more difficult to achieve than in normal circumstances, it is useful to try to be clear about the situation. As discussed in the section on Yom Kippur, it is important to hold on to the notion that this is not your fault. Cancer is not a punishment sent by God because you have been hurtful to people in your life. Nor is the more contemporary version of this belief helpful either. That version says it is because of smoking, what you eat, etc., that you have cancer. Either of these versions of "it is all your fault" can only be devastating to a person who is ill. Since the willingness to fight against the illness can be a factor in healing, it is critical for the patient not to assign blame. This is not to say that we have no responsibility for our health. Smoking cigarettes, for instance, is deleterious to our health and a matter of choice. A person with a diet heavy in fat should feel some responsibility for her heart attack. Yet in most situations, the connection between our behavior and illness may be unknown or only one of many factors.

The flip-side error of blaming yourself is to have too much faith in yourself. If you only fight it hard enough or get the right doctor or think the right thoughts, you can defeat the cancer. This is a contemporary version of a belief in miracles. Somehow this will not happen to me. Since "this" is death, the truth is it will happen to everyone. The problem, of course, is that miracles rarely happen. At some point people with this belief in a miracle run out of steam when it does not happen. They then feel they are unworthy and basically that it is all their fault.

It is extraordinarily difficult to fight the disease with all your strength and yet remain realistic about your situation. This is to acknowledge what could be and yet be determined to make the best of it by fighting for your life as long as you can. The Torah values life above all else. Thus each moment of life is to be cherished as a precious gift.

The religious question ultimately is not why is this happening to me, but rather how will I respond to what is happening to me? Will I be able to continue to affirm those things that I value? Will I respond to others appropriately rather than with misplaced anger at my fate? Will I appreciate the caring of my family and friends? Will I appreciate the gifts of the skills of the hospital staff and the blessings of the advancements of modern medicine?

What of God? If we no longer have a theology that says that God has sent the illness to us, then there is no reason to be angry with God for inflicting this on us. God, then, can be your companion through this experience. God's promise is to never leave us abandoned. In the rabbinic metaphor, God suffers whenever we suffer. Illness exists in an unredeemed world. We all suffer and God, the unity underlying the world, suffers with us. If God created the world as an act of *hesed*, "loving-kindness," then every moment of pain is a negation of that creating impulse. Being aware of the Presence of God sitting by the side of our sickbed does not make the pain go away or change the prognosis, but it tells us in a powerful way that even in illness we are not alone.

*Terminal care and living wills*    The advances of modern medicine have challenged Judaism's overarching value of life. Modern medicine's ability to sustain life has raised questions about when life is no longer worth living. When do we cease taking extraordinary measures to keep the body alive when its functioning is limited? Is prolonging a life that is experiencing great pain the correct thing to do? How does Judaism respond to questions concerning the end of life and living wills?

The basic attitude in the tradition is summarized in the *Shulhan Arukh*, the classic code of Jewish law:

> If there is anything which causes a hindrance to the departure of the soul as the presence near the patient's house of a knocking noise such as wood-chopping or if there is salt on the patient's tongue, and

these hinder the soul's departure, then it is permissible to remove them from there because there is no act involved in this at all, but only the removal of an impediment. [*Yoreh Deah,* 339:1]

This approach differentiates between taking active measures to end life, which is forbidden, and not engaging in measures that prolong life, which is permissible. This has been understood by contemporary authorities to mean it is permissible not to take extraordinary measures to keep someone alive. Thus resuscitation is not required if the patient and/or the family have expressed their wishes not to resort to it. The harder questions are related to what to do when someone is already on a form of life support such as a respirator. The respirator may have been attached at first to help with breathing while the patient was recovering. However, now the respirator is keeping the person alive. Can it be disconnected? If the person has stopped eating and is only being sustained nutritionally through intravenous feeding, can that be stopped? Of course, these questions are being asked in cases where there is no hope for the patient's recovery. The basic question, then, is are we prolonging a painful existence for the patient or even only a semblance of life for someone who has lost consciousness, who is beyond help, who is in a coma, or who has no chance of recovery?

Trying to balance the value of life and the quality of that life has raised difficult questions. Since the specifics of a situation are critical, any decisions on how to apply these principles to a particular case should be made in consultation with both your doctor and your rabbi.

To address these situations ahead of time is both legally and emotionally helpful to loved ones. After all, there is nothing abstract about a decision that a child is making about a beloved parent lying in pain. It would be easy to feel guilty no matter what is done. Thus it is important that you discuss with your family how you would want to be treated. Too often, by the time such decisions are necessary the patient is not capable of making them. Expressing your wishes removes some of the burden from loved ones. It can also reduce the potential conflicts among family members who may disagree about treatment. Besides talking about it, you should leave your specific wishes in writing. You may do this in two forms. First, prepare a living will that sets out your wishes in general and your decisions regarding some specific treatments. Second, make out a health care proxy that designates one person who will make decisions on your behalf if you cannot make them. A good idea is to combine the two by choosing a health care proxy with whom you share as much as possible about what your wishes would be in a variety of scenarios. This avoids the problem of the living will not being specific about your particular medical circumstance.

## Divorce

Over him who divorces the wife of his youth, even the altar of God sheds tears. [Talmud, *Gittin* 90b]

Divorce is a recognition of the failure of the hopes and dreams that a couple had brought to their marriage. As such, it is sad moment even if both partners feel it is the right thing to do. The Jewish tradition recognizes that a divorce can come about for a variety of valid reasons. A Jewish divorce is also a mutual action to the extent that no one is declared at fault, as can be true in civil divorce procedures. Traditionally, just as marriage is seen as a religious act, so too is divorce. A marriage in Judaism involves a legal bond and can only be dissolved through Jewish legal procedure. Thus there is a Jewish divorce procedure that involves a *get*, "a bill of divorcement," a document given by the husband to the wife. Traditionally, a civil divorce cannot terminate a Jewish marriage. The *get* procedure focuses on the legal aspect of a Jewish marriage. Its purpose is to dissolve the legal commitment of the couple to each other. It is a counterpart to the traditional text of the *ketubah*, the marriage contract. Both are legal documents rather than giving expression to emotional or spiritual experiences. While the legal nature of the *ketubah* is often given only a minor focus in the wedding ceremony, the *get* is the sole focus of the divorce procedure. This may be due to the central concern here, which is that this marriage be dissolved. The traditional authorities want to prevent any possibility of people remarrying and having children while still being "legally" married to their first spouse.

The upshot is that unlike how the tradition deals with weddings and especially with death and grief, here the ritual is not always useful in helping people deal with the emotional difficulties experienced in divorces. Ultimately, the experience can be little different from visiting your divorce lawyer, except that, being more arcane, it seems even less relevant.

This is not to discourage you from doing it. There is a legal element that is critical to take care of here. Just as you would want a civil divorce, I would urge you to have a Jewish divorce. Also some people find the ritual of the *get* emotionally powerful, despite its legalistic character. For some it provides a final ending to the marriage. For this reason, some rabbis will encourage the husband or wife to talk about what getting the *get* means to them.

The above critique is just to acknowledge that Judaism has failed to develop an appropriate ritual for this life-cycle moment. Recently there have been some attempts to introduce such a ritual; given the frequency of divorce, it should be a high priority on the agenda of the leadership of the various denominations. The Reconstructionist movement has developed an alternative egalitarian *get* procedure. It expresses the sense of loss in the divorce as well as urging the couple to respect their on-going common commitments if there are children involved. It should also be noted that the Reform movement accepts a civil divorce as a Jewish religious divorce.

*The* get *procedure*    The traditional procedure basically consists of the writing of a *get,* which is then handed over by the man to the woman. This is done before a *beit din,* a Jewish "court" consisting of three rabbis. Again, since there was concern that no small mistake be used to challenge the legality of the document, it is written with great care. There are also long-standing traditions of how exactly the writing should be done, with what ink, and so forth. Thus someone trained to do so writes the *get* document by hand. Since in premodern times there were no easy ways to identify people, the names of the couple needed to be exactly correct in the document. For absolute certainty, nicknames are also included in the document.

There is a lengthy ritualized question-and-answer that basically establishes (over and over again) that you are doing this of your own free will and that you are authorizing the writing of the *get* on your behalf. Nearly all of this exchange involves only the husband, since traditionally the husband is the one who must initiate the *get* process. In the midst of this, the scribe writes the text. Then the husband and the wife confirm that they are doing this of their own free will. The two then face each other. The wife removes any rings (so the document will touch her hands directly) and holds her hands together palms up. The husband then drops the *get* into her hands and says: "This be your *get* and with it be you divorced from this time forth so that you may become the wife of any man." The wife then lifts up her hands and walks a short distance (to show she has received the *get*). The *get* is then taken by the rabbis of the *beit din*, who slice it a number of times. (This is to prevent its being used by someone with the same name. Before surnames, it is easy to imagine that often there was more than one person named Joseph married to a person named Sarah.) The divorced couple receives a *petur*, a document stating that their marriage is dissolved and that they are "free" *(petur)* to remarry.

To arrange for a *get*, call a rabbi. Many rabbis will not themselves do a *get* procedure, but they can direct you to those who will. (To ensure there are no problems with the legality of the *get*, only rabbis who are expert in these laws will issue one.) In many Orthodox communities, there are *batei din* ("courts," the plural of *beit din*) who regularly do this procedure. The Conservative movement has a number of rabbis especially trained in the procedure.

When you contact the rabbi who will organize the procedure, he will explain to you what is involved and the cost. The simplest way is for the couple to appear before the *beit din* at an arranged time. However, sometimes the couple does not want to be in the same room with one another during the *get* procedure. (Actually, the wife can wait in a separate room until the last part of the ritual. For some people even this is too painful.) Other times the husband and wife are living at a significant distance from each other. The *beit din* can arrange for its representative to meet with the husband in another location or to have its representative deliver the *get* in another location. Thus it is not necessary that both—or in some cases either—appear in person before the *beit din*. The whole procedure can be done through an authorized agent of the *beit din*. The agent is a local rabbi who in turn will convene another *beit din* to witness and make legally valid the part of the procedure done before the agent. The local rabbi and *beit din* do not have to be experts in Jewish divorce law. They only have to follow the standard procedure for getting the husband's authorization for issuing the *get* or for delivering the written *get* to the wife.

*Some issues*    Based on the verse "and he writes her a bill of divorcement" (Deut. 24:1), the tradition states that the *get* procedure needs to be initiated and authorized by the husband. The wife cannot initiate a *get*. However, she can refuse to receive it. This is why most of the formulaic script of the procedure involves him and not her. This tradition is not only jarring to egalitarian sensibilities, but has created a serious problem in the traditional Jewish community. A husband can refuse to agree to give a *get* to his wife, and there is nothing that can be done about it. She can never remarry and has the status of an *agunah*, "a chained woman," meaning she is still technically married to her husband. What makes matters even worse is that he can legally remarry even without a *get*, because polygamy is allowed, as we know from the biblical stories of the patriarchs. Despite a thousand-year-old ban against polygamy by a noted rabbinic authority, the biblical precedent cannot be ignored. There is no such biblical precedent for a wife to have two husbands.

While this is not a new phenomenon, the rise in divorce rates and modern sensibilities have made this a major issue in the Orthodox Jewish community. The situation has only been exacerbated by cases of husbands using this law to extort money from their wives. There is significant pressure on Orthodox rabbinic authorities to come up with a solution. At this moment, they have resisted all such pressure, though some have taken to using social pressure on the refusing husbands to "persuade" them to relent. One prominent figure in the modern Orthodox community, Rabbi Emmanuel Rackman, has courageously created a *beit din* that stretches the law to create as many loopholes as possible to free women from this limbo status. He has not been joined by anyone else even from within the modern Orthodox wing of the traditional world. The Orthodox authorities maintain that these ancient procedures cannot be changed, much as they might like to change them. This has not been a problem within the Conservative movement, since, in the case of a recalcitrant husband, the *beit din* ultimately will "annul" the marriage. (Some Conservative Jews use what is called the Lieberman clause in, or a letter of intent with, their *ketubah* that empowers the *beit din* to act if necessary in divorces.) Frankly, the injustice of this situation is a stain on the Orthodox community. I am certain that the great authorities of the past would have had the courage to devise a solution, as they did in other areas where the tradition was so completely at divergence with its goal. After all, the point of a *get* is to dissolve a marriage between two people who are not compatible, not keep one of them locked forever in a painful nonrelationship.

*An important note*    This is another area where the denominational divide in Judaism creates problems. Often Orthodox authorities accept as a legitimate *get* only one issued by an Orthodox *beit din*. It is not because the Conservative movement uses different procedures; it is because they are Conservative rabbis and therefore considered by the Orthodox to be nonlegitimate religious authorities. This can especially be a problem in Israel, where issues of personal status are in the hands of the Orthodox Chief Rabbinate.

*My own experience*    We had an Orthodox *get* at my wife's request. It was strange to be before three rabbis whom I had never met to go through this personal procedure. They were from the ultra-Orthodox wing and so it felt particularly like being in a foreign territory. They tried to make me feel comfortable, but there was nothing asked about the relationship and no opportunity to share what I was feeling. It was an entirely legal process. My wife waited in another room. By then our civil divorce had come through and we had both accepted its reality. Unlike some other people's experience, the writing of the document did not take a very long time. One interesting moment of clashing cultures came when I was asked my wife's Hebrew name. I told them. Asked how I knew, I replied that is how she is called up for an *aliyah* to the Torah. Even though *aliyot* for women were foreign to the Orthodox authorities, they accepted that as proof of her Hebrew name.

It was the moment that I was facing my wife and told to drop the *get* into her hands that moved beyond the legal nature of the procedure. We both felt a sadness at the end of our marriage, which seemed finalized at that moment.

The other experience I want to share was how people responded to my divorce. Because I was a congregational rabbi who had been a member of the community even before becoming its rabbi, the divorce was a very public affair. My wife and I sent out a letter announcing it to the congregation to prevent rumors and misinformation. We also did not try to get our friends to choose sides. Nevertheless, people seemed at a loss for how to respond to us.

There is no structure, as there is with death, for the community to be supportive of someone going through a divorce—no tradition of bringing food, making comforting visits, or helping to make a *minyan*. There is not even a general tradition, as there is with those who are in the hospital of *bikkur holim*, visiting the sick. This is because of the paucity of ritual around the divorce and because divorce as a common life-cycle event is a contemporary phenomenon.

In difficult situations, even well-intentioned people do not know what to say. In case of a death, except in very rare situations, saying one is sorry is always appropriate. But a divorce is more complex. Individuals getting divorced may be happy about ending a bad relationship. Or they may be opposed to the divorce that their spouse has demanded unilaterally. I found that a lot of people, not knowing what to say, said nothing to me. The ones who understood said something like: "I do not know what to say but this must be difficult for you. Let me know if there is anything I can do."

A divorce is also often unsettling to other people's marriages. When a couple we thought had a good marriage divorces, it shakes our sense of what we know. Thus part of the response to my divorce had to do with their lives. A number of acquaintances came up to me and told me that they had been divorced. Others who had been friends dropped me as though I had the plague. People in the congregation expressed anger toward me that seemed to have no cause. Were they upset that I was divorced while they were still stuck in unhappy relationships? Had I failed to live up to their ideal notion of a rabbi with a wife and two and a half children? (I actually had three.) I joked with a friend that half the people who knew my wife and me were surprised by the divorce. The other half said they were not surprised and half of those were lying.

Like anyone going through a major life change, a person experiencing a divorce needs support. Each of us is different in what we need and how willing we are to express that need. Each divorce is unique. Yet part of living in a caring community means reaching out to those who may be in need. It is the way of *gemilut hesed,* loving-kindness.

The greatest spiritual challenge in a divorce is to go through it without being consumed with anger or vindictiveness. Each divorce story is different, but most are ripe with the opportunity to be hurtful to your former partner. This is particularly true if the divorce is not really a mutual decision. The noninitiator will feel betrayed even if there is no "other" person involved. Individuals will often feel helpless. No one likes to feel deprived of choice. A person may feel like the victim.

Even if the divorce is, or seems to be, mutual, there can be lots of recriminations over who is at fault. While most of the time the fights over material things have nothing to do with the things, at times there are serious issues at stake that could significantly affect the financial future of each of the parties. Ultimately, it is hard to have someone with whom you entered into a relationship with dreams and love now become an adversary over the division of the acquisitions of your failed marriage.

It is hard to be angry or in a great deal of pain and not strike out at the other person from such a place. Let me encourage you not to lose perspective and to try to hold on to one guiding principle and a few associated truths.

The guiding principle is that you are both adults. Your children, if there are any, are not. As parents, your responsibility as always is to care for and protect your children. You have no right to use them as pawns in the war with your ex-spouse. This is true even when your ex-spouse is only feeding them hot dogs or letting them stay up until midnight. They can survive anything like that. They cannot so easily survive being placed in the middle or fundamentally losing a father or a mother. Only if it is a matter of real importance, such as physical safety, can you break this principle. One of the prices of a divorce is that your ex-spouse now gets to raise your children in the manner she or he wants without needing your approval.

The hardest truth about a divorce is the pain that you cause your children, even when the divorce is relatively amicable. Almost every divorce happens for the sake of the husband or wife. On that level it is a selfish act, though an act that may be necessary not just for the adults' well-being but in the long run for the children's. However, in the short term, you get to be out of a bad marriage. The children must live complicated lives, often shuttling between two homes and two parents. It is never easy for them.

*The other truths are well known*    You rarely get what you really want in a divorce, even if you end up with the vase or the antique chair. Often what you want is to still be married or you want the other person to stand up before everyone you know and admit complete culpability. Or maybe you want revenge for all the accumulated hurts of the past, the divorce being the icing on the cake. The only thing you can get are material possessions that, even if now they are imbued with other meanings, will with the passage of time revert back to just being things. In the end, the chair is only a chair. Getting his favorite chair will only in the end get you a chair and an opportunity to hurt him. It is a war that cannot be won. All you can do is wound each other.

In the process of wounding the other person, you have to ask yourself what that does to your soul. Do you really want to live in the land of hatred? In what ways does that burden you? Is it worth it?

In the end, what you need is to move on with your life. Even if the other person initiated the divorce, the truth is you cannot and do not want to be married to someone who does not want to be married to you. Divide the stuff in a way that seems mostly fair. (No two people will ever define *fair* exactly the same way in such a situation.) You cannot have everything. You do not want everything, for that would be pretending that in some peculiar way the marriage was still intact. Anything that seems somewhat unfair, write off as part of the cost of ending the marriage. You need to move on, even as you may mourn the loss. Staying focused on the stuff, engaging in constant skirmishes, is a way of holding on to something that is over. Whether you want it that way or not, that is the truth of the situation. Hopefully, by facing the truth, you can then see clearly what is just a chair and what is really an issue of fairness.

## Other Hurdles

While illness and disappointment in relationships are two of the larger hurdles we can encounter on our journey in the desert, there are many other challenges. The loss of a job, feeling stuck in the wrong job, difficult relations with a child, and tragedies are all possible stops on the way. At some point in our travels through the desert, we begin to see a narrowing of possibilities. We become cognizant of all the paths not taken. There are places we have not visited, experiences we have not tasted. We may also feel a downscaling of expectations. I may never be famous, or be the best in my profession, or be a multimillionaire, or discover a cure for cancer.

We encounter disappointments big and small in our journeys. While it may be the daily disappointments that frustrate us, it is the more long-standing ones that are like corrosive acid on our souls, such as when we feel stuck in a job, or feel dissatisfied with a career, or feel our marriage is stale or just okay. Life just seems too routine or meaningless—not bad, but not as satisfying as it ought to be.

How, then, do we not only go on, but live fully in the face of these disappointments?

This view of life may not be a reflection of your lack of success. Rather it may be a more realistic understanding of the nature of life. The truth is most people will not be famous or be multimillionaires. This realism can also reflect a clearer sense of what your life's goals actually are. Maybe being famous is not important to you anymore.

There is an oft-repeated story about the Hasidic master Zusya, who is weeping upon his deathbed. When asked by his disciples, why are you crying? he answers: I am afraid. Afraid of what? Zusya replies: I am afraid that when I get to heaven they will not ask me "why were you not Moses?" but rather "why were you not Zusya?"

Instead of seeing all the things we are not, let us focus on who we want to be. For much of my adult life I wanted to be famous. Even after I had several books published, by my own standards I was not famous. People did not recognize me when I walked down the street. Nobody asked me to be on a national TV talk show. Even in the Jewish community, other people were asked to speak at some major conference or given some elaborate tribute. I remember once talking with my therapist about being famous. I asked him: Doesn't everyone want to be famous? I told him I knew someone who had a fairly routine job of delivering packages. I could not understand how people lived knowing they would not be famous. Being a good therapist, he never really answered the question. It took me years to understand that not everyone wants to be famous. It took me many more years to understand that my chasing of fame was going to be endless and thus always a failure, since there was always more fame over the next hill. The real truth was I did not want to be famous. I was looking to other people for my own self-validation. Ultimately, I would either give it to myself or have to live without it.

This truth came to me around my fiftieth birthday. I looked back and wondered where the last fifteen or twenty years had gone. I had always thought I would be very sad upon reaching fifty because I would feel my life would only go downhill physically from there. I had always dreaded becoming old (even more than death, I thought). Instead, I came to a much better sense of who I was and still wanted to be. The words of Kohelet (Ecclesiastes) stating that all is a striving after wind and a vanity of vanities felt profoundly true. True, that is, about the chasing of fame and other such illusory goals. Since this was also the year of the millennium, I was struck that almost all, if not all, of the people who were world-famous today would be unknown a thousand years from now. Life, in that vein, is a vanity that in the end is reduced to dust. All things do pass away, even the memory of them.

What, then, became important was not whether I was famous but how I lived my life. What mattered were the relationships I created, not how much wealth I accrued. What mattered was the caring and healing I could create, not by discovering a cure for cancer, but just by living in a holy way. Upon turning fifty I came to a place of satisfaction about my life. This was translated into a lack of desire to possess things. To be honest, spending money easily had never been my forte. A number of years ago I finally permitted myself to buy books. Over the years I have acquired a fairly extensive Judaica library. Now, at fifty, I discovered I did not feel the necessity to buy more books to make my library "complete." Recently, when I visited my local Judaica bookstore, they asked me whether I had moved, since they had not seen me in so long.

This sense of having enough things played itself out in other areas as well. I am something of a collector (of inexpensive things, of course). My two big collections are old, mostly Yiddish, signs from the insides of synagogues that are closing, and Hasidic music tapes (I have over three hundred). I always wanted to have a complete collection, particularly of the tapes. I think somehow having every Hasidic tape would deep down make me feel I am in control of my life. It would be to achieve perfection through completion and thus somehow outwit life's imperfections, including its biggest imperfection, death. Turning fifty, I no longer felt that drive for completion. I still collect because I enjoy it, but it has assumed its rightful place as a hobby and nothing more. I look around my home and see what I have and feel satisfied. Psychologically, there are no empty spaces on my walls calling out to be filled. Maybe it is having much of what I want that allows me to stop wanting. Perhaps that is a potential blessing of the age of Be-midbar. I am no longer at the beginning of my story or even occupied with becoming my own person. I can now more clearly differentiate between want and need. I can also more clearly avoid the confusion between liking a painting and trying to obtain some larger intangible goal through owning that painting. Such clarity does not mean I no longer want anything. After all, while everything may end up dust, there is every reason to enjoy the beauty and the pleasures of the world in the meantime. It is a matter of perspective regarding what is important and essential and what is simply enjoyable.

What is essential to live in the desert? A mode of transportation and water. A mode of transportation can be translated as that which will carry us through the Be-midbar years. What is it? I believe it is a sustaining community that cares for each other in moments of need. To be alone in the desert is terrifying. To be part of a caring community does not remove the adversities we may encounter, but it does make them more bearable. How? Community reminds us that we are not alone. We are part of the human race, whose lot is both joy and sorrow. We share our humanity and our need for each other. *Lo tov heyot ha'adam l'vado,* "it is not good for the human to be alone," is an essential description of the human right from our beginning.

How do we create community? We begin by being born into the community of family. (Unique to the community of family is that you have no choice of who is part of that community. Nor can you easily leave it.) In our Exodus years, we begin to enlarge that circle to include friends. (While lovers are the ones who most sustain us in our travels, they are a different category from friends and community.) It is in our Be-midbar years that we look to create a community beyond a few friends. Judaism stresses community as a context for living. After all, prayer takes place in a *minyan,* a community of ten, rather than in isolation. Wherever Jews have lived they have created community structures to take care of each other. Whether visiting the sick, preparing the body for a funeral, or taking care of the poor, the Jewish communities did not just rely on individual initiatives. They created structures often called *hevrot,* "societies," to organize a communal response to the needs of individuals.

> We have been taught that a disciple of the wise may not live in a city that does not have the following ten institutions and officials: a court . . . a charity fund . . . a synagogue, a [public] bathhouse, a [public] privy, a physician, a scribe, [a ritual slaughterer], and a teacher of young children. [Talmud, *Sanhedrin* 17b]

> If people reside in a town for thirty days, they become responsible to contribute to the soup kitchen; three months, to charity; six months, to the clothing fund; nine months, to the burial fund; and twelve months, for contributing to the repair of the town walls. [Talmud, *Bava Batra* 8a]

Each of these funds was run by volunteers who recruited others to help take care of those in need. This care was not just for the poor. As discussed earlier, *gemilut hesed,* deeds of loving-kindness, can be performed on behalf of anyone. It is the emotional support and not only the financial aid that is part of a caring community. It is obvious why such support could be helpful to someone ill or grieving, but it is also beneficial at moments of great joy, such as the birth of a child or a wedding. On happy occasions, that support can be helpful because the celebrants are so busy. It is also the case that people want to share their happiness with their community. Ultimately, to be part of the community means to help to "repair the town walls," that is, to participate in activities that will strengthen and protect your community (for more on visiting the sick, see pp. 398–400; for comforting mourners, see pp. 455–56).

How to find a community? Communities come in many sizes. They are often larger than a circle of friends and therefore can undertake larger activities. Communities are open to new people joining. They try to take care of everyone within them, not just the popular or powerful. The most common type of community in Jewish life is the synagogue. They can also be found in Jewish Community Centers, in groups like Hadassah, in independent fellowship groups such as *havurot*. Communities can be informal in structure or institutions with staff and dues. Forms of community exist wherever people get together on a regular basis, whether taking a class together or playing volleyball. Community is built at least as much by informal activities as by formal ones. A good example of informal community building is inviting someone over for a meal. This is known as *hakhnasat orhim*, "hospitality to guests."

### *Hakhnasat Orhim*, Hospitality

Hospitality is greater than a visit to the House of Study; it is greater than welcoming the *Shekhinah* (God's indwelling presence). The hospitable person is rewarded in both worlds. [Talmud, *Shabbat* 127a]

In the tradition, Abraham and Sarah are considered the models of hospitality. Their tent had door flaps on each side so that visitors could enter from any direction. They would not wait for guests to "knock" but rather would rush out to greet strangers and invite them to wash off their journey's dust. It is striking that these people, the first Jews in the world, would be known particularly for this quality, for hospitality, of all possible good qualities—peace, humility, generosity—was what characterized Abraham and Sarah.

Why? Why is hospitality greater than greeting the *Shekhinah* or visiting the House of Study? Perhaps because it is too easy to become isolated and retreat into the world of study and intellect—or to retreat into the world of contemplation of the holy. Hospitality requires an interaction between people, a bringing together of souls and hearts, an opening up, a getting to know better, a connection to the world outside yourself.

To be hospitable is to make room for others, to move over; to do *tzimtzum*, "contraction," as God did in creating the world, to open a space for others in your life. It is not a vacuum that is created by this contraction, but rather a space that bespeaks welcome, that makes others feel at home, that crosses chasms of isolation and connects our souls to others. In that space we learn about others and ourselves *and* the *Shekhinah*, God's Presence, whenever we are really present to each other. In that contraction, making space, and making welcome, we create new worlds as did God in that original *tzimtzum*—worlds of connection, meaning, stories, food, laughter, and sharing. Thus it is certainly true that hospitality is greater than study or even welcoming the *Shekhinah*.

### The Water of Joy

The second element we need in our journey through the desert is water. What is the water that will sustain us in the face of life's adversities? Happiness, patience, and serenity.

In our frantic search for something to quench our thirst, we overlook the water all around us and drive ourselves into exile from our own lives.

> We can travel a long way and do many things, but our deepest happiness is not born from accumulating new experiences. It is born from letting go of what is unnecessary, and knowing ourselves to be always at home. True happiness may not be at all far away, but it re-

quires a radical change of view as to where to find it. [Sharon Salzberg, *Lovingkindness* ]

Surely, the Instruction which I enjoin upon you this day is not too baffling for you, nor is it beyond reach. . . . No, the thing is very close to you, in your mouth and in your heart, to observe it. [Deut. 30:11, 14]

The water that will sustain us is that which nourishes our souls. It is the water of joy, gratitude, and compassion. With these three attributes we can not only avoid being overwhelmed by life's difficulties, we can experience life at its fullest. To attain these qualities, we must first see clearly. This means understanding that joy will not come from having a larger house, more money, or greater fame. There is nothing you can possess that will give you more than temporary happiness. Life is full of experiences like gourmet meals. They bring pleasure that should be savored, but it is a short-lived pleasure. Other people hope that there is a book or a teacher that will reveal the secret to living a happy life. The best teachers reveal to the student only what they already know. The secret to happiness is not far away. It lies within you.

### THE TREASURE

The story is told of Rabbi Isaac of Cracow, who lived in poverty. Once a voice in a dream told him to go to a certain bridge in Prague. Under that bridge, he would find a treasure. Rabbi Isaac ignored the dream until he dreamt it three nights in a row. He traveled to Prague, but was prevented from exploring under the bridge because it was guarded twenty-fours a day. After a few days, the captain of the guard had Rabbi Isaac arrested for suspicious behavior. When asked by the captain what he was doing, Rabbi Isaac replied: "I heard a voice in a dream telling me to look for a treasure under this bridge."

"Hah!" laughed the captain. "Only fools listen to dreams. Why I myself in a dream last night heard a voice saying that I should travel to Cracow to the home of some Jew named Rabbi Isaac and look for a treasure in his fireplace. What a joke."

Rabbi Isaac was released by the captain, returned home, and indeed found a treasure buried beneath his fireplace.

Moral: As in *The Wizard of Oz,* the treasure/answer is not far away. You possess it already.

Happiness comes from an acceptance of the way of the world. It is a world of blessings and curses. We cannot make the blessings last no matter how hard we try to grasp them. We cannot avoid the curses no matter how fast we try to run away. The "trick" then is to be present to the moment. In being present, we can be aware of the blessings we enjoy every day. The purpose of *berakhot,* blessings, as we learned in the "Eating and Food" chapter, is to express gratitude for the gift of food. The practice of saying *berakhot* is a way to cultivate an attitude of thankfulness for the blessings of the everyday. Thich Nhat Hanh, the Vietnamese Buddhist teacher, talks about nontoothache days. We must always be grateful that today is a nontoothache day. Happiness is enjoying what we have.

We are warned against the opposite attitude by the last of the Ten Commandments: "You shall not covet your neighbor's house: you shall not covet your neighbor's wife, or his male or female slave, or his ox or his ass, or anything that is your neighbor's" (Exod. 20:14). Envy is an enterprise that has no end. It is like trying to fill the Grand Canyon with dirt using only a teaspoon. We always seem to be measuring ourselves against those around us. We wonder why another is rewarded but we are not. Often, we feel the reward was undeserved. "I am a much harder worker than Joe; why was he chosen to go to the conference in Bermuda?" Even if we do feel that the other person deserves the reward, we are then envious of that person's talents or personality. "I wish I could be as outgoing as Jane; then more people in the office would like me." Or we look down on other people so we can feel superior. "Boy, is he stupid!" No one seems to be our equal. We find it hard to be happy at another's success or good fortune. We also find it hard to refrain from feeling smug about another's misfortune or failings. I would encourage you to experiment by paying attention to how many times in one day you enter into this competition. Buddhists call this the comparative mind, that is, a mind that is never happy with what it has. In our society it is probably more accurate to call it the competitive mind. Instead, the Jewish tradition encourages us to rejoice at another's good fortune. As we have seen, this is an understanding of the *mitzvah* of "Love your neighbor as yourself," that is, to wish for your neighbor all that you would wish for yourself. Even more basically, the tradition encourages us to move away from envy, in its classic teaching: "Who is wealthy? A person who is satisfied with his lot" (*Ethics of Our Ancestors* 4:1).

Being satisfied with your lot is not a recipe for passivity. Sometimes this attitude as expressed in Jewish sources in the past seemed predicated on a faith that everything that happens to you is God's will.

> Once, while on a journey, Rabbi Akiva came to a certain place where he looked for lodging but was not given any. He said, "Whatever the Holy One does is for the best." So he went off and spent the night in the open field. He had with him a donkey, a rooster, and a lamp. A lion came and ate the donkey, a weasel came and ate the rooster, and a gust of wind came and blew out the lamp. Again he said, "Whatever the Holy One does is for the best." That same night, brigands came and took the people of that city into captivity. Said Rabbi Akiva to his disciples, "Did I not tell you, Whatever the Holy One does is for the best?" [Talmud, *Berakhot* 60b]

For Rabbi Akiva, all the misfortunes that happened to him prevented an even worse thing—being seen and captured by the brigands. Let us leave aside that the story is very different if you are the townspeople, the donkey, or the rooster.

The problem for me in that story is that I do not believe that everything that happens to me is God's will. I do not believe that a tragedy occurs because I deserve punishment or because there is some unknowable plan that can make sense of life's terrible injustices. I do not have the faith of Akiva that everything that happens *is for some ultimate good*. I think some things are simply bad. Yet, like Akiva, I want to attain a clear perspective on what is happening. Akiva understood that he had spent an uncomfortable night and lost a donkey and rooster. But that is all it was. It was not the end of the world. We spend so much time worrying about what will be, and obsessing on what was, that we lose track of the present. If you are like me, you spend time rehearsing dramatic speeches in your head to tell off people who have wronged you. Usually I finish the speeches by revealing that I have just been diagnosed with a fatal disease giving me only weeks to live. After all, I want them not only to be wrong but also to feel *really* sorry. Countless scenarios of "what ifs" play out in my mind, almost all of which are very unlikely to happen. It is a pointless exercise. These are speeches, after all, that I will never give (never mind that they would never have their desired effect). It is more than just daydreaming or imagining some fantasy like pitching a perfect game. It is a worrying about the future. While it may have some use in processing some of my anger or fears, it seems like gnawing the same old bone over and over again.

Happiness lies in being grateful for what you have. For more often than not you have all you need.

"You give it open-handedly, feeding every creature to its heart's content" (Psalm 145:15). I never understood that verse from the daily liturgy. There seem to be a lot of people who are not content. (There are also a lot of people who do not have enough to eat.) I now understand it, though not as an absolute statement. For the most part, we are created with what we need: the ability to love, a mind for understanding, a means to communicate, a body that enables us to enjoy the pleasures of the world, hands with which to create, and so on. We have all we need if we would only see it that way. Happiness comes from seeing all that you have. Happiness is something we give to ourselves. Sharon Salzberg writes: "A loving heart will give you more happiness than anything you crave." Satisfaction is the key to happiness. The Psalmist maintains that God has given each of us enough to make our heart content. If you think what you need is always just beyond your reach, then no matter how much you manage to grasp in that outstretched arm, all you will get is a discontented heart. Rather be grateful for what you do have.

What about when things go wrong, when you make mistakes or

someone is hurtful to you? It is said of the people of Israel that we are *rahmanim bnai rahmanim,* "compassionate people, children of compassionate people." We are second-generation (and many more) people of compassion, of *rahmanus,* "compassion" in Yiddish. We need to have compassion for ourselves and for others. We are human beings created with choice. We have the ability to make a mess of things. We know ourselves intimately and have some understanding of why we get angry unreasonably or have trouble being generous. It is usually not just out of mean-spiritedness, but rather because of factors that lie within the complexity of our personality. If we have even just a glimpse of who we are, then we should be able to understand the complexity of other people. We can then come to a place of compassion toward them. To take an everyday example: You are driving in the left lane and someone just ahead of you in the right-hand lane makes a left turn, forcing you to slam on the brakes. You curse them and yell, even if it is only to yourself, "You idiot!" But do you really think the other driver deliberately makes left turns from the right-hand lane? Perhaps they didn't see your car, or they were unfamiliar with this area and just saw the name of the street they had been looking for. Haven't we all made such dangerous maneuvers because we lost track of where we were or suddenly saw our turn? Why not assume it was a mistake instead of a deliberate attempt to make you angry?

Even in more complex instances, when the person does want to hurt or anger us, coming from a place of compassion allows us to better deal with the situation. Sometimes it will make us think of our role in prompting the offense. Even in circumstances where the offense seems unprovoked, having compassion may prevent us from getting stuck in endless replays of the situation. By acknowledging that this person is careless or mistaken, but we are all flawed, we enable ourselves to move past plans of revenge.

There is a variant teaching to "Who is wealthy? A person who is satisfied with his lot." In *Avot de-Rabbi Nathan* 23, it is taught: "Who is wealthy? A person who makes an enemy into a friend *(oseh son'o ohavo)*." Ultimately it is in the richness of our relationships that we create lives of happiness. To turn an enemy into a friend is to remove the burden of hatred or even ill will that entangles us in a swamp of negativity. Instead, we are engaged in a relationship of mutual caring and giving. It is possible to live our lives as if at war. No matter how high and secure the walls of our castle, we are always aware somewhere that we are at war. We exist on the defensive (if not on the offensive). Suspicion and anxiety abound. But it is also possible to live at peace, letting forgiveness and understanding be the language of communication. At peace we can live lives unconstricted and open to all that will be. Compassion and gratitude allow us to live lives with open hearts and joy.

It is also possible to live life as a grievance collector or happiness miser (one who keeps happiness safely stored away in a vault). Such misers live a *farkrimpt* (constricted) life, never enjoying what they have because their focus is always elsewhere. But it is also possible to live a life of loving-kindness. Unlike everything else in this world of limited resources, we have an infinite capacity to love. We can never reach the limits of our ability to have compassion or love. We never have to say that we are empty of love. That infinite capacity is one of the ways that we are created in the Divine image. Our hearts are like *ein sof,* the "limitless" that is the name for the true nature of God for the Kabbalists. By striving to live a life of *rahamim,* "compassion toward others and ourselves," we will fill all our years with the wisdom and happiness that is just waiting to be discovered in our hearts.

### Mitzvot Bein Adam le-Atzmo

Commonly, the *mitzvot* are divided into two categories: Those that are *bein adam le-makom,* "between people and God," and those that are *bein adam le-havero,* "between people." The first can be described as the ritual commandments and the second as ethical commandments. Yet Rabbi Joseph Soloveitchik, a leading rabbinic scholar of the twentieth century, following in the tradition of the Gaon of Vilna (eighteenth century), posited another category: *mitzvot bein adam le-atzmo,* "commandments between a person and his or her self." Let me suggest that one way to understand this third category is as related to *middot,* "character." Beyond how we interact with God and with other people, we spend a great deal of time interacting with our interior world. *Middot* is the tradition's word for the good characteristics that we want to cultivate. These good characteristics not only make us more compassionate to other people, they also make us emotionally happier and healthier. (See "The End of the Day," pp. 94–102, for more about *middot*.)

These *middot* are broad ways of being. They go beyond a specific *mitzvah*, commandment. After all, the Torah does not say we should refrain from anger, nor does it specifically say that we should be nice to other people. This category of commandments concerning our inner selves suggests that the basic aspects of our personalities are also parts of what the Torah wants us to do and be.

Nahmanides, the medieval Bible commentator, puts it this way in his explanation of "Do what is right and good in the sight of the Lord, that it may go well with you" (Deut. 6:18):

> At first Moses stated that you are to keep God's statutes and testi-
> monies which God commanded you, and now Moses is stating that
> even where God has not commanded you, give thought, as well, to
> do what is right and good in God's eyes, for God loves the right and
> the good. Now this is a great principle, for it is impossible to mention
> in the Torah all aspects of people's conduct with their neighbors and
> friends. . . . But since God mentioned many of them, such as "do not
> go about as a talebearer among your fellows" (Lev. 19:16) . . . and
> the like—Moses reverted to state in a general way that, in all matters,
> one should do what is right and good, including even compromise
> and going beyond the requirements of the law. Other examples are . . .
> that one's conversation with people be pleasant. Thus people should
> seek to refine their behavior in every form of activity, until they are
> worthy of being called "right and good."

There are no limitations to what the Torah asks of us. There really is no such distinction as religious and secular. All activity, all life, is part of Torah. In each moment and in every activity we should strive to do that which is right and good. If we do, the verse tells us it will be good for us. Traditionally, this was understood as meaning God will reward the righteous. For me, it means that *tov* is the reward for *tov,* that is, good is its own reward. For by doing good, we live a life of harmony and peace rather than discord and anger. We create our own spiritual environment. It can be an environment so polluted with negativity that it is hard to breathe or an environment redolent with the scent of the wonders of the Garden of Eden.

# DEUTERONOMY/DEVARIM: AGING

When Moses realized that the decree of death had been sealed against him, he drew a small circle around himself, stood in it, and said, "Master of the universe, I will not budge from here until You void that decree." Wearing sackcloth, he persisted in prayer and supplications before the Holy One until heaven and earth—indeed, all things made during the six days of creation—were shaken.

What did the Holy One do then? God had it proclaimed at every gate of every firmament that Moses' prayer be neither accepted nor brought up to God's Presence, because the decree concerning him had been sealed.

Still, as the sound of Moses' prayer to God above grew even stronger, the Holy One summoned the ministering angels and commanded them: "Go down in haste, bolt all the gates of every firmament." For Moses' prayer was like a sword, ripping and tearing, and nothing could stop it.

In that instant, Moses said to the Holy One, "Master of the universe, known and revealed to You is the trouble and pain I suffered on account of the people of Israel, until they came to believe in Your Name. How much pain I suffered because of them, until I inculcated among them the Torah and its precepts! I said to myself: As I witnessed their struggle, so will I be allowed to witness their reward. Yet now that Israel's reward has come, You tell me, 'You shall not go over this Jordan' (Deut. 3:27). Thus Your Torah, which asserts, 'In the same day you shall give the day worker his hire' (Deut. 24:15), You manifestly turn into fraud. Is such the reward for forty years of labor that I labored until Israel became a holy people loyal to their faith?"

The Holy One replied, "Nevertheless, such is the decree that has gone forth from My Presence!"

Then Moses said, "Master of the universe, if You will not let me enter the Land of Israel, allow me to remain [alive] like the beasts of the field, who eat grass, drink water, and thus savor the world—let me be like one of these." At that, God replied, "Enough. Speak no more to Me of this matter" (Deut. 3:26).

When Moses saw that his prayer was not heeded, he went to implore heaven and earth, saying: "Entreat mercy in my behalf." They replied: "Before entreating mercy for you, we should entreat mercy for ourselves, for it is said, 'The heavens shall vanish away like smoke, and the earth shall wax old like a garment' " (Is. 51:6). He then went to implore the sun and the moon, the stars and the planets, and the mountains and the hills. Each time they responded that they needed to plead for their own passing existence.

Then he went to implore the sea and cried: "Entreat mercy in my behalf." The sea replied: "Moses, why is this day different from former days? Are you not the same Moses, who came to me with your rod, smote me, split me into twelve paths, when I could not withstand you because the Presence was proceeding at your right? What's happened to you now?" As the sea reminded Moses of what he was able to do in his younger years, he cried out in anguish, " 'Oh that I were as in the months of old' (Job 29:2). [O Sea,] at the time I stood over you, I was a king in the world, but now, though I prostrate myself, no heed is given me."

Then the Holy One said to Moses: "Moses, I have sworn two oaths: one concerning Israel—after they followed the doubting reports of the spies—that I would destroy them from the world; and the other that you are to die and not enter the Land. The oath I had sworn concerning Israel, I set aside at your plea when you entreated Me, 'Pardon, I pray Thee' (Num. 14:19); and now you entreat once again that I set aside My oath to comply with your plea 'Let me go over, I pray Thee' (Deut. 3:25). Choose which oath you want me to set aside!" When Moses our teacher heard this, he said: "Master of the universe, let Moses and a thousand like him perish, but let not a fingernail of one person in Israel be hurt."

Nevertheless, Moses said to God: "Master of the universe, shall the feet that went up to the heavens, the face that confronted the Presence, the hands that received the Torah from Your hand—shall these now lick dust?"

The Holy One replied: "Such was My thought from the very beginning, and such must be the way of the world: each generation is to have its own interpreters of Scripture, each generation is to have its own providers, each generation is to have its own leaders. Until now it had been your portion to serve Me, but now your disciple Joshua's portion to serve has come."

Moses said to the Holy One: "Master of the universe, if I must die to vacate my post for Joshua, let me be his disciple." The Holy One replied: "If that is what you wish to do, go and do it."

So Moses rose early to be at Joshua's doorway, where Joshua sat and interpreted Scripture. [In order to hide his identity] Moses stooped and put his hand over his heart [thus covering his face with the crook of his arm]. At the same time, Joshua's eyes were veiled [by God], making him unable to see Moses so that Moses would be humiliated and come to be reconciled to his dying.

In the meantime, when people came to Moses' doorway to study Torah and asked, "Where is our teacher Moses?" they were told, "He rose early and went to Joshua's doorway." They went and found him at Joshua's doorway—Joshua seated and Moses standing. They said to Joshua: "What has come over you, that you allow our teacher Moses to stand while you sit?" When Joshua's eyes were again clear and he recognized Moses, he rent his garments, cried out, and wept: "My master, my master! My father, my father!"

Then the people said to Moses, "Moses our teacher, teach us Torah." He replied, "I no longer have the authority." They: "We will not leave you." Then a Divine voice came forth and commanded the people, "Be willing to learn from Joshua." With that, the people submitted to the command to sit and learn from Joshua's mouth.

Joshua sat at the head, Moses at his right, and Aaron's sons at his left, while Joshua taught in Moses' presence. At that session, the tradition of wisdom was taken away from Moses and given to Joshua.

When they went out, Moses walked at Joshua's left, and as they entered the Tent of Meeting, the pillar of cloud came down and formed a partition between the two. After the cloud departed, Moses went over to Joshua and asked, "What did the Word say to you?" Joshua replied, "When the Word used to reveal itself to you, did I know what it said to you?"

In that instant, Moses cried out in anguish and said, "Rather a hundred deaths than a single pang of envy. Master of universes, until now I sought life. But now my soul is surrendered to You." [Adapted from Midrash, *Deuteronomy Rabbah* 7:10; *Tanhuma, Va-ethanan,* #6; *Yalkut, Va-ethanan,* #821]

In this midrash, Moses represents every person who is facing death. He tries prayer, but no matter how powerful the prayers, God will not listen. The failure of prayer represents the powerlessness of human efforts to stop death. Even as Moses' prayer tears apart the heavens, it remains ineffective. The same would be true if Moses had turned to medicine or wealth. No matter how powerful humans are, neither they nor their endeavors can defeat death. Perhaps, too, God does not want the prayer to reach heaven, because God knows that even God cannot change the decree of death. It is the way of the world.

Moses then appeals to God's fairness by asking to be repaid for all his years of devoted service. Moses begs to be allowed to enter the Promised Land as a beast. Death, however, does not have to do with fairness. Nor can life be prolonged by making some deal, whether that deal is to live on in some other form or to live on through fame or fortune.

Moses then turns to others to intercede on his behalf, including the heavens and earth, and the mountains and hills. They all say no because they need to plead for themselves, for even they will pass away. Does Moses understand that message? Do we? All things will pass away: you and I, and eventually even the earth, the moon, the sun, and the stars.

Moses then turns to the sea, which snaps back, reminding him how he had split the sea. Moses is anguished, remembering when he was young and powerful, when seemingly he could do anything. In the face of death, we too turn our minds back to moments when we felt powerful or successful or to moments when our future with the possibility of everything still seemed to stretch endlessly before us.

God, who must be tiring by now of Moses' pleas, hits upon a strategy that will remind Moses of who he really is. God tells Moses that he has a choice. Either God can revoke the decree, thereby allowing Moses to enter the Land, or God can restore the decree to destroy the people. Of course, Moses, leader and shepherd of the people for so many years, eloquently responds: "Let Moses and a thousand like him perish, but let not a fingernail of one person in Israel be hurt."

Yet even after being reminded of the mission of his life, Moses irrationally and cleverly perseveres. He also reminds God who Moses is, the one who received the whole Torah directly from God at Sinai. Can someone who has attained such spiritual heights, can he now lie in the dust? God responds by saying that this was God's plan right from the beginning of the world. God's plan is apparently not just that everyone will die. God goes on to say that death allows the world to continue to grow and change. Even when it comes to Torah, each generation needs to have its own interpreters. This suggests that the fact that Moses heard it all directly from God is not a reason for Moses to continue to live; rather the opposite. All things change, including the Torah. If Moses lived, the Torah would be stuck in the past. More broadly, this statement by God reminds us that all things need room to grow and therefore what comes before needs to die to make room for the new. Thus death is a necessary part of life, for it creates the space for new life.

In his final appeal, Moses is willing to relinquish all of his authority to Joshua. If that is why he is to die, then he will make space for Joshua's leadership. Moses tries to live this new life, but realizes he cannot do so without envy of Joshua's relationship to God. At last Moses accepts his fate. Why?

He finally understands that he can neither stop the future nor hold on to the past. Not only would that prevent Joshua and the future from moving ahead; it would also end up distorting who Moses had been. Moses wanted to remain a leader who cared more for his people than for himself. He wanted to remain a leader who was more modest than any other person. His words "Would that all the Lord's people were prophets, that the Lord put God's spirit upon them!" (Num. 11:29) were still true to his deepest self. He understood that he must now move offstage.

Most of all, Moses understood all that he had accomplished in his life. He could be proud of his legacy. Death would not diminish that legacy. His life was finished. His work was complete, even though he would never make it to the Promised Land. After all, while we treat this midrash as talking about death, its focus is on something else. Moses is not asking that he be spared from death. He is asking that he be allowed to enter the Promised Land. However, the Promised Land lies across the barrier of death. Moses, like everyone else, will not make it. He can instead look back over his life and reflect upon all he has accomplished. He can share the wisdom of what he has learned with the younger generations. If he can do that successfully, then he will stand upon the mountain of his life and see the Promised Land stretched out before him.

## The Challenge of Deuteronomy

This is the challenge of the Book of Deuteronomy. This book is basically a long farewell address to the Jewish people. Moses reviews the past and urges the Israelites not to lose sight of their responsibility to uphold the covenant between God and Israel. The book ends with the people about to enter the Promised Land and with the death of Moses.

The vision of Deuteronomy sees this time of life for all people, not just Moses, as a period of reflection on all that has gone before, of attaining insights into our life story. With this reflection comes the sharing of our accumulated wisdom with family and with the next generations. It is a time of gathering and harvesting all that has been planted. Yet it is also a time of giving and sharing rather than accumulating. It is the time when we no longer need to establish who we are. We do not need to build a home, a business, or a reputation. Our generativity does not come from giving birth to children. We may still be building. We may be taking care of grandchildren, but we are no longer driven by the desire to accomplish everything.

It is the time of retirement when we enter a world where expectations are unclear. What are we supposed to do now that we are past raising children and having a career? Is this just an extended vacation, a reward for our hard labor? Or are we really being pushed aside to make room for the young future? Are we "out of sight, out of mind," as we stand too near to death, making younger folks uncomfortable? After all, hasn't the slide begun toward an increasing lack of energy, mind, and health, leading to the inevitable?

Moses shows that this time of aging can be full of life and meaning, not just trivial "keep-the-seniors-busy" art projects. Rather than a time of shrinking possibilities, our later years give us more time for reflection, more time for interior work, more time for being rather than doing. Our task is to look back on our unique life story. With the perspective of age, we can try to see more clearly where we have been. With a tolerance for youthful and middle-age mistakes, we can reexamine those less-than-shining moments in our lives. What can we learn from what happened, now that we are not in the middle of losing a job or ending a relationship?

### Our Lives, Our Treasury

Imagine if everything of significance we remember is in boxes in a very large mansion called Our Life. Inside one box might be a memory of a teacher embarrassing us in third grade; in another, a memory of our winning an award. We know that we will be moving from this mansion and in preparation we need to go through all these boxes. In the rooms containing boxes of pleasant memories, we will linger over each box filled with a treasure. However, there are many boxes up in the attic or down in the cellar filled with unpleasant memories. We try to postpone going to the attic or cellar. Yet in the back of our mind those unpleasant boxes remain and require great effort to ignore.

More important, we cannot finish our life task without opening those boxes. Particularly if these are old boxes, we may be ready to examine them in a new light. Why have I carried the memory of being embarrassed by my third-grade teacher all my life? Can I discard it now? What about the hurtful comment that Jack made to me thirty years ago? Why was it so important to me? At the time I thought it was totally uncalled for, but looking back, did I do anything to provoke it? Do I have some understanding of why Jack might have been in an angry place at that time unrelated to me?

The process of examining these broken pieces of your life is not to simply say, "Boy, is it stupid to be mad at such a little thing so many years later." Rather, the truth is these things do have some significance to you or they would be long forgotten. By reexamining these past hurts experienced or caused by us, we can come to a more complete understanding. This understanding can lead to a forgiveness of both the other and oneself. Many youthful indiscretions are just that. We can look back at ourselves and see how immature or unwise we were, but be tolerant since we were young (or even middle-aged). Old age provides the perspective that gives us wisdom, that shows us what is important over the long haul, and that lets us be forgiving.

The truth is even if we never go up into the attic, those boxes and all they contain are present in our lives. Being righteous or in the right does not free you from being stuck in a permanent tango with the one who hurt you.

There are few people in the Bible with more of a right to carry a grudge than Joseph. Almost killed by his brothers, he is sold into slavery. Near the end of the story, Joseph tells his brothers that he forgives them. He says: "Have no fear! Am I a substitute for God? Besides, although you intended me harm, God intended it for good, so as to bring about the present result—the survival of many people" (Gen. 50:19). Looking back on his story, he does not dismiss what his brothers did to him, but he does see it in the larger context of his life. This too is the perspective of age.

Looking back, we can see that unexpected paths did bring us to good places. Even when they did not, we can see the unexpected turns in the road not as defeats but just as part of our journey. Instead of focusing on what might have been, we see all that has happened to us as part and parcel of our lives. Some things we could have done differently. Others were not in our hands. Yet in the end this is the life we both created and were given. Age gives us Joseph's perspective: You just never know what was for the good and what for the bad. As Joseph says, "Am I a substitute for God?" This suggests leaving the judgments about our own and others' behavior to the True Judge. After all, the irony of Joseph's comment is that the Israelites were saved from the famine, but in a few years would experience slavery in Egypt. One tradition holds that the slavery came about because of the brothers' animus toward Joseph. Yet it also came about because of Joseph's rise to power in Egypt, otherwise the Israelites could have returned to Canaan after the famine was over. Joseph's success, seemingly a good thing, was part of the sequence leading to the slavery of the Israelites in Egypt. For age teaches us, as well, that all stories go on. THE END never comes, only perhaps a conclusion to a chapter. Our stories begin long before we were born and we have an impact on the story that will continue long after we are gone.

## The Opportunities of Aging

This broader attitude helps us to face death as well. Instead of spending our last years in denial of death, we come to see it as a part of living. Depending on our belief about life after death, we can conceive of images about what will happen after. Whatever we believe, aging can allow us to see our place in the unending saga of life. Instead of trying to be young (when we are not), we can accept the natural life cycle, which can free us to enjoy our lives more fully.

For in the perspective of age, we are also able to explore things we have been too busy to explore or to recapture parts of ourselves that we put aside earlier in life. Are there aspects of ourselves that we gave up in order to start a family or that were too impractical when we needed to make a living? Aging gives us the opportunity to follow some of those agendas. It is often said that people's characteristics become exaggerated as they grow older. This often suggests that annoying personality traits become more extreme. Yet it could also be seen as a celebration of the uniqueness of the lives of each and every person. It is the opposite of adolescence, when we are so concerned about fitting in and being like everyone else. Now we can be who we are, each in our uniqueness, each carrying the treasures of our life's experiences.

Beyond a reflection of our past, a coming to terms, and a healing, aging is also about the sharing of the wisdom accumulated in a lifetime. We can use our time to help others, to tutor, or to mentor. We can become elders in a society that desperately needs elders. As elders, our role is not to talk about the good old days and how bad today's kids are. Instead, it is to share what we have learned by offering hands and hearts to help others on their own journeys. Rabbi Zalman Schachter-Shalomi talks about "saging" rather than aging (see *From Age-ing to Sage-ing,* by Zalman Schachter-Shalomi and Ronald S. Miller [Warner Books, 1995], a very good presentation on this whole subject). Elders or sages have a real role in the world. Our society, with its fast pace and rapid mobility, could especially benefit from the wisdom of those with the perspective of age.

## Some of the Lessons of Deuteronomy

*It may be time to refine our defining stories*    We all have stories about our lives that we use to define who we are, what we value, or what we dislike. In the period of Deuteronomy, we can reexamine those stories and see perhaps how we fit them to suit our purposes. Now, from a distance, we can retell them closer to the way they actually occurred.

Near the beginning of Deuteronomy, as Moses is recapitulating the past, he retells the story of the spies. Back in the Book of Numbers, God tells Moses to send out people to spy out the land of Israel. The spies return with mostly negative reports. In response, the Israelites despair of being able to defeat the "giants" living in the land. A disappointed God then decrees forty years of wandering for the Israelites so that this unfaithful generation will all die in the desert. Strangely, when Moses retells this story in Deuteronomy, the spies are sent not at God's desire but rather at the people's! One way to understand this is that when Moses tells the story in Numbers, he is embarrassed by what happened and so places the blame on God. But now in Deuteronomy, protecting the people and the leadership's (including Moses') reputation does not seem critical, so Moses tells the true story that it was the people, not God, who wanted the spies.

Thus we may be more ready to acknowledge mistakes, but even in that acknowledgment treat them like our misbehaving children rather than ammunition to berate ourselves.

## Size does not count

> It is not because you are the most numerous of peoples that the Lord set God's heart on you and chose you—indeed, you are the smallest of peoples. [Deut. 7:7]

Certainly, what you are blessed with makes a difference in life. Being beautiful, smart, or athletic can change the direction of your life (just as being born with obstacles and handicaps can also affect a life). Having a lot of money can sometimes make life easier and more enjoyable. Yet ultimately, it is the choices we make about how to live our lives that will have the greatest impact on the quality of those lives. If we live lives of caring and holiness, with an appreciation for our blessings, then it will be in the smallest things that we discover the wonder of this world.

## What really matters

> Remember the long way that the Lord your God has made you travel in the wilderness these past forty years, that God might test you by hardships to learn what was in your hearts: whether you would keep God's commandments or not. God subjected you to the hardship of hunger and then gave you manna to eat, which neither you nor your ancestors had ever known, in order to teach you that a person does

not live on bread alone, but rather that a person may live on any-thing that comes from God's words. [Deut. 8:2–3]

Our lives are filled with the travails of our journey. Some of those travails are the daily annoyances of life. Others are difficult chal-lenges. This is how we are "tested" to know what is really in our heart. Is it a heart of awareness and compassion? Or is it a constricted heart filled with envy or anger? God provides us with blessings in this world, though these blessings are not always as obvious as manna falling from heaven. These blessings are to teach us what is essential—holiness and caring rather than thinking we live by bread alone. What will sustain us in this world? Our possessions, the trinkets of the trades we pursued in our life? Or the words of Torah that we heard expressed by God at Sinai? Too often, we think it is the "bread" that we need to carry us through the desert, though the real truth lies elsewhere.

### The holiness of monotony

[God] who fed you in the wilderness with manna, which your ances-tors had never known, in order to test you by hardships. [Deut. 8:16]

The wording of this verse differs from the previous citation and sug-gests that the manna itself is a hardship! One suggestion is that, despite its miraculous nature, having manna for food every day became mo-notonous. This was true even though according to tradition manna was supposed to taste like anything that you wanted it to taste like. Yet no matter how it tasted, eating the same-looking food year after year must have been boring.

Thus manna is symbolic of all the miraculous blessings of life that we come to take for granted as one year follows another. Sunshine, health, relationships, music all become like manna. Deuteronomy re-minds us that life does not stretch forever and we should celebrate the blessings of the everyday.

### Do not become set in your ways

> Circumcise [cut away], therefore, the thickening about your hearts
> and stiffen your necks no more. [Deut. 10:16]

The danger in the passage of years is that a hardening of our emotional arteries can take place. Routine cuts deep wrinkles in the face of
our souls. We become habituated to the ways we have repeatedly done
things. Deuteronomy challenges us not to stiffen our necks by becoming
more set in our ways. Instead, we should strive to be open to each new
day by removing the accumulated layers surrounding our hearts. Those
layers urge caution and make us fearful of the unknown. More than that,
we should see this time as an opportunity to explore what we did not
have time for in our career and in our family-building days. Deuteronomy continues by reminding us to be like God and befriend the stranger
(Deut. 10:19). We are to look back to our youth when the world was un-
explored territory, when, as adolescents, we felt like strangers to our
body, to our family, to our world. Remembering what it felt like to be
strangers will help us be compassionate to others who feel like strangers
in strange lands. One step further is called for here: we are to befriend
that which is strange to us—the new, the unfamiliar, and the untried. This
too will keep life refreshed and renewed rather than stale and routine.

### It is all within reach

> Surely, the Instruction which I enjoin upon you this day is not too
> baffling for you, nor is it beyond reach. It is not in the heavens, that
> you should say, "Who among us can go up to the heavens and get it
> for us and impart it to us, that we may observe it?" Neither is it be-
> yond the sea, that you should say, "Who among us can cross to the
> other side of the sea and get it for us and impart it to us, that we may
> observe it?" No, the thing is very close to you, in your mouth and in
> your heart, to observe it. [Deut. 30:11–14]

The wisdom of a long life tells us that there is no Answer that lies in
some place too difficult to attain. Wisdom is right here. It is found in

the Torah, God's gift and guide to the Jewish people. It is found in the experiences of a lifetime. It is close to you because it literally is to be found in your mouth and in your heart. All you need to do is "observe it," that is, be reflective on the past, be aware of what is, and be open to the future.

### Choose life

> I have put before you life and death, blessing and curse. Choose life.
> [Deut. 30:19]

We have a choice. The choice is not whether or not to die. The choice is how to live. Do we live by constantly choosing life over death, blessing over curse? Do we live a life of ethics and caring and do we "hold fast" to God and thus to a sense of holiness and meaning? If we do, then we are promised that "you shall have life and long endure upon the soil" (Deut. 30:20). A long life does not mean that you live to be a hundred; rather, it means it is a life full of meaning and purpose.

If you follow the sage advice of Deuteronomy, then you will be like Moses: "Moses was a hundred and twenty years old when he died; his eyes were undimmed and his vigor unabated" (Deut. 34:7). Moses still led a life of awareness (eyes undimmed) and one where he was ready to cross over into a new land. He continued to lead his people and to share his wisdom right up until the end. Yet he remained human just like the rest of us, as reflected in the midrash that began this chapter. One last midrash on his death:

> It is taught: "So Moses the servant of the Lord died there" (Deut. 34:5). Is it possible that Moses, while still alive, would have written, "So Moses . . . died"? The truth is, Scripture up to this passage was written by Moses; from this passage on, Scripture was written by Joshua son of Nun. . . . But R. Simeon said . . . Is it possible that the Torah scroll is short of even a single letter? [Moses was supposed to have written every word of the Torah as he heard it from God] . . .

Rather, the meaning is that, up to this passage, the Holy One dictated, and Moses repeated the words and wrote them out, but from this passage on, the Holy One dictated, and Moses [without repeating the words] wrote them down with tears in his eyes. [Talmud, *Bava Batra* 15a; *Menahot* 30a]

# DEUTERONOMY/DEVARIM: DEATH

God told the first human not to eat of the tree in the center of the garden, "for in the day that you eat it you shall surely die." Having eaten of the tree of knowledge of good and evil, Adam and Eve and all their children were doomed to die. With knowledge comes death. Given the power to do good or evil, we have become Godlike, and yet we remain human and thus mortal.

We spend much of our lives desperately ignoring the fact that we and everyone we know—and for that matter everything we create and touch—will pass away and be no more. When we are young, death seems to dwell in another universe, only occasionally and very tragically striking down someone our age. As we reach middle age, death is no longer such an unfamiliar visitor. Enough people we know or have heard about are embraced by death that we begin to see holes in the panoramic tapestry of our individual lives. In middle age, our bodies begin to feel aches and pains. Not since adolescence, when our bodies changed so much, have we paid attention to them except for concern about our appearance and our physical attractiveness to others. Now this trusted and reliable (and therefore taken-for-granted) companion begins, just begins, to fail us. However, the future is clear. If we see our life's journey as climbing a mountain, then we are over the peak and beginning the descent. Life, which seemed filled with endless possibilities when we were young, now seems to have ever-narrowing horizons. I catch glimpses with my peripheral vision of my life's new companion, someone there but not there before, death. Death becomes only more familiar, more present, as we age. The holes from the loss of acquaintances, friends, and loved ones in the tapestry of our lives grow ever more numerous, until large gaps begin to appear, until for some there are more holes than tapestry. And in the end, we, all of us, come to THE END in the story of our life.

Death, the dark twin of life, is the great challenge to our attempt to create a life of meaning. But just as death cannot be separated from life, so our response to death cannot be taken out of the context of our whole life. Death can make "sense" in the context of the life we have led, in what we believe about our purpose in life (and thus in death), in what we believe about God, in what we believe about our souls, and in what we believe comes after death.

Imagine our world if everyone lived forever. There would be no place for change to happen. No incentive to finish anything in our lifetime. No sense of the preciousness of life itself. Or imagine a world where death was inevitable but you could choose the day of your death. The uncertainty of our lives would be removed. As much as we try to ignore death, deep down we are always conscious of death, and that consciousness is an important motivating factor in our lives.

Death is an inherent part of the life of our universe. On one level death has to happen if change and growth, and maybe even progress, are to happen. Whether in our personal lives or in work, in groups, or in a nation, things must pass away if an eternal gridlock is not to occur.

Death, then, is the way of this world, a world not of stasis but of change. Just as the natural world experiences the death of nature in winter, only to be followed by a new rebirth in spring, so everything that shares this planet comes to its end.

For humans, death is a return. Our bodies return to the earth from where they came. Dust to dust. Our spirit, our soul returns to the place it came from, to God. In one midrash there exists a place where all the souls wait to be assigned to human beings. When they are called by God, the souls resist leaving the world of the spirit to enter the world of materialism, but in the end they have no choice. At death the soul, that part of us which is in the image of God, returns to the world of the spirit and is united with God.

As much as we might see death as accomplishing our life's goal—achieving a union with God—death is never eagerly anticipated in Jewish tradition. We are called to redeem the divine sparks of this world, to make it a better place, to make ourselves better people, to strive to feel God's Presence. God says: "I have set before you this day life and death, therefore choose life." Judaism is life-affirming. It is why the emphasis even in traditional Judaism is on life in this world rather than life in the world to come. Death is the great enemy of life and the great challenge to a spiritual life, to finding meaning in life.

Faced with death, we may find some understanding in the notion of death as part of the natural process of life or of death as the return of the spirit to God. Yet when someone we care about dies we can only feel a sense of loss, a disbelief that that person will never be here with us again. Any death reminds us of our own mortality: most of us stand before this Great Unknown with fear and trembling. Death seems so unfair, most of the time coming too soon, always coming too cruelly, to the living and the dead.

### Facing Your Loss

Death brings us grief. We mourn, most of all, the end of a relationship with someone who mattered to us. Death is always incomprehensible, always unbelievable, despite the knowledge buried deep within us that each of us and everyone we know will die. We grieve because of our mortality. If Judaism calls upon us to live a holy life, to repair the imperfections of the world, then a death reminds us how imperfect the world really is.

We grieve most of all because so much of our lives that has been interwoven with the one who has died is now brutally torn asunder. A piece of us is lost with each loss. A hole appears, a black hole, which is filled with an overwhelming sorrow. We look for answers but there are none. There is only comfort, memories, and life itself that goes on. You go outside and people are still hurrying to work, birds still sing, the world is the same except for you. For you, the world has changed. It will never be the same and yet it is still the world.

Beyond the ache that tells you how much you miss the deceased is the knowledge that you were together and always will be. For a time you touched hands and hearts. His voice still echoes within you. She is a part of you forever. The love that was, the memories that do not fade, are a gift that can never be lost. For their memories are surely a blessing.

Death as part of the life cycle has two stages in the Jewish view. In the first, until the funeral is over, the deceased is at the center and the mourners are the enablers for the deceased to make sure everything is done appropriately. At this stage, the community's role is only to attend the funeral. In the second stage, after the funeral, the life-cycle event is now focused on the mourners, and the community becomes the enablers and the comforters.

### Kavod ha-Met, Honoring the Dead

When a person dies, her soul, that which made her who she is, that which gave her personality, is gone. Yet Judaism requires a respect for the body that was the container of the soul during its lifetime. Also, death is part of the natural cycle, and therefore a corpse is to be returned to nature. "From dust you are, and to dust you shall return" (Gen. 3:19).

These two principles have led to a number of traditional practices.

*Burial*   Burial should take place as soon as possible. It is considered disrespectful to leave a body unburied. Burial also allows the grieving process to begin so that the mourners are not left in a prolonged limbo. It is permissible to postpone a funeral if it is being done for the sake of the honor of the deceased, that is, to let more people know about it or to allow relatives coming from a distance enough time to arrive.

*The coffin*   A plain pine box is used as the *aron*, "coffin." The term *aron* also means "ark." An analogy is being made between the coffin and both the ark that carried all living things in Noah's time and the ark that holds the Torah scrolls. A Torah scroll and a human being are the two holiest things in the world according to Judaism's system of values. A wooden coffin is used because that will allow the natural process of the return of the body to the earth to take place. A metal coffin would slow down this process and therefore is discouraged. Another principle is operating here as well. In rabbinic times, rich families would dress the corpse in fancy clothes. It became so expensive to keep up with the Jonathans that some people were just abandoning corpses. Rabban Gamliel, a talmudic sage, declared that both the coffin and the clothes should be simple and the same whether for the poor or the rich. For death, equality and simplicity seem appropriate. (In Israel, where the earth itself is considered holy, coffins are not used, rather the covered body is simply wrapped for burial.) Some synagogues have a covering used at all members' funerals, which conceals the coffin (and so makes the choice of casket less significant).

**Takhrihin,** *shrouds*  Traditionally, Jews are buried in plain white shrouds. As mentioned above, it was seen as vanity to think that wealth made any difference in the face of death; therefore everyone was buried in the same garment. (Some people will have other clothing put on over the shroud.) Some place the *tallit* of the deceased on the corpse.

*Closing the coffin*  It is considered part of *kavod ha-met,* "honoring the dead," not to view the corpse. There is a naked defenselessness about a corpse. Also, just as with the practice of prompt burial, not viewing the body is another step in helping mourners move toward accepting the reality of what has happened. There might be a temptation to "hold on" to the body as if that would enable us in some fashion to hold on to the deceased. Rather, the deceased needs to become a memory. The soul and spirit are gone. Earthly remains are just that; they are not really our loved one.

*The* **hevra kaddisha**  *Hevra kaddisha,* "the holy society," is the name for the organization that prepares the body for burial. Since helping to bury the dead is considered an especially praiseworthy *mitzvah* (commandment), the society is called "holy." The *hevra kaddisha* takes care of the ritual preparation of the body. Basically a ritual of *taharah,* "purification" through washing, is performed. There are separate societies for men and women. Recently some liberal synagogues have formed these societies, which had in the past only existed in traditional communities. Ask the funeral home director or your rabbi how to request their services. The funeral home often does not provide a traditional funeral (*hevra kaddisha*, shrouds, and plain pine box) without a direct request.

**Shemirah**    Out of respect for the dead and for the body, the corpse is not left alone, even overnight. *Shemirah*, "watching," is the term used for the process of ensuring that the body is not alone until the funeral. Traditionally psalms are recited by a *shomer*, a "watcher." The *hevra kaddisha* or the funeral home can arrange for *shemirah*. Unlike *taharah*, which requires knowledge of the specific rituals, *shemirah* can be done by friends who desire to express their affection to the deceased in this manner. (The corpse is in a casket during the *shemirah*.)

## The First Stage of Mourning

Traditionally, on hearing of a death, you should say *barukh dayan ha-emet*, "Praised be the True Judge." Even at the moment of death, a Jew is called upon to affirm her belief in God, creator of life and death.

There are a number of steps in the mourning process. While everyone who knew the person who died will grieve, the mourning customs are incumbent upon the immediate relatives. We are to mourn for our parents, siblings, spouse, and children.

**Aninut**    The first stage of mourning is called *aninut*, "bereavement." It encompasses the time from death until burial. It is a time of shock and disbelief; therefore, the tradition exempts the mourners from the standard daily religious obligations related to prayer such as wearing *tefillin* and the act of prayer itself. The tradition recognizes that the mourners will not "have the head" to perform these *mitzvot*. This also allows them to devote their time solely to the arrangements for the funeral.

Planning a funeral is difficult, though for some people it provides a needed focus during this period. If the deceased made plans ahead of time, by discussing what kind of funeral he or she wanted, or by leaving written instructions, the planning process is easier. It is also useful to have a friend who is not so emotionally overwhelmed help with the arrangements. This can be especially helpful when dealing with the funeral home. Other friends can be given your personal address book to contact people to let them know of the death and the time of the funeral.

During this period, the rabbi will visit to gather information from the family for the eulogy and the funeral service.

**Halvayat ha-met,** *accompanying the deceased* It is considered a great *mitzvah* to accompany the dead on the final journey back to the earth. It is considered a mark of love and respect. In ancient times (when communities were smaller), the whole community would stop working to accompany the dead.

*The funeral service* The funeral service, as mentioned, takes place as soon as possible. The service is simple and brief. It includes the recitation of a psalm or two; an appropriate reading; the *hesped*, "eulogy"; and *el maleh rahamim,* "the memorial prayer."

The immediate family usually arrives forty-five minutes to an hour before the funeral. Customs vary about what takes place before the service. One custom is for the mourners to sit in a reception area rather than where the service itself will take place. As friends arrive they sign a booklet that is later given to the mourners (often the mourners are in a daze and are unsure of who was present). If friends arrive early they will stop to see the mourners. People should simply shake hands or hug the mourners, express brief condolences, and then go to the chapel for the service. Right before the service begins, everyone will be asked to proceed directly to the chapel, leaving the family alone in the reception room. (Funerals start promptly.)

**Keriah** Traditionally, the mourner tears an article of clothing, either upon hearing of the death, immediately before the funeral, or at the cemetery. This is called *keriah,* the Hebrew word for "tearing." Most commonly today it is done right before the funeral service begins.

The mourners stand and recite the blessing: *Barukh atah adonai eloheinu melekh ha-olam dayan ha-emet,* "Praised are You, Eternal One, our God, source of the universe, the True Judge." The mourner then tears the garment. Usually the garment is a shirt, a blouse, or a sport jacket, and the tear is made near the lapel. Some people will tear a tie or scarf. The initial cut is made by a razor or knife (the funeral director has one) and then the mourner should extend the tear by pulling at the two sides. The garment is torn on the left side for a parent, on the right side for all other relatives.

There are a number of other physical acts and sounds that are part of the mourning ritual. The act of tearing a garment clearly expresses the inner tearing that the mourner is experiencing. The heart, as it were, is exposed. Wearing the garment later during the *shivah*, the seven days of mourning, reminds both the mourner and anyone who sees her of her status as a mourner. It starkly states that outer appearances are unimportant in the face of death.

A more recent custom is the wearing of a black ribbon or performing *keriah* on a black ribbon. While capturing some of the symbolism of the traditional *keriah*, some people feel it lacks the personal connection that gives the ritual of *keriah* its power.

*The service*    After *keriah*, the family enters the chapel as everyone stands. After introductory remarks, readings, or psalms, the person officiating will give the *hesped*, "eulogy." Often this is a rabbi, though anyone can give the eulogy (or, for that matter, lead the funeral service). Sometimes a number of friends or relatives will speak, in addition to or in place of a rabbi. The eulogy should try to capture what was special and characteristic of the person who died. While it may be tied into that week's Torah portion, or speak of Jewish attitudes toward death and grief, good eulogies will make vivid the character and life of the deceased. They will present a picture of the whole person, including her faults, while stressing her good qualities. A good eulogy should make those who didn't know the deceased wish they had.

The service concludes as everyone rises for *el maleh rahamim* (named for its first three words, "God, full of mercy"). This is the memorial prayer that asks that the soul of the deceased be bound up in the bonds of life and come to rest in peace. Following informational announcements about the burial, *shivah*, and/or donations to *tzedakah*, the pallbearers either carry or accompany the coffin to the hearse. Customs vary whether the mourners precede or follow the casket. Friends can again briefly greet and console the mourners before they enter the cars that will take them to the burial. (As the funeral parlor will tell you, it has become standard for mourners to use a limousine. Obviously there is no Jewish requirement to do so. On the other hand, it should be equally obvious that an immediate mourner should not be driving.)

*Burial*    The service at the cemetery is brief. Though many state laws now require or encourage cemetery workers to carry the casket from the hearse and lower it into the grave, traditionally mourners and friends did this. The pallbearers sometimes carry the casket from the hearse to the grave. (Some cemeteries require the pallbearers to sign a waiver for injury insurance claims. This should be done upon arrival at the cemetery, at its office.) In traditional communities there is a custom to pause seven times on the way to the grave while reciting Psalm 91. One interpretation of this custom is to show a reluctance to say good-bye to the deceased.

The coffin is lowered into the grave, sometimes with the aid of a mechanical device. Of the various tasks during the burial, this is the one most frequently done by the cemetery workers, because it needs to be done carefully. A recent practice is to lower the casket and cover the grave with a grass cover before the mourners walk to the grave. This seems an unnecessary attempt to mask what is happening—a burial. Life is not all green.

After being lowered, the casket is covered with earth. Everyone who wishes should place a shovelful of earth into the grave. It is the final sign of love and respect and a last act of service for the deceased. The sound of the earth hitting the casket is one of the powerfully affecting sounds of the funeral service. There is a custom that the first person to put earth into the grave turns the shovel upside down to pick up the first earth. This is both an expression of reluctance to accept this reality and a metaphor for their world being turned upside down.

(Traditionally, those attending the burial fill in the whole grave. However, it is hard work and takes a fair amount of time, and can be emotionally difficult for the mourners. Therefore, some have the custom of putting in only enough earth to cover the casket. Others put in as many shovelfuls as people want and then stop. In either case, the cemetery workers will finish filling in the grave after the burial service.)

In very traditional services, a long prayer called *tzidduk ha-din,* "a justification of the heavenly decree," is recited. At most funerals this is not said, but rather a reading or short prayer such as Psalm 23 is recited. The *el maleh,* memorial prayer, and the recital of *kaddish* often follow this. For mourners this is the first time they recite *kaddish,* a prayer associated with mourning. The *kaddish* is a prayer that praises God and nowhere mentions death or mourning. Yet, over time, it has become the central ritual associated with mourning. *Kaddish* has a number of versions (see *"Avodah:* The Path of Prayer," pp. 176–205); this one is called *kaddish yatom,* "the mourner's *kaddish*" (literally, "the orphan's *kaddish*"). The mourner's *kaddish* is usually not recited at the funeral service at the chapel unless there is a concern there won't be a *minyan,* a quorum of ten, at the cemetery. (There is another version of the *kaddish* specifically for recital at the burial, but since its additional words are less familiar, many people recite the mourner's *kaddish* instead.)

There is a custom of ending the burial service by having everyone (except the mourners) form two rows, an effort to make mourners feel supported and embraced. The mourners pass between the two rows. People can offer condolences, or a comforting touch or glance, or recite the traditional expression "May you be comforted among the other mourners of Zion and Jerusalem." This custom helps the mourners leave the grave and head back to the car, and also symbolizes the shift in focus. During the funeral the focus has been primarily on the deceased; now the focus shifts to the mourners.

A recent notion has arisen that only relatives and close friends should go to the cemetery. Traditionally, everyone would go to both the service and the cemetery. Nowadays, some cemeteries are a fair distance away and more difficult for many people to travel to. People will make their own judgments whether to go or not. However, people should not feel that they are intruding by going to the cemetery unless the family specifically requests a private burial.

Some people wash their hands upon leaving a cemetery. Some cemeteries have an outdoor faucet near their entrance. Other people will wash their hands before entering their homes or the house of *shivah*. This custom is a remnant of biblical laws of *tum'ah*, "impurity." Contact with the dead was a primary source of impurity in the Bible and required rites of purification. Nowadays the laws of impurity are no longer observed, but the custom of hand washing enables us to mark the transition from a place of death back into the world of life.

*Cremation*    Death is seen as part of the natural process of life. Therefore, the tradition not only advocates wooden rather than metal caskets but also opposes cremation. The tradition maintains that the body should naturally decompose. Many rabbis will not officiate at a cremation and some cemeteries will not allow the burial of the ashes. Some rabbis will officiate at a funeral service if the cremation takes place after the service.

*Embalming and autopsies*    The body should be left in its natural state. Embalming is not allowed (except in unusual circumstances). Traditionally, an autopsy is considered a violation of respect for the body. Therefore, autopsies are to be avoided unless (1) required by law when the cause of death is unclear or (2) a doctor maintains that new medical knowledge might be acquired that could help future patients. In North America, autopsies are often routinely performed, partly to give medical students an opportunity to learn about the human body. Some states allow families to refuse autopsies for religious reasons in most situations. Organ transplants that will be of benefit to other human beings are a *mitzvah* and in a different way *kavod ha-met*, "respectful of the dead."

*Flowers*    While some rabbinic traditions allow for flowers at funerals (see Talmud, *Berakhot* 53a, *Bava Kamma* 16b), the contemporary traditional practice in North America is to discourage their use at funerals. This lack of flowers reflects the themes of simplicity and starkness at the funeral. Some rabbinic opposition to flowers seems to have been based on flowers' being an imitation of Christian funeral practice.

Flowers are commonly used in funerals in Israel. Many families encourage people to donate to the deceased's favorite charity in lieu of sending flowers.

## The Second Stage of Mourning

**Shivah**    Once the burial service is over, a new period begins with *shivah*, the traditional "seven" days of mourning. The focus shifts; the mourners are now placed center stage. The tradition recognizes that grief takes place in stages and encompasses many deep emotional feelings. These include not only grief but also anger, guilt, despair, and even relief. *Shivah* is time set aside for the mourners to experience and express all those feelings. The mourners begin to move past the initial shock of the death with all the feelings of disbelief. Reality begins to set in, but a reality that is too painful to be believable at times.

The tradition has created this time for the mourners, and the community is called upon to help make this experience possible. The community is asked to take care of the mourners' needs, especially preparing meals for them. The community is also asked to be a comforting presence during the *shivah*. But the style, tone, and emotional ups and downs of those seven days are to be set by the mourners. Traditionally, you enter a house of *shivah* in silence and sit down in the room with the mourners. You wait for the mourner to begin the conversation. Many people feel awkward during a *shivah* visit and struggle for appropriate words of comfort. Yet the wisdom of the tradition is to ask us to focus not on our awkwardness but on what the mourners need. Silence, crying, expressions of grief, laughter, sharing of fond memories, the repetition over and over again of how the death occurred, and talking about everything else but what has happened, will all occur at a *shivah* as the mood or needs of the mourners change.

*Shivah* can sometimes be a challenge for a mourner who is accustomed to acting as a host or hostess. During *shivah*, lots of people will visit your home, but you are not supposed to focus on their comfort. (Traditionally, you do not offer them food or act in any regular hostly manner.) As a mourner, your concern is focused inward. It can be difficult for those who are used to being caregivers to accept being cared for. *Shivah* is an extraordinary time created to deal with extraordinary circumstances. As a mourner, you should allow yourself this time just to be present to all the feelings that will inevitably arise.

What follows is a description of the laws and customs regarding mourning, yet it should be noted that each situation is unique. Each mourner will respond to a death based on their own emotional makeup and relationship with the deceased. Some deaths are more tragic than others. In some there was a long painful illness or a period when the person was no longer really aware of their family. There can be feelings both of relief and of guilt for those emotions. There can also be a sense that the mourning has already taken place.

You can experience guilt for not having done enough or not being there at the end or having had a recent disagreement with the deceased or because you are alive and they are not. You can also feel guilty for making a decision to terminate extraordinary care or for not making that decision. You can experience anger at them for abandoning you, or at the doctors for not having done enough, or at a relative for not coming through, or at God for causing or allowing this happen. You can experience depression at your loss or because you have come to acknowledge your own mortality by staring death in the face.

This is a period of great emotional stress, and mourners will sometimes direct these feelings at one another. Old competitions between siblings might be reawakened. People will compete in the "best child" contest or the "who suffered most" contest. The opposite also happens. People who have been at odds sometimes reconcile when they perceive the pettiness of their differences in the face of death and loss.

The Jewish mourning ritual does not resolve all of these feelings and tensions. It could be argued that a traditional *shivah* could exacerbate tensions by keeping all the mourners together in tight quarters for seven days. On the other hand, it does gently force the mourners to face this process with each other and with all the people who come to visit them. Otherwise certainly some people would retreat into a bleak solitude and either try to deal with this all on their own or make strenuous efforts to ignore what has happened. In general, there is much wisdom, health, and healing in the mourning practices. *Shivah* does create both a space and a structure to allow for and call forth both grieving and comfort. Being confronted with a steady stream of visitors, though at times overwhelming, provides both you and the visitors an opportunity to share memories of the deceased. The visitors assure you that you are not alone in your grief and loss. They provide what may be the only comfort possible, the love and concern of friends and community. Facing death, the living join together in affirming life. Facing death, we humans huddle together, giving warmth to one another to keep out the cold of the surrounding night.

**Shivah** *laws and customs*    Upon returning from the cemetery, as mentioned, there is a custom of washing your hands before entering the house. Once home, the special candle for *shivah* should be lit. (The funeral home will provide one.) Candles are seen as symbols of the soul because of the verse "The light of God is the soul of a human" (Prov. 20:27). The candle will burn for all of *shivah*. There is no blessing said for lighting this candle.

The meal eaten upon return from the cemetery is called *seudat havra'ah*, "the meal of consolation." Often friends prepare the meal while the burial is taking place. There is a tradition of serving hard-boiled eggs as part of this meal. One interpretation is that eggs have no mouth and thus are like the mourner silenced by grief. Another is that the roundness of the egg symbolizes the unending cycle of life and death. Friends may also prepare the home for the *shivah* by putting a pitcher outside the door for washing and by covering the mirrors.

Covering the mirrors is an old custom. One explanation of it cites an old folk belief that the departing soul might be trapped if it looked in a mirror. Another is that during *shivah*, a mourning period, there is no need to be concerned about how you look to the world.

Traditionally, the mourners remain at home during the *shivah* period. The effect of this is to keep the mourner within a world of mourning. It can be disconcerting to go out into the world and be greeted with "Have a nice day!" by people who are unaware of your loss. Since the reciting of the mourner's *kaddish* begins with the burial, a *minyan* for morning and evening services is sometimes held at the *shivah* house so *kaddish* can be said. As a symbol of the low state of feelings, mourners sit on low chairs or on "boxes" (provided by the funeral home). Since leather shoes were traditionally considered a luxury, slippers or sneakers are worn instead. As mentioned, friends prepare meals for mourners. Mourners continue to wear the torn garment or black ribbon from *keriah*. They do not cut their hair or shave.

During the Shabbat of *shivah* the public observance of mourning is suspended. Friends do not pay *shivah* calls. Mourners sit on regular chairs and are allowed to go out to attend synagogue services. The ribbon or cut clothing is not worn. (No *shivah minyan* is held during Shabbat.) However, Shabbat still counts as one of the seven days of *shivah*. (In some traditional synagogues, mourners are formally greeted during the Friday night service.)

*Shivah* ends on the morning of the seventh day. The day of the funeral counts as the first day of *shivah,* so if the funeral takes place on Thursday, *shivah* concludes Wednesday morning following the morning service or the equivalent time.

Mourners conclude *shivah* by taking a walk "around the block." This symbolizes their reentry into the world, since it is the first time they have gone out (except for Shabbat) during *shivah*. Upon returning, the *shivah* ceases, including all its rituals.

Our description so far is that of a traditional *shivah*. There are many people who observe *shivah* differently. Some do not observe *shivah* for all seven days—a frequently used alternative is three days, which has some basis in rabbinic tradition. Some will observe *shivah* (or at least encourage visitors) only during certain hours, such as the evening. Others will observe only a day or just an evening of *shivah*. While everyone will make their own determination of what is right for them, I would urge you to err on the side of more time for *shivah,* no matter how private a person you may be. It can be helpful not only to you but to people who knew the deceased and want to mourn as well. There was an elderly man in my congregation who had no close relatives. He was someone toward whom I felt fondly as well as grateful for his generosity to the synagogue, though we were not close. When he died, his business associates neglected to notify the synagogue. We found out weeks later. Those of us who knew him felt cheated of the opportunity to say good-bye to him at his funeral and mourn his passing. As the immediate mourner, your needs come first, but you should understand that other people also want to mourn even if it is on a very different level of intensity. As much as the *shivah* is for the mourners, it is also a structured way for anyone who knew the deceased to mourn as well.

Some people will begin the *shivah* at the home of the deceased, but then want to return to their own home in their local community to share the loss with their friends. A practical suggestion: transporting a lit *shivah* candle is not a good idea, but people feel uncomfortable about blowing it out and relighting it. Ask the funeral home for an extra candle that you can take with you when you return home mid-week and light the new candle when you reach your house.

Not everyone observes all the traditional *shivah* rules. Some people will sit on regular chairs or will go outside during *shivah*. Despite the fact that it is only a custom, many people cover the mirrors.

**Menaheim aveilim,** *comforting the mourners*    It is an important deed of loving-kindness to pay a *shivah* call. Your role is to comfort the mourners. This seemingly impossible task is accomplished simply by your presence. It is not by saying some magic words that will ease the mourners' pain. To be surrounded by friends and family enables the mourner to feel connected to the web of life despite feelings of grief. Your presence, your physical touch, the sympathetic expression on your face, will make a difference. Unfortunately, we sometimes say the wrong things out of awkwardness or a desire to be helpful. Comments such as "Everybody has to die sometime," "Well, he was ninety-two," "Time heals all wounds," or "I know how you feel because I went through this when my mother died" may be partly true, but they are of little comfort to the mourners. Their world is destroyed; the fact that everybody dies is irrelevant to them. Someone mourning the death of her mother does not really care about all the other people who have lost their mothers. Such statements are only helpful if the mourner feels that they are true. If the mourner feels the deceased lived a long life or went quickly without pain, etc., then you can echo back those sentiments. Otherwise it is possible that the mourner feels the opposite. "My father was ninety-two but he still had many good years to live."

What should visitors say? You should be sympathetic. "This must be so hard." "I feel so sorry for you." "Is there anything I can do?" You want to affirm the mourners' feelings rather than appear to deny them by minimizing the loss. Visitors should contradict the mourners only, for example, when the mourners are feeling unreasonably guilty for not having done enough for the deceased. Share stories about the deceased if you knew him or her. If true, remind the mourners how much the deceased loved them. Remember, it is your presence that brings some comfort in a situation where ultimately there can be no complete comfort.

The length of your visit depends on your relationship to the family, the number of mourners present, and the cues given out by the mourners. An average visit is no more than an hour. While it is a traditional custom to say, "May you be comforted among the other mourners of Zion and Jerusalem," upon leaving, many people say good-bye using their own words. Visitors show themselves to the door.

**Sheloshim**　The next stage of mourning is the *sheloshim,* the "thirty"-day period. It is actually only twenty-three days, since the *shivah* counts as the first seven days. Basically, the mourner's life returns to its normal routine, such as going back to work. *Kaddish* is still recited. Traditionally, mourners will not attend celebratory events like parties or weddings during *sheloshim,* especially if there is likely to be live music and dancing. Some traditional Jews continue not to shave or get a haircut. *Sheloshim* ends on the morning of the thirtieth day. For all relatives, except in the case of the death of a parent, the ritual of mourning, including the saying of *kaddish,* is over.

*The year*　When a parent dies, the mourning practices of *sheloshim* continue for a year. Traditionally, you do not attend celebratory events. You continue to recite *kaddish.* The custom has developed of saying *kaddish* only for eleven months, not twelve. There is a tradition that the deceased go to a purgatory to cleanse themselves of their sins. The holier you are, the less time this takes. The maximum amount of time in purgatory is a year. Thus to say *kaddish* for a year implies your parent needed a whole year to be purified. Whatever its origin, saying *kaddish* for eleven months has become the widespread practice. Observing it means that we experience nearly a complete year's cycle for the first time without our loved one. Jewish holidays, secular family holidays, or birthdays are all particular markers of the loss.

Why are the mourning practices longer for parents than for a spouse or any other relative? The tradition does not give a reason, but it can be surmised that it is an acknowledgment of all that parents have given to you and another reflection of the ideal of "honoring your father and mother."

*Unveilings*   The unveiling of the gravestone is a recent ritual; therefore, it has no real traditions attached to it. Many people do it around the first anniversary of the death, but it can be done earlier or later. There is no set liturgy and many rabbis now encourage families to do the unveilings on their own. A typical unveiling could include a Psalm or two, a brief sharing by those present, and the recital of the *el maleh* memorial prayer. Only family members and sometimes close friends attend an unveiling.

*Yahrzeit and Yizkor*   The anniversary of the death (not the funeral) is known as the *yahrzeit* (from the German for "year time"). It is customary to light a candle that burns for twenty-four hours (commonly known as a *yahrzeit* candle). It is also customary to recite *kaddish* on that day. If the Torah is read on that day, it is customary to ask for an *aliyah* and have *el maleh*, the memorial prayer, recited. In many synagogues you can also do this on the Shabbat preceding the *yahrzeit*. Some traditional Jews fast on a *yahrzeit*. *Yahrzeit* is observed every year.

Yizkor (from the word for "remembrance") is the communal memorial service that is said on Yom Kippur and on the final day of festivals—Pesah, Shavuot, and Sukkot. (In the case of Sukkot, Shemini Atzeret is considered the final day.) It is an opportunity for the community to remember all of our deceased loved ones. While some have the custom not to say Yizkor during the first year after a death, you can say Yizkor as soon after the death as you want.

*Festivals and mourning*   It should be noted that festival days (*yom tov* days) bring to an end *shivah* or *sheloshim*. The rules about this are complicated, and you should consult with your rabbi for guidance. If a funeral takes place during *hol ha-moed,* the intermediate festival days, *shivah* begins only after the festival is over.

*Non-Jewish relatives*    If your parent is not Jewish, you can still recite *kaddish* and observe mourning practices. In fact, *kaddish* can be said for anyone you feel very close to. For example, the Talmud tells of students saying *kaddish* for their teachers.

*Suicides*    According to the tradition, suicides cannot be buried in the regular part of a Jewish cemetery. This is because suicide is seen as a terrible violation of the sanctity of life. Contemporary practice diverges from this and allows such burials to be treated regularly. This is based on a better understanding of and sympathy for what might cause someone to commit suicide. Technically, it is justified by the principle that a person can only be punished for something done through an act of free will. This would not apply to someone who is "driven to suicide."

*Abusive parents*    While the tradition strongly encourages the honoring of parents, it recognizes that in extreme cases parents can forfeit that honor because of behavior such as sexually abusing their child. As mentioned earlier, there are halakhic opinions that a child does not have to say *kaddish* for such parents. Consult with your rabbi.

## Life After Death

Judaism has a number of beliefs about life after death. Scholars maintain that there is little evidence of an elaborate notion of life after death in the Bible. There only seems to be a vague notion of a shadowy underworld known as Sheol. By the rabbinic period, a complete doctrine of life after death is developed, in part as an explanation for the suffering of the righteous and the prosperity of the wicked in this world. The rabbis answer that everything is set right in the world to come. The righteous are rewarded and feast and study with God. The wicked are punished in hell. Accompanying this belief was a notion of a messianic era, when Israel would be restored to its land. There would come a time of peace when the lion and the lamb would lie down together. This notion was based in part on some of the prophetic visions for the end of days. Added to this notion was a belief in the resurrection of the dead. In the end of days, all the righteous would be brought back to life by God to live forever in this messianic time. Among some mystics there was even a belief in some form of reincarnation. Different rabbinic teachers stressed different aspects of these notions over time. Some downplayed the supernatural elements; others elaborated on the details of the afterlife and the end of days. In modern times these notions have not been as central to Jewish thought.

The scientific rationalism of the modern world has been a challenge not only to the belief in the resurrection of the dead but to all the beliefs connected to life after death. Future salvation has receded as the reason to be Jewish. Instead, emphasis has been placed on living a moral life in this world. Still, there is a range of beliefs about the afterlife, from its nonexistence to some version of the traditional view. In between, some people believe that while the deceased are no longer individuals with individual consciousness, the souls of those who have died become part of a universal human consciousness or become once again part of the Divine "soul" that encompasses everything.

### Facing Your Own Death

For some of us, death will catch us unawares. For others, we will hear its footsteps long before it comes to our door. For those who will have time to prepare for death, what should be done? Whatever your belief about afterlife, death is a potentially terrifying journey into the unknown. Frankly, it is with some hesitation that I talk about what might be done to prepare because I have not faced it myself. Yet, with that acknowledgment, let me share some wisdom that I have gleaned from the tradition and experience.

There is a tradition of saying *vidui,* the "confessional" (usually associated with the High Holidays) in the moments before death. Hearing a final prognosis often gives a person a great deal of clarity. Suddenly, many things that seemed important become trivial. Old hurts and feuds in the valley of the shadow of death seem petty and pointless. It often becomes clear what needs to be done and said in the time remaining. Perhaps it is repairing broken relationships or ensuring that family and friends know the love you have for them that too often remains unexpressed. In the face of death, we move beyond assuming that people know how we feel about them to making sure they know how we feel. Letters can be written to be read after we are gone. There are of course practical things that can be done to make the "afterward" simpler for the survivors. Even more important are the nonpractical things that you can do.

If you have family, what can you do to ensure that your death or your inheritance does not become a divisive experience for your family? Would not Jacob have done his family a service by gathering all his sons together before his death to ensure that the brothers understood that Joseph was not interested in revenge after he was gone? What can be repaired? What bad feeling will be taken with you to the grave instead of left behind? What questions can be answered about what you said in your will while you can still answer them? How can you make clear that you love your family members equally and in your mind the vase for Susie and the chair for George are of equal worth? Which of your possessions have no particular meaning so that your family can dispose of them if they so choose without feeling guilty?

One of the challenges in facing death is to move beyond seeing it as a clever enemy out to get you, to move past a superstitious notion that to say the word out loud is to invoke it. Death, while in many ways the enemy of all we hold dear, is also part of the natural rhythm of life. Death does come to us all. We are not to welcome it, but we do need to face it. How? By talking without hesitation about our preferences for our funerals. By making a will and telling family members where it will be. By not pretending it is still far away and therefore not doing and saying what needs to be done and said.

There is a tradition of writing an ethical will that gives expression to what you would like your legacy to be. What are the values you want to encourage? What is the wisdom that you want to leave behind? What are the important stories of your life or people that you want to be remembered? What are the regrets and mistakes? What are your possessions that have significance because of what they mean to you? What are causes or charities that you would like to be supported after your death? Wonderful examples of such wills that date from the Middles Ages to contemporary times are found in *So That Your Values Live On: Ethical Wills and How to Prepare Them,* edited by Jack Riemer and Nathaniel Stampfer (Jewish Lights, 1991). Like a regular will, it makes sense to write an ethical will long before it is obviously necessary.

Ultimately facing death involves coming to terms with your life. It means realizing that despite your failures, you tried and often succeeded in doing the best you could. It means trying to enjoy the moments, no matter how few, with loved ones or just with life itself that you still have. It really is a time to see the glass as half full rather than half empty. It is a time to have faith—faith in yourself and faith in the One who waits to embrace you on the other side.

## A CONCLUDING TEACHING

> Abraham was now old, advanced in years, and the Lord blessed Abraham *ba-kol*, in all things. [Gen. 24:1]

What does it mean to be blessed "in all things," *ba-kol*? After all, Abraham's life, like that of all human beings, was filled with triumph and tragedy. Sarah has just died. Why now is Abraham described as being blessed in all things?

Let me suggest that to describe Abraham as blessed with the aspect of *ba-kol* is a reflection of the spiritual greatness of Abraham. Despite everything that had happened to him in life, he experienced his life as full with blessings. Abraham is the person of faith who is willing to leave everything behind to journey to an unknown land. It is his faith in God that carries him throughout his life and brings to him, near the end of that life, a sense of years well lived and a life blessed with everything.

Can each of us achieve that same sense of blessing? Perhaps, but it is a very difficult spiritual state to attain. Instead, we are to strive for the spiritual state encapsulated in the Hebrew word *emet,* "truth." Psalm 145:18 (the *ashrei* prayer) says, "God is near to all that call upon God, to all that call upon God in truth *(emet).* What does it mean to call upon God in *emet,* thus enabling us to come close to God?

The word *emet* is made up of three letters: *aleph, mem,* and *tav.* If you take away the *aleph,* which, as the first letter of the first word of the Ten Commandments, *anokhi,* "I," stands for God, you are left with the word *met,* meaning "death." If you take away the last letter, *tav,* which stands for Torah, you are left with the word *im,* meaning "if." Without one you are left without God, without the other you are left with a world that is conditional. Everything is "if," there are no rules, no set definitions. *Emet* then, as truth, encompasses everything from A to Z, from *aleph* to *tav,* the whole Hebrew alphabet. Truth is all-inclusive.

When we come to pray to God, we need to come in truth. The truth about ourselves is everything. Sometimes we bring forth only the good parts of ourselves. Other times all we can focus on is how terrible we are, how much a failure. Yet the truth about us is not just the extremes; it is everything. It is both what we proudly display and what we try to hide in the shadows. It is not just the extremes; it is the extremes plus everything in between. The everything in between is represented by the other letter of *emet,* the letter *mem.* All together they make up *emet,* the truth. When we can perceive clearly who we are in all our complexity, then we can come close to God through that truth.

To make this explanation of the word *emet* perfect then, the letter *mem* should be the middle letter of the Hebrew alphabet. *Mem* then could say that truth is found when we come to the exact middle point of our selves. To find truth, then, would mean to be completely balanced. To achieve Maimonides' ideal of the golden mean of not being too generous or too stingy but rather being perfectly balanced.

But *mem* is not the middle letter. *Mem,* then, as it were, tells us that we need to strive for balance and the clarity that comes with it, but most of us will not achieve it. At best, we will reach the letter *mem,* which is close to the middle of the alphabet. So *Emet* is not a perfect truth but an imperfect truth about ourselves.

What is the middle letter of the Hebrew alphabet? Since the alphabet has twenty-two letters, it actually has two middle letters, *khaf* and *lamed,* the two letters that make up the word *kol,* everything. Thus we have returned to our starting point.

Abraham at the end of his life has achieved the blessing of *ba-kol,* of everything. His whole life is framed by the letters of *lamed* and *khaf.* At the beginning with those two letters he is told *lekh lekha,* "go forth"; at the end of his life these two letters are reversed, so he is blessed with *kol,* "everything." The blessing of *ba-kol* means that Abraham has achieved a clarity of vision to see all of life as a blessing from God. He has attained the golden mean; thus he has "everything." He has an equanimity about life. For us, who may never achieve that level, we strive for a coming close to God in truth. A truth that validates who we are in both our failures and our successes. Yet even as we come close to God, we desire to move beyond the acceptance of our present flawed reality and strive to be one of the children of Abraham. We seek nothing less than to be blessed with *ba-kol.* Then, like Abraham, we too "shall be a blessing . . . and all the families of the earth shall bless themselves by you."

Part Five

# AFTER DEUTERONOMY: LIVING IN THE PROMISED LAND

# ISRAEL:

# TOWARD A TORAH OF ZION

Most attempts to define our relationship to Israel have rested on the ever-changing shoulders of the political situation. Without negating the importance of politics, let me posit another model—a religious metaphor for the ways Jews might relate to Israel. This model would serve no matter what political party was in power in the State of Israel and even if a final peace agreement was reached between Israel and her neighbors, and even if harmony existed between the various denominations of Judaism. Ultimately, our relationship to Israel is religious in nature, not political or nationalistic. What is needed is a new religious Zionism that would affect both Zionism and Judaism.

This new Zionism would reflect the beliefs of those for whom the Diaspora is a permanent reality. This Zionism would recognize that *galut*—the spiritual alienation of the Jewish people—is a condition that exists everywhere, even in Israel. Yet even after affirming a Jewish life in the Diaspora, we still must face the question: What of Israel? Is there no difference between living in Boro Park or Des Moines and living in Jerusalem? Do the phrases *Eretz Yisrael, Zion,* and *If I forget you, O Jerusalem* have no special meaning to us?

The challenge, then, is to create a metaphor that takes into account both the Diaspora and Israel, a metaphor that posits both as being of equal importance and yet different. The struggle is to speak of two centers, of two paths, or two Torahs, without implying even subtly the superiority of one over the other. The answer to this challenge is hinted at by a strange phrase we chant when we take the Torah from the ark: *Ki mi-tzion teitze Torah . . . ,* "For out of Zion shall go forth the

467

Torah, and the word of God from Jerusalem." Doesn't Torah come from Sinai? What is this Torah from Zion? This verse points us to the metaphor of two Torahs. The symbols for these two Torahs are the two mountains in Judaism, each a center of religious experience and revelation: Mount Sinai and Mount Moriah (or more simply, Sinai and Jerusalem).

## Mount Sinai

Mount Sinai represents for us 2,500 years of Diaspora Judaism. The Revelation at Sinai is the single most important event in the history of the Jewish people. Yet the establishment of the covenant between the Jewish people and God took place at Sinai, outside the land of Israel. Sinai, then, serves as a reminder that the experience of exile predates the establishment of the first Jewish state.

According to tradition, three revelations took place at Sinai. The first involved Moses at the burning bush. The bush that burns and is not consumed is a multilevel symbol of Diaspora Judaism. The bush has been interpreted to represent: (1) God who suffers with us in exile: *Bekhol tzoratam lo tzaar,* meaning "In all their sufferings, God suffers" (Isa. 63:9). Even at our lowest moments, as symbolized by the humble bush, God is with us. (2) God is everywhere, even in the most humble bush, and not just in one particular mountain or country. The bush was chosen because it was in a *makom hefker,* "a place without any owner," therefore freely available to anyone who would turn aside to seek it. (3) Finally, God is revealed through *shalom,* "peace," that is, through the living together in harmony of two different, seemingly antagonistic entities. The fire and the bush exist together, yet neither is consumed. Until the Jews are accepted throughout the Diaspora and are no longer seen as alien, even in Israel, Jews are not safe. Fire and bush, Jew and Gentile, and all other disharmonies must coexist in peace for God to be revealed.

The second revelation at Sinai was of the Torah, the climactic experience of the Jewish people. Sinai proclaims that the covenant between God and Israel is expressed in Torah. The Jew lives in the *daled amot shel halakhah,* "the four cubits of Jewish law," which have served as the portable home of Jews everywhere—even in Israel. All of us stood at Sinai so that each of us heard that revelation, each in her or his own way. The struggle to understand that Torah and to make it our Torah has been the occupation of Jews for centuries.

The third and least well known revelation at Sinai is that of Elijah (1 Kings 19). After his dramatic defeat of the prophets of Baal on Mount Carmel, Elijah, threatened by King Ahab, flees to the desert. God tells Elijah to stand upon the mountain. Then the Torah says:

> And behold, God passed by, and a great and strong wind rent the mountains, and broke in pieces the rocks before God, but God was not in the wind; and after the wind an earthquake, but God was not in the earthquake, and after the earthquake a fire; and after the fire a still small voice.

This too is the revelation at Sinai. No longer the trumpets and thunder of the revelation to the whole people, but rather the still small voice piercing all the noise and confusion to reassure the lonely person of faith. It is this revelation to the individual, obtainable by each of us on rare occasions, that is also part of the metaphor of Sinai.

Thus Sinai comes to represent the suffering of the Jewish people and of God in exile. It stresses the necessity for the acceptance of the Jewish otherness by the nations. It bespeaks a revelation of humbleness, of the quiet revelation to the individual, of a revelation free to all who seek it. Foremost, Sinai is the revelation of the Torah, a setting out of how the individual should live in and help create *darkhei ha-shem,* "God's ways."

## Jerusalem

Two sets of symbols are associated with the other holy place of Judaism, with Jerusalem.

The first set is that of the *akedah,* "the sacrifice of Isaac," by Abraham on Mount Moriah, traditionally identified with the Temple Mount in Jerusalem. The *akedah* stands for sacrifice—the willingness of Abraham to sacrifice his son, and the willingness of Isaac to be sacrificed.

The second set is associated with Jerusalem as the City of David. Its eternity is linked with that of the Davidic dynasty, and thus, Jerusalem represents political sovereignty. With all the ambivalence that the tradition carries toward kings in general, and to the kings who succeeded David in particular, Jerusalem remains the City of David, a symbol of Jewish independence.

But Jerusalem is also the site of the Temple, God's dwelling place. It is a place of magnificent splendor and grandeur, reflecting God's greatness and power. Most of all, for almost the last two thousand years, Jerusalem has symbolized the messianic future. Its very name contains the word *shalom*—denoting completeness and peace. In that future, the Davidic line will be restored and the Temple will be called "a house of prayer for all peoples."

For in that messianic time we will see the fulfillment of the verse *Ki mi-tzion teitze torah . . . ,* "For out of Zion shall go forth the Torah, and the word of God from Jerusalem." This verse, recited during services, is taken from the prophets Isaiah and Micah. Both of them place it in the context of their visions of the future redemption.

> It shall come to pass in the latter days that the mountain of the house of God shall be established as the highest of the mountains, and shall be raised up among the hills; and peoples shall flow to it, and many nations shall come and say: "Come, let us go up to the mountain of Adonai to the house of the God of Jacob; that God may teach us God's ways and we may walk in God's paths." *For out of Zion shall go forth the law, and the word of God from Jerusalem.* God shall judge between many peoples, and shall decide for strong nations afar off. They shall beat their swords into plowshares and their spears into pruning hooks, nation shall not lift up sword against nation, neither shall they learn war any more; but they shall sit every person under her vine and under his fig tree, and none shall make them afraid. [Micah 4:1–4, see also Isa. 2:3ff]

This is the dream of Jerusalem. *This is the Torah of Zion*—a Torah of sovereignty and of peace, a Torah that encompasses all the nations of the world and as such is no longer just the Torah of the Jews. Jerusalem, then, emphasizes a physical place. It symbolizes independence and sovereignty. It stands for supreme sacrifice. But most of all, it is the metaphor for the messianic future.

## Sinai and Jerusalem

Each of these Torahs, the Torah of Sinai and the Torah of Jerusalem, has its strengths and dangers, and each requires the other for completion.

The great sin of the land of Israel, as proclaimed by the prophets, is that of idolatry. There is a temptation to think that other gods, objects, or the land itself are to be worshiped. Boundaries become walls marking the end of our domain, our concern, and our God. Ownership becomes everything. The other temptation is to think that in the sword rests salvation, to trust in the slender reed of foreign alliances or one's own power rather than in the Almighty.

The great sin of the Diaspora is idolatry of the self. Here it is easy to believe that feelings and thoughts are everything, materialness is nothing. We easily drift into realms constructed solely out of ideas, where animals fall into pits and one ox gores another, where castles float on air until a catastrophe brings them crashing down.

Thus the Diaspora can revel in the ethereal—revel in powerlessness. Israel can revel in earth and blood—revel in power.

The Diaspora strives to establish an eternity in time. Shabbat comes to free us from the prisons of time that we have created, to release us into a period of timelessness. Israel, on the other hand, tries to create an eternity in space. Jerusalem comes to free us from the prisons of space because it cannot really be owned. The Temple was built on land belonging to two tribes, not one; and therefore it symbolically belonged to all the tribes. Those who served the Temple were the Levites, the one tribe that had no inheritance in the land. More broadly, the prophet Isaiah spoke of a future vision of Jerusalem as a house of prayer to all peoples. Jerusalem, then, symbolically belongs to everyone. Without the Diaspora, it would be too easy to trust in our might, and in politics, and in the land. But the Torah of Sinai cries out: Trust neither in princes nor in your armies: "Not by strength, nor by power, but rather through My spirit says the Lord" (Zach. 4:6).

Without Israel and the Torah of Zion, we might continue to glory in powerlessness, championing our persecution as a sign of our moral superiority. We might continue to hold high the failure of the nations (particularly during the Holocaust) as proof of our righteousness. We might blame the faults of history on the Gentiles, and retreat to battle only on the plain of ideas, rather than on the Plains of Abraham.

In Israel, the Jew must proclaim the universal amid the particular. Therefore, the Jewish State must be unlike all other states. In the Diaspora, the Jew must proclaim the particular amid the universal. Therefore, the Jew must always be partially the alien other.

The Torah we received at Sinai is the Torah we have lived for 2,500 years. It is a teaching of how to live in an imperfect world. The Torah of Sinai is laden with compromise. The Torah of Jerusalem looks to the future. It is a teaching of how to create a perfect world. The messiah, then, will come to Jerusalem, not to Crown Heights or Washington, D.C.

The Torah of Sinai is much clearer, having been explored and observed by us for so long. *The Torah of Jerusalem needs to be created.* It is in Israel, in the Jewish State, where each decision is ours—from sewage to peace—that most of the Torah of Jerusalem will be created. In Israel, the Jews bear responsibility for the nature of the state. It is the flip side of the majority/minority equation of the last two thousand years. Others' fates now lie in our hands. The treatment of the minority, the barometer with which we continue to measure the nations, is now the barometer to judge us. This shall be the Torah of Jerusalem or its failing.

For after all, Mount Sinai is the mountain that one cannot ascend; its boundaries are marked forbidden. Mount Moriah is the mountain one *must* ascend to affirm the love of God and the willingness to sacrifice. Sinai is open only to individuals such as Moses or Elijah, and only as individuals can we make our way up that mountain. Jerusalem, on the other hand, is open to the whole people. It is the Jewish nation, which is to ascend in pilgrimage, to make *aliyah* by going up to Jerusalem.

And yet, in the Diaspora, we too make an *aliyah—aliyah la-torah—*

we are called up in the synagogue for the reading of the Torah of Sinai. Both *aliyot,* "ascendings," are necessary. As individuals, we must ascend Mount Sinai and as part of a people we must ascend Mount Moriah.

Nationalism and spirituality, universalism and particularism, ethe-realness and concreteness, powerlessness and power, majority and minority—in each of these dualities, as in many others, Diaspora and Israel together maintain the equilibrium. We must live in both. To use these metaphors is not to say that there cannot be spirituality in Israel, or nationalism in the Diaspora. Within each of us there exists both Sinai and Jerusalem: but these metaphors do bear relation to the reality of our different existences. The Torah of Jerusalem, with its messianic striving, can exist here just as clearly as the Torah of Sinai already exists in Israel.

In our time, we have seen the restoration of Israel, returning the balance of the equilibrium. Let us not now wish away the Diaspora as an embarrassment from the past. Or, to use a different set of images, Israel has claimed the symbol of Masada as an important component of its national myth. The slogan "Masada shall never fall again" expresses the determination of Israelis to overcome their enemies. Yet for the last two thousand years, the Jewish people have ignored the story and symbol of Masada, and have chosen a very different image from the period of the Second Temple. That image is the story of Rabbi Yohanan ben Zakkai, who through a ruse left a besieged Jerusalem to negotiate with the Roman enemy. When offered a concession, Yohanan ben Zakkai did not ask for the Temple or a remnant of an independent state. Rather he asked for permission to save a number of scholars and to establish an academy in the town of Yavneh. Unlike the zealots of Masada, he chose Sinai over Jerusalem. It is because of him and the rabbis of Yavneh that the rabbinic tradition survived and flourished. It is because of that tradition that we as Jews are here today. For Yohanan ben Zakkai to have chosen Masada would have meant a glorious but final end to the Jewish people. We must not now deny Yohanan ben Zakkai and his image.

The challenge is to have both Masada and Yohanan ben Zakkai. We must enlarge Israel's national myth beyond Masada to include Yavneh.

Similarly, it is our task in the Diaspora not to become lost in the potentially ethereal world of Sinai Torah; we must continue to see Masada looming in the not-so-far distance.

We must continue to say: "If I forget you, O Jerusalem, let my right hand be forgotten!" (Psalm 137:5).

But we must also recite: "My child, do not forget My Torah, your heart should keep My commandments" (Prov. 3:1).

Remembering both Torahs, we shall then merit to see the time when the word of Adonai shall go forth from Sinai and from Jerusalem.

# ECOLOGY

Living a spiritual life goes beyond working on our inner selves or our interpersonal relations. A spiritual life includes caring for our world. In contemporary society, our relationship to the world has come into clearer focus because of our understanding of the science of the environment. The ecological or environmental movement has raised concerns about how the inhabitants of the modern world and technology are treating the planet earth. Some from within this movement have placed the blame for the pollution and wanton destruction of the earth and its resources on the Bible. They claim that the Book of Genesis encourages the notion that the whole world is here for the benefit of human beings to do with as they see fit. They point in particular to the verse "Be fertile and increase, fill the earth and *master* it, and rule the fish of the sea, the birds of the sky and all the living things that creep on earth" (Gen. 1:28). It is interesting to note that a study of how this verse was understood by Jewish and Christian commentators throughout history reveals that only the first part of the verse absorbed the attention of the commentators. "Fill the earth and master it" had a different connotation to premodern people. Much of the world was uninhabited and dangerous. Human beings constantly spread out, creating new areas of settlement. Human history has often involved the struggle for settlement against an inhospitable wilderness. It is only in the modern world where that struggle has (for the most part) been won. Now we are in danger of running out of room on an overpopulated planet. Having defeated the wilderness, we are radically changing the world and its ecosystems.

How then should we live in the world and with the world? There are two streams of thought in Judaism in answer to that question. The first takes an anthropocentric view, seeing human beings as the most important creatures in the world. Yet along with this centrality comes a responsibility to all the other inhabitants of the earth. The second stream is closer to the views of "deep ecologists" who maintain that all creatures and even inanimate objects have values and rights.

Those advocating the anthropocentric view point to the Genesis story as proof that human beings are the climax of creation. In general, the Torah's message is addressed to human beings. If so, perhaps then we can do whatever we want to the world. The Torah sets limits on our power through the *mitzvah* of *bal tashit*, "do not wantonly destroy":

> When in your war against a city you have to besiege it a long time in order to capture it, you must not destroy its trees, wielding the ax against them. You may eat of them, but you must not cut them down. Are trees of the field human to withdraw before you into the besieged city? [Deut. 20:19]

The rabbinic tradition expounded upon this verse to prohibit not just the destruction of fruit trees during war, but any act that causes damage or loss. "One who smashes household goods, tears clothes, demolishes a building, stops up a spring, or destroys food on purpose violates the command: You must not destroy—*bal tashit*" (Maimonides, *Mishneh Torah*, Book of Judges, Laws of Kings and Wars 6:10). Wanton destruction of the world around us is clearly prohibited.

The principle of *bal tashit* together with a reading of the first chapters of Genesis has led to a notion of human stewardship of the earth. Thus in Genesis we are not only called to master the earth, we are placed in the Garden of Eden "to till it and tend it" (Gen. 2:15). We are to *avod* and *shamor*, "work and tend" the earth, and to watch over, protect, and preserve it. As humans we live in relationship to the world and its creatures, not independent of it. That relationship is made explicit in Gen. 2:19, when God brings before Adam all the creatures of the world and Adam names them. God creates the world through word. In naming the animals, Adam re-creates this world by expressing a relationship to all living things. To name something in the Torah is to know its essence, to be on intimate terms with it. Adam makes clear his stewardship by naming every single creature with whom he shares the earth. In the light of this act, the world becomes not just the setting for the human story, nor just a place for our use (or abuse); rather there exists a responsibility and a relationship to this ark filled with life that we call earth.

> In the hour when the Holy One created the first human, God took the human and let the human pass before all the trees in the Garden of Eden. God said: "See My works, how fine and excellent they are! Now all that I have created for you have I created. Think upon this, and do not corrupt and desolate My world; for if you corrupt it, there is no one to set it right after you." [Midrash, *Ecclesiastes Rabbah* 7:28]

## The Problem of Plastic Trees

In the contemporary debate about the ethics of ecology, a basic question often asked is why save a certain plant or animal. The answer often given is that this plant may be of future benefit to humanity; for example, it may contain within it a cure for a disease. Another explanation is that this plant is part of nature, which humans enjoy and therefore should protect. The answers focus on some potential benefit to human beings. But what if humans decide they can do without the spotted owl or for that matter cockroaches? What if humans decide that plastic trees are more aesthetically pleasing than natural trees? What if thousands of jobs would be created by flooding this valley and destroying an endangered plant species? Wouldn't an anthropocentric view urge that the human good takes precedence over nature? A pristine wilderness is not objectively better than midtown Manhattan. It is only our perception that creates definitions of what is rare and beautiful.

This critique becomes even sharper when applied to the traditional concept of *bal tashit*. This *mitzvah* prohibits wanton destruction. The traditional commentators clearly state that destruction for a purpose is not prohibited by *bal tashit*. As the *Sefer ha-Hinukh* says: "It is certainly permitted to cut them [fruit trees] down if any useful benefit will be found in the matter: for instance, if the monetary value of a certain tree is high and this person wanted to sell it" (Commandment 529). *Bal tashit* is defined in a very anthropocentric fashion; that is, if the destruction is for the benefit of human beings, then it is permissible. It should be pointed out that the source of this prohibition is a situation of war. Destruction is taking place all around the fruit trees. What the prohibition of *bal tashit* does is to set limits on the destruction allowed even during war. From this the rabbis developed a general notion that if there are limits on destruction during war, there should be limits on all wanton destruction, not just of fruit trees, even in times of peace. In both war and peace, the focus seems to be on purposeless destruction. Human benefit seems to be the overarching principle. Therefore, some have looked at other Jewish texts to move beyond this anthropocentric view. A number of concepts lend support to an ecological ethic "beyond anthropocentrism."

## Beyond Anthropocentrism

*Whose world is this, anyway?*

> Our rabbis have taught: It is forbidden for a person to enjoy anything of this world without a *berakhah* [blessing]. . . . R. Levi contrasted two texts. It is written: "The earth is the Lord's and the fullness thereof"(Psalm 24:1); and it is also written: "The heavens are the heavens of the Lord, but the earth God has given to human beings" (Psalm 115: 16). There is no contradiction: in the one case, it is before a blessing has been said; in the other case, after. [Talmud, *Berakhot* 35a]

*Berakhot* are said before we eat in part to acknowledge that this is God's world, not ours. Reminding ourselves that God is at the center is especially appropriate at those moments that we use the physical world for our own benefit, as when we are eating. Thus all anthropocentrism is tempered in Judaism by the acknowledgment of the Creator. We may have a lot of power in this world, but, at best, this world is on loan to us. We are only the managers, not the owners.

### This world is bigger than both of us

> Rabbi Tanhum ben Hiyya taught: The sending of rain is an event greater than the giving of the Torah. The Torah was a joy for Israel only, but rain gives joy to the entire world, including animals and birds—as it is said: "You take care of the earth and irrigate it . . ." (Psalm 65:10). [Midrash on Psalms 117]

If there is one thing most precious, most holy, and all-encompassing to the people of Israel, it is the Torah. Yet for Rabbi Tanhum, the simple and "natural" phenomenon of rain that constantly recurs is greater than the unique event of the giving of Torah. Why? Because it affects the whole world, especially birds and animals, who presumably don't benefit from Torah, and also perhaps because rain sustains and gives life to the world. What is significant in this world goes beyond what is important to Jews or even all people. The world is larger than human need, knowledge, or even perception.

### To everything there is a purpose

> Our rabbis said: "Even those things that you may regard as completely superfluous to creation, such as fleas, gnats, and flies, even they too were included in creation; and God's purpose is carried out through everything—even through a snake, a scorpion, a gnat, or a frog." [Midrash, *Genesis Rabbah* 10:7]

Everything in creation has a purpose, and that purpose goes beyond any usefulness to humans. Since every creature was created by God, all share the same status. The *Sefer ha-Hinukh* (#294) comments on the verse "You shall not slay the mother bird and its young in one day"

(Lev. 22:28): "At the root of this precept lies the purpose that a person should reflect in their heart that the watchful care of the Holy One extends to all the species of living creatures generally . . . and permanently." All creatures are part of God's providence. Nahmanides interprets this and similar commandments as teaching us that while we are allowed to ritually slaughter animals, we are not permitted to cause a species to become extinct. For Nahmanides, to destroy a mother with its young is considered as if you have destroyed a species (see his commentary on Deut. 22:6). There is also a specific prohibition, called *tza'ar ba'alei hayyim*, against causing unnecessary pain to animals.

The book *The Palm Tree of Deborah*, by Moses Cordovero (translated by Louis Jacobs, 1960), takes this attitude another step. It validates the existence of all creatures and also calls for a concern for all of them. Cordovero bases his writing on a story found in the Talmud, *Bava Metzia* 85a:

> The intestinal sufferings of Rabbi Judah the Patriarch came to him because of a certain incident, and left in the same way. What was the incident that led to his suffering? Once a calf was being taken to slaughter when it broke away, hid its head under Rabbi's robes, and bellowed in terror. Rabbi Judah said, "Go! For this is why you were created!" Then they said in heaven, "Since he showed no compassion, let us bring suffering upon him." And how did Rabbi Judah's suffering depart? One day a slave was sweeping the house and was about to sweep away some weasels. "Leave them alone!" Rabbi Judah said. "It is written: 'God's compassion extends to all of creation' " (Psalm 145:9). Then they said in heaven, "Since he has shown compassion, let us be compassionate with him."

This story contradicts the classic anthropocentric notion. The calf is clearly not just created for humans to eat it. Even though it is permissible for humans to eat the calf, that is not the sum total of the relationship between people and the calf. The calf has feelings that must be taken into account.

Concerning this story, Cordovero writes:

Furthermore, a person's mercy should extend to all creatures, neither destroying nor despising any of them. For the Supernal Wisdom
is extended to all created things—minerals, plants, animals and humans. This is the reason for the Rabbis warning us against despising
food. In this way, a person's pity should be extended to all the works
of the Blessed One just as the Supernal Wisdom despises no created
thing for they are all created from that source, as it is written: "In
wisdom You have made them all." This is the reason Our Holy
Teacher was punished for his failure to have pity on the young calf
which tried to hide near him. . . . In this way, a person should despise
no created thing, for they all were created in Wisdom. A person
should not uproot anything that grows, unless it is necessary, nor kill
any living thing unless it is necessary. . . .

This valuing of all things can be found in Maimonides, the great
Jewish philosopher of the Middle Ages. He writes in his seminal work
*The Guide for the Perplexed:*

It is likewise thought that the finality of all that exists is solely the
existence of the human species so that it should worship God, and
that all that has been has been made for it alone so that the heavenly
spheres only revolve in order to be useful to it [the existence of humans to worship God]. . . . Now if the spheres exist for the sake of
people, all the more is this the case for all the species of animals and
plants. However if this opinion is carefully examined . . . the flaw in
it becomes clear.

He points out the flaw: if the worship of God by humans is the purpose of creation, then why bother creating all those things which are
unnecessary to make that happen? Therefore, Maimonides continues:
"It should not be believed that all the beings exist for the sake of the
existence of humans. On the contrary, all the other beings too have
been intended for their own sakes and not for the sake of something

else." Maimonides concludes that as important as humans are to the universe, each thing is created for its own sake, for some purpose of God, *not* just to be used for human purposes (*Guide for the Perplexed* 3:13).

This attitude toward the world receives its fullest expression in the classic school of Jewish mysticism known as Kabbalah. According to Kabbalah (see pp. 489–91 for a fuller explication of Jewish mysticism), the world was created by a cosmic explosion that scattered divine sparks of holiness everywhere. These sparks are hidden in the materialistic debris of that explosion. God is then found everywhere *in* the world—at the same time that God exists *beyond* the world. Traditionally, when we do a *mitzvah* we are then bringing back together parts of the divided Godhead. Or more simply, our words and deeds are either redeeming the world *(tikkun olam)* by freeing the divine sparks or sinking those sparks deeper in the mud of human folly.

The world is one world, with every deed a pebble thrown into the lake of endless reverberations. What we do each day and each hour matters. The universe is a "unity amid unbelievable diversity." Nowhere is that unity more apparently manifest than when looking at the environment. For the trash we dispose of here shows up in India, the pollution we create here causes acid rain in Canada, the aerosol can of yesterday puts in danger all future generations in an ozone-thinning world.

No human can live without having an impact on the environment, both human and ecological. What then are we to do? The ideal is not to retreat to the woods and live without electricity or cars. There is no such thing as the natural state of humans; that is what makes humans unique. We have *choice*, not just instinct. After all, should we live without cooked foods or the planting of fields, neither of which is natural? If the ultimate value is to strive for the natural, shouldn't we then destroy all culture?

## An Environmental Ethic

Judaism is about making choices. It is a system of moral pluralism within the context of the Divine. Saving the environment raises difficult situational questions to which there are no hard and fast answers. Instead, we need to engage in the creation of an environmental *halakhah* that sets out values and principles to weigh in making decisions related to environmental questions. These principles can begin with the traditional principle of "do not wantonly destroy," but we have seen the limitations of that principle. Therefore, new principles need to be developed reflecting the approaches set out above that give value to all creatures and all creation, not just the human.

Three areas suggest themselves:

*1. Simple living*   Part of the source of the environmental crisis is the conspicuous consumption of our society. Our numerous appliances consume enormous energy resources. The manufacturing, packaging, and selling of consumer products use up other resources. The amount of garbage we produce overwhelms our means of disposal.

Some medieval Jewish communities issued sumptuary laws. These regulated the amount of money that could be spent on clothes or on parties or feasts. Such laws existed for a number of reasons, but one was to discourage conspicuous consumption. Some Hasidic communities have continued this tradition to prevent keeping up with the Joneses (or rather the Goldsteins) from making weddings ever more expensive. These laws could serve as a model for us to police ourselves in regard to our consumer purchasing. There is nothing that we buy that does not also come at a cost to the environment. We should constantly ask ourselves, do we need this item? Need can be broadly defined to include things that give you pleasure, but the question still remains.

*2. Tum'ah, impurity*   This is a category that fills much of Leviticus, but that has fallen into disuse (see pp. 365–66 and 450 for the exceptions). *Tum'ah* can be understood as meaning a pollution of our surroundings. An opposite concept would be that of *kavod ha-aretz*, "respect for" or "honoring of the land." A basic source for these concepts can be found in the flood story.

The earth became corrupt before God; the earth was filled with lawlessness. When God saw how corrupt the earth was, for all flesh had corrupted its ways on earth, God said to Noah: "I have decided to put an end to all flesh, for the earth is filled with lawlessness because of them: I am about to destroy them with the earth." [Gen. 6:11–13]

Finding that the deeds of humans have corrupted the earth itself, God decides to destroy everything, to cleanse the earth in the waters of the flood, the birth waters for a new world. What happens after the flood? Noah and his family and the animals of the ark are to reestablish the world. But some things have changed. God has established a covenant that God will never bring another flood to destroy the whole world.

I now establish My covenant with you and your offspring to come, and *with every living thing* that is with you—birds, cattle, and every wild beast as well—all that have come out of the ark, every living thing on earth. [Gen. 9:9–10]

The promise not to destroy the world is made with all life, not just humans. It is now up to us humans whom God has given power over the world to make sure that we do not pollute the world and thereby bring a flood or any other form of nature run wild that could bring an end to all living things. The rainbow, then, may be a sign that God will no longer destroy the world, but it is also a warning that we humans have now been given that power either to respect *(kavod)* the earth or to pollute it (make it *tameh*) and cause its destruction.

3. *Shabbat and sabbatical*    A number of people have suggested the biblical sabbatical year as a model for developing an environmental ethic. Giving the land a rest every seven years is an obvious environmental concept. The challenge is to expand the concept into other than agricultural areas and to suggest some practical ways to observe this concept.

Similarly, Shabbat has been seen as a day of environmental rest. It is a day when we refrain from our attempts to "master" the world. Shabbat law can be understood as an attempt for us to have as little an impact on the world as possible. While there is less than a perfect fit with traditional Shabbat laws (leaving your lights on all Shabbat is definitely not ecologically sound), they do call to us to stop working, slow down, rest, and celebrate the spiritual aspects of life. A challenge would be to rethink some of the aspects of Shabbat law to align it more closely with an ecological Shabbat (see "Shabbat," pp. 103–34).

One interesting side note in this regard is the category of *muktzah*. In traditional *halakhah,* these are objects that it is forbidden to use or even move on Shabbat, such as pens and money. *Muktzah* includes things that are not needed. Thus, twigs lying in your yard should not be moved, since there is no particular purpose to moving them. Basically, it encourages us to leave the world at rest. To use an analogy outside of Shabbat, it would discourage sitting on the grass and idly pulling leaves off a plant. This is to suggest that what we learn from the details of the laws of Shabbat can help shape how we act in the world all during the week.

### An Ecological Practice

An overall principle for living an ecologically correct life would be to try to negatively affect the earth as little as possible. Often we talk about desiring to leave our mark on the world, that is, we don't want to pass through our life without anyone noticing. Some of us strive for fame and imagine that thereby we can attain immortality. When it comes to living in harmony with our natural surroundings, our goal is the opposite: to move through life like a gentle wind through a grove of trees or maybe even as a gentle spring shower nurturing our planet.

To do this we should apply some of the principles described above. In order not to waste, we should make the effort to recycle as much as possible. In the products we buy, in the resources we use, we should make choices that diminish the waste of natural resources. We should strive for simpler living. Do we need to have a VCR with every TV? Do we need this new gadget? Can we walk instead of drive? Do we leave lights on, or the air conditioner running, when we are not at home? Together these small choices can have a significant impact on our environment.

One final midrash on our place in the world:

Why did God create loathsome reptiles and creeping things? . . . God created Adam and brought him into the world. And God created Adam for no other purpose than to serve God with a whole heart and God would thus find contentment in him and in his descendants after him until the end of all generations. But then after Adam complied with the command to be fruitful and multiply, one [descendant] worshiped the sun and the moon, another worshiped wood and stone, and thus every day Adam's descendants came to be deemed by God as deserving annihilation. Nevertheless, upon considering all the work of God's hands in the world of creation, God said: "These [human beings] have life, and those [other creatures] have life. These have breath and those have breath; these have desire for food and drink, and those have desire for food and drink. Human beings ought to be deemed as important as cattle, as beasts, at least as important as the variety of loathsome reptiles and creeping things which I created upon the earth." At once God felt some measure of contentment and resolved not to annihilate humankind. And so you see that reptiles and creeping things were created in the world as a means of humankind's preservation. [Midrash, *Eliyahu Rabbah*, ch. 1]

# AFTER THE WORDS: GOD

There is a very minor festival that falls on the fifteenth day of the month of Av. The Talmud discusses its origins.

> Rav Dimi bar Yosef said in the name of Rav Nahman: The fifteenth of Av was the day that the generation of the desert that had been condemned to die ceased dying. Mar adds: As long as the generation of the desert had not finished dying, God did not speak to Moses in God's customary intimate manner. [Talmud, *Taanit* 30b]

As punishment for believing the negative reports of the spies about the land of Israel, the adult Israelites in the desert (except for Joshua and Caleb) were told by God that they would all die without reaching the Promised Land. (See Num. 14:26–38.) Forty years of wandering ensued. According to a grim midrash, each year on the ninth of Av, every Israelite adult would dig a grave and sleep in it for that night. Each year a part of the desert generation would die. In the morning those who were still alive would arise, only to repeat the ritual again next year. In the fortieth year, the few survivors of that generation knew with certainty that their time had come. Yet that night no one died. Thinking they had miscalculated, night after night they lay in their graves until they saw the full moon on the fifteenth of the month. Then they realized the date must have passed and God had finally relented on the decree of death. Therefore, the fifteenth of Av became a minor festival. According to Mar, there was an even greater reason for having a minor festival. For the saving of their lives was a reason for those peo-

ple to celebrate, but the restoration of the intimate relationship between God and Israel was a reason for everyone to celebrate (see Deut.
2:16–17). That made it worthy of a continuing annual celebration.

This teaching suggests something important about the human-divine
relationship. Death gets in the way. No matter how close we may feel to
the Holy One, we know that we will die and that God will not die. Like
the desert generation, we walk around with an awareness of the decree
that none of us will enter the Promised Land. Our relationship with
God remains impaired by that knowledge. Even the relationship of a
Moses to God is impaired by the death that exists in the world. Yet we
still strive for that relationship.

Just as mortality impairs our relationship with God, so too does the
limitation of our intellect impair our ability to describe and define God.
That has not stopped people from trying. There have been countless
attempts to set out a Jewish theology about God. A survey of the varieties of Jewish belief over the centuries would be a book in and of itself.
Yet the goal of a spiritual life is to stand in the presence of the Holy.
Each of us needs to strive for some understanding of what we mean by
the word *God*.

Monotheism is the cornerstone of rabbinic theology, which begins
with the Oneness of God. There is only one God in the universe; by
definition all other "gods" are false. God is all-powerful (omnipotent)
and all-knowing (omniscient). The rabbis were not particularly concerned with the question of whether God could create a rock that was
too big for God to lift. However, they were concerned with how God
could be omniscient and yet allow humans to have free will. They expressed this paradox with the notion that "all is foreseen and yet we
still have choice." The free will of humans was essential in creating the
rabbis' moral universe. For Jews, this meant a commitment to a *brit*,
"covenant," with God. This covenant obligated Jews to observe the
613 *mitzvot*, "commandments," as set out in the Torah. In turn, just as
God redeemed the Jewish people from slavery in Egypt, God would
continue to care for the Jewish people. This covenant worked on an individual level as well. Individuals who were righteous would be rewarded. Those who were wicked would be punished. Thus God not

only created the world, but continues to intervene in the world and in the fate of individuals.

This belief in reward and punishment raised the question as to why innocent or righteous people suffer. The rabbis offered a number of answers. The most common was that whatever inequities existed in this world would be corrected in the world to come. The righteous would enjoy God's blessing in the afterlife, while the wicked would suffer punishment. For the rabbis, this meant that evil was not an independent force (since there is only one God). They were not particularly troubled with the question of how God could kill the innocent, since they had faith that there was ultimate justice in the universe.

For the rabbis, our relationship to God consisted of trying our best to observe the *mitzvot* and, more broadly, to live righteous lives. We could approach God through prayer and ask for what we needed and for God's blessings. When we messed up, we could do *teshuvah*, "repentance," and ask for God's forgiveness. Hopefully, God would respond with mercy.

The medieval Jewish philosophers tried to merge this rabbinic theology with their own philosophical beliefs. They struggled with a variety of problems but ultimately remained within the traditional framework of rabbinic theology. For instance, Maimonides was very troubled by the anthropomorphic descriptions of God in the Torah. He did not believe that God had an outstretched hand or could come down on Mount Sinai. He maintained that basically nothing could be said about the nature of God except as metaphor. We can "know" God only by seeing how God acts in the world. Yet this view does not diminish for Maimonides a belief in the theology of the rabbis as outlined above.

## Jewish Mysticism

There has existed another strand in Judaism alongside that of "rational" rabbinic Judaism: Jewish mysticism. We have clear evidence in the Talmud that some of the great sages such as Rabbi Akiva were mystics. This early mysticism seemed to focus on the mysteries of creation as well as Ezekiel's vision of the chariot and God. In the Middle Ages, mysticism reached a new stage with the publication of the *Zohar* in the thirteenth century. The *Zohar* set out what is commonly called Kabbalah. Kabbalah was further developed in the sixteenth century by Isaac Luria.

Though there are a number of approaches, one common version of the Kabbalah attempts to explain how this material world came into existence. For the Kabbalists, God is indescribable—a completely spiritual "being." One name for God is *ein sof,* "limitless." God as *ein sof* is completely beyond the comprehension of human beings. We can only know God because God created the world in order for humans to know God. To make that possible, God also "exists" in attributes. These attributes of God are called *sefirot.* There are a total of ten. The *sefirot* serve as a bridge between the unknowable spiritual God and the God who interacts constantly with the material world and is thus knowable by humans (for more detail about some of the *sefirot,* see pp. 245–49).

In this doctrine, there is a danger of the *sefirot* being perceived as independent forces. Some critics of the Kabbalah saw it as a step away from monotheism in the direction of the trinity of Christianity (though in this case with ten "gods"). But the Kabbalists stressed that the *sefirot* were just our descriptions of aspects of the One God.

The Kabbalists could be said to combine both transcendental and immanent notions of God. God as *ein sof* is certainly transcendent beyond our knowing. Yet the *sefirot* describe God as immanent, that is, present in this world.

How, then, did the world come into being? In one version, God withdrew to create a space for the world. This act of withdrawal is called *tzimtzum,* "contraction." Then God's spiritual energy began to flow back into the world, but it was too strong for the world to contain it. This led to a cosmic explosion scattering sparks of holiness throughout the world. We live in the world that follows that "big bang."

Our purpose in life and our relationship to God are different for the mystics than for the talmudic rabbis. We are still supposed to live a moral life, but our real task is to redeem the sparks that have been embedded in the material world. We are to redeem them and thereby repair the world *(tikkun olam).* Freed from their "imprisonment" in the material, the sparks are reunited with the Godhead. In one common metaphor of the Kabbalists, the female and male aspects of the Godhead have been separated and our task is to reunite them. The *mitzvot*, then, are not just good deeds or even God's commands. Our observance of the *mitzvot* has cosmic significance. How we act in the world can help bring the universe closer to redemption or help deepen the cosmic exile of the Divine sparks. Beyond doing the *mitzvot*, coming close to or even achieving union with God is the ultimate goal of the mystic.

In certain ways, the mystics took much of rabbinic theology and underlined it. Thus the mystics stressed how God animates everything in the universe. They maintained a strong sense of the underlying unity or at least striving for unity of the universe. Nothing is random or accidental. The most radical mystics said that nothing really exists except for God. The fact that our experience seems to deny this is a paradox. While from our point of view the world exists, from God's point of view nothing exists except God.

## Modern Views

In the modern world, philosophers challenged much of the traditional rabbinic theology and its mystical counterpart. There now exists a wide range of Jewish theologies, from those that still uphold the traditional notions to those that deny many of the premises of traditional theology. The underlying challenge of modernity to traditional theologies comes from its emphasis on the importance and authority of the individual. In the traditional model, authority comes from God and is interpreted by expert scholars (the rabbis). Modernity trumpets the personal autonomy of individuals. This attitude, combined with biblical and talmudic modern scholarship (see "Torah: The Path of Study," pp. 139–75), has undercut the authority of the halakhic system. If the Torah was written by humans over a period of time, what is its authority? Yet it is more than a rejection of the foundations upon which the rabbinic system rests. It is a rejection of the notion that we are servants of the king/God. Instead, as autonomous individuals with a sense of both our power and our responsibility, we become our own actors on the stage of the universe. We are partners with God. (This active role is not so distant from the concept of *tikkun olam* for the mystics.) This notion of the individual has an impact on all the modern Jewish theologians even within the modern Orthodox world. While the modern Orthodox world upholds the authority of the *halakhah*, one can find the human element both in revelation (Moses, not God, writes down the Torah) and in the acceptance of the covenant in contemporary Orthodox theological writing. Outside the Orthodox world, personal autonomy is the dominant view, especially in the way Jews live their lives, despite what the theologians might say. There is a spectrum of views on the authority of *halakhah* and of the biblical text.

The larger challenge of modernity is to the "supernatural" notions about God. Scientific rationalism has challenged such beliefs as the afterlife, miracles, and the idea that God intervenes directly in the life of individuals. Accordingly, all contemporary Jewish theologians, regardless of denomination, downplay the afterlife and/or miracles. Even in the Orthodox world it is commonly understood that the world works by the rules of physics. We live in a world of cause and effect. If you knock a glass off a table, it will fall to the floor and break. Except in a few segments of the ultra-Orthodox world, a belief that things can be caused by unseen agencies such as demons has disappeared. Yet before the modern period, the belief in demons as a possible explanation for a glass falling out of a cabinet by itself was widely held by Jews. Though the Talmud and the tradition are replete with stories about demons and suggestions on what to do about them, even in traditional circles there is a widespread acceptance of the modern way of looking at how the world operates. Yet Orthodox theologians would argue that God is not limited by the rules of nature, but can act above nature, that is, in a supernatural manner.

More fundamental than the question of miracles is the question as to whether God intervenes in the daily lives of individuals and communities. There are a number of theologians who hold this view. They maintain that God is supernatural, but just as we cannot fathom "who" is God, we cannot fathom how exactly the system of reward and punishment works in the face of contrary evidence such as the death of a child.

On the other hand, there are those theologians who deny the supernatural aspect of God. Mordecai Kaplan, the founder of Reconstructionism, posited the idea that God is the force that makes for good in the world, meaning that when we human beings act to do good, that is God acting in the world. Harold Kushner, in his book *When Bad Things Happen to Good People,* puts the modern dilemma simply but eloquently. He either can believe in a God that rewards and punishes but therefore is not a "good" God, since the innocent die; or he can believe in a God that is good but that does not control everything that happens in the world. Kushner chooses the good God who is natural, meaning that God acts only through the "natural" order, in particular through the caring deeds of people.

Between the traditionalists and Kaplan and beyond, there exists a wide spectrum of theologians reflecting a Jewish version of all the contemporary schools of philosophy and theology. One viewpoint that deserves particular mention is feminist theology, which challenges at once the imaging of God as male, hierarchical notions of God, and the transcendent nature of God. Some feminists see the notion of duality as leading inevitably to inequality. Two sources for further reading are *Contemporary Jewish Thought: A Reader,* edited by Simon Noveck (Bnai Brith, 1963); and *Standing Again at Sinai: Judaism from a Feminist Perspective,* by Judith Plaskow (Harper San Francisco, 1991).

## My Own Theology

I think a place to begin is with the Book of Job. Job raises all the challenges about the relationship of God and humans. The book ends with God speaking to Job out of a whirlwind. All the questions about God and theology have answers that can be found in the whirlwind out of which God speaks to Job. All Job's questions about evil and innocence are our questions, magnified by the six million of the Holocaust. Some of the answers certainly lie in what God says to Job: Were you there when I created the world? Do you know how it works? However, these answers are only reflections of the real answer. Out of the whirlwind comes the answer, but it cannot be heard; the whirlwind itself is the only answer we shall ever hear. All we can hear is the noise of the destruction in the whirlwind, the Holy One's speech is lost. But Job knows that the Holy One did try to speak to him, and therefore that there is an answer. Most of all, Job knows that there is a Divine Presence who cares and calls to us across the chasm.

Is the Holy One's voice then never to be heard? No, it can be heard in many places and has been heard in many times. Most often it is not found in thunder or lightning, or in the earthquake, but in a still small voice. The voice is calling to each of us at all times, but most of the time we do not hear it. We are, after all, the people who fled Sinai rather than hear the voice of God. We want to hear the voice and yet we are afraid to listen. We encounter the Holy One at Sinai and then rush to build a Golden Calf out of what we thought we heard. We try to concretize God, to capture that which is fluid.

What can we say of God? Nothing? Definitely. God *is* nothing and also everything. God is immanent and transcendent. The Kabbalistic model is for me the most useful. God is both out there and in here. To say that God is only one of those is to limit God. For me, God's most important name is "the Holy One," for God is the only *one* in the universe. God is unique.

*Tzimtzum,* "contraction," is a useful metaphor not only of how the world could be created in the presence of a God who is everywhere, but also of how the world continues to work. God gives us space just as we need to create space for the other people in our lives. Over time our understanding of the relationship between God and humans has shifted. Originally God was parent and we were very dependent children. Without the flood, we would never have realized that the pollution or the destruction of the world was possible. God needed to take us out of Egypt to show us that redemption and freedom are possible. Similarly, without Sinai, we might never have known that revelation was possible. Having been shown all these things, it is now in our hands to destroy all living flesh and even end the seasons with our nuclear weapons. We can bring redemption or enslave. We can hear the Voice and try to make a Torah for our times. Over time, we have become partners with God in working toward repairing the world.

Rabbi Ishmael was one of the talmudic sages martyred by the Romans. Under torture, he cried out bitterly and his cry shook the heavens and the earth. Then he cried out a second time, and this cry shook the very throne of God. The ministering angels said: Such a righteous person should die so cruelly! Is this the Torah and its reward! A *bat kol* (heavenly voice) called forth and said: One more cry and I will turn the world into *tohu u-vohu* (chaos). Rabbi Ishmael was silent and died.

Creation stands in contradistinction to *tohu u-vohu*. To create the world God had to make separations. God also had to allow humans the freedom to act for evil as well as good. We need to know that there is an order to the world, but also to know that order is not only impossible, *it would return the world to its primeval chaos*. And so Rabbi Ishmael, like Job, was silent.

Our comfort is to know that God accompanies us into exile. God is within the whirlwind. We are not alone. Only God remains alone. There is only one One. All the rest of the earth partakes of many dualities that lead to multiplicities. Knowing there is a One is meant to comfort us. It is also meant to show us that there is a unity amid the unbelievable diversity of our universe.

As humans, we are very twoish. Originally, we were created as a unity, more directly in God's image, since the first human was both male and female. Perhaps we were too like God or perhaps too unlike the rest of the world. Then male and female were separated into two different creatures. Since then we tend to see the world in dualities: male and female, mercy and justice, Shabbat and *hol* (weekdays). The problem of dualities is that they lead easily to hierarchies, beginning with good and evil. This duality transforms even neutral and equal dualities into better and worse, e.g., night and day, female and male. God's oneness calls upon us to look past all dualities to see both the multiplicity and the unity in the world. Humans strive to regain their lost unity by striving to come close to God, the One. "Hear O Israel, Adonai our God, Adonai is *One*" is the most important statement we can make about God.

*Idolatry*    What else can we say about God besides God's oneness? God speaks to Moses from the burning bush and tells him of his mission to free the Israelites from slavery. Moses asks God: When the Israelites wonder who has sent me, what should I say? God responds: Tell them My name is *ehyeh asher ehyeh*, "I will be what I will be." This name suggests that God cannot be easily encapsulated. It also suggests that God is in the process of becoming rather than just being. There are no limitations concerning God, including the way God has been in the past. God is an ever-changing and evolving God. This can be an unsettling notion, which is why people will seek an idol—an image of God fixed in stone.

Idolatry is often dismissed as an ancient sin. It is belittled as a primitive worship of stone or wooden images. Yet idolatry is actually a common error. I am not speaking here of a contemporary notion that instead of worshiping images of stone, people worship the god Mammon. Certainly, there are people who have placed at the center of their lives money, fame, or beauty instead of the Holy. I am suggesting idolatry is more subtle and prevalent than that. In the Torah, after the ten plagues, the crossing of the sea, and the Revelation at Sinai, what do the people do? They build and worship the Golden Calf. After all the miracles they had witnessed, how could they do this? I remember thinking when I studied this story in high school that if I could experience such miracles, all my doubts about God would be resolved.

In fact, the Israelites' desire for a Golden Calf is a common mistake and desire. It is a quest for certainty and a desire to hold on to what you can see. The Israelites took all they had learned and experienced about God and turned it into one form, one image, and one fixed idea: a Golden Calf. Upon seeing the Calf, they proclaim (Exod. 33:3): "This is your God, O Israel." This, and only this, is your God.

Idolatry is anything that we try to hold in place. It occurs when we worship partial truths instead of the One. For God is a God of change and the system of Jewish practice is called *halakhah* from the root meaning of "going," for the way is a journey, not a set of fixed laws.

This journey leads across a narrow bridge. On one side lies a chasm of partial truths, of many gods. On the other side is the chasm of believing that there is only one true path and all the others are false. This too is the sin of the Golden Calf: to decide that this is the only way and to try to fix it in the inflexible form of a calf.

God is, after all, the God of Genesis, of the universe. To claim that there is only one way to be holy, only one Torah true path, is to deny the essential nature of God, who is God of all creatures and creation. In a midrash it says that God looked into the Torah and used it as a blueprint to create the world. That primordial Torah, God's Torah, in distinction to the Torah of the Jewish people, is spoken in seventy languages because it is given to the whole world and to all people. Each will understand it in her or his own way. How can there be so many paths, some of which are contradictory to another? As mentioned in "Torah: The Path of Study," pp. 139–75, the Talmud uses the principle of *eilu ve-eilu divrei elohim hayyim,* "both these and those are the words of the living God," in regard to the disputes of the Schools of Hillel and Shammai. The differences between these two schools became so great it was as though they had two different Torahs. Yet they stayed within one community because of this principle. They believed that both spoke the words of God, even when they upheld contradictory positions. For there is a deeper underlying truth encompassed by a "living" God that includes all of creation. As the prophet Isaiah says, "God . . . forms light and creates darkness, . . . fashions peace and creates evil." Surely there are many paths to God. To define only one way as the true path is to deny the divinity found in every place of this world. This is the other form of idol worship: the worship of absolute assuredness. It is the danger of the written Torah without the ongoing oral Torah.

There is a tension here, for Judaism is about attachment rather than detachment. Yet it is an attachment *(devekut)* to God, who is both eternal and ever changing. Too often we try to attach ourselves to an idol— to make something eternal. We try to hold on to a moment or an object. We fruitlessly strive for an aspect of immortality: we put our name on a building, write a book, or act as if we are in our twenties when we are decades older. The truth is that all things pass away. Everything is transient. Even love is not forever. Only God is forever.

Yet in the face of life's transience, we are neither to create idols nor to become detached from everything. You could think the safe thing to do in the face of mortality is not to get involved in the first place, to avoid the inevitable loss by never letting yourself love or care. Instead, the Jewish model is one of *devekut,* of "cleaving," not just to God but to all of life. We are to engage in life. This *devekut* is not a desperate clinging to life, but an attachment to the flow of life. We are to enjoy life even as we know it is fleeting. Living life is learning how to float with the river's current and allow it to take you where it will. Too often we spend a lot of energy trying to swim upstream. We imagine that if we try hard enough we can get back to the garden. But we cannot. An angel with a fiery sword blocks the way. We can only go forward into life. That is why a midrash tells us that the Torah begins with the letter *beit,* which is enclosed on three sides. The only opening is forward into the rest of Torah.

In the modern world, we have learned well how to be dedicated, driven, and attached, except it is too often to all the wrong things. It is "misattachment" that is the problem. We need to seek attachment to the holy, that which will give meaning to our lives. If we can do that, then we can enjoy what life has in store for us and take pleasure in its blessings as long as they last. We can see life like our breath, flowing in and out. We do not try to hold our breath. All of life then, both blessings and misfortunes, will be as natural as our breath. How do we find the way? By cleaving to Torah, which is a tree of life.

*Torah*   Amid the thunder and lightning, the blaring of horns and dense smoke, the whirlwind of Sinai, the Voice is calling to us. It is speaking Torah. What was heard at Sinai? Some say only the Ten Commandments, not the whole Five Books of Moses. According to another tradition, only the first two commandments. Still others say only the first word, *anokhi,* "I am." A fourth opinion is only the first letter of the first word, the *aleph,* the mystery of the sound of a silent letter. According to the tradition, the Revelation at Sinai had two purposes. The first was to tell us that a relationship exists between the people of Israel and the Divine. The I-Thou encounter happened. We need to live our lives in the light of that encounter and to strive to reconnect again with the Divine. The second purpose was to tell us that revelation has content. We need to discover that content—the content that is contained in the silent letter *aleph.*

In our striving to hear the voice of the Holy One, our experience, like that of the Holy One, is an ever-changing one. There are times we feel close to living a moral and ethical life, and other times we see how far we have strayed from our ideals. At one moment, we feel pride at our emotional and psychological growth, and literally the next moment we despair about how awful we can be. We feel we are in the presence of the Holy One and then abandoned by God in our darkest nights.

In the eighteenth century, Hasidism saw this ebb and flow as a reflection of the true nature of spiritual life. Hasidism maintained that it was impossible to always stay at the elevated heights of spiritual existence. Hasidism uses the term *ratzo ve-shov,* "going back and forth." Taken from Ezekiel's vision of the chariot (Ezekiel 1:14), the phrase suggests constant movement. It acknowledges that the reality of the spiritual life is not about trying to climb higher on the spiritual ladder. Rather the life of the spirit necessarily involves movement: a movement in many directions including an up and down.

It is also a spiritual life that is played out in the world of the everyday. It is, as set out in this book, *avodah she-be-gashmiyut,* "spirituality through the everyday." Our service of the holy, our lives of meaning are to be made manifest in each present moment.

The Torah is an *etz hayyim,* "a tree of life." Driven from the Garden of Eden, humans can taste of eternity only through the *etz hayyim* (or its equivalent in other religions). It is meant to grow and develop. Unless you tend a tree and prune it and water it, a tree will die. Building a high fence around it might prevent certain predators from getting at it, but it will stunt its growth and at some point will strangle it and kill it. The Torah is black fire on white fire; it is also trendy and contemporary.

The Torah commands each of us to write a *sefer torah* which, on a metaphorical level, is the *sefer torah* written by our lives. Each of us, individually and together as communities and as peoples, will write this generation's Torah.

According to the mystical tradition, each Jew has one letter of the Torah, our own special letter that we are to learn and develop and raise up to the Divine. Each person's Torah is unique and different. This vision that each of us has a letter of the Torah is empowering but also frightening, for it means that today with so many Jews distant from Judaism, whole parts of the Torah are being left unread. Furthermore, that vision means we need every Jew to be able to read the whole

Torah. Lacking even one Jew—one letter—the Torah scroll is *pasul*, "incomplete and invalid."

What about Jewish continuity and the future?

"Leave it to Israel; if they are not prophets, then they are the children of prophets" (Talmud, *Pesahim* 668).

## God and Truth

What if what I have said about God does not resonate with you? What if you have a lot of questions about what you believe about God? One more teaching:

> R. Joshua ben Levi said: Why were they called the men of the *Great Assembly* [an institution with the highest religious authority of the Second Temple period]? Because they restored the crown of God's attributes. For Moses had said: *ha-eil ha-gadol ha-gibbor ve-ha-nora,* "the great, the mighty, and the awesome God" (Deut. 10:17). Then Jeremiah came and said: Aliens are destroying God's Temple, where is God's awesomeness? Jeremiah omitted the attribute of awesomeness. Daniel came and said: Aliens are enslaving God's children, where is God's might? Daniel omitted the attribute mighty. The men of the Great Assembly came and said: On the contrary, God's mightiness is that God subdues God's inclination to be angry and is long-suffering to the wicked, etc. [Thus the men of the Great Assembly were known as great for restoring these descriptions of God to the first blessing of the *amidah*.]
>
> How could Jeremiah and Daniel dare uproot the tradition [of describing God with these attributes] established by Moses? Rabbi Eleazar taught: Because they knew that the Holy One is Truth, and therefore they would not lie about God. [Talmud, *Yoma* 69b]

In the face of their experience, Jeremiah and Daniel could not resort to the pious descriptions about God. While later authorities restore those descriptions, our text gives Jeremiah and Daniel the powerful last word. God most of all "wants" truth from us. God wants what we believe, not what we think we should believe. God understands there is much in life that seems to deny the holy, that too often we can only hear the sound of the whirlwind. In the end, we are left only with our truth and our faith.

Unlike my ancestors who believed with a perfect faith, *ani ma'amin be-emunah shevurah,* "I believe with a broken faith"—yet with a belief that somewhere the Heart of the world is waiting for all the holy sparks to find their way home.

## A Final Midrash: Why Did God Create the World?

One day a long time ago, and yet maybe it was only yesterday, God decided to create the world. First God created the angels to have someone to pretend to talk to.

God said to the angels: "I don't know why I want to create the world. I have this longing—but for what I don't really know. Maybe the longing is to have someone to talk to who is more independent than you angels. Some being that is more than an extension of myself. Maybe I want to be surprised."

So God began to experiment with creating all kinds of beings. Finally, God said: "I will make a creature like me that encompasses the whole of creation. I will begin at the beginning with the dust of the earth, but this creature will stand erect with its head in the heavens so it will be made of both earth and sky. This creature will grow like the plants, will eat like the animals, *and* will have a piece of *me, tzelem elohim,* be created in 'My Divine image.' It will be called Adam, 'human,' from *adamah,* 'humus,' the one who encompasses all of creation."

"But—" said the angels.

"But you are right," God said to the angels. "We cannot have any confusion here. There is only one God. Therefore, this Adam will not live forever. Yet its domain will be of the earth and it will know all things and so name them."

"But—" said the angels.

"But," said God, "while the whole earth will be Adam's, there will be a tree in the middle of the garden whose fruit Adam will be forbidden to eat."

And so Adam was created.

"Who am I?" Adam asked.

"Well," God said, "you are like me, an encompasser of the world—except you are not—and—well, Adam, you will figure it out over time."

"But," said Adam, "I am lonely."

"Lonely," pondered God. "Maybe that is why I created the world. Maybe that was My desire. Not to be alone."

"Lonely," echoed the angels.

"Yoo-hoo," said Adam, waking God from God's reverie. "Remember me, Adam? I'm lonely."

"Well," said God, "we have each other."

"Yes," Adam replied, "but you just explained how we are not the same. How about this? I noticed the animals are either male or female. I am, too, except it is all mixed together inside me."

So God knocked Adam on the head. While Adam slept, God divided Adam into male and female. Upon waking, Adam and Eve introduced themselves and then went off talking and trying to understand each other.

God, seeing Adam and Eve more interested in each other than in Godself, felt jealous.

"Maybe that is why I created the world, to experience jealousy."

"Jealous," echoed the angels.

God silenced them with what we would call a look.

Adam and Eve enjoyed each other's companionship, but they felt something was missing. So they asked God: "Why did You create the world?"

God mumbled something that sounded like, "I don't know," and then left Adam and Eve. God went off to try to puzzle this out.

And that is why what happened happened. You know the story: the snake, the apple, etc.

When it was over, Adam and Eve knew that they were naked, knew they felt deep longing and desire for each other, and sensed the pain, anger, and disappointments that would be part of this longing and desire.

Adam and Eve understood that what they felt was more than a cure for loneliness, more even than sexual desire. They felt love. Love for each other. Love for Eve, who gave the first gift in the world, an apple.

Love in the protectiveness they felt toward each other in the face of God's wrath. Just love—one for the other.

And that is how love came into the world.

Love was the only thing in the world truly created by humans. For unlike everything else humans would create, love is a creation of something out of nothing. When God felt the love between Adam and Eve, God knew why the world had been created. God understood the need to create humans in order to make the one thing God could not create alone: love. Now, all God wanted was to love and to be loved.

And all this happened a long time ago, or maybe it was yesterday.

## A FINAL *KAVANAH*

How did the world begin?

For Jewish mystics the world began with an act of withdrawal. God did *tzimtzum.* God contracted to leave space for the world to exist. After this *tzimtzum,* "withdrawal," some divine energy entered the emerging world, but this divine light, this divine energy was too strong, overpowering the worlds that tried to contain it, and the universe exploded with a cosmic bang. Shards of divine light, of holiness, were scattered everywhere in the universe. The sparks of holiness are often buried deep in the cosmic muck of the universe, they are difficult to behold and yet they are everywhere, in everyone, in every situation. They are the life and meaning of the universe.

We live in this world of shattering. We feel in our bodies and in our souls the brokenness of the world, and we feel at times the resonance in ourselves of that initial cosmic shattering. Our bodies, like that primordial world, try not to contain, but rather to hold on to the divine light and energy flowing around us and in us. But as in the world's origin, our bodies are too frail, made only frailer with the passage of time, and so we begin to leak our divine image/energy. Perhaps, then, illness is really the leaking of our souls. In this world of shattered hopes and expectations, we search for wholeness.

Moses shattered the first set of tablets, the first set of the Ten Commandments. And then he got a second set that he helped to write. When the ark was constructed for the sanctuary, the rabbis tell us not only the whole second set of tablets was put into the Holy Ark, but the pieces of the first set as well.

Wholeness comes not from ignoring the broken pieces, or hoping to magically glue them back together.

The shattered coexists with the whole; the divine is to be found amid the darkest depths and the heaviest muck of the universe. Every moment has the potential for redemption and wholeness.

Our brokenness gives us that vision and the potential to return some of the divine sparks scattered in the world.

# A NOTE ON SOURCES/GLOSSARY

The translations of talmudic and midrashic texts are taken from *The Book of Legends,* edited by Hayim Nahman Bialik and Yehoshua Hana Ravnitzky, translated by William Braude (Schocken Books, 1992). This is a wonderful collection of material arranged topically. Occasionally, I adapted the translations to fit the context of this book.

The translations of a number of the Hasidic and mystical texts are taken from an important anthology, *Jewish Spiritual Practices,* by Yitzhak Buxbaum (Jason Aronson, 1990). These citations include quotations from the following books or authors: *Kitzur Shnei Luhot ha-Brit* (p. 83), the Apter rebbe (p. 78), *Midor Dor* (p. 202), Yitzhak of Vorki (p. 202 and p. 203), Hayyim Azulai (p. 202), Likkutei Hadashim (p. 207), *Darkei Tzedek* (p. 226), Abraham of Slonim (p. 277), *Menorat Zahav* (p. 231–32), *Sh'ar ha-Kedushah* (p. 230), *Emunat Tzadikkim* (p. 244), *Mazkeret Shem ha-Gedolim* (p. 231), *Tzadok ha-Cohen* (p. 279), *Ateret Tiferet* (p. 535), *Zichron l'Rishonim* (p. 542). (The page numbers refer to pages in *Jewish Spiritual Practices.*)

The story at the beginning of the introduction is from *The Gates of the Forest* by Elie Wiesel (Holt, Rinehart, and Winston, 1966).

The excerpts by Rabbi Jeffrey Salkin found in the chapter on work are taken from *Being God's Partner: How to Find the Hidden Link Between Spirituality and Work* (Jewish Lights, 1994). The quotation from *Tanna de-Bei Eliyyahu* in the same chapter is from the edition edited by Meir Friedmann (Vienna, 1902).

The quotation from the Rebbe of Mikolayeve in the chapter on food is from Louis Newman's *Hasidic Anthology* (Schocken, 1963).

An earlier version of the Israel chapter appeared as "Toward a Torah of Zion" in *Tikkun* magazine (July/August 1993), vol. 8, no. 4.

I have translated the words *melekh ha-olam* that appear in Hebrew blessings as "source of the universe." A traditional translation would be "king of the universe" or "sovereign of the world." Theologically, neither of the traditional translations reflects my understanding of God. I have also translated traditional texts with the assumption that when they spoke about Jews or people that they were referring to women as well as men.

## A Brief Glossary

*Aliyah*—1. The honor of being called up to stand alongside the Torah reader while the Torah is read during services. 2. Leaving the Diaspora to live in Israel.

*Amidah*—The central prayer of Jewish services.

*Berakhah* (pl. *berakhot*)—Blessing(s).

*Halakhah*—Jewish law and practice.

*Mitzvah* (pl. *mitzvot*)—Commandments or ritual and ethical practice.

Shabbat (pl. Shabbatot)—The sabbath.

# PERMISSIONS ACKNOWLEDGMENTS

Grateful acknowledgment is made to the following for permission to reprint previously published material.

*Jason Aronson, Inc.:* Excerpts from *Jewish Spiritual Practices* by Yitzhak Buxbaum. Reprinted by permission of Jason Aronson, Inc.

*Jack Canfield:* Excerpt from *Chicken Soup for the Soul* by Jack Canfield and Mark V. Hansen. Reprinted by permission of the author.

*HarperCollins Publishers:* Excerpt from *The Jewish Holidays: A Guide and Commentary* by Michael Strassfield and Betsy Platkin Teutsch (Illus.). Text copyright © 1985 by Michael Strassfield. Illustrations copyright © 1985 by Betsy Platkin Teutsch. Reprinted by permission of HarperCollins Publishers.

*Jewish Lights Publishing:* Excerpt from *Being God's Partner: How to Find the Hidden Link between Spirituality and Your Work* by Jeffrey K. Salkin. Copyright © 1994 by Jeffrey K. Salkin (Woodstock, VT: Jewish Lights Publishing). $16.95 + $3.75 s/h. Order by mail or call 800-962-4544 or on-line at www.jewishlights.com. Reprinted by permission of Jewish Lights Publishing, P.O. Box 237, Woodstock, VT 05091.

*Danny Siegel:* Excerpt from "A Blessing," from *Unlocked Doors* by Danny Siegel (Pittsboro, NC: Town House Press, 1983). Reprinted by permission of the author.

Illustration credits: *page xx:* "Shiviti," by Phillip Cohen, United States, 1861, paper-cut and ink, HUCSM 39.17, from the HUC Skirball Cultural Center, Museum Collection, Los Angeles, CA, photography by

John Reed Forsman; *page 136:* David Rosengarten, courtesy of the Museum of Ethnography and Crafts, Lvov, Ukraine; *page 224:* Created by the author, based on a paper-cut by Aaron Katlinsky; *page 298:* Susanne Schläpfer-Geiser, courtesy of Paul Haupt Publishers, Berne, Switzerland; *page 464:* Mordecai di Moshe Guzlan, courtesy of Musee d'Art Juif, Paris, France